Dark Psychology and Manipulation

2 in 1

Learning the Art of Persuasion, Emotional Influence, NLP Secrets, Hypnosis, Body Language, and Mind Control. With Secret Techniques Against Deception, Brainwashing, Mind Control, and Covert

Robert Pope

© **Copyright 2020 - All rights reserved.**

The content contained within this book may not be reproduced, duplicated or transmitted without direct written permission from the author or the publisher.

Under no circumstances will any blame or legal responsibility be held against the publisher, or author, for any damages, reparation, or monetary loss due to the information contained within this book, either directly or indirectly.

Legal Notice:

This book is copyright protected. It is only for personal use. You cannot amend, distribute, sell, use, quote or paraphrase any part, or the content within this book, without the consent of the author or publisher.

Disclaimer Notice:

Please note the information contained within this document is for educational and entertainment purposes only. All effort has been executed to present accurate, up to date, reliable, complete information. No warranties of any kind are declared or implied. Readers acknowledge that the author is not engaged in the rendering of legal, financial, medical or professional advice. The content within this book has been derived from various sources. Please consult a licensed professional before attempting any techniques outlined in this book.

By reading this document, the reader agrees that under no circumstances is the author responsible for any losses, direct or indirect, that are incurred as a result of the use of the information contained within this document, including, but not limited to, errors, omissions, or inaccuracies.

TABLE OF CONTENTS

BOOK 1: DARK PSYCHOLOGY 4
PREFACE 4
INTRODUCTION 9
CHAPTER 1 DARK PSYCHOLOGY SECRET 14
CHAPTER 2 DARK PSYCHOLOGY 101 30
CHAPTER 3 A DEEP DIVE INTO THE DARK TRIAD 36
CHAPTER 4 MANIPULATION – A TWO-WAY STREET 48
CHAPTER 5 DEFENSE AGAINST MANIPULATION 71
CHAPTER 6 HYPNOSIS -THE ART OF SELF-HYPNOSIS 81
CHAPTER 7 THE TRUTH ABOUT HYPNOSIS 98
CHAPTER 8 ANALYZING BODY LANGUAGE TECHNIQUES 107
CHAPTER 9 THE ART OF PERSUASION 124
CHAPTER 10 THE ULTIMATE GUIDE TO ENHANCE YOUR PERSUASION TECHNIQUES 137
CHAPTER 11 DECEPTION IN DARK PSYCHOLOGY 150
CHAPTER 12 THE ABCS OF BRAINWASHING 188
CHAPTER 13 HOW TO HANDLE THE MANIPULATORS IN YOUR LIFE 203
CHAPTER 14 HOW TO PROTECT YOURSELF AGAINST DARK PSYCHOLOGY 219
CHAPTER 15 MYTHS AND MISCONCEPTIONS ABOUT DARK PSYCHOLOGY 227
CHAPTER 16 FAMOUS DARK TRIAD PERSONALITIES 236
CHAPTER 17 THE WAY WE THINK AND MIND CONTROL 248
CONCLUSION 266

BOOK 2: MANIPULATION **269**
INTRODUCTION **269**
CHAPTER 1 THE MANIPULATION ETHICS - COULD MANIPULATION BE GOOD AND BAD? **271**
CHAPTER 2 THE ART OF MANIPULATION **284**
CHAPTER 3 LAWS OF MANIPULATION **291**
CHAPTER 4 I THINK I'M BEING MANIPULATED! **301**
CHAPTER 5 IDENTIFYING MANIPULATION TECHNIQUES **320**
CHAPTER 6 THE DARK PSYCHOLOGY OF MANIPULATION **330**
CHAPTER 7 HOW TO RECOGNIZE A MANIPULATIVE RELATIONSHIP **345**
CHAPTER 8 MIND CONTROL **358**
CHAPTER 9 BRAINWASHING **366**
CHAPTER 10 BRAINWASHING AND DARK PSYCHOLOGY **384**
CHAPTER 11 HYPNOSIS **394**
CHAPTER 12 PRACTICAL USES OF HYPNOSIS TECHNIQUES **411**
CHAPTER 13 NEURO-LINGUISTIC PROGRAMMING **417**
CHAPTER 14 THE ART OF PERSUASION **431**
CHAPTER 15 PERSUASION TECHNIQUES TO HELP YOU INFLUENCE OTHERS **448**
CHAPTER 16 ALL YOU NEED TO KNOW ABOUT PERSUASION **467**
CHAPTER 17 DECEPTION – A FORM OF MIND CONTROL **474**
CHAPTER 18 LESSONS ON DECEPTION **485**
CHAPTER 19 BODY LANGUAGE - UNDERSTANDING HOW OUR BODIES COMMUNICATE **491**
CHAPTER 20 WAYS TO PROTECT YOURSELF FROM EMOTIONAL MANIPULATION **495**
CONCLUSION **513**

Book 1: Dark Psychology

PREFACE

Congratulations, and thanks for purchasing this Book.

Recently Dark Psychology has attempted to uplift the human spirit with a good deal of popular Dark Psychology terms such as "Positive Dark Psychology" or maybe the many books released telling the masses the best way to behave to direct a fulfilled existence. Could life be as simple and easy as reading the right Book, and following some fundamental ideas, as well as things, are going to be okay for you as well as me?

This particular guide is different, and we shall check out the "Dark" Psychology secrets of the human brain, how to defend yourself against Manipulation, Emotional Influence, Persuasion, Deception, Mind Control, Discreet NLP, Brainwashing and Hypnosis as part of the daily human psyche which emerges in us all from time to time - that part of our being which finds pleasure, glee, and excitement in the dysfunctional portion of our existence.

Just how can society reconcile with this dark side? I use the term "Dark" to relate to people in society that oppose the social norm. For starters, let us look at exactly how we can find the "Dark Side" of mental notion and behavior. We want a measure to find out what's natural and what's considered abnormal behavior.

The very first measure is community norms; what this means is in any kind of society, what's regarded as normal behavior is provided by a set of circumstances which confront our belief. For instance, in Western culture, to strike someone else violently is regarded as a criminal act as well as one that's repulsive to a peaceful society.

Nevertheless, we condone violence whenever the individual is given societal permissions like a soldier at the action of war, a policeman in the act of apprehension associated with a risky criminal, a citizen defending the family of his from a significant risk coming from somebody else. These double standards could be misinterpreted in many ways.

The soldier that commits war crimes, including genocide, the policeman that utilizes violence to intimidate a witness while selecting them or maybe the citizen that violates someone else rights to further the role of theirs in a particular way. Additionally, how can we as a society determine what's wrong and right, that has the power to determine these rights, do laws follow moral conviction, or perhaps will they come to be the defence of the poor against the good or perhaps the rich against the bad?

Virtually all communities agree which killing another human being is actually against a moral code - it's wrong to kill. It must be penalized by an act of equal severity, by the society which supports the ethical, legal stance imposed on the masses by the lawmakers of its.

To the majority of societies, this continues to be a religiouss code of conduct like the ten commandments of the Christian faith, along with other of such systems from Buddhism to the Muslim Koran. Belief in divine reward, as well as punishment, is mirrored in the legal language as well as laws have seen when the bedrock of any civilized nation of women.

It's having acknowledged these rules why then do women conveniently deviate from these morals, laws as well as religious guidelines which provide us all to live in a peaceful society governed by agreed principals of actions that guard the person against danger, abuse, and hurt?

The third measure of behavior is the fact that not every laid down religious ideas or law are ideal, but those daily sets of behavior the English would relate to as "manners" or even being "polite." The conduct or also way of behavior which conforms to practice recognized as that of an excellent fellow member of a society that knows the way to conduct themselves in the organization of others to a set of requirements that are viewed as the mark of an advanced civilization.

These are often observed in the etiquette of table manners such as opening a door for a female and permitting her to pass first, the recognition that it is a man's duty to defend as well as protect females. Now in certain cultures, female's rights have cast doubt towards seeing females as sexist, also consequently demeaning to a female's freedom. Nevertheless, behaviors are viewed as the mark of being fresh breed and on top of the echelons of society, whether they're conventional English or maybe a Japanese tea ceremony.

To have functional societies, differing methods of managing our behaviors, possibly through law, morals, or maybe socially acceptable norms are essential. However, humans still manage to display a wide range of dysfunctional behavior which usually affects one and influences others to the level in which the culprits of this particular behavior view themselves as being above the law, moral codes as well as the etiquette of the majority of society.

Now, about the art of manipulation and how to defend yourself against it!

Have you ever gone into a confrontation feeling so sure in yourself, then walk out feeling confused but with no good reason why the other person should persuade you? Have you ever gone out of a conversation and agreed to do something for somebody, but couldn't figure out why you first agreed? Odds are, you exploited. Whether you were playing on your emotions or using persuasive words, you were brought to believe in or act on something you initially were not entirely agreeable with. Before you started the conversation, you could be totally convinced and so sure of yourself, but midway, you found yourself losing words, confused, frazzled, and disoriented.

Manipulation may feel like you are being manipulated, and leave your abilities in doubt. Being continually manipulated will leave you angry, demoralized, and sad and wonder how you have not seen this coming. Nevertheless, could you have prevented it, if you knew how to analyze the signs that indicate that somebody might not be good?

Manipulators exercise their influence by taking advantage of your emotions and distorting your mental perceptions to control and gain advantages. They are preying on your vulnerabilities and taking advantage of you by communication tactics designed to confuse you so that before it's too late, you don't see what they are. Identifying whether you are being manipulated to protect yourself from being exploited is essential, and facilitating a healthy balance of power in relationships. And it starts with learning how to analyze the people.

Another way of telling if you're being fooled is through body language. The sturdy, non-speakable, and subtle signs that speak volumes when you know what to look for. Through observing the transmitted movements, postures, and facial expressions, one can recognize and understand the full meaning of what someone is trying to say or not. Learning how to evaluate someone will produce some exciting discoveries, and more importantly, open your eyes to the signs that you can be taking advantage of so that you can take action to avoid or entirely stop the advances. There are fantastic tips and detailed chapters that can help you manage dark psychology traits and also defend yourself against manipulators.

Can I be a victim of manipulation?

You could be if you missed out on the signs that were signaling when someone was trying to take advantage of you. There's a lot of reasons people try to manipulate others. People exploit most of the time to get the most out of this relationship. Whether it's through wordplay, body language, or pulling emotional heartstrings, manipulators work to control and force others to do things for them.

The act of deception can sometimes happen right in front of us, and we don't even know it. Why? For what? Because we miss the signs, signals, and signs of the body language that indicate that this person may have more than the eye can meet. We've all been guilty of manipulation in one way or another. And, we were the target of the underhanded tactics of a manipulator. But what if there has been a way of analyzing the intentions of a person based on body language?

Many things create manipulation: convincing words, body language, and tone of voice are all channels for deceptive messages to be transmitted or communicated. But does manipulation do harm? Or is it the case that a little harmless persuasion is not going to hurt anyone? Why is manipulation wrong, and what if it is manipulated for the good of the one?

How to Examine People can guide you through what manipulation means, and delve into the human mind 's dark psychology. Learn how to analyze and figure out body language quickly and quickly give yourself the upper hand. Call someone's bluff and evaluate better the relationships and circumstances you are in, and most importantly, learn to separate manipulation from persuasion. Looking for a better understanding of the human mind's dark psychology, and how to identify the subtle signals of body language around you? This book has all the answers you 're looking for.

If you are ready, then let's get started!

INTRODUCTION

It is hard to think of psychology as dark. Most people want to believe they are good people, which means they wouldn't have a dark side to their minds. They aspire to bring good into the world; they forget their darkest feelings and conceal their dark secrets. Unfortunately, we can't just put those dark feelings aside for too long. It's similar to bottling up negative emotions pushing your dark thoughts deep into your mind; eventually, both explode. You can find yourself losing control when you erupt with emotions in the form of crying, yelling, or having a mental breakdown. It's more subtle when the dark side explodes. Most people don't even know they were letting loose their dark side.

Some people are still aware of their dark side and are using techniques such as deception to satisfy their dark needs. A person doing this could be deemed narcissistic.

Have we got a dark side?

No matter how hard we try to deny it, or how much we try to conceal it, there's a dark side we all have. Sometimes, you know your dark side and let it come out in the clothes you wear, the makeup you put on, how you treat people or how you isolate yourself from society. Often, with what you say or do, you don't know the dark side is coming out. You should know that it does not mean you are a terrible person just because you have a dark side. It doesn't mean you want to hurt somebody or you don't think that people are evil. There are plenty of social and cultural myths about having a dark side entails. Most of these stereotypes come from people categorized as "bad" by people who commit crimes, narcissists, Satanists, and others.

There are positive aspects that can come from the dark side of a person. They might find, for example, that they love horror movies, which give them lots of adrenaline. It is something that helps them stay motivated and relax throughout their day. Seeing the dark side brighten during Halloween is always enjoyable. Those who have a dark side and love this trip will make some of the best haunted houses, or labyrinths you'll be going through. It's also good to have a dark side when you like being afraid.

Your dark side becomes an issue if you wish to physically, mentally, or emotionally harm someone. If you try to manipulate their minds through coercive means to better your life, it becomes a problem. You don't care what it does to them, because other people don't generally care about you. This is when there can be a dangerous and criminal dark side.

The Truth About Dark Psychology

One of the biggest reasons that people fight dark psychology is that they don't fully understand what it means. Dark psychology is more than the actions and feelings of any person. It examines why people are preying on other human beings. Like psychology, there is an effort to find a reason why people think and behave the way they do. For dark psychology, the main distinction being that it focuses on whether a person would deliberately hurt another human or animal. Dark psychology, for example, looks at why millions of Jews were killed by Adolph Hitler during World War Two. Those studying dark psychology are asking what made Hitler tick the way he did? What did Hitler aim for the Jews?

Dark psychology can help you understand somebody too. For example, if you sense your significant other is manipulating you, you should learn about their tactics and why they are doing this. This can not only help you understand the person but also protect yourself. You should start counteracting the actions of your other significant ones. This will, of course, make them angry. It will also throw them off their game, however, which will give you more control.

You may not realize someone's using dark psychology. No matter who you are, at one point or another, you have manipulated a human. While this may have been to benefit them, it is still known as a form of dark psychology. It's not truly dark, though. You use general psychology when you manipulate someone to help them, which is what therapists do with their clients. Even though some of the tactics might be dark, this is not considered by many to be a significant form of dark psychology. Before you start looking into the dark psychology, it is always important to distinguish between bad and good psychology. Psychologists are stating there are four dark personality traits to help you distinguish. These traits are frequently found in people following dark psychology.

1. Narcissists

Narcissists are probably the most prevalent example of people participating in dark psychology. They are described not only as a feeling but also as truly believing that they are better than others. They like being the focus of attention and believe they are among the most important people. Many people feel that they think a narcissist is delusional. They don't care what other people think, though they typically are. What matters to them is what they think, and that they all agree with it.

2. Machiavellian

They are known as master manipulators, who are somebody who uses negative manipulation always to get what they want. At some point in your life, you've probably met a Machiavellian and found they cheated you out of cash, lent credit for your job, bullied you, or just made you feel useless. While narcissists are also known to be manipulators, at the game, Machiavellians are more thorough. They will also participate in white-collar crime once they have achieved what they want. For instance, if someone works their way up to the CEO by deceptive tactics just to start stealing money from the company, they're a Machiavellian.

3. Everyday Sadists

You've probably heard in the news recently about a murder or another crime which made your stomach feel sick. You hear of an everyday sadist when that happens. We are people who want to and enjoy causing harm to other humans or animals. Often they will look for jobs where they can participate in this behavior and find a way to get away with it, usually manipulative. We don't know if someone gets hurt, how much damage we inflict, or even whether they kill somebody. They participate in these actions because it is a pleasure for them.

4. Psychopaths

Many people misunderstand the distinction between sadists and psychopaths, as they may all enjoy harming others. However, to help explain their behavior, psychopaths are often diagnosed with various mental disorders. When it comes to their acts, they are also considered to be a little darker. While sadists can often experience emotions that can cause them not to engage in such activities, psychopaths do not usually feel such emotions. The biggest emotion they feel is the happiness they get when someone's being brutalized. Psychopaths also do not reason about their acts as do other enigmatic personalities. They appear to do whatever they feel good about right now. Charles Manson is one of the most known psychopaths.

Unfortunately, we can't alter the fact that there's dark psychology going on in the world, no matter how hard we try. It's just like the world has got bad and good people. There is nothing you can do to rid yourself of it.

Most people may try to disregard the dark psychology to live a more comfortable existence. That's not something that you should be doing. When you start overlooking life facts such as coercion and crime, you can get yourself stuck in a web created by a psychopath or narcissist. That can take you down a very dangerous and dark road. You need to know that there is dark psychology and you can understand what it is, and shield yourself from it as much as possible.

That doesn't mean you need to feel nervous about dark psychology, either. Before you were even born, it did exist. People often do not study dark psychology so that they can protect themselves; however, you can. They are studying dark psychology to understand what makes people like Charles Manson, Ted Bundy, and Adolph Hitler tick. What makes them believe their acts will help them get away? What makes other people, ordinary people who care for others, decide to follow their ways and become just as dark and malicious, more importantly? The Nazi soldiers, for instance, were under Adolph Hitler's influence. The majority of these soldiers were German regulars who once lived and spoke to Jewish citizens. They then begin to believe what Hitler said, which made them turn on people they once thought were kind and hardworking citizens.

CHAPTER 1 DARK PSYCHOLOGY SECRET

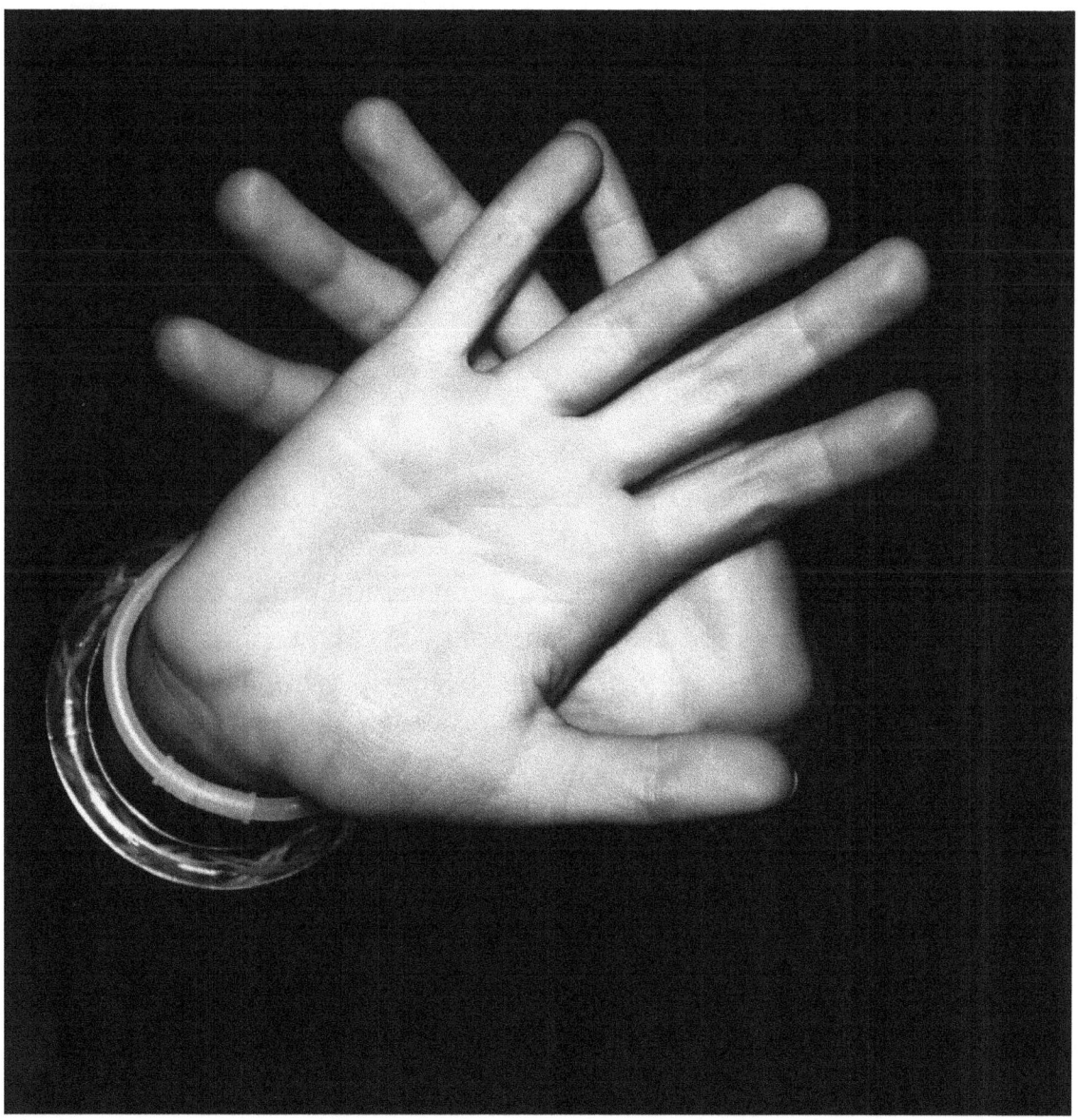

Dark Psychology is the research of the human condition as it pertains to the mental dynamics of individuals to prey upon various other individuals driven by deviant and criminal drives, which lack objective as well as common assumptions of instinctual drives as well as social sciences principle. Every one of humanity has this possibility to victimize some other humans as well as living creatures.

Even though many restrain or perhaps sublimate the tendency, some people act in these impulses. Dark Psychology seeks to recognize those thoughts, feelings, perceptions as well as very subjective processing methods, which lead to predatory behavior that's antithetical to contemporary understandings of human behavior.

Dark Psychology assumes that criminal, abusive, and deviant behaviors are purposive and have some logical, goal-oriented motivation 99% of the moment. It's the remaining 1%, Dark Psychology areas from the Adlerian concept, and also the Teleological Approach. Dark Psychology postulates there's a region in the human psyche which allows several individuals to commit atrocious acts with no purpose. With this concept, it's been coined the Dark Singularity.

Dark Psychology is a common component of the human problem. This particular construct has exerted influence throughout history. All cultures, societies, and also the individuals that live in them maintain this specific facet of the human problem. Probably the most benevolent individuals recognized have this specific world of evil, but never act upon it and also have lower rates of brutal thoughts as well as feelings. Dark Psychology puts forth the idea the near era owner draws to the "the dark hole" of perfect evil, the not as likely he/she features a goal of reasons. Dark Psychology describes the psychopath as being a predator devoid of remorse for the actions of his.

The study of Dark psychology

Dark Psychology posits that all humanity has a reservoir of malevolent intent toward others ranging from minimally obtrusive and fleeting thoughts to pure psychopathic deviant behaviors without any cohesive rationality. The Dark Spectrum is called this. Dark Psychology calls Dark Factor the mitigating factors that act as accelerators and attractants to approach the Dark Singularity, and where the heinous actions of a person fall on the Dark Continuum.

Dark Psychology is a topic that this writer has been struggling with for 15 years. It was only recently that he finally conceptualized the meaning, theory, and psychology of that human condition dimension. Dark Psychology includes all that makes us who we are linked to our dark side. There is this common cancer in all cultures, all faiths and in all humanity. From the moment we are born to the time of death, inside us, there is a side lurking all that some have called evil, and others have described as criminal, deviant, and pathological. Dark Psychology presents a third philosophical construct that takes a different view of these behaviors from religious dogmas and theories of contemporary social sciences.

Dark Psychology assumes that there are people who do the same actions for power, money, sex, revenge, or some other known intent. Without a target, they commit those horrid acts. Simplified, the goals don't justify the ways. There are people who, for the sake of doing so, abuse and harm others. The capacity lies inside all of us. The area which this writer explores is the potential to harm others without cause, explanation, or purpose. Dark Psychology assumes that this dark potentiality is incredibly complex and even harder to define.

Dark Psychology believes that we all have the capacity for action by predators, and that capacity has access to our emotions, feelings, and beliefs. We all have this ability because you can read in this text, but only a handful of us act upon them. At one time or another, all of us had thoughts and feelings about wanting to behave in a brutal way. We have all had ideas that we want to harm others without mercy seriously. Unless you're frank with yourself, you'll have to admit that we've all had ideas and emotions that what to do wicked things.

Regardless of the truth, we consider ourselves to be a kind of benign species; one would like to think that such thoughts and feelings will not exist. Unfortunately, both of us have these ideas, and fortunately, never act upon them. Some people have the same thoughts, feelings, and perceptions but act on them in both deliberate and impulsive ways. The apparent difference is that they act upon such thoughts when others have only brief thoughts and emotions to do so.

Dark Psychology claims that this type of predator is purposive and has some logical, purpose-oriented motivation. Religion, philosophy, psychology, and other dogmas have been convincing in their attempts to describe Dark Psychology. Most human conduct relating to evil actions is indeed purposeful and goal-oriented. Still, Dark Psychology suggests that there is an environment where persistent behavior and goal-oriented motivation tend to become nebulous. There is a spectrum in victimization in Dark Psychology ranging from thoughts to total psychopathic deviance, with no apparent logic or intent. This spectrum, Dark Spectrum, allows the Dark Psychology theory to be conceptualized.

Dark Psychology addresses that part of the human psyche or universal human condition that helps predatory behavior and can even animate it. Some of the characteristics of this behavioral tendency are its lack of apparent rational motivation, its universality, and its lack of predictability in many instances. This essential human condition is believed by Dark Psychology to be exclusive or an extension of evolution. Let's look at some straightforward evolutionary tenets. First, consider that we evolved from other animals and are the perfection of all animal life at present. Our frontal lobe allowed us to become the creature at the apex. Now let us presume that being apex predators doesn't exempt us from our animal instincts and predatory existence.

If you adhere to evolution, assuming that this is valid, then you conclude that all action relates to three primary instincts. The three main human drives are age, violence, and the instinctual desire to self-sustain. Evolution follows the evolutionary tenets of the fittest species and its reproductive cycle. Our specie, as well as other creations, behave in such a way as to procreate and live. Aggression happens to mark our territory, protect our territory, and ultimately win the right to procreate. It sounds logical, but in the purest sense, it no longer forms part of the human experience.

Dark Psychology believes this dark side is always unpredictable. Unpredictable in knowing who is acting on such risky urges, and even more unpredictable to the extent others can go negated with their sense of justice. Some people rape, assassinate, torture, and violate without cause or intent. Dark Psychology speaks of behaving like a predator pursuing human prey without clearly specified reasons for such acts. We are incredibly dangerous to ourselves as human beings and to every other living creature. The reasons for this are numerous and attempts by Dark Psychology to investigate certain hazardous elements.

The more readers can imagine Dark Psychology, the more prepared they are to have their chances of human predators being victimized. It is necessary to have at least a minimum understanding of the Dark Psychology before continuing. As you continue expanding this construct through future manuscripts, this writer will go into detail on the most important concepts. Six concepts are then required to understand Dark Psychology fully and as follows:

1. Dark Psychology is a part of the human experience as a whole. This construct has exerted historical influence. All cultures, societies, and the people that reside in them preserve this facet of the human condition. Known to the most benevolent people, they have this realm of evil, but never act upon it and have lower rates of violent feelings and thoughts. Dark Psychology is the study of the human condition, as it relates to the emotions, feelings, and beliefs of peoples linked to this inherent capacity to prey on others without pure definable motives. Since all action is purposeful, goal-oriented, and conceptualized by modus operandi, Dark Psychology puts forth the notion that the near-age individual draws to the "black hole" of pure evil, the less likely he/she is motivated. Although this writer believes that pure evil is never achieved because it is infinite, Dark Psychology believes some come near.
2. In its latent form, Dark Psychology may be underestimated due to its potential for misinterpretation as aberrant psychopathy. History is full of examples of this latent tendency to manifest itself as active, destructive behavior. Modern psychiatry and psychology define the psychopath as an unrepentant predator for his actions. There is a continuum of severity in Dark Psychology posits, ranging from thoughts and feelings of violence to severe victimization and violence without reasonable purpose or motivation.
3. On this continuum, the Dark Psychology's severity is not deemed less or more heinous by victimization behavior but plots out a range of inhumanity. Comparing Ted Bundy and Jeffrey Dahmer would be a straightforward illustration. Both psychopaths were severe, and their acts were heinous. The

difference is that Dahmer committed his atrocious assassinations for his insane desire for companionship when Ted Bundy was murdered and sadistically caused suffering from pure psychopathic madness. On the Dark Spectrum, both will be higher, but one, Jeffrey Dahmer, can be best understood by his desperate psychotic need to be accepted.

4. Dark Psychology assumes that every human being has a potential for violence. This potential is innate in all humans, and various internal and external factors increase the likelihood of manifestation of this potential into volatile behaviors. These actions are aggressive and can act without purpose at times. Dark Psychology believes that the predator-prey relationship is corrupted by humans and lacks its motives, which are assumed to be innate as part of the living organism of the earth. Dark Psychology is simply a human phenomenon and no other living being experiences it. Among other living organisms, aggression, and mayhem that occur, but mankind is the only species that can do so without intent.

5. An awareness of the underlying causes and triggers of Dark Psychology will help society to identify, diagnose, and potentially minimize the dangers inherent in its impact. Learning Dark Psychology concepts serves a twofold function, which is beneficial. Accepting that we all have a capacity for evil helps those with information to lower the risk of its eruption. Second, understanding Dark Psychology's tenets ties in with our original evolutionary intent of striving to survive.

The Dark Side - Dark Psychology Secret

What possesses the male that kicks the dog when he's disappointed by a society which pens the existence of his. What feelings does he release at that moment whenever the dog screeches as well as howls in fright and pain? Precisely why does he smile as well as additional wish injury to the dog and enjoy the sight of an animal in distress? On-lookers think outraged by his sympathy and behavior for the defenceless dog for which this male has sought to cure cruelly and with no remorse. Who's this male? Precisely why he's all people from time to time.

All of us lose the sense of ours of logical ideas as well as mental calm as we grapple with life's lack or unfairness of ability. On the flip side - wait - because of this male is wealthy, has all his requirements fulfilled, but still feels great delight in kicking as well as seeing the dog suffer at the hands of his. A feeling of power at the power of his to cause pain, as well as the pleasure at feeling superior to other lesser humans whom he sees as incapable of taking whatever they like and therefore end up his servants and workers. This outstanding positional thinking results in the absence of empathy or sympathy for other people as just fools that acknowledge the dominance of the type of his as lawmakers and leaders.

The case mentioned above is simply too provide an insight into behavior that breaks our three methods of societal norms, law (hurting a defenceless animal) moral (the taboo on mindless behavior viewed as wrongdoing) socially acceptable behavior, (while every person could lose their kick and temper the dog of theirs, the majority of will feel pangs of remorse and guilt). At this point, nonetheless, we meet individuals that believe no guilt, no remorse, and find out themselves as exempt from laws they don't go along with.

After example, we've to check out the criminal. Criminals are typically viewed as the rejects of society as they've come from flawed backgrounds, disadvantaged households, and poor parental upbringing. In the community, probably the most significant damage done to the general public is frequently from a business crime like pension fund embezzlement, stocks, and shares insider trading in addition to theft of wealth and assets by CEO as well as government officials.

This so-called white-collar crime is frequently undetected and also the hardest to bring to justice. Each day criminals tend to be more visual to the public as their crimes result in localized distress and help make the press cry for civil authority and police action. Thus, many laws are actually about a visual criminal who is very easy to learn as well as comprehend.

Punishment of visual crime is straight forward and also dealt with each day in our media and courts. How can we distinguish between the two kinds of criminal - the so-called victimless crime of white-collar criminals that see no immediate victim or maybe the murderer that while in an armed robbery kills as well as maims individuals who oppose his will to steal what he desires of society and also the distress they leave behind?

So just what does Dark Psychologist have to point out about the deviants that don't see the actions of theirs as an issue to themselves and think other people who don't take control of the life of theirs as sensitive and subsequently deserve to be victims of people who are smarter, stronger or perhaps a lot more amazing? Do the media usually cry all about the passive masses which acknowledge the status quo and also in the same paper would condemn the nearby individual who took the law and creates their own hands maybe to avenge a few wrongdoings against them or perhaps the families of theirs?

The very first location that Dark Psychology expounds the reasons powering this deep behavior of others is actually "developmental" that upbringing is actually at the route of this particular behavior, that the dog kicker wasn't loved or even looked after rightly. That during the formative years of theirs, these were subject to cruelty, sexual abuse, or maybe lack of social training that the same transgressors were victims of bullying at school and consequently required to act out the frustration of theirs on people in a society which are weaker than themselves.

There's proof amongst brutal criminals which they usually possess an additional Y chromosome (males) that provides them a high quantity of testosterone, leading to violent outbursts towards frustrating circumstances in which they use fear as well as terror as the secret to getting what they need.

Nevertheless, as a fraction of violent criminals, this's statistically minute while in the standard prison population, this might be greater. Most inherited exploration so much has to lead to speculation regarding genetic elements but without firm evidence to back up the claims. Probably the most frequently cited research is the fact that twin research in which twins separated at birth have very high incidences of comparable behavior as well as results.

This then is the propositional job which makes Dark Psychology difficult to continually find as a proper perspective or maybe a deterministic means of the planet which perhaps it's in fact that normal behavior amidst people would be to be a tendency, violent, deceitful, and cruel towards criminal behavior under an assortment of circumstances. Those morals are a luxury of a settled society where everybody is equal both economically and within category or caste.

The Dark Psychology Of The Survivalist

You will find those especially in the USA which sees the conclusion of modern society as a genuine possibility whether they advocate nuclear annihilation (today much more likely bio-warfare) or maybe the description of capitalism leading to civil strife as well as cultural chaos. These individuals are usually called survivalists. They save weapons against the unrestrained hordes that would roam the nation in the event of a civil breakdown as well as meals for the chance of shortages brought on by the economic meltdown.

(Looking at two009 in the USA numerous survivalists would argue they have an excellent case). The survivalists assume they have got a simple right to protect themselves as well as the families of theirs of the situation of societal breakdown as well as lack of safety laws. On events, these groups come into conflict with present authorized statutes, which become enforced by federal authorities, including the FBI.

Consequently, the survivalist's mentality is actually while on the one hand of conflict with society and in the other viewed as a real attempt at managing one's fate against succeeding catastrophes. After all, insurance companies survive only on that premise by itself - and ironically will be the first never to endure an economic breakdown of capitalism as seen by the failure of many banks between 2008/9 across the globe. Today the most favoured films at the box office are disaster movies, those where flood, sun flares, biowarfare, other catastrophes, and alien invasion result in the interpersonal breakdown of society. The heroes of the films are usually the ingenious survivalists that, through violence, protect the kin of theirs from all comers.

Precisely why does the public find these individuals as appealing, as hero's and still the actual survivalists are vilified as public enemies of the status quo? Judging by the good results of these films, everyday individuals recognize that the description of modern society is something which could happen or perhaps is whether the reality is inevitable so that they seem to these films as a kind of optimism for another future which can come around by the demise of the daily world of theirs.

Dark Psychology As Evolution

For human history, all individuals began as survivalists as hunter-gatherers roaming the land, searching for readily available animals for warmth and food. As time goes by, we come across these societies settle into agro cultural settlements that create leaders, laws, and rules moral code. As they create as well as expand, these settled societies create a religion, music, and art to compensate for a small presence within the constrictions of the real society they've created.

From these beginnings, land, and rightly start to become essential. The possession of products plus chattels becomes crucial to development. As time goes by, these settlements become cities, towns, and villages, which ultimately create nations with boundaries. Survival becomes right now the team and not the person as was human's instincts from the outset of time. Nevertheless, eventually, these societies fade as well as crumble away.

Most people fail as they develop into empires that dominate the poor with an edition of their religions and laws. Nevertheless, something history teaches us all is the fact that societies do disappear for all kinds of reasons. (Greek, Roman, Egyptian in the ancient world as well as British, French, Japanese and German empires in the contemporary world).

Most of those societies had the one thing in typical they didn't envisage the demise of theirs. Nowadays, an American and European couldn't picture the fall of the USA or the EEC; however, these latest contemporary empires have the Achilles heel of theirs, "Capitalism." Even though Karl Marx discovered the evils of capitalism and its eventual disaster, he couldn't have seen just how it'd grip the contemporary world to such a place that wars over gas and oil would rule the two1st century.

The majority of the failures could be attributed to mismanagement, though it was a loss of confidence in the monetary system by ordinary people who caused a rush on failure and funds to service crippling debt through little return and high-interest rates on investments. When individuals panic, they go into survival mode - they take care of themselves initially.

Dark Psychology Of Fear

Exactly why the mental perception of any risk causes organism effect? The solution is actually in human anatomy, more precisely, in the causes of pain appearing. Is mental pain much like an actual one? Exactly how pain occurs? With physical pain, all is pretty sharp. We don't take into account natural motor reflexes that are carried out under the command of the spinal cord. Exactly how mental pain takes place? The organism of ours has some element as self-regulation of all the physiological processes; quite merely, brain responses on the shift in the chemical processes in the body.

Most likely, under the influence of feelings of the organism happens some sort of change, for instance, in blood composition, then it's transmitted to the brain, and once again the resulting impulse from the human brain is actually transmitted to one of the organs, and hence pain takes place. Allow it to call the mental root cause of the soreness.

At this point, we ought to comprehend precisely how emotions impact the shape of the organism. It's essential to recognize the complex business both of the central nervous system and mentality. For that purpose, there's a demand for a specialist.

For instance, if you worry about the darkness, you are afflicted by heartache, woodiness for blossom, the distress of the throat. You feel as someone stops the breath of yours. Right here, you worry, not darkness itself but a factor that could stand in the darkness. It's based on received info about it throughout the daily life of yours. You worry that something can play the devil along with you. A bit of kid never fears darkness until he was told what could be in it. Allow it to call mindful fear.

This kind of phobias as fear of a concrete circumstance or maybe object, which scares you with something and rises the sensation of horror and fear, are usually referred to calculated fear since you are feeling this particular fear in the outcome of the unfortunate encounter of yours or maybe wrong info received from someone. What are the dynamics of this fear? Just how does this fear happen? Which food do I think? Lack of confidence, Embarrassment, Dejection, Inactivity, Anxiety, Blame, Injury, Consternation, Pressure, Panic. You believe issues in the blossom of yours. Breathing difficulty. Cold sweat. These physical and psychological sensations in the body of yours. And this means that fear is interconnected with various other negative emotions. One factor causes an additional, comes out of the other, but means the same thing.

How about subconscious fear or even, in other words, an underlying fear not depending on the experience? What could it be? This may be the worry of the uncertainty, fear of the unidentified. For instance, kids worry noises, unfamiliar items. In general, out of the real start of human history, folks always had been frightened of inexplicable acts of nature. Or maybe the fear of theirs depended on the phenomenon seen before?

For instance, fear of the future that is unknown, fear of potential fantasized adverse events. How can we discover that these are terrible occasions? We compare attainable occasions with seasoned negative ones. It turns out we worry about unfamiliar items since we fear strange negative things. We don't fear excellent unfamiliar items since they arouse joy. When we believe fear, all the significant events we do forget. Put simply, when we consider an unknown occasion in the head of ours, a terrible picture appears, as a result, occurs a sensation of fear-based on negative first skilled fear. It indicates that fear of the unknown factor is a calculated fear.

Remorse Regret And Sorry - A Triad Of Dark Psychology

Remorse, Regret, and Sorry are three words essential to adaptive living. These three words, when practiced, improve the likelihood of all the public interactions achieving success. Refusal and ignorance of this mental triad lead to deviant and criminal actions with victimization as the modus operandi. The words "I am sorry" are actually among the most potent and complicated phrases expressed in communication.

Since the start of civilization, this particular phrase has been a part of all cultural and societal exchanges communicated through different languages. "I am Sorry," will regularly be essential to community relationships. The idea of this particular term concretely illustrates how most individuals are fallible creatures. Words, as well as actions, can offend briefly or perhaps inflict a life long mental scar void of healing. Understanding the significance as well as the origins of "I am Sorry" will help the viewer comprehend this useful term.

The expression, Sorry, is an adjective with a wide range of meanings defining several communications conveyed in interpersonal relationships. Originating from a reductionist standpoint, as well as adding the identifier, I am, makes the phrase a kind of phrase and apology of regret. The definition of apology is an expression of regret for causing another person pain or difficulty. The definition of regret means feeling contrite or perhaps remorse approximately one's actions. Remorse, as well as regret, are two emotions individuals, generally speaking, have a difficult time admitting and experiencing.

Remorse is yet another essential phrase to recognize the phrase succinctly, "I am sorry." Without the experience of remorse, it's not possible to communicate regret for one's misdeed(s) sincerely. Remorse is described as a feeling of sincere regret as well as guilt for leading to someone's damage. Based on the damage committed, the severity of remorse can range from subtle to terrible. The societal intent behind remorse is usually to educate individuals on actions not appropriate in social interactions.

Without having the experience of remorse, individuals can not find out to change their actions leading to a far more conducive way of life. Since the start of history that is documented, civilization has written poetry, songs, music, and other types of communication to explain as well as express the experience of remorse. Without remorse for wrongdoings, society couldn't exist, and isolation will be central to human existence. The man being is a social creature flourishing just surviving inside a team dynamic. As part of this evolutionary framework, interaction and remorse of regret are equally necessary and encouraged for the survival of all men and women, the homo sapiens.

Given the essential goal of regret as well as remorse to humanity, the expression "I am sorry" is usually confounded by suspicions of sincerity. An individual's character, as well as integrity, is a barometer of sincerity, as well as the effect of talking remorse is directly attached to the person's intention. If perhaps integrity is deemed questionable, then tries to apologize could effortlessly be construed as misguided void of truthfulness.

Character, as well as integrity relevant to being genuinely remorseful, are tied to past, present, as well as future actions following the misdeed(s) of theirs. Some are unforgivable while many are acknowledged, provided precise succeeds are showed following his/her misdeed(s). The result of actions after a misdeed is freshly learned behaviors decreasing the possibility for repetition of the particular misdeeds.

An analogy to illustrate human fallibility not addressed, altered, or perhaps redirected would be the individual that is suffering from alcoholism. Even though the alcoholic is secretly conscious of his/her drinking brings about anguish and pain to others, he/she goes on drinking, making use of a bunch of defence mechanisms including denial, displacement, and minimization. Interested in the gradual demise of trust, integrity, and his/her character by others, the alcoholic might go years before experiencing remorse and abstaining from potential alcohol usage. The procedure for recognition, rehabilitation, recovery, regret, and remorse illustrates the road all individuals must go through in the procedure for good man adaptation.

Without regret or remorse for actions deemed hurtful by others, the probability for good change is minuscule. Because of the depths of the human brain, you will find significant defence mechanisms prepared to protect someone from feeling regret for the actions theirs. The capacity to say, "I am sorry," as well as imply it takes an inner tank called conscience. Conscience is described as a moral sense of wrong and right. This particular mental construct impacts a person's behavior and encourages purposeful behavior.

Self-awareness, thinking, and consciousness are all pertinent facets of the conscience. This particular construct is a cup of water ranging from empty to full—many people's tanks of conscience range from zero to Filled. As stated before, an integral part of the human condition is proclivity as well as fallibility to participate in non-functional behavior (s) - the less conscience a particular person possesses, then after he/she is actually at risk for victimizing others. Probably The severest effect of lacking a vessel of conscience will be the criminal, deviant, or maybe sociopathic brain.

The phrase "I am sorry" is actually among the most crucial phrases active in the personal experience. By the start of time as well as ad infinitum after that, the procedure of rehabilitation, remorse, regret, and recognition will often be a barometer for man adaptability. Familial guidelines, philosophies, religions, and laws for raising kids are targeted to control and lower human suffering.

THE GOAL IS QUITE SIMPLE AND EASY TO PRACTICE USING FIVE STEPS.

- Expect others to be offended because of the variability of perceptions filtering all human interactions.
- Whether guilty or innocent, causing others harm, initiate an apology followed by empathy for the expertise of theirs.
- Verbalize a program for not offending down the road.
- Introspect after and begin a paradigm shift decreasing the possibility for future offending action(s).
- Never forget, learn to forgive, and foster mutual respect.

What If You Need Out

The bottom line is that using any of those negative tactics of dark psychology in a relationship is a form of abuse. Suppose you are being manipulated or psychologically influenced to the extent where you have to find a way out of the relationship physically, emotionally, or psychologically. It won't be easy, and you may feel like you are making the wrong decision. After you leave them, you may find yourself going back to your significant other because, as you will get yourself to believe, "it wasn't that bad" and "they promised that they'd change."

Firstly, you have to know they won't be able to adjust overnight. It will take years for them to change and a lot of counseling. If they want to change, which is not usually the fact, then you need to make sure that they go to a counselor and recognize when and when behaviors change.

Second, although you may not feel it right now, you can get out. You have the backing. Even if you've become isolated from friends and family, there are always support groups, shelters, and non-profits willing to help you get back on track with your life. It won't be easy, because you're going to have to get to the point where you start building your confidence again. You have to feel like you're not wrong and people want to help you. This is something that master manipulators and mind controllers are trying to take away from you as it gives them the upper hand, and they feel you can never find your trust again. You can prove them wrong, though. You can fight against this, and you're going to come out on top.

CHAPTER 2 DARK PSYCHOLOGY 101

Identifying A Predator

Your favorite work colleague maybe someone you get along with or someone who pretends to get along for their benefit. How is it that you say the difference?

- **They are incredibly charming.**

Often, the most powerful predators are incredibly charming. They know how to do the right things and say the right things, so they come across as attractive to others. Based on their ability to get into the good books of anyone under a few well-placed compliments and smiles, they come off as highly likable. When you meet a charmer like that, they'll make you believe you're the core of their universe. They will pay attention to you, make you feel unique, and will pull all the stops to impress you. This is an art form learned for many charmers. They had years of practice to make the Mr. Charming act great.

When two normal people meet without hidden agendas, the interaction that is taking place is natural, sometimes awkward, and often superficial. That is, instead of deep heartfelt conversations, there is likely to be a whole lot of small talk to fill the silences. The latter conversations come after you got to know each other a bit better. Be wary to someone who wants to divulge charmingly some needless detail that paints them as this ideal human who is unable to make a wrong move. Be careful of anyone who has the perfect answer to every question. Finally, be careful of someone who appears to move through social interactions easily. This type of person may be a well-meaning social butterfly, but there's also a chance they're putting on a show you're going to pay a lot for.

- **Possession is the order of the day**

Have you ever come across someone who acts as if they are owed something by the world? That kind of person has to have at whatever cost what they want. They'll throw a tantrum if they don't, and make us pay for it. Human predators are also people entitled. This is why they often have no problem getting at whatever cost what they want — even if it means hurting others. The world is in its debt, after all, and this debt must be repaid even if it means stepping on a few or many toes along the way. At the workplace, entitlement is exercised in the form of a colleague who believes they deserve a promotion for whatever reason they come up with. This type of employee will go to great lengths to ensure that the boss gives them the promotion they believe they've earned even if they're barely pulling their weight at the bureau. They are going to try to make everyone else look bad and unworthy of the promotion. If they don't get their way, and the promotion goes to someone else, they'll make that person their enemy in their life. How could that person take their promotion off after all? It'll never happen to this entitled employee that they'll probably have to work harder to raise ranks.

- **They enjoy managing**

Most people like to have some control over certain aspects of their life. Wanting to be able to call the shots is normal, within reasonable bounds. The issue begins when a single person thinks they need to call the shots in their lives and the lives of others. Most manipulators are Freaks of Science. Some of them have subtle ways to express that control, while others can't be bothered to make it less obvious. If in your life you've got a control freak, you probably already know it. Power freaks are also impossible to ignore due to their tendency to get interested in just about anything and everything. Control freaks at the workplace have a very difficult time delegating to others, even when they need to. They want to run every show because they know it's theirs to reap the reward.

The inability to admit when they are wrong is another sign of a control freak. Human beings are prone to error, and accepting you are wrong requires a certain level of grace. This is something of a grace that most freaks of control lack. One reason people who love being in control find it difficult to admit error is because they see it as an admission to being weak, which contradicts their idealized self-image that they are better than anyone else. If you are ever involved in a control freak, debate, don't expect to win, they always win in any battle that involves a control freak. If they don't win, the winner will become the newest enemy to be defeated, whatever may come.

Control freaks tend to nitpick anything and everyone else, measuring them by the superior expectations they set for themselves. A control freak will have an opinion under the sun about anything, even if that opinion is uncalled for or even unsolicited. Their criticism is harsh and frequently makes others feel worse. This is a way for them to take control; if you make someone feel insecure and low, you have a greater chance of getting them to meet your demands, whatever they may be.

Control freak is not, as you might have guessed, the official psychological term for those individuals. Rather, this is a term used in informal circles to describe whoever has an obsessive desire to get others to comply with it or to control others. While the need for manipulative power over others motivates this unnatural need for control, there are several root causes for this sort of behavior.

Freaks of control also have personality disorders, which cause them to act as they do. A personality disorder is characterized as a behavior pattern that deviates from what is considered natural behavior. To recognize this kind of behavior as a personality disorder (and not just a teenager with a bad day), it must occur regularly, to the point that it is deep-set in the life and everyday choices of the offender. From time to time, everyone has their bad days where they make poor decisions; every day an adult with a personality disorder has a bad day. Adolescents are also diagnosed with personality disorders. In some people, it could take longer to arrive at a diagnosis.

Three personality disorders are likely to cause a person to become obsessed with being in control of others. These include antisocial personality disorder, personality disorder with histrionism, and personality disorder with Narcissism. People with antisocial personality disorders often have an exaggerated sense of self-worth and, if at all, very little empathy for others. As such, they are often predisposed to control others without feeling any kind of sympathy or mercy. Conversely, people with histrionic personality disorder love attention. They're going to go to whatever lengths to get us to pay attention. They have to be in full control of the show even if it means lying to get this kind of attention about everything in their lives. Attention is the means to and the result of their control over others. In short, it's a song they can dance to forever.

Narcissists love control because they believe that they are better than anyone else and that they have the right to control that. There's just no way a narcissist can get your way. If you're engaging with a narcissist, whether at work or in a personal relationship, the only answer that you'll ever be able to say is yes. Narcissists thrive on control because it nourishes their infinite desire to be the biggest deal in any room they are in.

Their feelings aren't genuine

Have you ever met someone who seemed very sweet and generous, but you were told by your instincts not to trust them? It's probably because your sixth sense could detect that it wasn't all that kindness and generosity. While the heart and mind can be fooled, the sixth sense is almost always able to pick out the truth from the lies. Human predators know that relationships are beneficial to certain emotions and behaviors. They know children are well-liked, and they take generosity to mean a person is good at heart. Predators won't care much about kindness but will go to great lengths to paint the image of perfection they require. They'll show up with home-baked cookies for community gatherings.

They will get the biggest check at charity events. They always get the brightest, warmest smiles. On the surface they will be the image of friendliness and hospitality in the neighborhood. That's why when they want to unveil their other hand, they still catch people unaware — the one that isn't as sweet and not as compassionate. Take a pinch of salt with you when dealing with someone who is going to great lengths to show they are a very good guy. Beware of what your gut is saying about this guy. You may be fooled by your ears and eyes, but the inner voice of reason will always have your back.

- **They like being the victims**

One of the easiest ways to divert attention from your misdeeds is to turn the spotlight on the wrongdoings of another person. Human predators perfected the art of the victim game. It allows them sufficient time to victimize another person while distracting everyone else. A person playing the victim will never make an apology for anything they do. If they are late, it's because someone else sent the invitation to the wrong meeting. If they lied, it is because their partner was aren't paying enough attention to them. If they hit another person, it is because they were made so mad by that person that it drove them to violence. It is always a story or something else.

The truth of the matter is the predator, never being the victim. They cannot also be the victim. After all, their lives and those of others have been orchestrated to suit their interests. But predators are also mindful that people want to feel bad for victims. As such, as long as it serves them, they can play the victim. With this understanding of how predators look, you may wonder what steps you can take to protect yourself. First of all, it's important to recognize that this first chapter only touches the surface of dark psychology and the players in it. The chapters that follow will dig deeper into peeling back the more intricate issues at stake. You'll have developed an even greater understanding at the conclusion of this deep dive about how manipulators and other dark characters work. This information will help you defend yourself and turn the tables accordingly, if necessary. You can still protect yourself, that being said, as early as now.

Basics to defend yourself from human predators

The first thing you need to understand is how to identify the predator. Two psychologists would later invent a name for this concept by the names of Paulhus and Williams in 2002: the dark triad. There have also been discussions and debates about the role that culture and society play in trying to understand the dark triad's identities. To put it plainly, behavioral scientists, psychologists, and scholars were keen to understand whether the Dark Triad persons were born or bred. Are we born evil and cynical, or are we becoming so because of the things we grow up to be exposed to? It has been noted that the dark triad has a significant genetic component to it according to numerous works done. The predator uses to conceal from you their real self. This, in the form of excessive gifts or forced affection, could be fake kindness and generosity. Watch out for anyone who finds himself too perfect. A wise person once said you should think twice if the deal is too good. If a person is found to be perfect and flawless, it is probably because they wear a mask. Once that mask comes off, you're going to be in a lot of trouble.

Second, know yourself in and out, so that you will never be blinded by another person. Everyone has spots that are vulnerable. If you do not know where your blind spots are, human predators will be open season. Predators are like sharks — one drop of blood, and they're like white on rice all over you. Get to know where you are bleeding from and keep this knowledge hidden far away inside of you until you are one hundred percent certain that this information can be trusted to a person.

The third way of protecting yourself from predators is to use the time to your advantage. According to World Bank statistics, the average life expectancy in the US in 2018 was 78, while that figure in Canada was 80. That means you have a very good chance of living past the age of seventy if you live in either of those places. So why is everybody so hurried about? Unfortunately, we're living in a world where everyone is in a rush to do something or go somewhere. In the midst of all this hurry, predators are preying on the desperate ones to catch up. If you hurry through things, you'll look back and think about all the mistakes you've made that you should have prevented. Use the time to your advantage when it comes to knowing someone, or understanding an investment. Predators like to inculcate fear in their prey by making them think they run out of time. You just don't run out of time. Time is with you. Use these wisely. If you pause to reflect every time you're faced with a decision, you'll find yourself making far better choices and avoiding the numerous traps that the predators around you have laid for you.

CHAPTER 3 A DEEP DIVE INTO THE DARK TRIAD

There is a phenomenon in the field of psychology, which is called the dark triad. The mysterious triad is a collection of three characteristics of personality, namely Narcissism, Machiavellianism, and Psychopathy. This set of three is called dark due to the typical malignant behaviors associated with those traits. The dark triad's dramatic contrast is the light triad, which is a topic and discussion for another book in itself. While the three traits stated on the dark triad in their own studies are distinct, it is shown that they often overlap in reality. What this means is that with blurred boundaries, a person who scores highly on the dark triad test will likely have all these traits present. It might be hard to tell, for example, where Narcissism stops and where psychopathy begins.

Discussions about the Dark Triad concept were initially begun in 1998 by three psychology experts who argued that Narcissism, Machiavellianism, and psychopathy occurred overlappingly in normal samples. Two psychologists would later invent a name for this concept by the names of Paulhus and Williams in 2002: the dark triad.

There have also been discussions and debates about the role that culture and society play in trying to understand the dark triad's identities. To put it plainly, behavioral scientists, psychologists, and scholars were keen to understand whether the Dark Triad persons were born or bred. Are we born evil and cynical, or are we becoming so because of the things we grow up to be exposed to? It has been stated that the dark triad has a significant genetic component to it according to numerous works done. That is, some born with a predisposition to the dark traits of the triad, however in terms of heritability, narcissism and psychopathy rank higher than Machiavellianism. That is when compared to a parent who ranks high on the Machiavellian scale, a psychopathic parent is more likely to transfer the trait to their offsprings.

The dark triadic traits have been shown to be well-represented in top-level management in the news, which may not be very pleasant to anyone who is employed. As the components of the dark triad are unpackaged in the parts below, it should become clear why this representation could be so. After all, very few CEOs, if any, arrived by playing nice to where they are.

The Dark Triad to Unravel: Narcissism

A story is told in Greek mythology about a young man named Narcissus. Narcissus was a hunter renowned for his striking, good looks. Narcissus did not have the time of day for them despite the adoration he received from his admirers and even pushed some to take their own lives to prove their love. While there are different versions of the story of Narcissus, all of them point to him being incredibly self-absorbed, which eventually ended up in him dying a death that was a punishment for his selfish ways. Thanks to the story of that young man, Sigmund Freud first coined the term narcissism. Freud, aptly titled On Narcissism in his famous 1914 essay.

Narcissism, in the simplest terms, is the excessive and obsessive self-admiration which a person has towards himself and his physical appearance. A narcissist is quite easy to spot because they easily give away their actions and beliefs. Asking yourself if you have a narcissist in your life? Here is what you should look for:

Narcissists like to feel superior, and often have the right to normal, healthy relationships involve a reasonable amount of giving and taking, whether they relate to work, personal, or business. Narcissists are not subscribing to that logic. They enjoy doing all the talking while somebody else does all the giving. They feel owed the things they demand, even if that is not the case. Narcissists are relentless in their pursuit to be at the center of attention and always right. A narcissist would never take responsibility for the job for everything that goes wrong inside a team.

Whenever a problem arises, the narcissist will deflect the blame from itself and place it on a different party. They believe themselves, after all, to be superior and unable to commit wrongdoing. If you're a narcissist dating, they're going to try and do it all about themselves. You have to eat whatever they want, do the things they want, and hang onto your life to make them happy. They're going to have no trouble doing all the things that ordinary people would frown upon because they're really doing you a favor in their minds by dating you. If you find these signs of extreme self-centeredness in an individual, you'll probably be dealing with a narcissist.

Narcissists are often perfectionists

Faults and imperfections are a normal part of life for many. If a party isn't going exactly as expected, most people have no trouble sitting back and enjoying it all the same for narcissists, that is not so. If anything isn't ideal for a narcissist, then it doesn't count. Narcissists seek perfection in everything they do because they believe they are flawless and therefore deserve the only perfection. If you're dating a narcissist, they're going to ask you for perfection as well as your dress, the way you speak, the kind of friends you have, the neighborhood you stay in, and just about everything. It'll be an ever-ending conquest you'll most likely lose. Seeing that perfection is often so difficult to get through in daily life, narcissists often end up miserable and frustrated.

Narcissists have an unflagging desire for dominance

When called upon, it is important always to be ready to take charge. This is a hallmark of great leaders. It helps to have a healthy sense of control over diverse aspects of your own life. You can't drift through life here and there with no sense of purpose or direction, after all. However, for narcissists, the need for control is more visceral — they have to be in control whatever may happen. Remember their considerable need for perfection? Well, narcissists feel they need to be in control so they can attain this perfection.

They actually can not have faith that other 'lesser beings' will be in charge, because then they will screw up everything. A narcissistic partner will want to dictate what kind of friends you can have, whether or not you should have a job, whether or not your friends can come to your home, and just about every detail in your life. You may find that, at the beginning of a relationship with a narcissist, you mistake this need for control for undying love and devotion. But you will begin to feel mistrusted and suffocated later on, and that will mark the beginning of the end. Narcissists in the workplace love to manage every aspect of the work of their employees. A narcissistic supervisor won't give his juniors any room to breathe and will do all they can to make sure he's the one calling all the shots.

Narcissists don't sense boundaries

Your boundaries are those guidelines you have set to determine how your personal interactions are going to proceed. Boundaries establish what is acceptable in your life and not acceptable. Boundaries are second nature to many. Most people, for example, will not take insults while they lie down. It's simply not acceptable to disrespect them in this way. Normal people are capable of recognizing limits in their daily lives. On the other hand, the narcissists have no time for such frivolities. A narcissist will have no problem intruding into your personal space because they believe they are entitled to be present. Because they believe these rules do not apply to them, they get a high from flouting social norms and rules, and nobody can do anything about it since they are superior to everyone else anyway.

How Do Others Control Narcissists?

Now that you can recognize a narcissist, you're likely wondering what the narcissist is doing to control you in your life. A narcissist's traits discussed in the previous section seem to be fairly easy to notice. How hard can it be to remember, after all, that someone is trying to manipulate you? The response is, it can be very difficult, particularly when this person disguises their acts as just looking for you. Most narcissists are usually very smart and can blend in their daily lives without calling attention to themselves. They can also be very talented and imaginative, and the beauty that attracts you to them will generally be that. When you're out there looking for a narcissist-shaped monster, you might not be looking for that talented and super creative friend who's always having a solution to everything. And yet, she might be the one narcissist in your life who only cares about winning irrespective of who gets hurt along the way.

Narcissists are also very keen liars, in addition to using their aforementioned characteristics to the best of their ability. Narcissists quickly master the art of deception in its various forms in a bid to be the star of the series. Deception is the way the narcissist throws you off reality, so they stay in control. In any case, they also live in a changed reality where they are perfect, and everybody else is inferior to them. Hence, deception is also a way for them to loop you into this endless narrative where they are the principal character.

The Dark Triad to Unpack: Machiavellianism

Niccolò Machiavelli, sometimes referred to as the founder of modern political science, was a Renaissance-era Italian who wore lots of hats. Machiavelli was amongst others a politician, historian, humanist, poet, author, and diplomat. Machiavelli composed his most famous book, The Prince, in 1513. Machiavelli, in this book, described and endorsed the use of unscrupulous means for gaining and maintaining political power. The term Machiavellianism arose from this work and its endorsements, which was used to refer to the kind of political leaders and tactics Machiavelli described in his book. This term was later borrowed from psychology experts to describe a personality trait characterized by a lack of emotion and a desire to achieve at the expense of others, be it through deceit, manipulation, or the flouting of common rules of decency and morality. A person who exhibits Machiavellianism is, in the simplest terms, willing to do just about anything if it means winning. Machiavelli is the reason why the ending phrase explains the means that exist.

Much work has been conducted since the adoption of the term Machiavellianism in psychology to determine precisely what drives the individuals who score highly on the Machiavellianism scale, otherwise known as high Machs. High Machs have been found to tend to value power, money, and competition above all else. High Machs place a very low premium on things like building a community, family, and even love. To those who score low on the Machiavellianism scale, otherwise known as low Machs, the reverse is true.

Strong Mach Characteristics

There are High Machs all around. In your current workplace, you probably know one, or even work for one. High Machs are driven and successful often. They have worked hard and intelligently to be where they are, often stepping on others' toes without apologetic action. If you know someone who is very successful and that everyone around you seems to fear, then you will probably be dealing with a high Mach. So, what exactly distinguishes an individual who scores highly on the scale of Machiavellianism?

The hate structure of high Machs

Structure comes with rules, and Machs has high rules of hatred. Ergo, likewise, high Machs hate structure. High Machs would rather be left alone while they go about making their own rules. They just abhor having to do something because someone else has said so. Rules make no sense to them, and the structure is in jail. Consequently, high Machs thrive in environments where they are boundless and free to be as creative as they wish. High Machs tend to prefer business environments as far as the professions go while shunning any profession that involves helping others. For example, High Machs makes a very effective salesman by counting on being willing to tell lies to sell a product if it earns them a commission. An individual who scores low on the scale of Machiavellianism could feel guilty of selling hot air to a consumer. Not so with a high Mach. As long as he is awaited with the benefit of a fat bonus and commission, a high Mach will ensure that customers give them their money in return for whatever they sell. In other words, for a high Mach, the result will always justify the process.

High Machs are high chances

While other people go through life smelling the roses and doing other clichés that make ordinary people happy, high Machs look at life as a challenge where they have to compete. They think of life as a giant chessboard where you have to get closer to winning with every move. High Machs, therefore, are highly opportunistic and will leap at every chance they will be able to grab for ahead. On the chessboard, they have no concern for others because they believe that there can only be one king while the rest remain on as pawns to be used as instruments for power and status attainment.

High Machs have an emotional detachment

High Machs have the uncanny ability to stay emotionally detached from any situation they find themselves in. They avoid commitments and often make relationship partners very frustrating. For High Machs, emotions and feelings are merely distractions that will prevent them from achieving their objectives. If you're married to a high Mach, when all family time is replaced with work commitments, you might find yourself very lonely. Work must be done to the high Mach in order to attain power and wealth. They don't care; they are neglecting their family. They just have to do what it takes to do. But this doesn't mean every workaholic is a high Mach. This is usually the case, however, more often than not.

High Machs are also more likely to have numerous sexual encounters because of their ability to detach their emotions from situations, often with people they are not well-known to. For that, there are two reasons. Oscar Wilde once said this: everything that's really about sex in human life, except sex. Sex is about might. No one is better at this than a high Mach who has persuaded yet another conquest to join him in bed. The second explanation for the multiple sexual partners is the emotional detachment capacity, which allows a high Mach to hop from person to person without having any kind of commitment to anyone.

High Machs are short of empathy

Empathy is described as being able to share one's feelings with another. Seeing that high Machs are not emotionally attuned to individuals or situations, it goes without saying that they are not exactly in the best position for being empathic. This lack of empathy also works to their advantage, in that they can easily hurt others to get ahead without blinking. After all, if you can not feel anybody's pain, in the first place, you really have no problem, causing them pain.

High Machs are good coworkers but not good friends

You want to get the teammate who will help you win the top prize in a sport or a debate. Due to their competitiveness and willingness to use any means to get ahead, High Machs make very good teammates in competitive scenarios. The same can not be said in relation to personal relationships. While a lot of people are going to rush to team up with a high Mach, not too many are going to be willing to date them or be best friends. This is just because they are not making very good friends. A high Mach will throw you to the drop of a hat under the bus, even if you're friends for years. High Machs then again don't really make friends — they just collect pawns and instruments for later use.

Small Machs are also uncanny

High Machs seldom place their hearts on their hands, thinking they're playing a game. They are difficult to figure out and are often found aloof. Most people often have no problem mixing and sharing their own bits of information with others. This is frivolous and unnecessary, a high find for Mach. Because of their emotional detachment, they have a hard time bonding and sharing with others. Also, since they believe that life is a game that needs to be played and won, they fear disclosing any information that could cause them to lose. As such, they tend to keep people at a distance, rather than let them in. Strong Machs also tend to be hated rather than respected and therefore do not have much room for hand-holding and other friendship-reserved niceties.

The Dark Triad of psychology

Psychopathy is a feature of personality marked mainly by a lack of empathy toward others. Psychopaths never show empathy for others, and will never feel guilt even though other people have been injured. There are numerous views about psychopathy, but most of them seem to agree on the three main features that distinguish a psychopath from any other normal individual. These three traits include boldness, lack of inhibition, and meanness that any other person would find uncomfortable.

Psychopaths are fearless and bold and are not afraid to venture into unfamiliar territory even when they may be in danger. Although these conditions usually stress most people, psychopaths can cope with these circumstances as if performing their everyday tasks. Psychopaths often have a high degree of self-confidence and social assertiveness that allows them to interact with people without the shyness or anxiety that others may have. Sometimes, when a horrific crime is committed, you may learn about the specifics of the crime and shudder while thinking to yourself: how could a person live with himself after doing so? It's business as usual for a psychopath to kill someone and then grab a sunny side up at their favorite cafe. This is not to say that all psychopaths have killed somebody. Some psychopaths then made their lack of guilt and vulnerability to certain crimes and transgressions.

Psychopaths exhibit poor control of the impulse because they can not control their urges. If a regular person has an impulse of some kind, they are always able to get it under control and speak out of that state themselves. For instance, if you're dealing with an annoying colleague who just won't be shutting up about their upcoming bridal shower, you'll probably be able to fight the urge to punch them in their face. On the other hand, a psychopath will often be overcome by impulse and will react without thinking twice about the cost of their decision. Psychopaths are prone to snapping in a simple way. Often one gets hurt when they snap.

Common decency, when dealing with others, demands a certain level of civility and kindness. This is not something of concern to psychopaths. While the majority of the population is concerned about love and compassion, the meanest person in the room would have no trouble becoming a psychopath. Depending on the circumstances in hand, they might be subtle or direct about it. In addition to these three main areas of commonality in their personalities, psychopaths tend to have other distinguishing features:

They represent risk-takers

This is related to their fearlessness and boldness. While everyone else is afraid of their safety, psychopaths are not spending two seconds worrying about security — theirs or anyone else. This characteristic is an asset when used for the right. On the flip side, taking such risks can be expensive, especially if someone else bears the burden of the risk. So it's no wonder that psychopaths who are nurtured in healthy settings tend to be successful entrepreneurs and politicians. They are genetically predisposed, after all, to take all the major risks in business and politics that will put them ahead.

They are absolutely charming

A psychopath puts on his best suit, wears the best smile on his face, and tells you all you need to hear, and you'll never be able to guess you've heard it from a psychopath. Although psychopaths can not feel or experience things the same way as everyone else, they are smart enough to know that people expect certain things to go some way. And while your date may not really fall in love with you after dinner, they know they should behave as if they are. Psychopaths are excellent students of life in that they can imitate normal behavior, enabling themselves to remain undetected for the longest period of time. Do not fall for a psychopath's charm — it's fickle, and it comes at a high price.

Often, they lack long-term targets

There's nothing exciting about long-term goals, at least regarding the psychopath. Psychopaths are living for the rush of adrenaline at the moment and are not waiting for a target to materialize for ten years. The perpetual bad boy who refuses to grow up and who is not committed to a healthy relationship may very well be a psychopath who literally can not surmount his inherited genes.

The Dark Triad Test

The Dark Triad Test is a measure of how one scores with respect to the three traits of Narcissism, Machiavellianism, and Psychopathy. The test is often used in different settings, and particularly by law courts and police. The dark triad test is also used by corporations to gage their employees. The main reason the dark triad test is applied is to determine the personality traits of an individual and possibly predict their behavior for the purposes of avoiding unsavory habits. It was noted that people who score high on the dark triad test are more likely to cause trouble and social distress, whether it's in the workplace or even in their places of residence. At the same time, these people will also likely have an easy time to attain leadership positions and gain sexual partners.

The dark triad test asks you to answer a series of questions on a range of topics, including how you feel about yourself and others, how you keep track of details you could use to harm others, and your general views on life, death, and social interactions, among others. The dark triad test, when self-administered, can be a fun way to gauge how you score on the dark triad test. When administered by law courts and police, the dark triad test may not be very accurate as the respondent may intentionally alter their answers to make them look better than they actually are.

This is a key limitation of the obscure triad test. If you're interested in taking the dark triad test, there are several online sites where you'll be able to complete a test in minutes. Be careful to take the test results too personally—sometimes, the answers you give are based on the type of day you are having and not on the type of person you are being. In any event, if you consider yourself a decent human being who always respectfully treats others and never harms others, you shouldn't be too concerned about what the test tells you. On the other hand, if you still seem to run into disagreements and disputes and have to talk yourself endlessly out of hurting others, then the answer you've been searching for all along might be a high score on the dark triad exam.

Addressing Dark Triad Personalities

They may not have taken the tests and brought you the results, but you probably know certain dark triad personalities in your life. That can be easily spotted.

CHAPTER 4 MANIPULATION – A TWO-WAY STREET

Renowned critic and often MIT linguist Noam Chomsky, one of the classic voices of intellectual dissent over the last decade, has compiled a list of the ten most popular and powerful tactics resorted to by the "hidden" forces to create a media exploitation of the population. The media have traditionally proven highly effective in molding public opinion. Through the media paraphernalia and propaganda, social movements have been produced or killed, wars justified, financial crisis tempered, spurred on by some other political forces, and even provided the trend of media as truth producers within the collective psyche.

Manipulation of the media is a part of our daily life. The media portray each event in a way that is comfortable for each one of them. Misunderstanding of the media-created truth in the audience can contribute to misjudgment and actions in humans. Not only do media have a social function, but they are also instruments for regulating public temperature. Media manipulation is about how news is interpreted, which depends on how people interpret a process and how they react to it. The media play varying degrees of a social role. They can talk about some things, and remain silent about others. That is precisely what makes them a new kind of force.

In closed and oppressive countries, media seek to convince the public that we must unconditionally embrace all of the government's political and social acts. And they are a part of the bodies of state control. Though the media are a conduit between the authorities and the people in open and democratic societies, they will provide the institutions with a two-way flow of knowledge to society and vice versa. Media rivalry leads to a distinction between news and facts, also called the manipulation of media

But how to identify the most effective approaches to recognize such psychosocial techniques that we definitely engage in? Fortunately, Chomsky was given the task of synthesizing and revealing these methods, which are much more obvious and complex but obviously all equally successful and demeaning from a certain viewpoint. Encouraging insanity, encouraging a sense of shame, encouraging diversion, or setting up imaginary problems, and then, somehow, overcoming them is only a couple of these.

There are tactics designed to direct whole populations. In many places, Sylvain Timsit is named. A quest elsewhere ends with the interdisciplinary French-speaking journal Les Cahiers Psychologie politique, and Noam Chomsky is mistakenly identified as the author. I don't know whether the tactics were or weren't initially intended satirically. It's more critical that the methods appear fairly straightforward, logical, and empirically measurable-with a little regular distance. Many persons may accept that their limited collection of themes and abbreviated knowledge bombardment not only depend on mass media.

Whoever does this and sees the world from the viewpoint of a liberal pluralism according to which there is no center of power, no hierarchy, and no law in society but several different groups of actors exercising their authority in a very balanced way such that those ideas that conform to the fundamental interests of the majority will probably reject the list.

What is Manipulation?

The first question which is frequently asked is, what manipulation is? In this guidebook, we will discuss manipulation in terms of psychological manipulation, which is a social influence that works by abusive, deceptive, or underhanded tactics to change the behaviors or perceptions of others or the subject. The manipulator will work to advance their own interests, usually, at the expense of someone else, so much of their manipulative methods will be devious, coercive, and exploitable. While social influence is not always negative in itself, when a person or group is being manipulated, it has the potential to harm them.

Social influence is usually perceived as something harmless, as in the case of a doctor working to persuade their patients to start adopting healthy habits. It extends to any social power that is capable of respecting those involved 's right to choose and is not unduly oppressive. On the other hand, if someone wants to get their own way and uses people against their own will, then the social impact can be negative and is generally looked down in. Psychological or emotional manipulation is viewed as a means of coercion and persuasion. This form of mind control can include many components, such as bullying and brainwashing. This will mostly be seen by people as being abusive or deceptive in nature.

Those who decide to employ manipulation will do so to try to control those around them. The manipulator will have some final goal in mind and will work through various forms of abuse to coerce those around them to help the manipulator reach the ultimate goal. They often involve emotional blackmail.

Those who practice manipulation will use tactics of mind control, brainwashing, or bullying to get others to complete the tasks. The manipulator's subject may not want to perform the task but feel they have no other option because of the blackmail or other tactics used. Most people who are manipulative lack adequate caring and sensitivity toward others, so they may not see their actions as a problem. Many manipulators just want to hit their final target and don't care about who got bothered or hurt along the way. Additionally, manipulative people often fear to get into a healthy relationship because they're afraid others won't accept it. Anyone with a deceptive attitude will also be unable to take responsibility for their own attitudes, concerns, and lives. Since they are not in a position to take responsibility for these issues, the manipulator will use manipulation tactics to get someone else to take responsibility.

Manipulators are often in a position to use the same tactics found in other forms of mind control to gain the influence they want over others. One of the tactics most used is called emotional blackmail. This is where the manipulator works to inspire sympathy or guilt in the matter they manipulate. These two emotions are chosen because they are considered the two strongest of all human emotions and are the most likely to spur others into the manipulator's desired action. The manipulator would then be able to take full advantage of the issue, using the compassion or remorse they have generated to compel others to comply or help them achieve their ultimate objective. The manipulator will often not only be able to create these emotions but will also be able to inspire degrees of sympathy or guilt that are far out of proportion to the current situation. This means they can take a situation like missing out on a party, seeming like the subject is missing out on a funeral or something really important.

Emotional blackmail is just one tactic manipulators employ. One of the other tactics that many manipulators have been successful is to use a form of abuse, which is known as crazy-making. Usually, this tactic is aimed with the hope of creating self-doubt in the subject being manipulated; this self-doubt will often become so strong that some subjects may begin to feel that they are going crazy. The manipulator will sometimes use forms of passive-aggressive behavior to bring about madness. They can often choose to show support or approval of the subject verbally, but instead, offer non-verbal signals that reflect conflicting meanings. Often the manipulator will actively try to undermine certain events or behaviors while loudly showing its support for the same behavior. If the manipulator is caught in the act, they use denial, justification, rationalization, and ill-intention deception to get out of the trouble.

One of the biggest problems with psychological manipulators is that they are not always able to recognize what others around them may need and will lose the ability to meet or even consider those needs. This does not excuse the behavior they are doing, but often others' needs are not taken into consideration or are not a priority for the manipulator so they can perform manipulative tasks without feeling guilty or shameful. This can make it hard to stop the action and rationally justify why the manipulator wants to stop it. Furthermore, the manipulator may find it difficult for them to form meaningful and long-lasting friendships and relationships because they will always feel used to the people they are with and will have difficulty trusting the manipulator. The issue goes both ways in building relationships; the manipulator won't be able to recognize the other person's needs while the other person won't be able to form the necessary emotional connections or trust with the manipulator.

Requirements to Successfully Manipulate

An effective manipulator must have tactics at hand, which will make them successful in using people to achieve their own ultimate objective. While there are several theories about what makes a successful manipulator, we'll look at the three requirements that George K. Simon, a successful author of psychology, has set out. The manipulator, Simon says, will need to:

1. Be able to conceal from the subject of their aggressive conduct and intentions.

2. Be able to recognize the vulnerabilities of their intended topic or the victims to determine which tactics are most effective in achieving their objectives.

3. Have some level of ruthlessness readily available, so they won't have to deal with any discomforts that may arise as a result of harming the subjects if it comes to that. That can be physical or emotional harm.

The first requirement the manipulator must fulfill in order to manipulate their subjects successfully is to mask their aggressive behaviors and intentions. If the manipulator goes around saying their plans to everyone or always acts mean to others, no one will stick around long enough to be manipulated. Rather, the manipulator must have the ability to hide his thoughts from others and behave as natural as is everything. Even those who are being exploited, at least not in the beginning, do not know it. The manipulator is going to be nice, behave like their best friend, and maybe help them out with some problem or another. The manipulator has enough information about them by the time the subject becomes aware of the issue to coerce the subject into continuing on. The manipulator will then need to be able to determine what the vulnerabilities are of their intended victim or victim. This will help them find out what tactics to use to achieve the end objective. Sometimes they can be the manipulator capable of making this phase with a little observation, and at certain times, they would need to have some form of contact with the subject before they come up with the full plan.

The third prerequisite is to be brutal on the manipulator. It won't be going well if the manipulator puts all of their efforts into it and then worries about whether the topic will end up being fair. If they cared about the topic, they are unlikely to be going through with this plan at all. The manipulator won't care at all about the subject and doesn't really care if any harm, either physical or emotional, occurs to the subject as long as the overall objective is met. One reason manipulators are so successful is that the subject often fails to realize they are being manipulated in the process until later on. They may think all goes well; maybe they think they've made a new friend in the manipulator. They are trapped by the time the subject knows that they are being used or that they no longer want to be a part of the process. The manipulator will be able to take advantage of many different tactics, including emotional blackmail, to get their way finally.

Victim Control

One thing the manipulator needs to be able to accomplish in order to see success is to control its subjects. There are some different explanations available to understand better how this can be achieved by the manipulator. Two of the theories to be discussed in this section will include those begun by Harriet Braiker and Simon.

Hardy Braiker

Harriet Braiker is a clinical psychologist who produced a book on self-help. She's defined five basic ways in her book that the manipulator can control his subjects. Including:

• Positive reinforcement
• Negative strengthening: Partial or intermittent strengthening
• Penalty
• Traumatic thinking, just that
• Gives one court

The first two tactics discussed include positive strengthening and negative reinforcement. The manipulator can use a number of techniques of positive reinforcement such as public recognition, facial expressions (such as a smile or a forced laugh), attention, gifts, acceptance, money, excessive apologizing, superficial compassion, which may include crocodile tears, superficial charm, and praise. The point of using such reinforcement is to give the person a reason to want to be a friend of yours. If you give someone a gift or some money when the time comes, they may be more willing to help you out. If you can make the subject feel bad for you, then later, they'll have the support they need to be on your side. The other form of strengthening that can be applied is negative reinforcement. In this tactic, the manipulator removes the subject from a negative situation as a reward for doing something else. An example of this would be, "You're not going to have to do your homework if you allow me to do that for you." Each of these has particular strengths and weaknesses that allow the manipulator to get out of the subject what they want. The manipulator will also use a mix of various strategies to get the things they want.

A manipulator can also employ partial or intermittent reinforcement. This method of strengthening is used to effectively build an environment of doubt and fear within the subject. Gambling comes as an example of this. While the gambler may sometimes win, overall, they will still lose some form of money, especially if they play for a long period of time. But the win is always enough to hold the target on the same course, long after they can't. The manipulator must use this technique at enough intervals to provide the subject with encouragement to keep the subject coming back.

Punishing is yet another method used to control the manipulator's subject. There are many different actions that might fit into this category. They include playing the subject, crying, sulking, using the guilt trip, emotional blackmail, swearing, threats, and intimidation, using the silent treatment, yelling, and nagging. The point of using this method is to make the subject feel like they have done something wrong. The subject will feel bad and want to make things right, with the manipulator falling right back in.

Finally, the last method Braiker mentions in her work are the one-trial, traumatic learning. This is where the manipulator explodes in the hopes of conditioning or training the subject in not wanting to contradict, confront, or upset the manipulator for the slightest things. Some of the tactics that could be used in this method include explosive anger, verbal abuse, and other behaviors that are intimidating and used to establish superiority and dominance over the subject matter.

We have also come up with a list of tactics manipulators need to use to control their victims successfully. Some of these are similar to those listed by Braiker but with some more details. It will encompass:

- Lying: Manipulators lying to their subjects really are wonderful. Often the subjects will find it hard to tell when they're being lied to at the time. When the subject discovers the obvious lie, it is usually too late to do anything about it. The only way the subject can ensure that their chances of being lied to are to look out for different styles of personality who are experts in the art of deception and lying. In order to get their way, the manipulator will lie about something, and for the most part, their targets will have no idea that it will happen until it is too late to do something about it.
- Omission lying: This one is similar with a few minor variations to the approach mentioned above. Omission lying is a bit more subtle, because the manipulator will tell some of the truth, but will withhold some of the key issues that should have been disclosed. This can also be called propaganda. The manipulator might say they need to borrow some money to get gas to buy groceries when they need the money to pick up some drugs or other illicit substances in reality. While using the money to buy gas, they have left out an important part, just as they said. Probably the subject wouldn't have given the money if they knew the end of the story and now they might get caught up in something illegal.
- Deception: Manipulators are Denial Experts. None of them will admit they did anything wrong, even when all the evidence points to them. They will always deny something and often make it look like the subject is the one at fault.
- Rationalization: This is when the manipulator uses an excuse to make them look good. They might say they did the act just because they wanted to support the subject. This tactic is related to the spinning technique, too.
- Minimization: This is a mixture of rationalization and tactics of denial. The manipulator will tell everyone their behavior is not really as irresponsible or harmful as the subject was thinking. An example of this would be when the

manipulator says an insult or taunt they've performed just a joke, and the subject should be

Don't take them that seriously.

- Selective attention or inattention: The manipulator works during this tactic to avoid paying attention to anything that distracts them from their ultimate goal. They are trying to trivialize it and make it look not as important to them as it really isn't. A case in point would be when the manipulator says, "I don't want to listen to this."
- Diversion: Not only are the manipulators good at lying to their subjects, but they are also experts in avoiding clear answers to questions asked. If somebody asks them a question they don't like or just want to know if they're lying to them, the manipulator will try to push the conversation in a different direction. The manipulator will often briefly give the question a vague answer before moving the conversation to another topic.
- Evasion: This tactic, with a few differences, is very similar to diversion. The manipulator will answer the questions given to them in this tactic, but they will use weasel words, vague answers, ramble, and provide irrelevant answers to the question. When they do, they'll leave the subject with more questions than answers.
- Intimidation: The manipulator will always try to keep the victim on the defensive to make sure they stay on the same team all the way through. This is often done by employing veiled, implied, indirect or subtle threats to the subject.
- Guilt Trip: Manipulators like using the guilt trip as a form of bullying to get the subject to do what they want. The manipulator will try to make the subject feel guilty in some way, such as saying the subject has it too easy, is too egotistical, or just doesn't care enough about the manipulator. That's it. This will lead the victim to start feeling sorry for the manipulator. The subject will then be kept in a position of submissiveness, anxiety or self-doubt, making it easier for the manipulator to use them still.

- Shaming: The manipulator's whole aim is to make the subject feel bad or have sympathy for them so that the subject continues to go along with the scheme. One way the manipulator can do this is by making use of putdowns and sarcasm to the shame of it. This technique makes the subject feel indignant. Most of the shaming tactics used are going to be very subtle and would include things like subtle sarcasm, rhetorical comments, unpleasant voice tone, or a fierce look.
- Playing as a victim: the manipulator wants to look like they are the victim, no matter what, even if they are the ones in control. When the manipulator behaves like the victim of their circumstances or someone else's actions, they may elicit compassion, sympathy, and pity. Most people won't be able to stand by and watch as someone is suffering, and the manipulator will find it easy to get those same people to work with.
- Vilifying the subject: this is one of the most powerful tactics that can be used since it puts the subject on the defense role almost instantly while at the same time, they are concealing hostile motives from the manipulators. The manipulator will try to turn things around, so the target appears to be the victim and the one who caused all the trouble. Then the subject will want to find ways to change this outlook and get back on the manipulator side, making it easy to use. Manipulators often hide their own agendas by making it look like the work they do is for some noble cause. They said only the mean thing about your outfit because the principal wants to start sprucing up the school look, and they wanted to help out. The term "just doing my job" would fit into that category as well.
- Seduction: Seduction may be used by manipulators to get the things they want. Some tools that would fit this category would include intensive support, flattery, praise, and charm. That's it. They get their defenses lowered to the subject. After a time, the subject will start giving its loyalty and confidence to the manipulator who will use it as they please.
- Projecting the blame: The manipulator is going to spend a lot of time blaming others for their problems. When this happens, it's often hard to detect so nobody can call them out on it.

- Feigning innocence: if the manipulator gets caught in the act of reaching their own agenda, they will try to suggest that it was completely unintentional if harm was done. They may even deny that they were doing anything in the first place. The manipulator will put an indignant look of surprise on their faces when caught. The aim of this tactic is to make the victim doubt their own sanity and judgment because it looks as if they were wrong.
- Feigning confusion: another thing that could happen when the manipulator is caught is that they could be playing dumb. This will happen if the manipulator tries to pretend they have no idea what the matter is about. They may also act as though they're confused when a critical issue comes up to them.
- Brandishing anger: When the manipulator uses anger, it's a matter of getting them to feel sorry or sympathy. The manipulator will be able to shock their subject back into submission if done in the correct manner. The manipulator really isn't really angry; they just put an act on to get what they want.

As can be seen, the manipulator can use a lot of tools to get to their final goals. These tactics will often be used in such a way that the subject doesn't realize what is going on in the beginning, and it will take them some time to catch on. When they do, the manipulator will be able to use some of the tactics that will be addressed in the next section in order to keep the discussion going in the right direction. The manipulator is skilled in using a combination of these skills to get the things they want and how much they harm the other person in the process doesn't matter to them.

Manipulation Techniques

A manipulator, as discussed earlier, must work to achieve its final target. To accomplish the ultimate objective, the manipulator can use whatever tactic they can to get people to do what they want. The five most common techniques that a manipulator will use to achieve their ultimate goals include blackmail, emotional blackmail, putting the other person down, lying, and creating an illusion. Those will be discussed in each of the previous sections.

Blackmail

Blackmail is the first technique that a manipulator would employ. Blackmail is considered to be an act involving unjustified threats to make a certain benefit or to cause a loss to the subject unless the demand of the manipulator is met. It can also be described as the act of intimidation involving threats of criminal action, threats of taking property or money from the subject, or threats of causing physical harm to the subject. The word blackmail has a long history; it was originally a term that meant payments that the settlers rendered to the area that bordered Scotland to the chieftains in charge. This payment was made to shield the settlers from the marauders and robbers who were going into England. It has since changed to mean something else and is an offense in the United States in some instances. Blackmail is more of a threat to the subject for the purposes of this section, whether physical or emotional, in order to coerce them into doing what the manipulator wants. In certain cases, Bribery is often known to be extortion. Although there are times when the two are considered synonymous, some differences do exist. Extortion, for instance, is when someone takes another person's property by threatening to do future harm if the property is not given. Blackmail, on the other hand, occurs when threats are used to discourage the subject from engaging in lawful activities. Those two events will work together at times. The person may threaten someone and may need money to be kept at bay and not cause harm to the subject.

To get what they want, the manipulator should be able to use this strategy. They will take the time to learn about their subject's stuff of a personal nature, and then they will use it as a means of intimidation against them. By threatening to spill an embarrassing secret or ruining their chances of getting a new job or promotion, they might blackmail their subject. Or the manipulator could work more threateningly by threatening to physically harm their subject or the family of the subject unless they agree to go along with the manipulator. Whatever the blackmail may be, it is used with the assist of the subject to help the manipulator reach their final goal.

Emotional blackmail.

Another similar tactic which the manipulator can use is called emotional blackmail. The manipulator will seek to inspire sympathy or guilt in its subject during this technique. These two emotions are the strongest for humans to feel, and they will often be enough to spur the subject into the manipulator's desired action. The manipulator will take advantage of this fact to get the thing they want; they will use the sympathy or guilt they inspire to coerce the subject into cooperating or assisting with them. Often the degree of sympathy or guilt is blown out of proportion, which makes the subject even more likely to help out in the situation. The point of using this sort of blackmail is playing more on the subject 's emotions. The target has a threat to contend with in daily blackmail, often involving physical damage to themselves or someone they love. The manipulator will work with emotional blackmail to inspire emotions that are strong enough to spur the subject to action. While the subject might think they are helping out of their own free will, the manipulator has worked to ensure they are assisting and bringing out the emotions whenever needed.

Putting The Other Person Down

The manipulator has other options available if they want to get their subject to assist in achieving the final goal. One technique that has quite a bit of success is when the manipulator can put his subject down. In typical situations, if the manipulator uses communication skills to get their subject down, they may run a high risk of making the subject feel as though they have been subjected to a personal assault. If the subject feels like they're being targeted, they'll be bristling and not able to assist the manipulator in the way they want. Instead, the target won't like the manipulator and will remain as far away as possible from them, making it very difficult for the manipulator to achieve their final objective.

This is why the manipulator won't just go around and put their subject down. They need to be more discreet about the process and find a way of doing it without raising red flags or making the subject feel like they're being attacked. One way you can do this is through humor. Humor can lower barriers, which might otherwise appear as humor is funny and makes people feel good. The manipulator will turn their indignation into a joke. Although the put down has turned into a joke, it will work just as effectively as if the joke was not present without leaving the visible scars on the subject.

The manipulator will often direct their put down in the third person form. It helps them hide what they mean more effectively, which offers a convenient way to refute damage if it comes back to haunt them later. For instance, they could start their put down with "Certain people think ..." If the target would still assume that the remarks were made about them, then the manipulator might end it with a throwaway line that might involve something like "present company except, of course." The idea of the put down is to make the subject feel less than the manipulator, somehow. It takes the manipulator to a new level and leaves the subject feeling as though it desired something. The topic is more likely to try to make it better and correct any errors they have made. This will put the manipulator in a position of power and will make it easier for them to get the subject to help.

Lie.

No matter what the manipulator's end objective is, lying is something they are an expert at and are going to do all the time to get what they want. There are several different types of lies that the manipulator can use to help them attain their final goals. One is that they are telling full lies, and others are omitting parts of the truth from their subjects. When the manipulator lies, it's because they know the lie will go much more effectively on their agenda than the truth would. Telling someone the truth might make them unwilling to help the manipulator out, and that would go against their plans altogether. Instead, the manipulator will tell a lie to convince the subject to do something for them, and it is too late to fix the problem by the time the subject finds out about the lie. Also, the manipulator could decide to omit part of the truth in the stories they tell.

They will say some of the truth in this process but will leave out other details that are unsavory, or that could impede the progress being made. Such kinds of lies can be just as risky as telling what the truth of the story is and what the lie is increasingly difficult. It's important to realize that anything they tell you when you're dealing with the manipulator can be a lie. It's not a safe idea to believe what the manipulator is doing, because they're only trying to manipulate and use their subjects to achieve the ultimate goal. The manipulator will do and say anything possible, even lying, to get what they want, and will not be sorry. As long as they get what they want, they don't worry too much about how it affects the subject or others around them.

Making an Illusion

Aside from lying, the manipulator would be an expert in building illusions that are more successful in achieving their final target. They will work to create a picture they want and then convince the subject that this illusion is actually a reality, whether it matters to the manipulator or not. To do that, the manipulator will build up the evidence needed to prove the point that works toward their goal. The manipulator will plant the ideas and the evidence into the subject's minds to start the illusion. If these ideas are in place, the manipulator will be able to step back for a few days and allow the manipulation to take place in the minds of the subjects during that time. After that, the manipulator would have more time to get the topic to go along with the strategy.

Manipulation is a form of mind control which the subject finds difficult to resist. Unlike brainwashing and hypnosis described in the preceding chapters, manipulation can occur in daily life and can occur in some instances without the subject having much knowledge or control. The manipulator must work discreetly to achieve their ultimate objective without making the subject become suspicious and disrupt the operation. The manipulator won't worry about who they're hurting or how others might feel, and most of them won't be able to understand the needs of their subjects. They just know they want something and that the topic they've chosen will help them get to their goal. The methods that are mentioned in this chapter are intended to help understand what goes on during the process of deception and how the mind of the manipulator can work. It is also best to try to steer clear of someone who may be a manipulator so that you are able to prevent this kind of mind control.

Diversion technique

The diversion technique is an integral aspect of social regulation, which is to deflect public attention from issues and critical improvements determined by the political and economic elites. Through the flooding method, endless distractions, and trivial details, the mind gets more docile and less important. The diversion strategy is also necessary to avoid mass interest in science, economics, psychology, neurobiology, and cybernetics. Here the keyword is "insignificance." Focus is an incredibly scarce tool. If a democratic society should be structured for the relatively little benefit because most people will be watching, then the majority must be concerned with these issues so that they do not interfere with particular interests. Under the word "bread and circuses," Juvenal of the Roman Republic attested to such a state of diversion.

Whoever values the choice of topics in TV, radio, newspaper, and fellow-person conversations should inquire about the relevance of particular topics to one's life or fellow-person life by reflecting on the conditions of long-term happiness in existence and then investigate whether the relationship of working time or energy expenditure to life importance can show some form of "inversion" of events.

In order to make those themes dramatic, there are exclusive deals in the store, tables of favorite teams, love affairs of the famous, neighboring child's name intrigue, medium-fat advantages compared to regular margarine and so on vs. the abolition of civil rights, slavery and attempted mass murder and secret wars by Western "models," war anchoring, sexism and precariousness in normative terms.

The Process of Forced Question, Reaction, And Solution

This approach is often called "Problem-reaction-solution." They establish a problem, a "situation" that will trigger a reaction in the audience so that this is the standard of the steps that you will embrace. For example: 'let us escalate urban crime, or organize bloody attacks to increase public acceptance of laws and policies that damage their freedom.' Or: create an economic downturn, so that the public may recognize the annulment of civil rights and the elimination of public services as a necessary evil.

When social issues are concocted in order to stimulate a particular need for ideology in the population, a solution in the political direction desired from the outset is made possible. A serious crime is committed, especially when people's living conditions worsen. Neoliberal proponents are highly creative, as seen in the example of government finance that was gradually undermined as public debts skyrocketed, and the requisite fear was generated with the help of the media and business lobbies to offer fake solutions in the form of debt brakes. These inevitably lead to follow-up problems (financing bottlenecks, economic inflation, more increase in government debts) that revitalize the old familiar idea of privatization as a subsequent remedy and broaden the sphere of control for massively concentrated private capital.

This includes privatizing, deregulating, and slashing state spending. Resistance to the revenue side of the state cuts comes from the beneficiaries of patronage and subsidies. Hence the emaciation or thinning would possibly begin with tax cuts on the revenue side to help the dictate of the empty treasury. This makes the explosion of state deficits as shown by practice. This sort of tactic can be seen in the ongoing "Euro-crisis." Economic recession is forced to cause mass unemployment by social cuts. Dismantling the structure of collective bargaining fuels wage cuts, which lead to corollary issues.

Naomi Klein gave many examples of the cycle in her book "The Shock Doctrine." Whoever sees the knowledge advantage of the elites over their diverse populations, particularly when the mass media acts as a "fourth hand" under resource scarcity and capital-connection factors and under a consensus mindset, does not need much imagination to understand how quickly disasters, catastrophes, and other problems can be exacerbated and manipulated in many areas.

Rating of Improvements

Gradually apply enough pressure, drop by drop, for a few consecutive years to make an unreasonable measure appropriate. It is in such a way that in the 1980s and 1990s modern, revolutionary socio-economic conditions were imposed: the minimal state, privatization, poverty, instability, mass unemployment, wages that do not guarantee decent incomes, several reforms that would have given rise to a revolution if they were implemented at once.

The understanding of the political processes of change often depends on their gradation, as is obvious for light, sound, and noise, etc. The economization of all aspects of life from today to tomorrow can not be implemented into the crisis. Rather, if the cost-benefit, business- and management-model is to become the all-pervasive social theory, it must be culturally sedimented through centuries by powerful institutions. These methods are implemented at a smaller scale as well. As for the case of the proposed cuts in the school's university area, the OECD publication recommends keeping state grants constant and not lowering them on account of the danger of protests of "watchful political" groups.

Postponing the changes

Another way of making an unpopular decision is to view it as "painful and important" in order at the time to win over public approval. Any potential sacrifice is easier to consider than an imminent sacrifice. First of all, because the remedy is not widely used; secondly, because the public, the people, are still inclined to naively believe that "all will change tomorrow" and that the sacrifice needed can be avoided. Which gives the public more time to get used to the idea of change and accept it when the time comes without resignation.

If the expected worsening of conditions is on the agenda for a large part of the population, the supposed reasons for this should be set out early. As long as the issue being built is not yet serious, there would be little impetus for civil society to look at the assertions. When it is extreme, the question that was built appears as a common reality. Demographic transition and global rivalry have been put at the forefront in Germany, while jobs, pension, and social reforms tend to be "painful" yet common needs in times of prolonged capitalist collapse.

Response In Language Understood by Children

Many advertisements targeting the general public use rhetoric, claims, characters with especially infantile intonation, frequently targeting frailty, as if the audience were a very young-age individual or mentally disabled. The more you try to fool the audience, the more infantile the adoption sound is. Why? For what? If an individual goes to a person as if she were 12 years of age or younger, then, owing to suggestive nature, the other person tends to reply or react with some probability without much thought as a person 12 years of age or younger would.

Vague messages are used to reveal negative subjects where something can be perceived about what's being said. For extreme criticism, no surfaces of attack do emerge. However, if the population is addressed directly, a simple language that renounces relevant information in a patronizing or solicitous sympathetic tone compels the collective counterpart in the position of the children. People are used to corresponding early on to some role models that are triggered by environmental incentives. With simple hierarchies and conduct patterns embedded in a strongly conservative culture, this technique can have the desired success in the form of unquestioned obedience and trustful acceptance that inspires faith.

Replace emotions with reflection

The puppet-masters do not want to trigger the thoughtful sides of the people. They try to emotionalize to touch the unconscious men. This is why so many of these messages are filled with emotional content. The aim is to trigger a sort of "short circuit" in the mechanisms of logical thought. They use emotions to catch the message's general meaning but not its particulars. This is another way in which they destroy the rational thinking potential of people

In evolutionary history, "Thought" as capacity is new. The basis of the human spirit is an emotional core that leads to judgmental forces at whose gates security guards of reason simply refuse their service. Inequality and inequality are growing rapidly; "competitiveness" and competition among the population are becoming the prime incentive of humanity, and German tank deliveries to dictators to quench rebellions are becoming the standard case.

Promoting Ignorance

Ensure the public is unable to grasp the techniques and strategies that are used to regulate and enslave. The standard of education offered to the lower social classes should be as weak and inferior as possible, so that it is and remains difficult for the lower classes to overcome the difference of ignorance between the lower classes and upper classes. Ignorance may involve a lack of knowledge and a lack of knowledge. Both conditions can be closely interconnected. Neglect can cause shame. Then, numerous possibilities to escape embarrassment will benefit not-wanting to know.

One can completely stay away from the milieus and themes of political power and keep the shameful awareness of one's lack of information out of the spotlight, or one can deny the importance of knowledge and leap out of the way in phrases like "nothing can change anyway!" "Nothing can be done!" and "the world runs that way!" which are appropriate like curtains wherever the relaxed atmosphere would otherwise be. There are patterns of human activity exploited by the state and capitalist power to the detriment of the majority of the population. There is a significant gap between the importance of information and expertise in economic relations. What's money, then? Within a national economy, what is the role of wages and productivity? What are the conditions for the distribution, and how did they develop? Who owns what, and for what? Why is there mass unemployment within a society, and how does it affect the pecking order or balance of power?

Strangely enough, these topics are rarely discussed in school, and commercial television or even in a non-controversial or fragmentary manner-although the concepts associated with them still have the last function to explain incisive macro-social shifts. "That costs jobs!" "We can no longer afford this welfare state!" "We need structural changes!" and "We need to increase productivity!" are heard. Comprehensive information here should be a political requirement (at least if democracy at the ballot box should not be limited to the blind motor act). However, people's systemic ignorance is fostered by private enterprise lobbyism, by media brainwashing or by that concentration of work, income rivalry, and status anxieties - that restrict the focus to the near environment.

Fostering Mediocrity

Any of the patterns and fashions are not only coming from anywhere. It's almost always someone who sets them in motion and supports them. They do so to establish homogeneous preferences, desires, and views. Such fashions and trends are actively marketed by the media. Most have to do with trivial, wasteful lifestyles, even ludicrous ones. They are telling people that this way of behaving is just what is in style. The standardized truth is to work, consume, take advantage of the possibilities of mass entertainment, and be honest in little things. People embrace the uniform truth and transmit it obligatorily to their fellow citizens.

Offer a poor conscience to resist

Make the person believe he/she is the culprit of their own misfortune and cause them to doubt their intellect, skills, or efforts. Instead of rebelling against the economic system, therefore, the person devalues and blames himself, creating a depressed state whose aim is to stifle action because, without action, there is no revolution. In an interesting book, Stephan Hessel, the renowned resistance leader and co-author of the Declaration of Human Rights, urged: "Be appalled!" He aimed at the discriminatory, anti-social, and power-centered circumstances of our time that fundamentally endanger humanity and pleaded for a dedicated and educated standard of living that uses civil disobedience.

To undermine the expectations of this kind of mentality, individuals must be given a bad conscience that paralyzes them in preserving conditions from the functional elite viewpoint. They are advised that they are deficient, or that human existence is poor altogether. The person is a greedy, gourmand, and lazy person. The person who doesn't think he is a "healthy guy." This implicit message can be heard in the varied TV entertainment[24], resounding in slogans such as "We have lived beyond our means" or in the devaluation and punishment of living conditions created by the social structure that was followed by a public rabble-rousing against socially deprived people.

The environment created here demoralizes large sections of the population as it directs the general aversion to those fellow persons who are bound to the social state rather than directing this aversion to the actual common causal agents of the suffering. This atmosphere breaks unity by calling everyone to a bad conscience and telling them to withdraw in the close environment so that they can be trustworthy and ready to accomplish it.

Knowing more about people than they know.

Science has given us access to this information about human biology and psychology over the last few decades. Yet, most people still don't have the information available. Just a small bit of information ever gets to the public. The bourgeoisie meanwhile has all the knowledge and use it as they please. Once again, we can see how ignorance promotes domination over the culture for the powers that be. The goal of these media influence tactics is to transform the environment into whatever the most influential people want it to be. We obstruct the skill and freedom of rational thought for everyone. Yet it is up to us to avoid passively letting them manipulate us. We have to wage as much war as we can.

Although in denial and confusion about social circumstances, all sorts of constant bombardment and market publicity magnets fix the populace, those who have nothing to lose and extensive resources [do little to avoid this according to the maxim "information is power. For example, think tanks work here as institutions receiving millions of powerful capital interests and generating dominant expertise through studies suitable for functional elites and decision-makers. If one sees the world as a causal network where an infinite range of causes and effects are linked together on the most diverse planes, organizations with immense resources create fantastic social intervention-knowledge through detailed documentation and statistical analysis (big information and information mining), not revolutionary scientific theories.

CHAPTER 5 DEFENSE AGAINST MANIPULATION

Self-defense entails negotiation as well as manipulation with the offender/attacker. In these situations, you are attempting to persuade the offender not to allow you to go. You are additionally attempting to de-escalate the situation to get away from and use force against him.

In case the offender has a weapon, attempt to persuade him to avoid using the weapon by stating that things will go healthier when he does not use it, or maybe the weapon is frightening you. After the weapon is no longer a problem, you can, in that case, decide to use force against the offender or even seek a chance to get away from.

When the assailant is in the home of yours, you can talk him into allowing you to visit the bathroom. Perhaps there's a window you can escape from in there. Or maybe you can get an additional way to get away from (backdoor, side door, several additional windows). Or perhaps in case you think that you can make use of force against him, go ahead. There's additionally the choice of only wholly flipping out on the assailant to scare him. Begin acting insane, scream at the top of your voice, wave your arms in the air, and begin running about like a maniac. The assailant may be freaked out by the behavior of yours, and he may only get the heck out of there.

Individuals do not love to consider that, but giving in to the attacker's demands can save the life of yours. It can likewise prevent you from being seriously hurt during the strike. Rather than thinking about this as providing in, think of it as passive spoken self-defense. You speak with the enemy as in case you already know precisely where he is coming from. You allow him to know you are not going to attempt to do Anything to tick him off. You decide to determine which method is the most excellent option for you. In the event, you do not see some chance for escaping, using force against the enemy, or only going insane. You definitely can try to have no option but to attempt to diffuse the situation so that you do not get killed or even seriously injured by merely speaking to the enemy to calm him down and allowing him to realize that you will not resist.

The best way to recognize a psychological manipulator

Occasionally individuals can act in a particular way that leaves others feeling powerless, as well as the victim of the game can wind up confused as well as disorientated without any idea just how it all took place. It has happened to everyone at several stages in the life of theirs as individuals attempting to get' one up on each other' is an all-natural process of leadership; nonetheless, in most instances, it's both sides which don't identify what's developing.

Right here, I am going to describe the "hit as well as run" technique of mental manipulation. This particular type of energy management is actually among the strongest as unless the target is quite powerful in will power and ready to risk looking out of place, the chances of success are stacked against achievement.

A hit and run technique is referred to as the following. Picture one partner (Person A) has invested an extended time planning to go out for the evening and take a great deal of attention and care but has poor self-esteem. The self-esteem problem might result in the individual to depend on the manner they look to feel valuable, but the inner fear of theirs is they're not up to scratch. As they come downstairs to their significant other or maybe friend, a friend of theirs could say a thing as "come on, are you getting prepared?

It's almost time to visit out! (Implying they don't seem) that is ready (This will be the HIT) Aimed to bring about from the person's fear that really, they're not up to scratch. When individual A then attempts to protect themselves by replying. "I am ready" the partner of theirs can turn back and say, "Great, you look great; we need to go then!" (This will be the RUN) If individual A then asks for reassurance and states, "well, do I look okay?" the partner turns again and says, "I merely said you look fantastic."

The insult has been positioned in individual A's mind, and they cannot come back from it, leaving them with a sensation of inadequacy all night, but giving the partner of theirs (individual B) in total control. The sole energy an individual has against this is recognizing it and genuinely ask themselves in case the attacker truly intended to cause pain. In case they did it, it might be an extreme situation and then be damaging to be near them based on in case they are going to change or even choose to. When dealing with or perhaps near a manipulator, the sole power is recognition; it's ill-advised to ward off them in case they can bring about fear in you as to when you're in fear, the essential innovative concept of yours will evaporate, and choices can be tough. Understand yourself! Know the enemy of yours! Know the game of yours!

Self-Defence Techniques

In a self-defense situation, you can disable or even limit the assailant by adjusting the joints of theirs. The little joints in the toes, as well as hands, are vulnerable since they're not so powerful individually. A significantly smaller defender can inflict immense pain as well as leverage. With this publication, I am going to explain how you can adjust these joints.

If you've previously bent or maybe jammed a finger or perhaps thumb backward or even to the side, you comprehend precisely how vulnerable an individual finger could be. And just how much pain may be involved? Professional athletes should continuously be conscious of maintaining the toes together to stay away from injuries. The hand as being a whole is pretty powerful, though the person digits could be manipulated with no a lot of pressure.

In a self-defense situation, you are able to make use of this to the benefit of yours. Often the attacker's fingers are going to be in a weak place. Grabbing one of their thumbs or fingers and using pressure will enable you to disable or even handle them. Disabling them will entail destroying the joint or even breaking a bone. Controlling them will entail keeping the continuous strain on the joint.

You've no question noticed one individual controlling another by a thumb. No matter whether it was an episode of the Three Stooges or maybe a fighting style demonstration. Though it appears amusing, it's a vital defense method as well as a means to discover how you can fight. Aikido is one well known martial art form that uses joint manipulation thoroughly for individual safety.

Joint manipulation could be utilized in several ways in case you're grabbed. When grabbed by the collar or maybe lapel, one easy self-defense strategy is using the thumb of yours to push the thumb of theirs down into the palm of theirs. This's a controlling method. With sufficient pressure, you can drive them to the ground. Yet another alternative is usually to get the thumb of theirs with the entire hand of yours and pressure it to the rear of the hand of theirs. This is a disabling method. The thumb of theirs could be dislocated, creating immense pain.

Precisely the same thumb methods could be used when you're grabbed by way of the wrist. On the other hand, the fingers of theirs can be manipulated as you can see them more comfortable than in case they're on the collar of yours. Fingers may be bent to the edge or perhaps back to the top part of the hands theirs. Dislocating a joint, tearing a muscle, or maybe tendon or maybe breaking a bone in the finger or perhaps hand will inflict plenty of pain for these people to release you.

These very same defense methods might be utilized anytime a digit is accessible. When you end up in a place to manipulate the toes of theirs, pull off the footwear of theirs as well as bend and twist. An elbow or maybe knee hit can be quite useful on the side or maybe inner elbow or perhaps knee dislocating it. Consider the boy or girl at school which would arise at the rear of you, and set the knee of his within the rear of the knee of yours. The rear of the knees isn't secure, and the knee of yours would twist forward each time.

These simple fighting styles self-defense methods don't take many years to learn. They may be a crucial weapon for female's self-defense. Practice them on yourself or perhaps a buddy or perhaps a training partner. You can employ them to protect yourself in many scenarios. They're can, effective, and quickly disable a significantly bigger attacker very easily.

Private Self Defense Against Manipulators

- **Become Assertive**

Private Self Defense has two types. The actual physical self-defense as well as mental self-defense. Part-one of this particular series looked at the psychological and social facets of self-defense. Part-two is going to be a continuation of part one; however, right here, we'll look into establishing actionable steps. Acquiring private self-defense against manipulators calls for an enthusiastic power to be assertive. When you're confident, it instantly loosens the command a manipulator has over your choices and views.

As previously discussed, lots of cult leaders work with a lot of the strategies (mentioned in part one) to solicit brand new followers and likely cause physical and economic damage to you and the family members of yours. Here are a few actionable actions you can take fighting against those that wish to manipulate you.

- **Tell Them You Feel Pressured**

Tell them you're feeling pressured, and you do not wish to do something. When the subconscious of yours is letting you know, anything is to speak, listen, and wrong up. The earlier you say Anything, the better. The way, it will not thrive as well as develop into a far more significant issue. Remember, you have the right not to feel pressured to do something you do not wish to do.

Ask Questions

Ask a series of probing questions. To ask questions might put the manipulator on guard and provide you with enough time to reorganize your actions and views. Think about using several of the following questions as a guide to probing:

a. What do I get out of that?

b. Does what you would like from me audio reasonable?

c. Do I have a say in that?

d. Are you asking me or perhaps telling me?

e. Does this appear sensible?

- **Refuse The Request**

If a person approaches you to do one thing you do not wish to, do not do it. In the beginning, this might look complex; however, getting assertive at this point might save the life of yours. Additionally, if you mention "no," the manipulator can become surprised and back down. When somebody does not get the idea which you're not interested, say no and walk away. You have the right emotions, thoughts, and behavior right to give no reasons or maybe excuses for justifying the behavior of yours. You have the right to change the head of yours and supply no explanation. You have the right to say "no" with no feeling guilty.

- **Confront The individual**

Confront the manipulator in a private setting. A public atmosphere might turn followers against you, or perhaps even worse, alienate one to a group-think mentality. You might then feel obliged and unwillingly comply with demands. If you create your thoughts known, it shows you're not readily convinced and might not be well worth the effort. Additionally, understand that the individual might not want to keep on the friendship. Do not feel responsible because once again, you have the right to have independent ideas and then to be the judge of the behavior of yours.

- **Do not Give Into Flattery**

Flattery is a superb tool of the manipulator. They usually use the self-consciousness of yours against you. When somebody praises, mainly when you have not done Anything to deserve it, doubt the purpose of theirs. It may be simple to fall victim to flattery; however, it has among the best resources a manipulator can make use of to manage your actions as well as views.

Simply Stay away from Manipulative People

You have the right to choose your friends. In case anybody causes you to feel manipulated, do not let them in your life affairs. Staying away from somebody does not suggest you have to finish a friendship; it just means you're working out much more manageable for the instances as well as circumstances you meet.

Psychological Influence And Dark Psychology Building

In an interaction, whether it's one on a single, or perhaps in a team, anyone who displays probably the most potent emotion is leading the interaction next and influences the emotion as well as Dark Psychology of all of the others involved. Consequently, in a two-person interaction, if one individual is actually showing heavy sadness and also the additional individual is reasonably joyful, the unfortunate individual can have a more significant effect of the interaction at a minimum in the beginning and can provide the emotion of the joyful man or women down towards sadness.

Today, this's not always a terrible thing in case the joyful person is aware that he or maybe she can still favorably affect the emotion as well as Dark Psychology of the other individual. By coming down to that person's emotion, the joyful individual has a much better chance to recognize as well as empathize with this person's emotion.

As a consequence of this, the unfortunate individual might start to feel much better, and also as the sad individual starts to feel good, the joyful individual might then start taking the lead and bring Dark Psychology and the emotion of the sad man or woman up towards a far more optimistic feeling. Humans are social creatures as well as the better the social interactions of ours, the much better we feel. From the mind of ours, we've what neuroscientists call mirror neurons, and mostly what they're there to do is help us tune into and copy the emotion of another person so we could better understand them. As we do this, we loop with each other's emotions, as well as the emotion builds in intensity. We also frequently than talk of quite similar ideas as well as principles.

Folks frequently instinctively lower the intensity of such excellent emotion of theirs as well as Dark Psychology to attune with the negative feelings of somebody that has a higher status. Nevertheless, it's not the status of yours, though the sturdiness of the emotion you opt to create that is going to determine the moods of yours and just how you influence others. Even in case you have a supervisor who's usually angry or perhaps stressed, it doesn't need to affect the mood of yours. In an interaction with him or maybe her, in case you displayed an even more powerful amount of excitement or calm, for instance, you will be probable to affect them and minimize the intensity of the emotion of theirs although they have a more prominent status.

Regrettably, though, this's unusual, as the majority of folks instinctively attune to the emotion as well as Dark Psychology states of the individual with the more prominent status, instead of choosing to empathize with the individual in case it's feasible after which point them to a far more positive emotion. Within any stage in an interaction, you're possibly being or even leading led. In case you're being led, be sure that it's towards a psychological spot you're prepared to go. Also, you will not usually have time to empathize with someone's Dark Psychology condition and emotion and might just have to decide to affect the other individual towards the emotion of yours immediately. The impact isn't just an essential one on a single but also in team scenarios. Allow me to make use of an instance of an impact within the team amount.

I am going to use the example of a fire. When there's a fire, obviously, as there's a risk, everybody will feel fear. In case one individual starts to panic, everybody else's degree of fear will boost when the panicking individual is leading the team with probably the strongest emotion. With this circumstance, panic will equal disaster as when you're gripped with a damaging emotion; you can't think obviously.

To avert disaster, a part of the team has to create a more intense positive emotion like determination or confidence and lead the team. The brand new mental leader will have to show the panicking individual as well as the majority of the number, which they're intensely self-confident and can now be leading the team. This will likely lower the amount of fear in the team as well as enhance trust as the team attunes to the brand new leader.

In the event, the firefighter starts to panic unless another person is somehow in the position to create an even more powerful amount of good emotion, the team is apt to have no possibility of averting disaster. Therefore if the stronger emotion leads the interaction, the emotions you intensely and consistently produce will affect how others view as well as react to you. In case you're happy, other individuals close to you are going to become more content. In case you're generous, other individuals close to you are going to become much more generous. When you're irritable, others around you'll be more irritable as they attune to the thoughtful leadership of yours. That's precisely why in the very long term, consistently satisfied individuals start maintaining relationships with other regularly happy individuals, and regularly unfortunate individuals maintain relationships with other regularly sad individuals, or perhaps not at all since others are finding it difficult to connect to them.

Happy, confident, proud, pleasant, pleased, etc. Write down what will you've to point out and just how you'd need to act to obtain the outcome. In case they're the type of individual that usually speaks about issues, think of ways of replacing the subject rapidly towards better endeavors.

Be sure you prepare yourself and commit to the result before the encounter and take thoughtful leadership (with a substantial real smile) once you see them.

Mental impact usually requires ability in mental literacy. We, emotional beings, are irrational, humans, meaning we don't consistently act in tactics that get us what we would like. Mental literacy is the capability to behave in tactics that move us closer to the results we want, particularly during moments that feel hard. Emotional literacy means we can feel soreness without soothing it with an exercise that will get us less of what we would like. Knowing intellectually, which logical activity is essential, doesn't always imply we can deploy or perhaps enact it regularly. An individual can find out precisely the current influence as well as the psychological IQ resources of the planet. Nevertheless, when psychologically caused by something, that very same visitor will act in tactics that mess with the outcomes of theirs.

Whenever we awarded incentives based on thank you cards received, we discovered that the individual with the most because of your cards usually had the most money collected. Precisely why did individuals pay us far more as well as take the children of theirs in to meet the bill collector of theirs? Simply because we gave that individual a feeling, they didn't get enough of somewhere else.

What's that feeling?

Exactly how individuals think about themselves near an influencer dictates compliance or perhaps commitment. So long as an individual uses someone else experiences small, they are going to reduce influence as well as determination.

Below are ways to raise mental literacy as well as impact in communication:

- Stop calming individuals down If an individual is upset, match, or even exceed the concern of theirs for the issue. With much more emotional parity, somebody upset starts to feel heard.
- Be interested instead of remedial We quite often attempt to correct another person's discomfort instead of listening. If the son of mine throws a container of water on the floor and states, "I HATE SCHOOL!" the initial reaction of mine is telling him, "school is great for you." If I ask him the reason he hates school, I will help him resolve the actual issue.

Feel empathy, then ask. Remember a moment whenever you experienced the same manner, and FEEL empathy first.

CHAPTER 6 HYPNOSIS -THE ART OF SELF-HYPNOSIS

We need support in today's ever-changing world to get rid of the routines and ease our fears. We should shift to conventional methods: doctors, government departments, and counter-medicine. We will converse with therapists and psychologists. We can go-it-alone, too. However, sometimes when nothing we do seems to be helping our situation, we need a little support outside of the box. It's time to talk about self-hypnosis. Where all other approaches have let us down, it can work. Self-hypnosis is a hypnosis connection. It merely substitutes the client for a hypnotherapist or other trained person. In other words, the client is the hypnotist too. Self-hypnosis, such as hypnosis, is a method of self-discovery and awareness. It is a way by which everyone can have access to the subconscious mind. You do so deliberately to alter the existing thinking pattern maintained by the subconscious. You are beginning to lay the foundations for progress in doing so.

The Self-hypnosis intent differs according to the needs of the person. The fundamental purpose of this technique is to help a person reach deep into his or her subconscious. You should retrain it to focus on and accept what you want to achieve in doing so. Some traditional self-hypnosis uses include:

- Stopping smoking
- Supporting the diet
- Strengthening your general self-image
- To help you surmount any doubts
- Halt issues like procrastination
- Help you overcome a phobia
- To help you memorize faster

Stage hypnosis

Stage hypnosis doesn't mean hypnotherapy. Hypnosis on Stage is just the use of hypnosis for entertainment purposes. In these shows, it is the art of the hypnotist to persuade the audience that hypnosis is a mystical and mysterious force. The more magic and mystery the show exhibits, the stronger. Knowing that what the viewer sees isn't a real and mystical show of the powers of hypnosis. Like a good show of magic, it's more happening than what you see or are told.

A significant, rarely exposed aspect is the influence of stage subjects that owe orders, not so much to hypnosis, but to a phenomenon called group or crowd anticipation. Psychologists know that when the individual is in a crowd or large group of people, it is much easier to anticipate, control, and assess an individual's behavior. There's a strong force called stage conformity, which significantly enhances the magical powers of the stage hypnotist. The stage subject(s) decide to go along with the hypnotist by stage conformity, not because of the hypnosis but because they don't want to let the audience down.

They follow the hypnotist's instructions to unimaginable ends, but not because they are in hypnosis, and have no choice. But because they want to impress the audience and escape personal humiliation as a result of a crowd caused by failing to do what they expect. It doesn't matter if they end up doing awkward things, like quacking like a duck; that is not the point. The better and louder they "quack," the more insane they become, the more the mind control of hypnosis comes off ... And the stronger they are performers. Instead of resisting the entertainer's orders, the audience would appreciate, support, and accept them more if they "go with series." Stage conformity can also be more substantial than the hypnosis effect. I can testify to what the feeling is like, having been a stage subject on two separate occasions.

Does hypnosis play a role in the theatre? Yeah, but more only to a certain degree. Hypnosis helps to help concentrate the mind in stage shows. Using hypnosis to concentrate and clear the mind for the time sets aside the multitude of conscious, frequently random, thoughts. A robust and concentrated mind is a compelling thing, once again. This, combined with stage conformity, does not make the job of the hypnotist quite difficult. You'll find that they can focus a lot of their energies on simply entertaining and animating the show. The more they can persuade the viewer hypnosis, the more engaging the performance becomes in mind control. And that's what's being presented; it's not what's happening.

Hypnosis is an extremely fun, physically stimulating, and calming activity. It's like taking a relaxed mental rest. It is easy to want to go along with the show as a stage subject because you feel that not doing so would end the fun experience of hypnosis in which you are. It's not contemplating, catching, or holding on to random ideas, the mind relaxes. That is not to suggest that the subject is asleep, in a coma, or that the consciousness has taken over. You are aware of what's happening, and you are aware of the sounds around you, maybe more so than in usual awakening consciousness. You know that you could wake up instantly if you really wanted to. But to what end? If the hypnotist understands your limits, it's just as well to go with the experience.

When subjects are asked to do or say something that runs contrary to their social, ethical, or religious values, they either wake up or simply disobey the hypnotist's order. In hypnosis, a person does nothing that they wouldn't usually do while they're awake, in the same sense, and environment. This once came into question with one stage subject who started to take off her clothes during the series, while the other subjects just went so far as that which is socially appropriate- attempting to "strip" but stopping just short of reaching the social norm. The hypnotist himself was very shocked and realized that the woman, which he did, had to stop. It wasn't until he figured out after the series that her profession was a stripper's.

The majority of hypnotherapists do not advocate or support hypnosis on the Stage. There is a clear split between hypnotizers and hypnotherapists on Stage. The explanation of why a stage hypnosis display works are understandable by presenting hypnosis as an unconscious state of sleep that lends itself to the mental power. This is an example of hypnosis. It serves to reinforce the unfounded, the commonly held idea that hypnosis is weird, weird, and abnormal- which it is not. You don't fall unconscious, and you're not in a trance, you're not in control of your mind. Hypnotherapists tend to use hypnosis as a tool to help people lead a happier, safer, and more fulfilling life. The stage hypnotists, in contrast, use hypnosis as the main prop in their entertainment shows. It is clear why there is a break.

Given the apparent similarities between the stage hypnotist and hypnotherapist, through administering hypnosis, the stage hypnotist unintentionally represents a portion of humanity. The stage show, along with television portrayals, fuel the widespread illusion that hypnosis is a powerful, magical thing that taps the mind's strength. Putting the pieces together doesn't take long. "Anything else I've done, why not use hypnosis as a last resort? It's weird, I don't know how it works (the fear of the unknown), but I don't mind … It could just fit. That is the line of reasoning that prompts several telephone calls into the yellow pages of the hypnotherapist listings.

In an ideal world, kids in school will be taught what hypnosis is and how it works. The importance and advantages of hypnosis would be recognized, and a more popular role in society would be for it. That, however, is not today's world. When it comes to educating the public about hypnosis, hypnotherapists have their job cut out for them. The long-term aim of the field would be mass education. Ironically, this hypnotherapist sees hypnotherapists showing off a lack of public education. Many hypnotherapist-written brochures themselves appear to lose educational information about hypnosis. I assume that several hypnotherapists favor "magical" and "mysterious" hypnosis, as this consistency will undoubtedly improve the clientele. At this point, it is very early to denounce stage hypnosis flat out.

Stage hypnotists are in a rare role for attracting thousands of people watching their shows. Stage hypnotists are encouraged to understand the high degree of impact they have on the effects of hypnosis and hypnotherapy, which can be used to inform and educate people. Maybe they should remind the audience at the end of the show what was shown, "We've had a wonderful time here tonight. I want every one of you to know that what you've seen is merely a glimpse of what a concentrated mind can do. Hypnosis is just as effective in helping to change the lives of people as well as entertainment. A hypnotherapist can use hypnosis to focus your mind on living a happier, healthier, and more rewarding experience.

How differs Self Hypnosis from Stage Hypnosis?

Known types of treatment are hypnosis and self-hypnosis. Such types of hypnotherapy are used to achieve a particular goal-one in which only the individual who wants to improve or pursue a cure and the therapist participate. The expectations set by both the therapist and the client are individualistic and intended to resolve a specific need. The sessions and themes are informal, private, and are performed in a comfortable and secure environment. If you're using self-hypnosis, you just need to know why you're there.

The most significant difference in the case of stage hypnosis is Stage. That is a performance by the public. Customers have paid the hypnotist/magician for seeing what someone would "transform" do. There is no "client" or stage prop to attain any personal objective except, maybe, for their few minutes of fame. The stage hypnotist may be deceptive and even exploitative to achieve his or her goals. The whole technique requires more than a little deception and even self-delusion.

Hypnosis Groups

In today's culture, four significant forms of hypnosis are used to hypnotize another person or to hypnotize one 's self. Classic hypnosis, Ericksonian hypnosis, NLP hypnosis, and self-hypnosis are the four primary forms of hypnosis. Every type of hypnosis is typically and different. The most common denominator between the four kinds of hypnosis is that they all begin to induce a hypnotic state by some form of hypnotic induction, including fixed eye induction or counting backward.

Modern Hypnosis.

Traditional hypnosis is the most common type of hypnosis and is most commonly practiced in the belief that with a little guidance and preparation, anyone can do it. This is often assumed that conventional hypnosis is the simplest type of hypnosis, as it is based on simple suggestions and commands. It is the method of hypnosis, commonly promoted with CDs and MP3s for hypnosis, along with tapes. Traditional forms of hypnosis communicate with the subconscious while in a hypnotic state and use direct instructions and orders to manipulate a person's attitudes, emotions, feelings, and acts. Definitions of these orders may be a sign of self-confidence, or of leaving a bad habit such as drinking or smoking. Because traditional hypnosis is based on suggestions and commands, it is often not regarded as being entirely useful for people with critical and analytical thinking processes. The conscious mind has a propensity to interfere with the transmission of suggestions and orders, to critique the messages and not to allow the subconscious to comprehend them completely. Modern hypnosis also forms the basis for stage hypnotism, which is common among partygoers and comedy club participants in today's culture.

Ericksonian Hypnosis.

Ericksonian hypnosis is based on the concepts Dr. Milton Erickson developed. This method of hypnosis is particularly useful for those who are wary of hypnosis, as it uses metaphors rather than direct suggestions. Metaphors enable the brain to think creatively and arrive at conclusions that may not be drawn by using the more subjective method of conventional hypnosis. Metaphors operate by a more nuanced way of comparing and contrasting two items than basic commands and suggestions. These often encourage the mind to wrap in a more organic way around an idea or a concept than a direct recommendation, which is why skeptics are often able to be hypnotized using this approach and not the conventional method. Ericksonian hypnosis uses metaphors, both isomorphic and interspersal. Isomorphic metaphors tell a story that has moral that makes the unconscious mind draw a one-to-one comparison between the story's morale and a problem or issue it already knows about. Interspersal metaphors use embedded commands which distract the conscious mind and allow the unconscious mind to process the metaphor 's message.

Ericksonian hypnotherapy makes further use of what is known as indirect suggestions. Indirect suggestions are much harder to resist because the conscious mind often doesn't even recognize them as suggestions since they usually disguise themselves as stories or metaphors. An example of an indirect opinion is - "Maybe your eyes will be tired as you listen to this story, and you're going to want to close them down because people can experience a pleasant, deepening sense of comfort as they allow their eyes to close and relax deeply."

Think of the following scenario: A five-year-old baby brings a large glass of milk carefully to the dining table. The child's parent warns in a stern voice, "Don't drop it!" The child looks up at the parent, stumbles, drops the bottle, and spills milk all over. The suddenly furious parent yells, "I told you not to let that slip! You're so sloppy. You're never going to know!" It is an example of hypnosis, as unintentional as it might be. The loud authoritative voice (the parent), having developed an altered state (trance) by indirect suggestion ("don't drop that!), has given out a direct post-hypnotic suggestion" (You're so sloppy. You'll never learn). "Post-hypnotic" even if the kid (and children always do) follow the idea, he or she will often see him or herself as clumsy. For the future, this post-hypnotic advice from the parent may well stick to the order, sabotaging the progress of the infant.

It's believed that Ericksonian is an effective strategy as well as high quality to crossing many people's conscious minds. It utilizes accounts called "metaphors" to take advantage of the subconscious mind.

These stories, also known as metaphors, are extremely seen as well as acknowledged by the conscious mind. When these accounts pass through the conscious mind, it then redirects to the subconscious mind to keep the metaphor. The subconscious mind then processes these metaphors and will quickly understand the actual value or maybe the good tutorial of the story. The subconscious mind will likely then change an older notion into a brand new one. It is going to create an innovative perception by what the story or maybe the metaphor is attempting to convey.

Hypnosis and NLP.

To obtain impressive results, NLP hypnosis incorporates neuro-linguistic programming (NLP) with hypnosis. NLP is a type of psychotherapy that links psychological processes to behavioral behaviors-basically; it relates what we do to the way we feel. Hypnosis is a method of consciously interacting with the subconscious, frequently bypassing the conscious mind; this ensures that the hypnotized person is extraordinarily suggestible and responsive to suggestions and alteration of thought.

In addition to self-hypnosis, NLP hypnosis is used to deal with problems such as self-confidence, self-esteem, and general mental well-being. NLP hypnosis is also used to defeat anxieties and conquer fears and phobias. This form of hypnosis is successful as it reverses or gets rid of the problem using the same thought process as fear or problem. The most popular NLP technique is maybe anchoring, and everyone has probably encountered it at some point. Was there one song that causes thoughts from the past when you hear it? If so, then the song is an anchor to those feelings. With NLP hypnosis, anything you want can be rooted in whatever emotions or mental states you want. For example, you can anchor feelings of self-confidence by touching your ear. You can just touch your ear and trigger those feelings of self-confidence and power if you feel nervous about something or are experiencing stage fright. When choosing an anchor (e.g., touching the top part of your right ear), it's essential to choose one that's specific, intermittent (if desensitization would otherwise occur), and that it's anchored to a prompt and unique reaction (if an association doesn't happen).

The flash is one more sophisticated technique for NLP hypnosis. It is used to dismantle a conditioned response, that is, to remove a link between two behaviors. For example, when they feel hungry, a lot of people tend to have a cigarette. With time, their minds will associate being hungry with having a cigarette, and when they are hungry, they will start craving for a cigarette. You can use the flash to remove that association. Another method in NLP hypnosis is called the reframe, which is used to alter a person's behavior. The consequence (what the person's goal is) is established. Then the subconscious is accessed and forced to replace one set action with another, which is appropriate to the conscious but would be more helpful to achieving the target than the previous behavior.

The benefit of NLP hypnosis is that you don't have to master the whole art to profit from it. Also, if you understand only one definition or NLP hypnosis technique, you can use it to change your life. The anchoring strategy is the simplest to learn, and we recommend you try it first. NLP hypnosis is known to be one of the most potent types of hypnosis when the techniques are used either separately or together.

Auto-Hypnosis.

As already discussed, self-hypnosis is done by oneself to achieve a deep state of relaxation by using some of the above forms of hypnosis. Self-hypnosis helps the mind to relax without a hypnotist or hypnotherapist and to enter a hypnotic state. Suggestions and commands are then made by yourself or by a CD or MP3 that will guide you through the session of hypnosis. Most people now choose self-hypnosis rather than controlled hypnosis, since their delicate and dominant subconscious minds do not trust others.

As the title indicates, this particular strategy depends on the subject inducing hypnosis on themselves. This's accomplished by the topic studying a set of methods, or even by listening to a recording. Many self-hypnosis is presented as hypnotherapy, and it is akin to severe relaxation and meditation. Hypnosis, as well as self-hypnosis, are incredibly similar. The crucial difference would be that the topic is focusing on the recommendations of theirs instead of that of another person. It's a commonly held the view that all hypnosis is the truth is self-hypnosis.

This's since the hypnotist might give the ideas, though it's the evaluation as well as interpretation of the ideas in the subject matter very own mind that heralds the outcomes. The hypnotist is just the car that assists the topic into a trance, though it's the topic that processes the info. No matter, the outcome is the same. Self-hypnosis may be used in a remarkably similar method to hypnotherapy, and it is good at overcoming mental issues, phobias, addictions, and stress. It's frequently utilized to advertise a state of deep rest simply.

Subliminal Message

When you try to make a change but don't seem to get results, there are limiting beliefs that block you, and you have to eliminate them and instill new ones. This cycle can only come about through the subconscious mind. Subliminal messages are the most powerful, most comfortable, useful, and friendly technique dealing with the root-the subconscious mind-directly. Subliminal messages have been thoroughly and from time to time studied and are known to be the best way to make significant changes. Anyone can perform this procedure, and its efficiency, results, and ease of use make it highly accessible and the most studied. Subliminal messages have become widespread among millions from a little-known technique that was used by the elite.

Although it's recommended to listen to subliminal messages before or during sleep, when the mind is in a receptive state, there are other efficient ways to use Subliminals during the day. Can the subconscious mind absorb the subliminal messages and be programmed while we are awake? Absolutely! During waking time, the brain functions with beta waves, but new information can still reach the subconscious mind.

New information gets to the subconscious all the time. The only difference is that we can communicate with the subconscious mind easily during alpha and theta waves production. During the day, we don't have to communicate deliberately with the subconscious; we can simply let it absorb the subliminal messages automatically. In addition to subliminal flashes, another highly effective way to use subliminal messages during the day is to play MP3 subliminal meditations in the background. You can cook, clean the house, take a relaxing bath, or watch your favorite TV show.

Enjoy Subliminal Sleep Messages

During sleep, subliminal messages will help you make positive improvements and stick with them for the long term. You can convert your 6-8 hours of sleep time into a personal growth seminar with minimal effort. Through opening your brain to subliminal messages, you can effectively spend one-third of your day to change the problems you deal with, and program your subconscious mind to get rid of harmful patterns of thought. Subliminal signals will drive you ahead more than ever! You may use subliminal messages in this way as do the most productive people. When you read the daily news online, you can gradually gain confidence; you will develop fantastic social skills and quickly learn to make new friends when checking out your favorite pie recipes. When checking your email box, you can program yourself to feel happy; you can build optimistic money paradigms while Facebook likes posts.

With only a few moments of listening, you can begin to feel the tension that leaves your mind and body behind. You'll be engulfed in a deep feeling of pure peace and be worry-free. Besides all the beautiful goals you can achieve through the use of subliminal messages, you can also improve your sleep and wake up with a positive spirit, energetic, fresh, and lively. Here at the Vortex Success audio library, you can find life-changing subliminal messages.

Watch the computer screen for the subliminal flashes

As you know, audio but even visually can relay subliminal messages. The subliminal visual signals will surface on your computer screen as rapid flashes. By using this subliminal messaging process, you can only spend a few minutes a day. The subliminal messages carry positive affirmations and are regularly exposed to them, creating a new neural network in your brain. The essence of this all is that you can be the person that you want to be. The subliminal affirmations will become your reality, and then you will let yourself become the healthy person that you have always wanted to be. For those subliminal messages in the form of flashes, the affirmations can be quickly expressed and made real. Setting the subliminal messages on your PC is simple; watching this video, scrolling down, and pressing the 'live demo' button to see how it's done.

Hypnosis Explained (Debunking The Myths)

Hypnosis is a straightforward and easy-to-explain mental phenomenon - however, frequently, it's wrongly portrayed as some kind of phony mysticism or dark magic. This particular absence of a good representation leaves numerous to throw "hypnotic wisdom" separate as pure fantasy or maybe hogwash, along with individuals who are hypnotized we usually think of as gullible or weak-minded though not any of this's real. I am hoping to take a brief couple of minutes of the time of yours to debunk several of these misconceptions surrounding hypnosis and ideally leave you with a more precise knowledge of what these phenomena are actually about.

Just before I move with debunking these myths, allow me to 1st create a fast definition of what I think hypnosis is actually: Hypnosis is a set of suitable interaction methods (often through the usage of indirect or direct "suggestions") for shaping one's beliefs, perceptions, feelings, and behaviors.

Despite this broad sounding characterization, this's what hypnosis is actually in a nutshell. Today let us get going.

Hypnosis Is the State Of Consciousness

Hypnosis isn't at all associated with any particular state of consciousness. The main reason individuals confuse hypnosis as a state of consciousness is the fact that we quite often connect the strategies of hypnosis as leading to a half-awake and half-sleep state. We picture individuals lying on leather sofas with their eyes shut and their understanding facing inwards to their "subconscious." Though the reality of the material is hypnosis may be utilized to increase understanding only as effectively as it may be used to contract to understand.

A great example of hypnosis running for "normal" consciousness is staged hypnosis. If a participant clucks like a chicken or maybe acts out a scene in Saving Private Ryan - it's not that the person is unconscious and being pulled by his or perhaps the strings of her such as a stuffed puppet - they're only in a situation in which they're comfortable acting out behaviors they usually would not do in front of a crowd.

They're not being "controlled" by the hypnotist - they're simply being communicated to quite efficiently. The participant's free is going to is still intact all over the entire session. A participant can provide his or maybe the person of her outside of hypnosis every time they choose, but why would they when they're having a lot of fun playing pretend?

All Hypnosis Is actually "Playing Pretend."

During stage hypnosis, participants are aware they're not a chicken or perhaps they're not really in the films. They understand they're acting (it so happens hypnosis can make individuals into great actors). But not every hypnosis could be considered "playing pretend." It is dependent on the dynamics of the recommendations provided. In case a suggestion is usually to "cluck like a chicken," then the individual is going to act it out. When the suggestion is actually "think of a period in the past of yours in which you felt confident" - that's not playing pretend - the individual is thinking about this and associating themselves within that moment in which they had been sure.

I go along with hypnotists that think that all hypnosis is self-hypnosis, which means that a hypnotist can't usually trick someone into doing a thing against their own will of theirs. There's usually compliance on each side of the interaction. The sole difference is hypnotists can evoke non-ordinary or unusual behaviors in case they learn the right method of communication.

This's partially true: scientific research does usually say that just 5 10 % of the population is suggestible to hypnosis. However, these experiments are mostly flawed because researchers just test participants with typical hypnotic inductions and generic hypnosis scripts. Hypnosis does not work in a one-size-fits-all way type through (since the usefulness of it comes out of the usage of our very own private and individual associations and understanding of language).

A genuine hypnotist can read through the patient of his, stray away from generic scripts, and find out the language most suggestive to that specific patient. There are also strategies in NLP (Neuro-linguistic Programming -a train which may be seen as "modern-day hypnosis") which allows NLP practitioners to find out an individual's language tendencies (sometimes called "trance words" or maybe "keywords") by simply asking the patient a series of questions. Put simply, with the correct hypnotist as well as the correct correspondence - anybody is suggestible to hypnosis.

Hypnosis Is Much like Meditation

This's a typical misunderstanding. Once again - hypnosis is a set of communication strategies. At the same time, meditation is a far more distinct procedure which is a lot more linked with one's state of mindfulness or consciousness. One can, nonetheless, use hypnosis strategies to help a meditative process. What's usually termed "Guided Meditation" might be regarded as a kind of hypnosis, and one can also make use of a degree of self-hypnosis (meaning no third party guidance) to increase and contract understanding into a specific hypnotic state?

But once again, hypnosis isn't about an individual's psychological condition - it's about an expression of suggestions or even ideas. Sometimes, a particular psychological state could be much more favorable to learning. That's the reason why frequently hypnotherapist opts to place the people of theirs to a calm state before getting into the majority of the session of theirs. Relaxed people often feel much more refreshed could focus more, improve the cognitive abilities of theirs, and consequently are more quickly learners. Phase hypnotists do not but wish to place the participants of theirs into calm states, however. That might be a dull show. Instead, they often wish to instill a feeling or perhaps a little joy of adventure - like the mood a kid will be in. Hypnosis isn't a genuine catalyst for chemical or physical changes within the body.

Simply for the basic fact that the human brain is made up of electro-chemicals known as neurons that shoot off between 50 two00 times a second makes something a possible catalyst for a substantial change within the body. All we have to do is consider food, and the brain chemistry of ours is changed. But much more virtually, folks wish to find out whether hypnosis can lead to physical modifications like an increase/decrease in body weight, the construction of muscle, and on occasion, even growth in breast/penis size. Generally, the solution is "yes, to several extents" to all these questions.

Hypnosis can not make your body do something it is not currently effective at doing effortlessly by itself. But hypnosis has been shown to help guide the body through specific changes with the usage of the suggestion for both behavioral changes (such as consuming less, inspiration to go to the gym) as well as direct changes within the body (changes in metabolism, the time it takes muscles to restore, and there have been cases of advancements in vision, and of course, penis as well as breast size development - hypnosis has been a show to be especially significant with blowing substantial changes in soft tissue).

Remember: hypnosis helps make modifications towards the body's maximum potential - it doesn't let you transcend the biological disposition of yours via a few "mystical fashion." Although there's a good possibility, hypnosis will disclose things about the body of yours you had been in the past ignorant of. Many skilled hypnotists, as well as hypnotherapists, would let you know you need to find a professional constantly. Though it will be hypocritical of me to state you've to accomplish this since I'm self-taught. I think everybody must help themselves with a little bit of hypnosis, so they can check out and find out the possibility for themselves.

Hypnosis is an all-natural occurrence - it's your natural right to check it out and additionally to check out the mind/body like an entire. You will find loads of videos, podcasts, and books to help you started with doing hypnosis - play around with so many as you would like, get a sense for the distinction of methods, and start to find out the basic concepts of what constitutes a hypnotist adaptable as well as useful. I'd suggest you start with learning self-hypnosis methods. Nothing too sophisticated. Only training inducing yourself throughout hypnotic suggestion into a state of relaxation or maybe a light trance.

You can additionally practice by analyzing generic scripts to a buddy or maybe a loved one and having them read through several for you too. They are not the very best items of the planet, but that generally makes them comfortable and harmless to learn with. Do not take the first of the studies of yours way too seriously, simply get a sense for the various phases of a hypnosis session: inductions, scripts, exactly how to rightly come out of a session.

Hypnosis generally evokes an enjoyable experience, but at times things go awry. Be acquainted with the way to end sessions fast in case you end up steering down a terrible route, particularly before you decide to dive into several of the more hi-tech methods as changes in the belief systems of ours or maybe the basic principles of the character of ours. I am hoping this provides you with a clearer idea of seriously what this particular hypnosis is about.

Hypnotherapy

Using hypnosis to promote healing or maybe a good improvement in any way is recognized as hypnotherapy. It's generally utilized to deal with mental issues to the brain, as this's precisely where hypnosis may be useful when effective, hypnotherapy can reprogram patterns of behavior to the brain. It will permit conditions like phobias, irrational fears, negative emotions, and addictions to be managed. Hypnotherapy may additionally be utilized to manage the sensations of pain, and hypnosis has been employed to do surgery on completely aware individuals who'd be in apparent agony if not for the usage of hypnosis.

Hypnosis may be utilized to help individuals. Hypnotherapy is utilized to encourage proper growth and help in healing. With mental issues, like depression, hypnotherapy may be incredibly useful. Phobias, addictions, and even all manner of irrational feelings could be selectively reprogrammed, and influence started on negative emotions. Hypnosis, as utilized in hypnotherapy, could likewise have actual physical consequences, the most apparent being the blocking of pain, permitting medical methods to be undertaken without the damage as well as risks related to anesthesia. Hypnotherapy typically merely makes use of really light hypnosis, not the full trance state used at the standard type.

Many individuals are completely awake, as well as entirely conscious. The crucial thing of the hypnotherapy would be that the individual should stay centered entirely on the treatment as well as listening to the terms the therapist is thinking. Maintaining a great rapport with the therapist is essential. When the individual doesn't have confidence in or even thinks the therapy won't work, then it'll fail. Nevertheless, if the individual is positive, and it is open-minded, the success rate is quite high.

CHAPTER 7 THE TRUTH ABOUT HYPNOSIS

When you hear about the word hypnosis, what is the first thing that comes to mind? The answer for many people is this: a Hollywood movie with an awfully executed scene complete with a hypnotist and his mythical swinging watch. Across the hypnotist is the unfortunate person who is about to be taken to a place in their mind they have yet to visit in more than twenty years. The truth is, the hypnosis is less dramatic in the real world. Hypnosis is, in the simplest terms, a type of conditioning involving growing a person's perception of their outer environment and increasing their inward focus. They respond more favorably to suggestions when an individual is under hypnosis because their critical thinking is impaired. That is why the movies will show a subject unquestionably responding to a hypnotist's commands.

Hypnosis has some science behind it, so this means understanding the workings of the human mind. The human brain is built in such a way that memories that regulate rational thought and subconscious mind are retained in the conscious mind. What the rational mind tells you is that is dangerous and stupid to cross a busy road without looking, while the subconscious mind is likely to tell you that losing weight is difficult because the memories of the last time you (unsuccessfully) tried losing weight are stored in it. Hypnosis works by altering and replacing the subconscious thoughts you have about certain things with better and more beneficial thoughts.

The Myths of Hypnosis and Manipulation Unravelled

It seems almost difficult to consider the use of hypnosis in our everyday lives, but the truth of the matter is that it is so. You may not have any swinging watches in your face, and during your waking time, your eyes may be open all the time, but you are most definitely hypnotized as you go about your daily life. How could it be? When was the last time you read a book that really made you lose track of what was going on around you? You were essentially hypnotized while you were in that state of being fully absorbed into your book. The high chances are you weren't just distantly aware of other people walking by you and living their lives. Rather, you were riding somewhere on a train, along with the main character's thoughts and acts. That is real-life hypnosis. No hypnotizers, no watches-just you, and your subconscious mind is taking a trip to an alternate universe.

Self-induced hypnosis is common also in children who are frequently slipping into this state several times a day, at least. That's why, while they watch their favorite cartoon series without any response, you'll call your boy. They don't want to forget you. They simply cannot hear you because they have tuned out the conscious mind and the world, and they exist in another world where they are fully tuned to the subconscious. During their performances, artists and athletes needing focused attention to perform excellently in their sport or art also often go into hypnotic trances. Many would refer to this trance as being 'in the zone.' What often happens is that the mind of the artist is so focused on what they are doing that throughout this time, nothing else matters. Writers also get in the zone when it comes to the writing process. When that happens, you can find the writer being transported to the world with which they have woven their thoughts. Incapable or unwilling to leave this world, the writer will churn thousands of words a day when they were previously unable to go beyond a few hundred words, thanks to the block of writers.

Some groups and individuals have mastered effective ways of utilizing hypnosis to their advantage when it comes to manipulation and mind control. Giving a long speech and having a long and almost never-ending lecture, for example, all have the effect of bringing the audience into a trance-like state. That may be due to boredom or fatigue, or a combination of both. When an audience is in this state, they are more pleasant and likely to sign up for whatever you offer. This is something that has been learned by many cult leaders, which will explain why many cultural meetings are so long which dreary. A cult meeting has rarely ended in a few minutes. If you conclude a meeting in 15 minutes, the minds of the attendees will still be sharp and questioning. But if you go on and on for hours, they start unknowingly sliding out of consciousness and will not be as opposed to your suggestions as they would have been in the first 15 minutes.

Another technique used to achieve hypnosis is to view contradicting knowledge as though it were not contradictory but absolutely rational. What do you mean by that? As described earlier in this chapter, there is a critical thinking part of your brain. By helping you process vital knowledge, this part of the brain is what keeps you alive and out of trouble. If this part of the brain is bombarded with contradictory information without sufficient time being given to process it, it shuts down. (That is why it's always so important to step back and process information especially when you feel like you're in a hurry to make a decision in any situation). If your rational thought has been bypassed, you are likely to follow any suggestions offered to you even if they may not be agreed by a normal-thinking person in harmony with their mind's logical pieces.

How to hypnotize someone without knowing them

You may use hypnosis in daily life to receive what you want from people without them suspecting what you are up to. One good thing about hypnosis as a manipulation tool is that it's subtle and leaves no evidence behind it. Unlike lying where you may find yourself trapped in your lies, hypnosis does not leave any traces behind. No one is going to walk up to you and accuse you of hypnotizing them. In the worst-case scenario, you can just be accused of getting away with it.

That Jake, they'll say, he's got a way with the ladies. What they don't know is that you've mastered the art of hypnotizing ladies doing just as you're saying. The first step to successfully hypnotize a person is to establish a connection with that person. You can very rarely hypnotize a stranger with whom you share no bond at all. It's relatively easy to form a connection with a person. You just need to watch and respond appropriately to your body language and theirs, and their facial expressions as well. The whole point of creating a bond is to make sure the other person is accessible to you and will react favorably to your subtle control of the mind, better known as hypnosis. Make use of any of the following tips to hypnotize them after making certain of the existence of some connection between you and your subject:

Tip # 1: Throw the familiar ones off

Humans love patterns. They are simple, predictable, and soothing to interpret. Patterns are a major component of the comfort zone and do not require much critical thinking. What patterns did you create in your life, and how do they support you? Patterns simplify life for many. Let's consider a simple example that can be interrupted with a person's intent to hypnotize. Let's say you and your spouse have a way of saying goodbye before work every morning, which involves a quick hug and a kiss on the cheek. You feel particularly philanthropic one morning and decide to replace your pattern with a tight, lingering hug and a full kiss on the lips. The mind of your spouse will be thrown into disarray because that's not what mentality is used to. You'll have a narrow window for a hypnotic command in the five seconds of confusion that will ensue in your spouse's mind.

Why don't you make lasagna?

Your spouse does react instantly, of course.

They would have sat back on any other day and considered the work involved in making lasagna, and would probably have suggested an alternative. On the day you throw them off your pattern, they'll say yes without too much thinking, because you've essentially shortened their conscious mind.

Tip # 2: Execute the Zeigarnik effect

The Zeigarnik effect in psychology is the concept that people are more likely to remember incomplete tasks than the ones that have been completed. Think about it: if you're going to do your laundry, you 're likely to have that thought lingering in your mind until you finally wash and put away all your dirty clothes. You will no longer have any interest in learning anything to do with laundry shortly after you have finished your laundry duties. The Zeigarnik effect was named after a Russian psychologist, who had been influenced by her professor to study the phenomenon. The professor, one Kurt Lewin, made the observation that the orders which were still unpaid could be remembered more precisely by a waiter.

In many scenarios, the Zeigarnik effect is used in everyday life. In particular, soap operas and television shows are keen to leave their viewers seeking more by ensuring each episode ends with a cliffhanger. When the episode runs out anticlimactically, your brain will store this as an incomplete task in your short-term memory. That's why you keep going back to your favorite soap opera because your mind tells you to complete what you started. As long as the incompleteness lingers in your brain somewhere, your attention will be drawn to that. Consider telling an exciting story with pauses in between during which you give them hypnotic commands to hypnotize someone using the Zeigarnik effect. This may sound something like this:

You won't believe what happened when I decided to go hiking with my friends last weekend. We walked up this rather lonely trail when all of a sudden we heard these strange noises coming from the woods [could you please shut the door for me] ... They sounded like a cross between a bear and a coyote, and they got louder and louder the further we went up the trail. Of course, we're getting really nervous at this stage, but [could you also file these documents for me] we knew there was no going back. There were four of us, and we were ready to fight anything that it was. You can ask your conversation partner to do pretty much whatever you want, without much resistance, throughout this storytelling. This is because their mind is focused on the story you're telling, and their brain is anxious to finish. They're your putty to deal with when they're in the trance-like state.

Tip # 3: Remain ambiguous

Ambiguity keeps a guess on your audience. If you want to linger in people's minds that you interact with long after the conversation is over, you have to strike a balance between being memorable and remaining ambiguous. Ambiguity leaves the mind wondering: What did he say exactly when he said this or that? You are in charge of the other person as long as their minds inquire. It confuses the conscious mind with confusion and vagueness. There are things that the conscious mind can not process, and one of them is the mystery of ambiguity.

Ambiguity in the world of dating and relationships can serve a particularly important role in persuading others to go out with or date you. Many relationship experts will agree that a bit of a mystery will serve a long way to keep things exciting. What doesn't explain most is why. The explanation of why mystery is so thrilling is that as long as a person's conscious mind has not completely processed and understood, you can still remain in their minds. While always making sure you are vague and enigmatic about one or two things, you will hypnotize your friend or lover into doing whatever you want them to do.

Tip # 4: Negative words have an even greater impact

The subconscious mind is often believed not to be able to hear negative ones. Any negative thoughts communicated to the subconscious mind are instead interpreted as positive. For e.g., if you were to tell someone, when I'm away, don't go peeking into my room, that person is likely to interpret this subconsciously as, when I'm away, go and pee into my room. This is possibly the reason why so many exasperated parents see their children tend to be doing the exact opposite of what they are told not to do. As such, if you are looking to get someone to do something without being too direct about it, you can use negative wording to hypnotize their subconscious mind. Rather than telling his friend:

Help me pack up for my upcoming relocation please come over.

Please consider:

You don't have to come over to help me pack. Throughout their day, the subconscious brain of your friend will tell her she needs to help you pack your move because that's how your statement was interpreted by the mind. Of course, whether or not your friend is really coming over is a question of how much emphasis she places on your relationship.

Tip # 5: Applicable keywords

Have you noticed how often sales copies or advertisements have this descriptive wording, which makes you imagine all the possibilities presented by a given product or service? When it comes to hypnotizing people, certain words hold a particular charm. For example, if you tell a person to imagine something, you're already sending them into a hypnotic trance, where they're tuned to their subconscious mind. They are more suggestible when they're in this state, and will likely do what you're asking them to do. If you don't believe this, look up any advertisement for travel destinations and have a listen. You'll probably be thinking of booking your next holiday to that destination at the end of it.

As long as something is imagined by the subconscious mind, then that particular thing gets programmed. This explains why some people are afraid of the dark — they've imagined the dark to contain bad things, and the fear remains real and present as long as that imagination is active. It also explains why people are scared of horror films. Think about it — nothing frightening about horror movies. They're just a bunch of ordinary people acting out fake scenes, so why are you so scared? Since your mind has dreamed that everything is real, that's why.

Protect yourself from Hypnosis

It is always welcome the occasional self-hypnosis in the form of a captivating book or movie. Once in a while, it helps to escape the harsh daily reality. But what may not be so welcome is the hypnosis brought on by other sources that you don't feel too comfortable with. How do you guard against the hypnosis that exists in your everyday life? For starters, it's important to recognize that you might not really be able to escape all the hypnosis that is present in your life. Combating would be too big of a war. That being said, as far as hypnosis goes, there are certain battles that you can win.

One of the things that will help you guard against hypnosis is to live by principle. Living by principle does not mean being stuck or relentless when you're supposed to be flexible. It just means knowing what you're going to accept, and what you'd rather forgo, rather than just going with the flow. If you're the kind of person in the interest of being easy going with the flow, you may find that you've drifted too far from the safe shore. Manipulators who use hypnosis to prey on others know how to attack those who are not securely anchored to something unshakeable. If you're the kind of person who, having been told to imagine how easier your life will be with Product X rushes to buy Product X unquestionably, you'll find yourself in your life with a whole lot of clutter. Having one or two principles on certain aspects of your life helps you make more conscious decisions that are not influenced by other people's actions or words.

There's a wise person who once said you'll find it when you go looking for something. The reason they hypnotize so many people in their everyday lives is that they don't really search for hypnosis because they can't even detect it. As long as you are aware of the fact that there is hypnosis, you will be able to notice it from a mile away and be consciously guarding yourself against it. You'll notice it when your partner tries to get you to agree to something you wouldn't usually agree with, and you'll notice it when your sly colleague tries to get you a favor. Being mindful of the fact that there are people out there who are doing their hardest to take advantage of you is going to go a long way to shield yourself from mind control.

The free will that is conferred on every human being living in the civilized world is a positive thing about life. Free will means you can choose what you want in your life and what you don't get through the doors. There are numerous channels in today's world that are used to influence you. TV, movies, movies, the internet, books, magazines, radio shows, music ... the list is endless. You are free to choose what you allow in your life because you can be sure that most of these channels are used to put you in a certain state of mind that is advantageous to channel owners. In short, you'll be able to decide what's filtered from your life. Pick wisely.

What is Hypnotherapy?

Hypnosis is sometimes used as a form of treatment for different conditions. When used in this way, hypnosis is called hypnotherapy. Hypnotherapy is essentially minded control where the person under control has given a clinical psychologist their consent for the same. As for other complementary methods of treatment, the effectiveness of hypnotherapy has divergent views. The fact that research on the same subject is very limited does not do the case for hypnotherapy any good.

Hypnosis as a method of therapy is used to help people break unhealthy habits like poor eating habits, as well as alcohol recovery, eating disorders, and even insomnia. Hypnosis is often used in childbirth, where pregnant women are encouraged to hypnotize themselves so that they can psychologically brace themselves for almost painless childbirth. This is called hypnobirthing and involves essentially programming the subconscious mind for pain-free labor.

CHAPTER 8 ANALYZING BODY LANGUAGE TECHNIQUES

As much as we want to believe that we are doing a pretty good job of masking our true feelings, little do we realize that our bodies are giving us away from more than we want. The silent language of human physics reveals more about what you're thinking and how you feel more than your words will ever do. When what you're saying out loud doesn't match what your nonverbal signs are saying, that's when anyone who's paying attention can see that something else is happening. If you know the clues to look for, reading the body language of another person-which is, to begin with, a very tricky affair-can be powerful leverage in your quest to determine who is manipulating you and who is genuine. Understanding the signs of body language can be beneficial if you are the one who attempts to subtly manipulate or persuade another to do what you need them to do as you are fully aware of the signals that are responsible for giving away your true intentions.

But reading body language isn't as simple as we might think. One signal might have several different meanings that generally change depending on the context and the other factors that may influence the feeling of that person. You might presume, for example, that a person who has his arms crossed in front of his chest while talking to you is either irritated or closed off, but if they were in a place they felt unusually cold, they might cross their arms to remain warm, and that's it. The next best thing you can do in a situation like this would be to watch out for the subtle signals to see if what they're telling you verbally is in sync with what their body is doing. When there is a mismatch, this is when you want to start paying more attention.

Body language is a fantastic skill to develop for those who have always been fascinated by what others think and feel about it. It can reveal a wealth of hidden information, the innermost secret thoughts that could be running through the mind of a person they don't want to know about anyone else. The information that no one can detect except you. Almost like a secret communication line between just you and the person you are watching. It's a fascinating subject, even more so because, admittedly, we all wanted to read someone else's mind at one time or another. Okay, there's a way to correctly do that now, except that you're not only reading their minds either but their entire body.

7 Techniques for Understanding Head to Toe Body Language

Quite literally, the language of your body. The facial expressions, contrary to what others would assume, are not the only dead giveaway as to how someone might feel. The nose, as they say, is just the tip of the iceberg, and there is much more to discover under the water. When we communicate, our whole body is involved in the process. Every aspect of your physical and mental state contributes to what's going on, but the parts you're aware of (the words you're thinking about saying) and those you're unaware of (the body language). There was fascinating research carried out by UCLA that showed how only 7 percent of human contact happens verbally. That means the words that we believe most contribute to the way we communicate matter less than we think. Especially when, according to the research, 55 percent of our communication comes from our body language while the remaining 38 percent is based on the tone of voice we use. This means that if you can learn to decipher that 55 percent that goes unspoken when it comes to interpersonal communication, you will have a significant advantage over everyone else.

TalentSmart, a leading provider of services for emotional intelligence, conducted a survey involving over a million participants. The results of those findings were intriguing, revealing that those who fell with the upper echelon ranks where the top performers resided were made up of those with high emotional intelligence Stages. To be precise, 90 percent of them. Among the many vital skills that landed them in that position was the knowledge they had to understand, decipher, and read all the unspoken signals and signals that occurred during the communication process as they knew how to read these clues properly.

There's one thing you need to keep in mind before you start diving into the seven techniques for understanding people and reading body language from head to toe.

Stop working too hard to look for signs you're too concentrated and critical. Remember, as much as everyone else, your body language can give you away. Stay calm and relaxed, be natural, and observe simply without being too critical and overthrowing all the indications you receive. Here are the seven strategies you want to use to decipher the deep emotions that others keep hidden:

• Strategy # 1-Lookout.

The appearance of a person is perhaps the most obvious giveaway and an immediate indication that you would like to pay attention to when you meet them. Do they have a freshly shined power suit? Are they ready to make a powerful impression, dressed in for success? Were they dressed for natural comfort, showing that they feel confident and relaxed? Are they seductively dressed on a first date, deliberately trying to get your attention? Have they an accessory on them that suggests they might be religious? Maybe like a cross pendant? There is a lot that you can take away from there just by looking at the way they look.

• Strategy # 2-Positioning.

Is the person you're talking to hold their head high trustingly? And are their shoulders slightly hunched, indicating they might feel vulnerable and uncomfortable? Are they walking in such a way as to indicate their indecisive feeling? Gathered in a crowded room, who strut about with their chest puffed out, making it known that they have confidence and maybe a big ego to accompany that? How about the person who is hiding in the corner trying to blend in so nobody will notice them? Observe whether the person leans to you in a conversation or tries to separate himself from you. In general, if we like them or are comfortable in their presence, we tend to lean towards a person subconsciously, and we try to set some distance when we don't like somebody. The most comfortable body pose to find is to cross the arms in front of the eyes, but attention should be paid to the toes too. If you note the toes of someone or the top of their leg pointing to you, this is a sign they feel relaxed with you. Besides watching the way they sit or stand when you are trying to decipher body language, keep an eye out for hand positioning. Someone who has their hands either in their pockets, placed behind their back or in their laps (if they're sitting down) might suggest they 're trying to keep something hidden.

- Strategy # 3-Nose.

    Nothing gives away how a person feels more than their facial expressions, from all the other physical parts of the human body. The feelings that are painted across our faces are more powerful than we might claim. The deep frown which shrinks the forehead. Thin, pursed lips. The crinkles around the eyes are always accompanying a sincere smile. A jaw clenched. These are all signs that indicate the feelings that may be going through the body of a person as you examine them, and if there were ever a place where you were searching for mismatched signals and signals, it would be the facial expressions. A verbal "yes" with pursed lips, a clenched jaw, and a subtle frown between the brows send a clear signal that this person is reluctant and unhappy to say " yes. A smile that doesn't quite reach the eyes and make it "crinkle" in such a way that only a real smile can let you know that this person is plastering for good measure on their face with a fake smile when, in reality, they wouldn't smile at all if they could getaway.

- Strategy # 4-Eyes. How often did you hear the sentence "look me in the eye and tell me the truth"? We work on the assumption that maintaining eye contact is more difficult for them when a person is lying. To some extent, there's some truth to that, but skillful liars wanting to cover up the lies they say purposely will deliberately keep eye contact, but that's also where they tend to slip up, and the most by overcompensating by holding onto eye contact for longer than they need before it is awkward since they are lying. On average, a person can keep eye contact from 7 to 10 seconds for anywhere, slightly longer if they listen to the speaker attentively. When a person looks at you with a look that makes you uncomfortable, particularly if it's followed by barely any blinking and entirely still body positions, that's your cue that something may not be right. This person might be lying to your face.

- Strategy # 5-Sound. Remember the other 38 percent that comes from the use of the tone of voice? That's the number four strategy to help you get a read about how to analyze the person before you. The tone and overall volume used during a conversation can give an insight into the emotions of a person. Is the tone calming, low and comforting to use? Talking to this person makes you feel completely relaxed and comfortable? Or is it short, sharp, abrasive, and clipped, which makes you feel indeed awkward as it gives you the feeling that this person is less than happy to have a conversation with you. The tone and sound frequencies we use to express speech generate vibrations and a person's tone has a way of influencing the way you feel, even though you do not think twice about it. Like the expression of the face, if some say "yes" but accompanied by a clipped, low tone, you know that "yes" isn't the real answer they wanted to give at all.

- Strategy # 6-Chest-We were also told to stand up straight, to keep our back straight, to stand up erect, and to maintain a proper position. There is a good reason for this counseling. In general, it's not only beneficial for your body, but it also indicates to others that you feel relaxed and in charge. A highly emotional person will have trouble thinking straight, let alone concentrating on standing up straight. If you encounter someone who appears to have a chronically saggy pose, followed by other signs they feel insecure when they are in the presence of others, it is a pretty clear sign that they suffer from low self-esteem. Hunched shoulders are a typical symbol of avoiding publicity if someone wants to.

- Strategy # 7-Hands. How a person's legs are positioned when they are either standing or sitting is essential indicators of what they think and feel. Getting them firmly crossed (not in a relaxed way) when sitting down, shows the feeling towards the other person "closed off." It tends to show when a person does not feel particularly comfortable, relaxed, or at ease during a conversation. For example, if a woman wears a skirt that may have turned out to be a little shorter than she anticipated when she sat down, worrying about a possible dysfunction in the wardrobe will translate into the rest of her body language because that's what her mind is concerned about. The conversation can deteriorate rapidly when its apparent discomfort becomes apparent, and when the other persons present during the conversation, misread the signals. People who deal with anxiety can unconsciously translate these messages in the form of foot-tapping or leg-shaking through their feet, which sends a deafening and clear message to everyone else around them that they feel anxious, irritated, or both. Because the legs of a person are the most supportive limbs we have, it's pretty hard not to notice when there is excessive movement.

Including using your eyes to search for all the hints you 're trying to find, there's something else you need to focus on when it comes to reading the body language correctly—the insight. Just when you are trying to listen to your brain, listen to your gut feeling and what it is trying to tell you. There's more to understanding than just relying on logic alone. Intuition and empathy will take you even deeper into their story than will let you see what your eyes are. One of the core competencies that those with high Stages of emotional intelligence possess is the ability to empathize with others. Sensing the emotional energy generated and determining what is happening using their intuition. The subtle signs of energy can be a powerful indicator of a person 's personality. Being around positive, optimistic people lift your spirits, improves your overall happiness and mood while being around manipulative and harmful individuals leaves you feeling drained and tired. The emotional energy that is released is often getting little consideration. Still, it is actually among the measures that you might use to get a read on what the personality of someone could be. If you've ever been around anyone who just seems to have a dark cloud hanging over them no matter where they're going or what they're doing, that may be the indication you need to know that person is someone that has a robust negative outlook, or that they may be deceptive.

Other Body Language Indicators ...

There is a myriad of ways to gauge body language, extending beyond the main seven strategies mentioned above. People are complex creatures with exciting personalities, and, like a good book, with every turn of the page, it becomes more interesting, especially when more clues are unraveled along the way you look deeper. Other indicators of body language to look out for when you try to analyze someone are:

- **Handshake-** Nothing like a secure, efficient, firm handshake to let you know when somebody feels relaxed and secure. But what if the reverse was the handshake? Limp, reluctant, and like they can't wait to release their hand when they touch it? While it doesn't necessarily have to mean anything specific, a handshake less than a firm could simply indicate that the person lacks self-confidence, feels uncomfortable, is non-committal, timid, or is by nature an introvert. On the other hand, cold and clammy hands could signal the person's feeling anxious and nervous, as we all tend to sweat a bit when we have those butterflies in our stomachs.

- **Microexpressions** — Tactic number 3 focuses on the more apparent facial expressions that occur during the communication process. Still, there is another dimension of what psychologists call show laws that play a vital role in letting us know how you feel. Maybe you're even thinking about what. These very tiny facial movements are known as micro-expressions and tend to focus specifically on the areas around the mouth and eyes. These micro-expressions, along with the rest of your facial expressions, can completely contradict what you're saying, and anyone capable of reading nonverbal signs can immediately pick up on that. An individual might feel they 're doing an excellent job of concealing the anxiety they 're having while trying to impress the individual they 're talking to. Still, the ever so slight pullback of the muscles around the mouth area will give away how nervous they're feeling inside. The dangerous thing about micro-expressions is that when a person feels nervous or anxious, they do not just happen. They occur when someone lies, too. It's not so easy to hide a little white lie when your little facial muscles are giving you away.

- **Raising Eyebrows**-There are only three main reasons (and emotions) to raise somebody's eyebrows. They feel either surprised, frightened, or worried. Try raising your eyebrows the next time you're in a relaxed and casual conversation with a friend, and see if it's easy to do. At best, you could come off looking strange. When someone talks to you and the conversation doesn't involve a topic that would either cause fear, surprise, or worry as they raise their eyebrows, keep up your antennas as something else could happen under the surface.

- **The Chin and the Neck**-Yes, even your chin and neck have their secret language that they're trying to tell the rest of the world. At the same time, you're unaware of it unless you make a conscious effort to focus on those two areas and what they're doing when you're having a conversation. If your chin juts out (usually or subconsciously) in front of you, others might get the impression you're either somewhat stubborn or obstinate. Just the way you hold your neck around someone helps them to know how you feel inside. Shy introverts who are uncomfortable in a large group of people tend to tuck their chin underneath so they're eyes fixed on the floor or avoid eye contact, while those who are confident and upright tend to have their necks straight up and hold high.

- **The Arm Cross** – We all know that the meaning has a part to play in the arms crossing, but, if you cross your arms during a meeting, for example, the indication you send is that you feel close to what the other person says. Even if they have a smile on their face, and they engage in the conversation as pleasantly as they do. How they feel when their arms are crossed in front of them is that they feel emotional, physically, and mentally closed to whomever they speak and what they're being told. This gesture is made so unintentionally most of the time, that it makes it the most revealing indicator of all. When Gerard Nierenberg and Henry Calero recorded more than two,000 negotiations as part of their research for their book How to Read a Person Like a Book, not one of those negotiations resulted in a deal if one (or both) parties had their legs or arms crossed during the negotiation.

- **Excessive Nodding**-At the risk of looking like a bobblehead, the only reason someone might be nodding excessively when you talk to them is if they were either concerned about what you thought of them, or if they are worried you might doubt their ability to keep up with your instructions (employees sometimes do this when the boss gives off a string of instructions, and they try to do so).

- **Firmly Clenched Jaw-**The only moment when someone's jaw is firmly clenched during a conversation is when they feel anxious. When you note that the words they say that make it sound like they're all right with an idea but their jaws are clenched when they're saying it, that's the signal you need that tells you they 're not as happy with the idea as they're leading you to believe it.

- **The Feet-**Another part of your body that could trouble you by sending mixed messages. When you tap your toes, someone may get the idea that either you're feeling nervous or you're in a rush to bring the talk to a close. Tapping your toes when you are trying to get someone else's attention is a way to get them to notice you without interrupting a conversation they might have. Toe-tapping is a way to indicate when you are pressed for time without writing it out specifically because you don't want to sound rude. There's a reason people tap their toes. Still, it doesn't necessarily mean it's the best method of communication, mainly because either way, you'll be viewed as disrespectful when you regularly tap, tap, tap on someone else. Imagine the feeling of having someone tap their toes at you.

Indicators of body language

How to analyze people based on their words, their manuscripts, their environment, and their emotions. How effectively you can deal with the people around you will depend heavily on your readability. You can tailor and adapt the messages you communicate to ensure that they are received in the best possible way when you develop the ability to understand others and the way they feel. That's what effective communication is all about at the end of the day, and the reason so many people struggle with communication is that they haven't mastered the skills they need to analyze the people they 're dealing with at a deeper Stage.

Analyzing Words

One significant aspect to look at is the body language. Another is by the words they use. The eyes (and the rest of the language of the body) may be the windows in the soul, but the words used are the gateway to the mind. The words that are spoken are chosen consciously and carefully, which then makes it a good representation of what is happening in the thoughts of a person. By listening to and understanding what someone else is trying to say, whether they're taking it or writing it out, we form bonds and connections. For certain situations, the words that are spoken are a direct reflection of the person's character, so if you know what to listen to, you will increase the chance of knowing their temperament, mode of thinking, and even behavioral patterns.

The reading of minds is not magic. It's a talent and one learned by those who taught themselves to search for all the right signs, one of which is to research the word usage that is being used. Take this simple example when a friend of yours tells you they have been awarded "another" recognition at the office. Here's another keyword, which is a sign they want you to know; this isn't the first time they earn honors and recognition. By deciphering the meaning behind the words, you then know that in this case, an acceptable answer would be to give them congratulatory praise for their successes, which is what they secretly wanted when they told you the news. If you know the right words to look out for, you could even catch someone in a lie. However, considering the context, you need to be careful and remember that verbal indications are not always 100% foolproof. The general indicators you'd be looking for may tip you as to whether someone is lying include:

- Repeat the question with you again. For the time being, they could be playing to make up a credible story.
- When they add qualifiers such as "to the best of my knowledge" to their sentences.
- Eviting the use of the word "I" to avoid involvement could indicate that they are not entirely honest.
- Using the present tense to speak about events that have already occurred.
- Some people use more formal language when they tell a lie. When anyone omits so many of their contractions, it may be a warning to keep an eye out for.
- Some liars (especially if they're guilty of doing something wrong) may turn to the use of "softer" words to cushion the deed done. For example, rather than using the word steal, what they might say is borrow instead. Captain Jack Sparrow has infamously opted to say "borrowed without permission" in the Caribbean Pirates movie to avoid revealing outwardly that he had stolen a ship.

Another way to analyze when a person's words have something to hide is by paying attention to the tone of voice and the speed at which they speak. Underneath the surface could be the indicators that give away something more:

- Speaking too quickly, which signals they may feel nervous or anxious.
- Too slowly speaking, which might indicate that they feel down, depressed, or not in the right mood to have an engaging conversation.

- Sighing as a sign of sorrow or frustration; Even tiredness, at times.
- A sudden change in the tone and pitch of the voice indicates a lie trying to remain hidden.
- A repeated tone of voice may be indicative of insincerity.
- Men have known in a romantic relationship to change the tone of their voice to signal when they are interested in a woman.

Study of their manuscript

Analysis of a person's handwriting is referred to as graphology, and the way we craft our words and letters can indicate more than 5,000 types of personality traits, according to the science of this subject. Graphologist Kathi McKnight, when she introduces them to this field, has her students write the sentence "she sells seashells by the seashore," and she gets them to write it out in the cursive format. There is a reason why she specifies cursive writing, and that's because it gives a better opportunity for graphologists to analyze the personality of an individual.

Everybody has their unique writing style, which is just as distinctive as their personalities. While graphology can provide a fun way to try to guess what the personality of someone might be like, it's not the most accurate measure out there, unlike, for example, reading body language signs. Although it might not be the most precise, it can still provide some fascinating details about a person when you're only trying to gauge them based on their handwriting. More prominent personalities tend to write in more giant letters while shy, introverted people prefer smaller printing. As for the ones writing in between? Ok, average-size handwriting is also an indicator that you have a better capacity to concentrate on the tasks you are doing. Other interesting clues to seek when you are trying to practice some of your graphology techniques include:

- Looking at the Space Between Words- The more significant the room, the more the individual who loves his independence and freedom would be. Those who prefer writing letters and squeeze words closer together generally prefer other people's company. If you have written your

sentences in such a way that the words seem to be crammed together completely, an analysis of that type of handwriting might suggest that your personality tends to be more intrusive.
- Writing Slants-If, your handwriting appears to slant to the right, you may be someone who wants to meet new people. To the left, it indicates that you prefer to work alone and that you are introspective and in the nature reserve.
- Pen Pressure Used-Do you know that even when you write with your ink, the type of pressure applied gives you clues about your personality? Pressure writing could suggest you're feeling tense, stressed, or even angry. On the other hand, a moderately applied pressure is a graphological indication of commitment. Those with the softest touch tend to be the ones with the most sensitivity and empathy towards others. Still, according to a study by the National Pen Company, soft pressure might also indicate that the individual lacks vitality.
- The Way You Dot Your I - The way you dot in your I appears to be higher up the page, handwriting experts suggest your personality can be one with an active imagination. On the other hand, an I that is carefully dotted is an indication of a detail-oriented, organized personality. If your I tend to slant to the left, you might be a procrastinator, and you're playful or childlike at heart if you dot your I with a bit of a circle at the top.
- Signature Legibility-Those with confidence, strength, and comfort in their skin tend to have the most legible signature. A signature that is difficult to read is often the property of someone who prefers their privacy.
- Letter Form-Smarter people prefer to have more pointed letters, whereas rounded letters tend to show a more imaginative and innovative personality.
- Speed-The speed you write at means something. Many who are hurried and don't want to waste valuable time tend to write more quickly, while

the more self-reliant and methodical individuals take their time writing down the words they want to say.
- Attach, or Separate-The Pen Warehouse, claims that those who are rational in making their choices prefer to write letters that are connected. Disconnected letters are an approach that appears to be written with more passion and imagination.
- The Baseline-This one can be read easily if the sentence is written on lined paper. Watch the angle of the sentences. If the writing has more of an upward slant to it, that means the individual is either in a positive or happy mood, while a downward slant, on the other hand, maybe a sign of exhaustion or discouragement.

Being Caught In A Lie

According to experts in handwriting, when a person lies, the slant of his / her handwriting (or any other feature for that matter) tends to change dramatically.

Environment Analysis

Human beings have always been sensitive to their surroundings, even from the time our ancestors roamed wild food hunting. As evolved as we have become, an innate sense of awareness about our surroundings still exists within us all, which is why we tend to look for environments with certain types of qualities that we're comfortable with. A typical example is when you're either trying to rent or purchase a home. Environment plays a significant factor in your decision, and your preferences for the type of environment you want will determine your decision to buy or rent the house you are inspecting. Other qualities that influence our decisions include not only safety and security but also the physical attributes of the environment. Quick everyone is looking for an atmosphere that is both physically and emotionally soothing. It's emotionally soothing to return home after a long day at the office because this is when you know you can relax and be yourself.

The environment can have a considerable impact on how a person reacts and responds. Put a person in an environment they are not comfortable in, and sometimes their reactions are nearly immediate, depending on the circumstances. For example, a claustrophobic person would immediately begin showing signs of discomfort, anxiety, fear, and wanting to escape feeling "caught up" is a smaller, confined space. Other ways for the environment to play a role in determining a person's response include:

- To encourage or discourage interactions. An encouraging, warm, and inviting space will make you feel more relaxed and comfortable enough to have an open chat.
- Motivate and influence your behavior. Everywhere you look, an office supply room that is dusty and crowded with stuff will make you want to dump your items and leave as soon as possible. On the other side, a compact supply room, ordered, clean, tidy, and spacious lets you stay quickly enough and spend time putting away your things.
- Influence on mood. An environment that is crowded, noisy, and full of distractions can make you feel restless and agitated, somewhere you're not likely to want to carry on a conversation because you don't like it. It's negatively affecting your mood.

Because the nature of the environment can have a significant impact on a person's way of thinking, feeling, and responding, where you analyze their body language will be an important consideration factor. You may not get an accurate reading of the body language if your subject is uncomfortable, not with the topic being discussed but with the surroundings in which they find themselves.

Analyzing feelings

Developing the empathy needed to understand and be sufficiently tuned to the emotional state of another can provide you with vital intelligence to help you navigate the relationship successfully. Those who have mastered the art of emotional intelligence have developed their empathic abilities and have turned that ability into knowledge that they can use in a social situation to give them the upper hand.

Here's what you need to keep in mind when trying to analyze somebody's emotions:

- Open Mind- You've got to keep your mind open and be a blank slate. Getting preconceived ideas or bias can only cloud your judgment, and can contribute to misreading the situation.
- Think Big Picture – Instead of focusing on every single gesture in the body language, think of the larger picture and do a comprehensive body scan instead, putting together all your information before drawing any conclusions.
- The benefit of Doubt-Seek to give someone the benefit of the doubt before making any conclusions about the feelings they experience. Remember also to observe the context and the environment, as this may affect their emotional state. If you are still uncertain about the signals that you are receiving based on their facial and body signs, consider asking them if all is right.

Factors to evaluate

How to tell people when they are insecure

In a business deal or any kind of negotiation for that matter, swooping in to win the deal depends not only on your negotiating skills and the talking points you've prepared but on your ability to analyze when that person is insecure or indecisive so you can make your move and secure your win. It can be advantageous to be able to spot insecurities in a negotiation because everything you need to do from there to secure the odds in your favor is to say the right things that resonate with your subject enough to convince them to jump the fence and come over to your side. Here are signs you want to keep an eye on that might give you some indication that the person feels indecisive or insecure about their choices:

• The concerns and worries still crowd.
• They don't seem to be settled with the decision they are currently leaning toward.
• They keep asking the same question repeatedly, almost as if they are having difficulty accepting the answers given.

- They reject your initial suggestion, but then return and circle again.
- They challenge you to think several times, or just what you think they should be doing.
- They may apologize for being indecisive and not yet in a position to make a decision.
- They're afraid to offend you or make you angry at their decision.
- They express concern that they do not know what the right thing is to do.
- They worry if their decision will reflect poorly on them.
- They feel uncomfortable thinking that they are being ganged up and pressured to make a decision.
- They can become aggressive if they feel threatened.
- They will attempt to impress you but seem nervous about it, and the insecurity shows through the tone of their voice.
- They worry they don't have the support they need.
- They are too preoccupied with what others might think.
- They're inclined to strive for perfection (or to be a perfectionist).

CHAPTER 9 THE ART OF PERSUASION

Merriam-Webster defines persuasion as the ability to convince while persuading is further characterized as moving to a belief, position, or course of action through argument, entreaty, or expostulation. To persuade someone to do something is to ask someone to do something in lesser words. Persuasion is an art form that someone trying to get people to do something will learn. It's an amazing tool to have, especially if you're constantly surrounded by people that every now and then need a bit of prodding.

On the other hand, deception is defined as the act of causing someone to believe that something which is false or invalid is actually true and valid. Deception is a form of self-manipulation and also an instrument through which you can achieve your goals of persuasion. So far as persuasion goes, this is probably where things get blurred. Debates have been going on for the longest time about the thin line between coercion and persuasion. There are groups that are fully persuaded of the malevolence of persuasion, while others claim that persuasion is a perfectly harmless way for people to get what they want. Manipulation theme in itself is a grey area for many people. Morality is subjective, depending on the metrics in which different societies and cultures placed in place. The question of whether manipulation is correct or wrong is one that should be individually answered.

That being said, some technological variations exist between persuasion and manipulation. Manipulation always has a strong self-interest, while persuasion may be done for a whole community's greater good. Consider the case of an activist who is persuading people to plant trees for the environmental good. Before they get the numbers, they would need to push and prod to make the tree-planting exercise a success. Some people may see this as manipulation, but in the end, the result of their efforts benefits the entire community. The art of persuasion, of course, presents a clear and logical argument for a particular case, whereas manipulation often involves the manipulation of facts aimed at distorting a person's perception of reality. In the end, persuasion and manipulation often serve the same purpose, which is to persuade them to do something you want them to do. The main difference is how the parties want to do it: there are all the cards on the table process, which is persuasion, and the process of manipulation of the secret cards.

The Persuasion Principle

In order to master the art of persuasion, you need to be aware of the underlying principles which will enable you to harness your influence. Generally, Human beings are a touchy lot; one wrong move and you're going to lose all ability to persuade people to join your team. You need to make strategic decisions that are guided by the fundamental principles that are needed. Reciprocity, consistency, social evidence, liking, authority, and scarcity are the six principles of persuasion.

Reciprocity Principle

Reciprocity just does to others as you would have them do to you. Reciprocity calls for respect and kindness as you go about your everyday experiences. It's a good thing to show kindness to others that makes others feel better about your interaction. Other than that, your way of earning chips that you can cash in later is to do well. If you have been very nice and kind to someone else, you have a better chance that they will be nice and kind to you.

If you are hoping to persuade a person, you must behave towards them in a decent manner. Speak a word of kindness, give them a favor, or even buy them a gift. They will be more agreeable later when you need to convince them to do something. After all, you have proved yourself to be a kind human being who cares for him.

The Cohesion Principle

Consistency in persuasion works this way: once you have convinced them to agree to smaller ones, people are more likely to commit to bigger tasks or favors. That is, if you get them to spring a puddle for you, you can get someone to swim oceans for you. A few studies have been done to support this hypothesis. For example, in one study, a group of researchers asked some homeowners to put up a hideous Drive Safely billboard on their front lawn. Very few homeowners declared yes. The researchers, however, had to take a different approach to the experiment: first, they got homeowners to agree to the small commitment to putting up a Drive Safely postcard in their home's front windows. Ten days later, they returned with the request for a billboard. This time, despite its lack of aesthetic appeal, more homeowners agreed to put up the billboard. The reason for this is that the homeowners subconsciously felt compelled to keep up with their earlier reaction.

The technique of foot-in-the-door compliance is premised on consistency. It means getting people to consent to a bigger request by first using smaller requests to check the waters. If you want to execute this strategy cleverly, your target will need to be trained to be consistent with their responses to your question. For example, if you want your employee to work the weekend shift, you might want to get them to agree to work the overnight shift — or vice versa, depending on which shift in your business is the least preferred one.

The Liking Principle

If a person likes you, they're more likely to fulfill your demands, no matter what that may be. A person who is unlike and who is also unlikeable will hear no more times than a person who is well-liked. But how is it that you get people to like you? The secret to being loved is a combination of three main factors, according to science. First of all, people prefer the ones close to them. You must find common ground with them in order for you to look close to the person you are trying to convince. For example, many foreigners have learned that learning and speaking the local language is the simplest way to become more likable. The other thing you need to be mindful of is flattery while making yourself more likable. If you are using it well, Flattery will open many doors for you.

Citizens prefer those paying attention to them. If you want to ask someone to do something for you, start by offering them a genuine compliment first. Just because this is called flattery doesn't mean you need to be effusive about it. Too excessive in your praise will actually be counterproductive to your need to be liked. Last but not least, be the kind of person that is usually pleasant and cooperative in achieving mutual goals, and you will be one step closer to being pleasant. If you're always stepping on the toes of others to get what you want, you'll have very few friends, and this won't help your case when you need to convince someone in the future. Remember, being pleasant and cooperative doesn't imply being a doormat. Sometimes, it simply means putting some little effort into helping a person achieve a goal that is important to them. For example, if a colleague struggles with a due report, offer to help them with the printing and mailing process. It's not a lot of work, but you're going to go from an uninvolved, unwritten colleague to a kind and helpful colleague. You can cash this chip later if you wish.

The authority theory

When compared to a complete newbie, a person who is an authority figure in a particular field will have an easier time influencing others. If you want to persuade more people to do something specific, you need to build your credibility by making yourself seem like you have expertise in whatever field you play. This principle is a key reason why professionals in their field display their diplomas. Think about it — when, for example, you step into a therapist's office, you would probably deliberately look out for the sort of qualifications they have hanging on their walls. If your therapist has a whole lot of credentials displayed in this way, you will probably feel a sense of comfort in their expertise and experience. As such, you'll quickly accept and follow any advice they have for you. Essentially the therapist has managed to influence you without even saying a word.

It's a fact that if you're the only one talking about it, your authority won't be taken very seriously. As such, you have to make sure, so to speak, that you recruit others to beat the drums on your behalf. Subtle ways exist to do this. You can identify a field in the office that you are passionate about, and become that field's office guru. This could be Microsoft Excel or Reporting for some people. The guy known as the Excel office guru will have a much easier time getting things out of people because they already know he knows what he's talking about. He has also proved to be likable and helpful by solving all of their problems with Excel, and his colleagues may want to pay him back in some way. You don't need to learn Excel to make your mark around the world. There are many other fields in which you can excel in and present yourself as a figure of authority.

Scarcity Principle

The laws of demand and supply are simple and straightforward in economics: when supply is low, and demand is high, prices rise. To translate this, the value of scarcity builds. If you are a business person who wants to persuade people to purchase your product or service, it helps to highlight the fact that the product is on offer for only a limited time. Furthermore, let the customers know that if they do not access this product on time, they will lose significantly. If the marketing message is packaged in this way, more people will be rushing to beat the time limit on your product.

It is important to become a scarce product yourself in the business and personal relations world. If you're not there for others whenever they need you, you'll easily lose your worth. If you want to maintain your aura of mystery and power around you, you must learn the art of being inaccessible and unavailable. When you actually appear, your word will be respected more than a person's word that continuously appears and speaks out of all importance and meaning.

The consensus theory

People look at others who are similar to them in everyday interactions for clues as to what to do or say. An individual who is a good influencer knows that buying into their idea is all it takes is one individual, and the whole crowd does. There are different ways you can apply the consensus principle to your benefit. For example, in an office setting, you can get a section of staff to agree to a cause and champion that causes their colleagues to do so. These colleagues are more likely to be convinced of the worthy cause because their peers have said so.

If you've ever purchased anything from Amazon, you might have seen that it includes a section showing the other items purchased by customers who ordered the product you just purchased. Why do you think this is so, and how does that segment affect you as a buyer? More often than not, you'll probably consider buying those other items because they were bought by these customers who obviously have similar tastes and needs to yours. Originally you may not have planned to buy the additional items, but just the fact that it was done by others will make you think you also need to. That is, in effect, the principle of consensus.

Insight Tips for Daily Use

If you are looking to influence people, simply understanding the principles underlying persuasion isn't enough. You also need to master the simple yet effective ways you can use those principles in everyday life. If you're a convincing guy, you'll have a much simpler time in life, and your desired goals can always be accomplished without having to jump through the hoops. Some of the tips to be more convincing can be quickly applied, while others may take a bit of practice.

Tip # 1: Seem confident

Trust does not come to us all, naturally. Some people seem to be confident more easily, while others are struggling quite a bit. Whether or not you are naturally confident, you need to ensure that you always appear assured to others. If you're nervous about how you look at a specific topic or your skills, nobody else needs to know that. Do not provide a platform for your insecurities to shine on. Instead, fake it until you make it.

In this country, there are people who don't know a lot of things and yet have managed to get hundreds of people to help them and their ideas. Rationale? They reflect the epitome of confidence. They step into the rooms as if they were their own. They speak authoritatively even when they're unsure what they're talking about. Trust means you know what you're talking about. People encourage people who know what they're talking about to believe themselves.

Tip # 2: Be careful in approach

Even when they allow themselves to be persuaded to do something, most people like to think that doing something was their idea in the first place. No one wants to believe that they have allowed a certain idea to be shoved down their throats. You have to be discreet in your approach to persuasion for performance. Consider starting with an anecdote rather than introducing a certain topic in full-on. If you are looking to get someone to buy into an investment, start by mentioning how you and your friends went on a cruise last weekend after receiving your Investment X payout. Don't even try to sell them that investment. Instead, get the other person to think about how they might have gone for the cruise too if they had invested in the investment vehicle. In short, entice people with your ideas without being too obvious.

Tip # 3: Be flexible in your procedures

The persuasive techniques aren't set in stone. Different people react to different stuff. The same person will also react to different methods differ depending on time and occasion. You need to know when to switch gears as appropriate. Sometimes you will have to work with the liking principle, and some other times, you will have to base your method on the authority principle. Reading social signals will enable you to determine what methods to use.

Tip # 4: Timing is All

If you want to convince someone to buy a house, if you catch them when they're shopping for houses, you'll get more success. Most things hold that true. If you want your crush to go from crush to partner, if you talk to them when they are looking for a relationship, you will have an easier time. You also have to master the art of knowing when the timing is right to master the art of persuasion. If not, you'll fall into the trap of harassing people to come to terms with things they're not interested in. No one likes a person who constantly plagues them into doing things, particularly in the strangest times.

Tip # 5: Interestingness is a plus

Most persuasive people don't get boring. No one pays a lot of attention to boring people. To converse with boring people is not fun. They're not engaging, and definitely, they're not memorable. If you want to win convincingly, you have to be an interesting person. The good news is that there are lots of interesting ways to be. You just have to recognize and emphasize something special about yourself for the world to see. It could be a talent or a hobby you're very good at. Maybe it's also your sense of humor or the way you dress. Maybe you'd even want to share your unique worldview with your audience. Whatever you're opting for, make sure it helps people remember you long after the conversation is over.

Tip #6: Listen more than you speak

You may imagine that being persuasive involves doing a ton of talking, yet this couldn't possibly be more off-base. So as to impact individuals, you should prepare yourself to be a persuasive speaker. Listening abilities fill two needs. In the first place, insofar as individuals are talking and you are listening, then it implies you are gathering critical information that you can use furthering your potential benefit. Second, individuals like a decent audience. Why? Since individuals love discussing themselves. Keep your mouth shut and your ears open, and you will be well en route to expanding your amiability remainder. In the event that you don't accept this is significant with regards to affecting others, allude to the standard of preferring as examined in the past area.

Sorts of Deception and How to Get Better at All of Them

Trickery comes in different structures, which are all expected to lose a subject reality. Toward the start of this section, we characterized duplicity as the demonstration of making somebody think something that isn't substantial or valid. In this area, we will investigate the various courses through which you can trick somebody, how to show signs of improvement at these strategies, and how to ensure yourself against misdirection in your regular daily existence.

Untruths

Untruths are the most famous type of trickiness. They are utilized each day during casual discussion, gatherings, seeing someone, in exchanges, when you need to escape an ungainly circumstance, and in pretty much any sort of discussion or situation. An untruth is essentially an explanation that is the direct inverse of reality. A case of an untruth would be telling your manager that your grandma has died so you can get empathetic leave when in reality, your grandma is a lot of alive, and you simply need a day away from work. Untruths are anything but difficult to advise - you simply need to discover the differentiation of reality and tell it.

Prevarications

A prevarication alludes to the utilization of a specific word or expression to change the importance of a sentence so as to move the expected message purposely. Evasions are not really utilized in regular discussions, albeit some shrewd individuals may figure out how to mesh them into their beguiling web. Prevarications are basically wit. They fall under the more extended term of the deception, which is characterized as flawed thinking, which is expected to cause a contention to appear to be better than it really is.

Instances of evasions incorporate the accompanying:

Dating my beau is a genuine cerebral pain. Anti-inflammatory medicine can cause cerebral pains to leave, so perhaps I should take ibuprofen to make my beau leave. I reserve an option to free discourse. Hence, it is directly for me to state what is at the forefront of my thoughts consistently. Prevarications are regularly an extraordinary wellspring of clever jokes that you can tell at each chance. For instance:

Two barbarians were eating a comedian, and one gone to the next and stated, "Docs this taste interesting to you?"

All joking aside, however, prevarications are not really your greatest concern with regards to misleading. Best case scenario, quibbles will acquire you some giggling your life; even under the least favorable conditions, you are probably going to wind up confounded, however, just for two or three minutes before you make sense of what's happening.

Camouflage

At the point when you participate in camouflage, you preclude information for motivations behind double-dealing. This is a favored type of double-dealing, particularly since it is anything but difficult to get yourself free in the event that you are gotten. You can basically account for yourself by saying that you neglected to uncover the specific certainty. Camouflages are some of the time alluded to as lying by exclusion. Suppose, for example, that you intend to purchase a house. You know a decent real estate professional, and you contact them with your particular necessities. The real estate professional has a couple of open units that fit your depiction, and you mastermind a site visit. Come the day of, you are intrigued by this one specific unit that is strategically placed close to your working environment, and extensive enough to suit you and your pooches. You need to make a proposal on it; however, you simply need one inquiry replied: for what reason did the last proprietor surrender the unit?

Your real estate agent reveals to you that the past proprietors chose to proceed onward to greener fields subsequent to living in the unit for a long time. In any case, the real estate professional advantageously excludes the way that the requirement for greener fields as required by the way that property estimations are declining in the specific territory that you need to purchase your home in. By precluding this critical certainty, your real estate professional persuades you to purchase the house. They didn't lie - they essentially would not tell every bit of relevant information. This is the idea of driving coverings.

Misrepresentations/Overstatements

A misrepresentation is an extension of reality. A few people don't prefer to come clean in its plain structure as it sounds exhausting that way. Or maybe, they will adorn it to where it is not really unmistakable. An embellishment or exaggeration resembles this: your companion places their cash in a little side venture that is giving them returns of $100 every week. Rather than your companion detailing precisely on their profits, he circumvents telling everybody that he is making can heaps of cash from his venture. Contingent upon the economy you live in, $100 might be a few cups of espresso and a pleasant supper or a fourth of the month's lease, however it barely the get-away paying, prepared to-resign fortune that your companion needs to cause it to appear. Truly, he is bringing in cash, yet truly, he is additionally extending the truth...perhaps to make you desirous.

Under-representations

Under-representations are the direct inverse of exaggerations. Under-representations are likewise alluded to as the minimization of truth and include making light of a fact with the goal that it doesn't appear as awful as it really may be. Under-representations are regularly utilized by individuals who are trying to claim ignorance about something or the individuals who need to support an, in any case, a silly choice that they have made. Abusers may likewise make light of reality when gone up against by or about their casualties with the goal that they can shed off some obligation regarding their maltreatment.

Suppose, for instance, that a couple who have been hitched for a long time commonly consent to have the spouse run the funds of the family unit. Sure about his better half's marketing prudence and money related insight, the believing spouse contributes perseveringly to their speculation kitty and lets the husband do all the contributions. Sadly, the spouse makes a couple of awful ventures that crash all their cash, leaving them with only a couple of months' checks. Detecting that something is not right, the spouse requests an update whereupon the man expresses that things are bad. Actually, the spouse has come clean: things are for sure, not great. What he has additionally done isn't expressed precisely how terrible things are. In the event that he was straightforward, he would have expressed that things are horrible and that they are near the precarious edge of money related hardship. For this situation, double-dealing by the type of modest representation of the truth has happened, and the spouse gets the opportunity to abstain from resting on the lounge chair for in any event one more night until the heaping charges ruin his disguise.

Since you know the various sorts of double-dealing, you should be considering how you can ace the craft of trickiness. First off, recognize that duplicity isn't actually a pleasant thing, to the extent profound quality and morals go. You truly would prefer not to base every one of your connections and communications on trickery since then you'd be detracting from the individuals around you and from yourself too. Certifiable connections that depend on trustworthiness and realness have a superior shot at withstanding the trial of time. That being stated, it is additionally important to recognize that life doesn't generally happen clearly. Now and again, there are different hues in the middle of that call for us to be inventive. On occasion, you may need to utilize double-dealing to get to where you should be. In such occurrences, you should be cautious about how you bundle your double-dealing.

Something you should be cautious about is your non-verbal communication. You may have the most intricate falsehood illustrated in your mind and convey it precisely as you had rehearsed before the mirror and still come up short at misdirection. Why? Since your non-verbal communication parted with you. There are sure body flags that will part with a liar. These incorporate the powerlessness to keep in touch, squirming, and in any event, stammering. A few people have been known to contact their noses at whatever point they lie. Watch out for this indication of lying and ensure you avoid them while you are turning your huge stories.

The second thing you should be cautious about while being efficient with the fact of the matter is the purpose behind the duplicity. Trickery merits the difficulty just If it makes you something you need or someplace you truly should be. Other than that, misleading is only a misuse of everyone's time. In the event that you start lying for the purpose, everyone is going to consider you an obsessive liar who can never be trusted. This will demolish any validity you may have fabricated, and you will never again be in a situation to control or impact individuals.

Never stir up your accounts. This is the surest method of getting captured. If you should beguile somebody, ensure that you have the whole story spread out in the event that you need to respond to any examining questions. You would prefer not to get trapped in an inadequate story that has a bigger number of openings than an angler's net. Most unpracticed liars particularly become involved with their snare of falsehoods since they can't recall what they said to who and when. If you should keep a scratchpad to follow your falsehoods, kindly do. It may very well spare you the shame of being trapped in lies.

CHAPTER 10 THE ULTIMATE GUIDE TO ENHANCE YOUR PERSUASION TECHNIQUES

Persuasive abilities may be learned from failure. Probably the most crucial component of the understanding malfunction is actually by defining it. Malfunction is identified by Giving up on the persuasive course of action or merely winging it without a game plan. Failure could additionally be identified by not making it while you did all you are claimed to do but do everything later to figure out why the persuasion wasn't made. In either case, you determine failure effective methods call for framework and scripting to the process of yours.

The dread of failure has stopped a lot more people before they've also started than other motives. It is the same reason that individuals continue operating in a task that they hate year after year. Often, entrepreneurs are going to say the most significant thing that took place to them is they had been fired or even lost a task which caused them to do for a brand new feature. You are going to battle failure in both definitions so long as you focus on the powerful capabilities of yours.

So just what does this have to do with persuasion results? Failure in specific elements or any other isn't just healthy; it's to be anticipated over time. The very best individuals in many industries near just seventy % would mean they fail thirty per cent of the time or perhaps did they. Would you believe it bothers an individual to walk away from a speech? This particular issue most likely is the emphasis of their long time after the persuasive speech of theirs, although they've let the pain of losing. They usually need to learn how to increase persuasion abilities.

The blunder is usually to allow someone else to define what a persuasive failure is usually to you in a great deal as they can say you're a failure. Loads of effective individuals nevertheless make silly mistakes every single day they've simply lost focus on what they know works, or maybe they've become lazy. Failure could be of great benefit for you as a human being by looking for out what does not work and just what does.

What might work for somebody else or a coworker doesn't imply that it is going to work for you, and that's okay as well. Sales achievement comes from you finding out what works for you. Persuasive abilities for every visitor could be different based upon the abilities of theirs and or perhaps demeanor. This's news that is great since you might be able to see persuasive abilities to dominate in the marketplace of yours that others can't. This describes precisely why you've seen or even heard other individuals do things that you can't duplicate, although you've tried.

Good results are a mystery for some since they let it be. For you to acquire persuasive capabilities, at times, you are going to have failed as well as be okay with this. In case you're afraid of good results, you won't end up having it.

There's at some point in which you've to become weak as well as seen as vulnerable to develop in nearly every element of the daily life of yours. Occasionally being susceptible suggests asking for help, failing, or maybe sometimes not being successful at the amount which you like and or even desire as quickly or even as fast as desired.

Several individuals are going to get to a place just where they believe they've failed. This's absurd also because, as a person, there'll often be a task that doesn't go through. Persuasion is an ever-changing, as well as by not knowing that regardless of how many successful methods or maybe persuasive abilities, you'll fail. The industry of yours in case it hasn't changed, however, it'll quickly that's precisely how business is evolution is an element of every occupation or even sector.

Dark Psychology Of Persuasion

Each day living creates a lot of things to be associated with persuasion. A lot of businesses would like the product of theirs to become the ideal seller in the industry, even though the service provider additionally requires the society to find out they can be found to supply assistance for these people that need the assistance.

For this, after that, persuasion is necessary to make others stick to the concept, including purchasing services and products they provide. The idea of persuasion is such a pervasive part in the life of ours that the Dark Psychology of persuasion gives a comprehensive method including the aim of persuading a person to internalize the concept and hence adopt that brand new concept or maybe attitude as the primary belief in the life of theirs.

The very first thing to do in the methods brought by the Dark Psychology persuasion is creating a desire. The demand is attractive to the fundamental demand of man, food, shelter, love, self-esteem, and self-actualization. You can create ideas with these fundamental things. Whatever it was always related to the way you can produce through an easy concept. In that way, your goals are going to be far more focused. The next in the Dark Psychology persuasion is creating an appeal to social demand.

The example of the strategy is perhaps a tv producer would like the product of theirs to be purchased. Chances are they create the offering that in case you've some television type. You are going to be in a position to be similar to a famous person, by making some celebrity as the ad icon. The use of loaded text, as well as pictures, is additionally mostly utilized to ensure that individuals will be "deception" to get the offering.

Three Modes of Persuasion by Aristotle

Virtually everyone heard of Aristotle. He is one of the most well-known classical periods of Greek philosophers. While best known as "The Father of Western Philosophy," he also developed three modes of persuasion: Ethos, Pathos, and Logos ("Ethos, Pathos & Logos-Persuasion Modes (Aristotle).

Ethos

Ethos is better defined as the personal character or ethical nature of the speaker. According to Aristotle, these qualities would include empathy, ability, and good intention. Together, they make the speaker trustworthy, which is the main objective of the speaker because they want to get the audience to listen. There are many ways the speaker can use styles, such as language, grammar, clothes, and achievements. The speaker needs to use the best terminology for the audience. They need to use the best vocabulary and talk at a level where their audience will understand it. For example, if they explain how to uninstall a beginner's machine, they do not use expert terminology as their own.

Their choice of clothing will also tell the audience about the character of the speaker. For example, if the speaker wears jeans and a shirt, the audience might think they're laid back or unprofessional. If the speaker wears professional clothing like a suit, the audience will think they're professional, successful, and pride in their work. Another way the speaker gets more convincing is by their achievement list. If they have substantial achievements in the field, the audience is more likely to believe the speaker.

The audience will pay attention to the facial expressions, gestures, tone of voice, and body movement of the speaker in general. If, for example, a speaker does not move around the stage and does not make eye contact, they will look less engaged. People might feel nervous, uncertain about what they are talking about, or uninterested in talking to them.

Pathos

When a presenter uses pathos, they use their emotions to try to persuade the audience. This is a common factor among many speakers at some point in their presentation. Depending on what they're talking about, presenters might open up with a personal story to get to the emotions of their audience right away. Other speakers will wait until later in their presentation as they feel this engages the audience. Emotions are used to make the audience feel closer to the speaker. They feel sympathetic because they understand what the speaker has been through. Another common emotion from speakers is to make their audience feel angry. Of course, this isn't about the speaker, but about someone else or a company.

Emotional tone, language, and meanings are the key features that effectively allow speakers to reach an audience through pathos. It is much easier to persuade someone through strong emotions because people often let their emotions guide their decisions. Aristotle thought it was important for the speaker to know their audience. People tend to get emotional about these subjects. For example, if you're in a wealthy society, the majority of the audience may not relate to problems of poverty or low-income housing, and many of them do not realize what it's like to live in poverty.

Logos

Logos is where the speaker uses justification or logic to persuade their audience. In other words, the speaker must offer an argument to win the audience over. This means that the speaker has to be incredibly knowledgeable about their subject. While love for the subject helps, it's what the speaker will use for pathos over logos. The audience convinced by logos wants to hear facts. They also don't care about emotional stories; however, you can always have a few. Aristotle said that there are two different types of facts to concentrate on in your presentation: the first form is scientific or artificial facts, which are formed by reasoning and knowledge.

The Ultimate Guide To Enhance your Persuasion Techniques

The energy of persuasion can open doors for you and come up with the road to good results much smoother. After looking at this book, you are going to have an array of effective methods at the disposal of yours. Probably the most effective methods have the origins of theirs in NLP (neuro-linguistic programming). These persuasion methods are derived from empathy - to persuade someone - you have to comprehend them.

Empathy-Based Persuasive Techniques

The very first and most significant thing you have to comprehend about the individual you're attempting to influence is precisely what the brain of their best response to - feel, visual, or maybe auditory stimulation. Knowing this can enable you to be persuasive by plugging into and feeding this particular desire.

Females generally respond better to feelings, however, not. Guys frequently respond very well to visuals, and several individuals are impacted by audio. To discover and that is the very best stimulation to focus the persuasion of yours, look at the way they talk. Can they say, "I see," "I hear what you are saying," or maybe "I feel that."? These are obvious examples; of course, the appropriate answer might be far more subtle and maybe a blend of two kinds of stimulation.

Alter the persuasion methods of yours depending on the mind type you're offering with; for instance, when persuading somebody who's "feel" orientated, focus on the way they are going to feel if they do what you're attempting to persuade them to. Do not attempt to tell them just what it is going to be like - you've to make them believe it. The more you are conscious of the individual you are coping with, the much more efficiently you are going to be in a position to focus the persuasive strategies of yours.

Mirror Based Persuasive Techniques

Matching the body language of yours, as well as your pose/position, is a subtle but amazingly effective persuasive method. You have to be subtle, and this might feel uncomfortable in the beginning, however, with a bit of exercise, you are going to see just how helpful this particular method, referred to as "mirroring," maybe at creating a rapport and easing persuasion.

Along with focusing the content of the persuasion of yours in a means that interacts nicely with the specific character style of theirs, you can additionally correct the language of yours as well as how you talk to place yourself on the Stage of theirs. Individuals react much better to persuasive strategies that are in their own "language" of theirs. Pick up on certain words they utilize as well as added them back on them, particularly adjectives. Consider their response, volume, pitch, and speed as similarly as you possibly can.

Other Persuasive Techniques

You will find a lot of different persuasive methods that you can focus on and build up. We suggest you learn the empathy/mirror effective methods, most notably, as these are the best. Nevertheless, the following methods may be useful additions to the persuasion armory of yours.

• **Persuasive Words**

There are lots of subconscious persuasive words that an individual may make use of. Frequently these will be a call to action: for instance, "Do that" or perhaps "Be this." Kind words as well as adjectives, for example, "Definitely," "Most," as well as "Effective" are extremely persuasive all on their very own.

Utilize "now" words including "today" or perhaps "at the moment" frequently to subliminally recommend urgency.

• **Rhetorical Questions**

Allowing the individual to believe for themselves is extremely motivating and can, therefore, be incredibly persuasive. Ask questions that engage them, and they instantly are open. This will even enable you to know more about them. Frequently this will persuade them they're making the decision when in reality, you've just steered them to this particular persuasion.

• **Eye Contact**

It's highly crucial to produce a great rapport with the individual you're attempting to persuade. Without eye contact, this's practically impossible. With non-threatening and consistent eye contact, you can develop trust. Include a real smile, plus persuasion will get so much easier.

Be Persuasive By Connecting Emotionally, Not Rationally

Anyone of politics will let you know - individuals just do not answer rationally. They react based on feelings. To persuade somebody, you should connect with them emotionally. Aristotle determined the three fundamental components of every persuasive argument:

Ethos: the credibility, knowledge, expertise, authority, and stature of the individual attempting to persuade.

Logos: the appeal of logic, reason, cognitive thinking, facts, and data.

Pathos: the charm to the emotions; the non-cognitive, non-thinking motivations which impact actions as well as choices.

All layers are, of course, necessary, though it's probably the psychological Stage which keeps probably the most energy of persuasion. We're psychological beings and are a lot more apt to be persuaded by the promise of feeling great as opposed to the promise of "something being correct."

The Moral Behind Persuasion Techniques

You might be thinking that using persuasion methods is immoral, underhand. You might find yourself with the dilemma of whether to utilize them on someone you enjoy. It is actually up for you exactly how you think about using effective methods, but remembers the following. Individuals must be conscious of the strategies and understand when others are attempting to manipulate them. If you effectively persuade somebody, you've just out-competed them.

Persuasion is optional. After practice that is very much, you might find that these effective methods just embed into the dynamics of the being. Might you feel guilty for making use of other elements of the individuality of yours, like talking confidently? A lot of the time, you'll be attempting to do what's most beneficial for these people regardless. The goal of connecting with someone psychologically is to learn what they need. Whenever you realize this, you're just persuading them to do something which they are going to want to do anyhow. And so, by the definition of its, persuasion isn't manipulation - it's merely bringing the point of yours across.

Individuals must note adequate to make their own choices theirs. Ideally, you need to be sure that you can make use of these effective methods to do what's appropriate for those concerned.

Power Of Conscious Persuasion

The key to the universe is the strength of persuasion. Persuasion is the one key element to getting everything you need, becoming rich, and having success in whatever. Without any persuasion, nothing gets done. It's about persuading yourself and others. Persuasion is all about moving consciousness, and once you can move consciousness, you can move something of the universe.

All persuasion is persuading to take action, whether physical or mental exercise. Most successful and wealthy individuals are masters of persuasion. You might have had particular concepts against using persuasion since you feel it's manipulation. But they're limiting beliefs that you have that are preventing you from achievement. The utilization of persuasion for wrongful purposes is manipulation, though the natural use of persuasion is actually for guidance. Consumers wish to be guided in a manner that makes them comfortable and eager to take action to help themselves. All of us want to be led into doing what is excellent for us by someone who could teach us the way.

Understand that notion generates reality. Persuasion is all about changing the perception of individuals to change the reality of theirs. It's about helping others to see things in a diverse way that they did not see before. To make use of persuasion, you initially need to persuade yourself about the usage of persuasion. You've to change the perception of yours of persuasion. If you are able to shift your beliefs and perception about truth to those who are successful and wealthy, you are able to utilize the strength of persuasion the manner they put it to use.

Probably the most powerful as well as important individuals on the planet are the persuaders. They have the potential to shift people's perception, choices, and beliefs about things. In the event that you would like to alter the planet, you've to alter the consciousness of individuals. Probably the most effective sort of persuasion is actually persuasion that moves individuals of the path that they currently wish to go. It's persuasion to show them the ways of getting that which they wish. You are able to persuade men and women to do something in case they believe it is going to satisfy them. In total persuasion, the objective is persuading individuals they have a particular desire, exactly how they are able to satisfy that motivation, and that it's really worth whatever they provide in exchange for that that will meet the desire of theirs.

Numerous locations teach persuasion in ways that are different; however, the basic concepts all come right down to a couple of that represent all of them. It's about getting attention and sparking curiosity and interest. In that case, it's related to arousing desire and convincing them to take a particular action to fulfill that desire. The crucial point that all persuasion deals with is actually convincing others about the importance of something. Something just has greatly based on the importance which you give it. Who's saying that a specific product is definitely worth a specific amount of cash? The fact is that everything in the universe is totally free. All of the items in life obtain the worth of theirs from the perception of individuals. The perception of worth is able to differ from one individual to yet another. You are able to develop some worth in anything merely by the way you cause others to perceive it.

Nothing in the universe is actually of any use to any being except by the consciousness that the being has towards it. All drugs medications wouldn't do the job to heal whether an individual thinks that they wouldn't heal, and the consciousness of theirs isn't in harmony for healing but illness. For an individual that has the consciousness as well as trust for healing, actually, a placebo would procure the outcome of healing. Nobody is able to get pleasure from anything until they have the consciousness to get satisfaction from that thing.

It's persuasion that makes the world go round. When individuals aren't persuaded to do anything, there'd be no movement of energy. There'd be no buying or even selling. When materials aren't being moved around, things can't be placed into the hands of those who could place them to use more effectively. The economy comes to a standstill when cash isn't flowing. When individuals keep what they've rather than offering it to get something far more, it'll just lead to stagnation, entropy, and degrading of the universe.

That's why the entrepreneurs, as well as sales promoters, are actually doing society a huge service. By convincing individuals in order to see value in food as well as to offer something different, whether it's time, information, or money to get it, they're encouraging the exchange of power. When power is replaced, that's when there could be experienced types as well as brand new combinations of energy designed for the majority around the globe to benefit from. The exchange of electrical power is the thing that supports the evolution of humanity and also the improvement of living.

The right way to great wealth is to create that much value as you can for other people. Since value is actually produced by perception, you are able to produce value by producing the perception of value. The higher the perception of the value you are able to produce and the greater number of individuals you are able to affect, the more you are able to produce an exchange of energy where cash flows for you in exchange for everything you provide. You are able to have all that you would like when you assist others get what they need, and that is by what you persuade them to want as well as get.

Learning Subconscious Persuasion In order to Attain Everything You Want

The subconscious persuasion is a situation of great value because in case you perfect it, it might make it easier to out of many unfavorable scenarios. Effectively, individuals that are different make use of various techniques of persuasion to get others to make the points they wish to be done, out of the usage of excessive force, a cajoling tone, and maybe by the use of powerful words.

You might employ persuasion as an instrument at the home, workplace, and so forth to realize the various objectives of yours in daily life and, much more so, attain the happiness which you've consistently hungered following. Keeping the strength of subconscious persuasion is going to place you in a place to gain insight into whenever the techniques of persuasion have been utilized in you. The thing you ought to understand about the strength of persuasion is the fact that primarily since you use your internalized capability of persuasion and that of reading through other people's gestures and minds. These items help make the entire process like a breeze, with results that are a fantastic guarantee.

It is likely you have numerous resources that you are able to utilize in the aspects of the initiation of the subconscious mind persuasion system. To start, you need to look at the voice you make use of. It's been proved which the usage of a voice that's a tad lower when speaking to someone is much more powerful whenever you wish to appeal to the subconscious mind of theirs. A low voice has the outcome of comforting that individual, and even more important, it will reduce the defenses of theirs ultimately, which leads to establishing trust in these individuals.

Subliminal Technology As A Therapy

Subliminal engineering is among the best therapies which may be utilized to improve the strength of persuasion. This's for the reason that this one is directed at the mental faculties, and better still, it's usually vital that you keep in mind that each performance that occurs in as well as the body is managed in the human brain. Thus, researching for more info is the key element. There are numerous resources for subliminal engineering. They are going to show you the way it may be utilized to boost subliminal persuasion. Know almost as you are able to.

The Following Are crucial Methods for Mastering Subconscious Persuasion

- The framing technique: No much better way to change the method of yours of categorizing, sorting, associating, and ultimately giving meaning to other facets of life, from items to events or perhaps behaviors, than that one. Framing has the outcome of swaying individuals towards the perspectives of yours. In order to frame persuasive arguments, use words that will conjure images in the brains of those you're addressing.

- The Mirroring Technique: This's mimicking the activities (the body language as well as movements) of the party you're engaging in persuasion. What you do is actually develop a sympathy sense by playing the job of the individual listening. This particular method, likewise referred to as the "Chameleon Effect," is much more successful since you use it subconsciously.
- The Timing Technique: Industry experts have proved the Subconscious Persuasion as being especially powerful when used to individuals following a very brain cracking activity. Just before placing a chat with an individual about a product they're likely never to agree to, think about beginning that discusses when that specific individual is mentally exhausted.
- The Reciprocation Technique: We're significantly compelled by the great measures which are given to us by individuals that are good in the lives of ours. Most likely, in case you do something great to the workplace, at home, or your neighbor, they'll additionally will you great for reciprocation. What you are going to achieve by this's that you'll enhance these interactions by the potential of the Subconscious Persuasion.

CHAPTER 11 DECEPTION IN DARK PSYCHOLOGY

Deception can easily be described as willfully misleading a person for a specific gain. When using this definition in the mental exploration context, deception takes place in which the investigation subjects, people who participate for a specific investigation, are actually supplied with misleading or maybe info that is false to record the reality of their behavior or responses. Particularly, in behavioral scientific studies, the significance of this shortage of understanding of the simple fact is actually ideal as it makes the ideal state of unveiling the reality.

The use of deception is quite explicit as the participants had been deceived of the reality of the investigation. Nevertheless, although this offered rich and accurate sources of information, which were extraordinary as well as contributed enormously to the behavioral Dark Psychology, there was a great deal of criticism as it had been viewed quite deceitful. This's as although there was no bodily damage for the participants, and it was a painful emotional encounter.

Deception Is actually Accepted Under Certain Conditions?

Firstly, deception has to be worn when there's not one other option for getting info that is accurate? Secondly, it shouldn't damage the subjects possibly physically or mentally, and? Finally, after the truth has been discovered (this procedure is described as debriefing, the place that the researcher uncovers the true goal of the research) and also the participants maintain for withdrawal, the researcher has to respect his or maybe the choice of her.

Drawbacks In Deceiving Participants

While the deception has the benefits of its of enhancing the mental pool of study and results in exact findings in which individuals genuinely respond to the predicament, it definitely has the drawbacks of its. In the very first place, prior to doing research, the informed consent of the participants has to be used. One of the primary objections is actually it violates the rights of the participant as the participant will be consenting to deception and utilized for study exactly where he or maybe she's unaware of the true objective.

An additional claim is it questions the whole thought of ethicality. Last but not least, this taints the picture of the general discipline as the use of deception may be quite demeaning in which individuals formulate bad attitudes to not just that specific study and researcher, though the whole community.

To sum up, it's correct that the use of deception is; actually, Dark Psychology offers dependable, accurate details as individuals screen real behavior. Nevertheless, deception must just be used at mandatory circumstances as it's a number of disadvantages to the researcher, the participants as well as mental study community in particular. In order to decrease the dilemma of ethicality, the participants have to be debriefed as early as you possibly can of the true nature of the investigation as well as the goals of its.

Advantages and disadvantages Of Deception In Dark Psychology

The advantages and disadvantages of deception in the mental present an incredibly complicated topic. On the outside, we're enticed to reject the notion of deception in mental investigation outright. Nevertheless, as you're likely to discover, everything is significantly less easy as deferring to that opinion each and every time. With regard to the idea of investigation, there's no question that ethics is actually among the important ingredients there's. This's definitely true for all types of psychological studies. The requirement for ethics in mental investigation is incredibly high. Many of us appreciate this truth.

Nevertheless, there are actually likely to be times in which ethics, as we understand the idea in broad terms, is actually going to be subject to a specific amount of manipulation. In terms of psychological research, this particular manipulation is actually crucial to a particular degree. Without a doubt, with regards to sociological or psychological experiments, there are likely to be circumstances in which you don't want the topic to find out everything. For the experiment to become meaningful and effective, you're likely to need to keep things that are certain from the patient at specific times during the experiment. This's a kind of deception. Could it be an important kind of deception? It can easily be.

But while deception might be crucial in a few areas of psychological research, the subject of ethics of that department of research is still a great topic of debate. Discoveries are now being made about the brains of ours, apparently every day. We've to keep this in mind, and we've also to think about the idea that deception in the mental analysis is actually effective at causing damage, unintentional, or perhaps otherwise.

Dark Psychology organizations and doctors around the world are continuously re-examining as well as updating the ethical codes of theirs, and there is a reason behind that. While we wish to accept the importance of a particular Stage of deception within specific research projects, we additionally need to continuously think about the advantages and disadvantages of deception in psychological studies.

As you are able to imagine, weighing the advantages and disadvantages of deception in the sociological or psychological study may surely make for complex considerations.

The Pros Of Deception In Dark Psychology

Deception Is recommended with no less than several of the mental tests being conducted, a specific amount of deception is crucial to producing the type of results that can make the whole endeavor important. Accuracy, as well as validity, are actually cornerstones to any mental research challenge. Lacking deception on no less than some Stage, it's tough to envision particular experiments reaching great ph Stages of both validities as well as accuracy.

The Intentions Are Good

Although this might not seem like a lot of a pro, it is crucial to know that deception in the mental analysis isn't an inherently evil idea. While generally there are almost certainly examples of deception being used to evil extremes, the truth of the issue is the fact that for the majority of part, the motives behind the usage of deception are excellent.

The Ends Can Actually Justify The Means Sometimes

If perhaps you think about the great history of breakthroughs attained by way of a mental research project, you are discussing substantial gains in the drive of ours to completely understand as well as foster the human brain. The deception continues to be a part of a lot of those experiments. At times, which deception runs to a Stage, which makes numerous folks uneasy. Nevertheless, think about breakthroughs. Carry out the ends justify the means? Many folks feel they do.

The Ethics Of Psychological Research Actually are Never Complacent

This means that the idea of values as they exclusively apply to deception in the mental analysis isn't fixed or perhaps incapable of evolution. Since the idea of deception in the mental analysis is such a vulnerable, complicated subject, it's a thing that associations and researchers alike are continuously working to look at as well as enhance. To put it simply, in case you compare the ethics inside mental study to the ethics practiced in mental investigation 50 or perhaps two0 years back, you are going to notice a marked impact.

A Lack Of Deception Can Sometimes Ruin Everything

Based on what the analysis is actually attempting to achieve, offering individuals everything in the way of info coming from the really beginning of the task can drastically alter the outcomes of the task. In several instances, it is able to totally ruin the entire point of the investigation.

A Universal Approach To Ethics Is Unrealistic

The needs of one research task may be totally distinct from the demands of another research task. Implementing common, iron-clad values that demand full disclosure right from the start may be fine for specific research projects, though it might prove to be extremely difficult for various other jobs. These're several of the more noticeable pros of deception in psychological studies. Nevertheless, the pros don't paint a total image by any means.

Cons Of Deception In Dark Psychology

There's a number of really good to be discovered in using deception in psychological studies. Nevertheless, several cons must be taken into consideration, as well:

- **Even The very best Of Intentions Can Go Wrong!**

The issue with deception in the mental analysis is the fact that even when researchers go into the task with the best of intentions, there's a bit of possibility for damage to the individuals. One of the more fascinating elements to a lot of the awful examples of the implications of deception is the point that in instances that are many, malice was probably the furthest point from the head of those to blame for the task.

- The Potential For Abuse Still Exists

Regrettably, despite strict values in place, it's feasible for a person or perhaps a team to abuse the idea of deception in mental investigation deliberately. Even under the very best of circumstances, there's also a threat opportunity with practically all research projects that utilize some type of deception. You will find mental chances to think about, along with community risks and other things.

The possible risk factor is able to change in seriousness from one project to the subsequent, but there's no getting around the reality that the threat potential is present in practically all mental research projects.

Does Knowledge Truly Develop a Bias?

A number of people think that just in the most severe circumstances would full disclosure develop a bias that might harm the validity of the study.

The Morality Of The Entire Concept Is Very Complex

There's basically no getting around the reality that we're discussing an extremely complicated moral idea. For many, it's absolutely impossible to come to a good solution, making a number of keen on eliminating deception coming from the research project type entirely.

Ways In order to Detect Deception

Lots of people think they understand how to identify deception. They depend on nonverbal cues or maybe actions that frequently speak louder compared to words. In fact, you will find body language signals which could help identify whether an individual is telling the actual story or perhaps not. It's frequently thought that you are able to see whether the individual is trustworthy or perhaps not by looking at the eyes of his. In case he appears straight in the eye, he's presumed truthful. Nevertheless, there have been situations in which nonverbal cues by itself have failed to identify deception.

Based on research, lying is actually a skill. It's a thing that may be discovered - a lot of love, biking, swimming, and driving. Pro liars have trained themselves to tell lies with a straight face, and they are able to take action with ease after extended hours of training. It simply takes patience to find out a skill. In case you would like to learn how to identify deception, it is best if you make use of some other resources along with reading body language signals by itself.

Relying entirely on nonverbal cues are able to result in misinterpretation. To tell the truth is extremely demanding to a lot of individuals. This's particularly true when painful and sensitive matters are concerned. For many people, discussions about sexuality lead to discomfort that they can't discuss casually or even look straight in the eye. With misleading nonverbal cues, individuals are likely to overestimate the capability of theirs regarding how to identify deception, which they turn out to be deceived themselves.

The procedure for lie detection is very tricky that individuals depend on technological resources to uncover the truth. This particular unbiased strategy might get a much better success rate compared to merely depending on nonverbal cues. Lie detection equipment is utilized by law in interrogating suspects or may be witnesses in crimes. These power tools demonstrate just how inept an individual's judgment is with regard to translating signals. Several of the most typical resources utilized to uncover deceptions are actually the polygraph and also the functional magnetic resonance imaging, normally known as fMRI.

The polygraph methods, as well as monitors a person's heart rate, epidermis conductance, and blood pressure. Modifications in the monitored information are actually related to a person's anxiety Stage. If a human being is nervous throughout the interrogation, then there's an enormous possibility that he's lying.

One more technological application that works for exactly the same objective is the fMRI. It utilizes brain scans to know how a person's thought process works and also includes signs which figure out if an individual is telling the truth or perhaps not.

Police investigators understand how to identify deception. They begin the task by asking non-threatening questions. These questions don't encourage an individual to lie. Chances are they move with the structured interrogation procedure. They evaluate and notice the changes in the brain's activity.

Once again, these power tools are sometimes not 100 % correct. To be subject to a lie detector test will cause a growth in the anxiety Stage as well as brain activity for just about any typical individual. This might result in a misinterpretation of information resulting in the realization that the individual is lying even in case he's telling the truth. He's merely self-conscious or perhaps might be apprehensive about the machine! It can swing each way. Pro liars can conceal the feelings of theirs of anxiety, while some individuals become stressed out by telling the truth! Nevertheless, individuals shouldn't wring the hands of theirs and give up on these resources. They appear to forget that the majority of people whom they're offering aren't skilled liars, and only a few individuals are available to deceive them.

Operating from such a bad mindset is only able to attract much more of these undesirable persons in the expertise of theirs. Let us be thankful that science has come up with those tools that could assist in knowing as well as understanding how you can identify deception.

Power And Control In Human Deception

As the devolution continues, day occurrences around the majority, as well as the U.S. of the planet, provide proof of control and strength in human deception. A continuing process of man regression of the imbalance of social equity, the few that adjust the materials manage to exert impact on those of lesser means. Lately, a prominent company magazine noted for reporting on power and wealth within the business, as well as government sectors, reported that 50% of earthly wealth. The continued decline of sensible materiality doesn't paint an optimistic photo.

Appropriately, there are actually associated indicators that not much more than 100,000 folks have a net worth more than fifty million dollars. By unbelievable contrast, at the bottom part of this human energy pyramid, is 70% that have under $10,000. From there, the revenue disparity gets gloomy, as poorer individuals encounter income losses, and richer ones show income increases. An additional study found in a UK news service that under 400 of probably the richest individuals possess greater than 50% of probably the poorest individuals.

While generally there are actually noble instances of charitable giving by a couple of on top of the echelons of wealth, recent studies are likely to show a decreasing trend. Several analysts recommend that poorer persons, by comparison to the wealthy according to a fraction of income, are actually providing much more in benevolent efforts.

Needless to say, there are actually arguments on each side of income inequality problems. What exactly are the implications for humankind? Apart from the abject realities, the probabilities for continued community degradation don't provide an optimistic future for the human race. Rather, the decline of the species invites eventual extinction.

For all those in power, on top of the echelons of wealth, the oligarchies foster collusive gambits that possess a lot of faceted expressions. By the illusions of contemporary education of the halls of academia to the blathering campaigning of career politicians, the superficiality of societal discourse slides into the regressive oblivion for which extinction looms near. Running a business, higher education, public service along with other human interactivity, the Darkinishing worth of fearlessly enlightened leadership suffer a similar fate. Leaders are disappearing, along with a self-centered feeling of "anti thinking" that perpetrates divisiveness.

In a society easily regressing to primal states of early reactivity versus intellectual preeminence, many have concluded leadership is actually scarce. Most are challenged to find and/or otherwise title a public office holder that exhibits remarkable capacities for directing on an increasingly risky planet.

A regressed collective of tyrannical "tolerance" for the arrogance of intolerance to others fosters a dishonest climate of political correctness. Nowadays, for example, it doesn't take much to unnerve or maybe usually terrorize a town, at state, a city, or perhaps the whole state. In the aftermath of a horrific event, multitudes effortlessly clamor for government assures of shielding subservience. A "lone gunman," a terrorist with a bomb, or maybe a disgruntled worker is able to have many citizens ready to sacrifice liberty for an impression of individual security. Handy scapegoats are too simple to conjure.

For anti thinking, steeped in the misconception as well as the magic of foolish conjecture and idle thinking, the numerous acquiesce to the numbing cerebral maladies of mass-market deception. Societies get what they need by consequence of piggish selfishness as well as slothful work. For the majority, instead of a greater sense of skeptical inquiry, sanctioned by a logical program of methodical studies, as well as the integrity of critical thinking, sincere discourse, as well as enlightenment, requires excessive responsibility.

In many cases, there's a quick appeal to alleged authority, as in merchandise promotions, the political campaign advertisement, as well as the questionable academic "experiment," etc. So-called public interest surveys, whatever the subject matter, don't say a lot, prove small and resolve nothing. At exactly the same moment, ghosts, goblins, and small green males become scapegoats for man immaturity.

Meanwhile, some are actually gauging the likelihood of finality and concentrating on two dynamics, which can result in a worldwide disaster. One of those is actually a mass pandemic, as well as the other is actually source depletion, which invites natural catastrophes. For the former, also by the contrivance of nature or maybe human manipulation, the social collapse might occur by means of terrible "killer diseases."

For which, today, physiological immunity is actually starting to be much more of a task for disease control mechanisms. Failure to anticipate, recognize, plan, and implement effective methods prior to calamity hastens the worst-case scenarios. While conjecture alleges catastrophes that can befall humans, a major component is still the gambit of control as well as strength in human deception.

Deep Psychological Mind Tricks - Crossing The Line Between Persuasion And Deception

Psychological mind tricks might be made up of strategic persuasive communication strategies to create a person doubt his values as well as beliefs. This could mislead a person to believe that what's right is actually wrong, and what's wrong is actually right. Mental brain techniques could seem crazy, though it really works. This will entail crafty persuasion as well as communication skills, which will inevitably affect someone's choices and views. Furthermore, the feeling of touch additionally plays a crucial role in this particular persuasion method.

Many people are currently making use of mental mind tricks and making obvious changes in the life of theirs, using them to the benefit of theirs. Unconsciously, you might not realize that a particular individual has already played mind tricks on you, and also you wake up uncertain of the activities which have just happened.

Mental Mind Tricks In Business

These're quite typical to salespersons that make use of these persuasion strategies to persuade customers to buy their services or products. This's getting one to think that what they're promoting is ideal for you. What they do is the fact that they are going to tell you things about the item, the way you are able to gain from it, the reason it's perfect for you, and just how you are able to cut costs by purchasing it. These intense exaggerations that could actually result in deceiving the potential purchasers of theirs.

Example: You're searching for an automobile to purchase, after which you meet with a salesman letting you know you are able to bring down the gas price of yours by fifty % in case you buy the automobile. Though the simple truth is, you will not. He is going to try to persuade you by providing "exclusive" offers just provided to you, though he's already provided the identical offer to prior purchasers.

Challenging Tactics Of Mind Control

Many advertisings make use of mental mind tricks to generate the audience of theirs to get the services and products being offered. To make you believe every person is making use of it and just minimal offers are left.

EXAMPLE: "The only product used by all Americans, you will not fail with it. Purchase right now and say goodbye to headache forever!"

What you've simply read above is actually a good example of an extreme exaggeration utilizing ad as a tool to persuade buyers to purchase the item, informing them which they will not encounter headaches permanently in case they normally use the service. All you're doing is suggesting the elements they would like to do anyway, as well as supporting them to recognize that those items are the very best options for these people.

Hence, mental brain tricks include strategic communication, persuasion, in addition to a little bit of exaggeration. Timing, as well as the feeling of touch, also are fundamental areas of this often-effective persuasion strategy.

When to Use Psychological Mind Tricks

You must understand the correct time, individual, and place to take rational mind tricks. In certain instances, specialists of the field can instantly find the techniques of yours, therefore firing back at you and resulting in an assortment of effects. Be sure you wear them at the right spot at the right time. Find out and evaluate the individual you are offering with original, as well as be worried about the interests of theirs before jumping into any deal.

Brain Control

A lot of individuals make use of the idiom "Mind Control" for things that are different. In truth, it's an extensive meaning which has many types. Mind control means seizing control of the head. The question is whose brain is now being controlled? You will find numerous diverse treatments of mind control that are used in any situation. Nevertheless, these methods might have been produced by different sciences. So the strategies which are utilized for managing other people's thought process are distinct from those to manage the mind of ours. That is the reason there are many brain management kinds.

Therefore if a person would like to change as well as manage the thoughts of others, then he should find out hypnosis methods as well as NLP (Neuro-linguistic programming). Even when NLP is a toolbox centered on individual growth, it can assist with understanding what sort of character the person you wish to influence is. For instance, utilizing a recognized NLP method, an individual can manage the thoughts of a particular person while he appears to speak to him as always. This particular technique is known as conversational or Discreet hypnosis.

Immediately after some time, the planted concept comes up as being a brand new theory to the other individual. Even though they believe they believed this on their own, in fact, you instructed them what you should believe, so in this way, you are able to manipulate as well as control the brain of theirs. Standard hypnosis from the various other side consists of the consent of the other individual so to allow you to hypnotize them and grow ideas in the subconscious of theirs.

Yet another hypnosis technique, which appears as brain manipulation, is the Stage Hypnosis. This's a method utilized by showmen hypnotists to adjust a "volunteer" participant. There's a debate in the event this's a mind control method or maybe a phony method.

For people that refer to mind management as a means to manage the mind of theirs, there are plethora means out there. A few commonly held ones are self-hypnosis, the Silva technique, Meditation, brainwave entrainment, and a lot more. Within the brainwave entrainment, management features a different sense as opposed to the very first two.

In self-hypnosis, one tries to induce the head of theirs into hypnosis. This ordinarily occurs with thorough visualizations by initiating the right hemisphere and reducing the frequency of the brainwave. These visualizations could be a simple symbolic means of obtaining the goals of theirs, quitting bad habits, slimming down, and other things. Self-hypnosis might be instructed or perhaps unguided. Guided ways that a person listens to a prerecorded instruction from a hypnotherapist to enter into a trance and be hypnotized. The web is filled with such items that are targeted for certain good reasons. A few common aims of the programs are giving up smoking, calming, losing weight, assisting with sexual problems, and other things.

Meditation approaches brain management differently. Even though the prior mind control methods activate the right hemisphere as well as the creativity of the person, the goal of meditation is simply the contrary; to stop the notion creation. You will find plenty of deep breathing methods. One simple one is concentration meditation in which a human being attempts to focus the interest of his to an inner (e.g., breathing) or even outside (candle flame) fixed-job.

The Dark Psychology Of Mind Control

To the box office hit "Inception," characters use a complex fantasy machine to infiltrate the subconscious of effective businessmen and manipulate the brains of theirs. In the traditional movie thriller "The Manchurian Candidate," the son of an active political household is brainwashed into attempting assassinations with implanted code words.

Although they take various methods, both these movies are actually about the Dark Psychology of mind control. These two instances illustrate exactly how this particular topic has captured the imagination of the general public. Imagination is a manifestation of truth, nonetheless, and there are numerous diverse types of techniques utilized to coerce individuals into different psychological states.

Underneath hypnosis, the body of yours is in a full state of physical rest. You start to be ready to accept suggestions, as well as the brain is effective at tremendous psychological awareness. Certain nurses make use of hypnosis to calm down people, removing the anxiety of theirs during methods as well as operations. Numerous others willingly undergo hypnosis to enhance the quality of theirs of life, by probing the subconscious of theirs to stop overeating or perhaps smoking.

Neuro-linguistic programming was established in the 1970s and required a mix of verbal and body language techniques to boost neurological abilities. Someone taught in NLP can utilize a range of techniques to coerce a subject into specific cognitive states. These techniques include the idea of "mirroring" a subject's non-verbal cues and "anchoring" a trigger term to elicit a specific state of mind.

The conscious brain perceives a typical stimulus. The subconscious perceives a subliminal stimulus. Advertisers often make use of this particular strategy. Visual pictures may be shown so rapidly you might not observe that they're there. Sound cues could be played at just below calculated listening volume, or perhaps placed backward. These pictures, as well as soundtracks, can infiltrate the subconscious of yours, giving the suggestive traces of theirs behind and influencing the behavior of yours down the road.

The Dark Psychology of mind control features an amazing history and likely frightening implications. It's really worth the time of yours to find out a lot more info relating to this debatable topic. It's the mind of yours, all things considered.

Gaining Mind Control to Enhance The Life of yours

Mind control isn't a procedure of making a private lose control over their behavior as well as views. And many mind control experiments aren't actually done via actual physical force as well as violence until you're in a P.O.W camp lol! Don't confuse brain management with hypnotism. Hypnotism, as well as mind control, aren't interchangeably identical. They're two completely different phrases. This particular technique of self-control used to be believed to be enforced by religious cults, types of politics, parenting, as well as the implementation of a false or incorrect set of actions. It's be also said that brain control has been related to two syndromes.

A battered female's syndrome and also the other is known as a Stockholm syndrome. This's NOT ACCURATE! Because psychological command has numerous positives to it too. It is able to assist you have far more sustaining as well as fulfilling daily life. And so, let us not look down after brain control merely yet. It has been pointed out this may a lot be the keys to becoming a much better individual. Occasionally a bit of brainwashing is actually required, since, with all of that moves on in one's life, the mind is able to get yourself a bit cluttered, and may utilize very good clothes. With the correct info provided to the brain, it could be a life-changing experience.

Mind control methods allow you to recognize as well as know more about yourself and the mindset of yours. This's what I'd love to call self-mindset analysis. Simply because we believe we understand how the brains work of ours, but in reality, we have not the slightest idea of what we're thinking, as well as, or even just how this particular thinking is actually hurting the actions of ours. Are we hindering ourselves from a terrific offer with these incorrect thought procedures?

It's favorable to getting a much better man or woman in case we know more about the brains of ours. You are able to see from brain control about just how you feel, are you processing the views of yours or perhaps will be your knowledge outdated. The main reason I say this's because as we live, we discover and in understanding out with the old and in with the latest. Things change; individuals change because our thoughts change.

When we do not clear the brains of ours of the clutter, we'll simply suffer from info overload, and most of that does is actually cause us to act irrational as well as ill-informed. Positive affirmations or even correct brain management, help you get help from damaging thought processing, as well as aids in helping achieve the objectives of yours.

Control of the mind of yours enables understanding and alertness of what's taking place. You are able to change the mindset of yours. It's a precise procedure. Use mind control to change actions that are holding you back, as well as gain possession of a far more dedicated fulfillment of your goals and wants. Mind control additionally produces a feeling of peace as well as strength. Many people make use of that method and build enhanced healthful, durable relationships. This can build one's' confidence. This brand new thought process is going to lead to far more focused behavior. Behavior management suggests regulating an individual's genuine behavior.

Information that is Right and thought management is a need. You are going to be in a position to make much better choices and examine some matter rationally. It will build the practice of obeying the 1st imagination of yours with no question. Reading, writing, as well as the meditation of the thoughts of yours, will aid you to learn the future of yours. Think about what you would really want from daily life and set out to achieve it; in case it is not aiding you to have a far more rich and fulfilling life than it's a misuse of time.

The very best Mind Control Techniques

What would you think of whenever you listen to the words -' Mind Control'? Will it seem supernatural or even a thing you are able to have? The majority of the folks believe it as something of the supernatural. The fact is that all of us could manage the brains of ours. It's we that run the brain and feed it with whatever we wish to. Controlling the brain is in the hands of ours. Exactly what are the most effective methods to control the brain of yours?' Why the hell must I be keen on controlling the brain of mine? Would not it be nicer? In case I can manage the minds of others?' If you are thinking on lines that are very much the same, you are completely wrong just since you can't control others' minds until you are able to manage yours! And in case you are thinking of world accession by managing the minds of others - you, in all probability, are actually watching way too many sci-fi films!

Observation

What's it that separates you from James Bond? Indeed, it could be the females and also the gadgets, but most notably, he's a learner and an enthusiastic observant. Indeed, you have to become an observant to master to control the brain of yours - look around; stop seeing. Begin observing!

Leadership

The very best of the frontrunners certainly understand the very best of the mind control strategies. Look at them - they're very popular. Do not you believe that they are able to manage people's minds? Provide it with a thought - much better, think as a leader does.

Concentration

The individuals who could manage the brain of theirs rightly are the highest businessmen, leaders, as well as sportspersons, to name a couple of organizations. What they certainly have in common is a way by which they are able to manage the brains theirs. If it were not for that element, they wouldn't have been exactly where they're today. Awareness, as well as focus, is the key element.

Winner

Consider as a winner does. He doesn't fear to lose - he takes it just as a component of the higher learning curve. A winner is regarded as the optimistic individual you would actually see. Be a winner.

Positive Attitude

This's crucial because until you've it, you don't understand just how to get it done. The more you are within the dark, the more you start to be susceptible to being a failure.

Exercise

Nearly all individuals misbelieve that in case they simply eat well and completely focus on what they're doing, they could accomplish anything they would like. Though the significant factor is the fact that in case they're unfit themselves - they can't take the stride for the strive. Working out the head of yours as well as the body is significant.

Yoga

Last but not least, this century-old all-pervasive information of Yoga is what's needed if you would like complete command of the brain of yours. It employs probably the most scientific postures and 'kriyas,' which help you ideal the brain control strategies. It isn't a popular advertisement gimmick. It's a procedure that each person should go through.

Using Mind Control

If you consider mind control, you might consider someone attempting to take control of another person's brain. The concept of getting a person to take action against their will might additionally come to mind, but are all of us using brain control each day of the lives of ours? Might it be the case we're making use of mind control without actually realizing we're performing it? So what's mind control, and just how can we favorably gain from the usage of it?

The concept of managing the brain has been the topic of several thinkers, but could it be feasible to manage the mind of yours to get much more out of life? Certainly, in case you think about individuals that are attaining things that are great in daily life, might it be since they've perfected the capability to manage the brain of theirs? It's been said that the brain consists of the objective head as well as the subjective brain, and getting greater command of the subjective could enable you to reach a lot more in life. So how could you access greater capabilities through this subconscious brain?

Finding out how The Subconscious Mind Works

The subconscious is actually believed to be the element of the head which deals with such things as the moving of the blood, the beating of the center as well as items that you don't purposely think about. It's been said it doesn't make conscious choices but just functions on the info that's been transferred to it by the conscious mind. It's likewise been claimed that the individuals that are inclined to attain things that are amazing in life can pass the desires of theirs to the subconscious mind. When it gets the motivation, it starts giving chores that enable you to attain the wants.

The Objections Of The Objective Mind

Any desire which goes to the subconscious mind has to work through the unbiased mind first, of course, if the objective thought process doesn't recognize the concept, then it won't be transferred to it. For instance, in case you mention an affirmation that I'm a millionaire, though you're not presently a millionaire, then the aim of yours might not recognize that thought, and hence won't pass the concept to your subjective or perhaps subconscious. And so to get the subconscious of yours to perform the brand new things which you want to do, you have to get the concept straight to you bypass and subconscious the independent brain of yours.

How Are you able to buy-Pass The Objective Mind of yours?

What exactly are the ways in which you are able to pass dreams and thoughts straight to the very subjective brain of yours? Among the techniques which were said allowing the ideas or maybe dreams straight to the subjective head as well as bypass, the objective brain is actually by use of subliminal messages.

The goal thought process doesn't identify these emails and go immediately by blinking the idea on the laptop display of yours for an extremely brief duration, say about a tiny proportion of a second. This particular duration isn't long adequate to be realized by the objective brain but tends to be recognized by the subjective. In this way, it's recommended that you can pass your dreams as well as goals straight to the very subjective brain of yours.

Mind Control - Things To Do To Make Anyone Do Everything You Want

You will find various kinds of mind control. Some entail simple manipulation as well as extortion, but these may be classified as a command instead of as managing the brain. The art of making folks do everything you need requires making them prepared to do what you would like. To recognize the next phases of influencing an individual to do everything you need, you've to find out what brain control is in the essence of its. It entails powerful persuasion, which affects the subconscious imagination, the element of the head that's to blame for the feelings of ours and actions which are not thought through. These include habits, instincts, values, beliefs, desires, and feelings. By mapping an activity into the subconscious and exploiting the functions of its, you are going to be in a position to make anyone do everything you like as well as enjoy it. Here's how you can do the step by step.

Get The individual To Listen To You

Precisely why would anyone listen to what you've to say, let alone do everything you tell him? For an individual to listen to you, you've to become important for him to in away. You can be a person he wants, and trusts or even sees as an authority. You can perform all these roles, provided you find out and learn the various mind control methods for the purpose. The most effective way to create a person as if you are building a subconscious link to the individual through creating rapport. This's done best although mirror-imaging as well as voice matching. Mirror the gestures the individual makes without him noticing. Match the pitch of the speech of his along with the pace with which he's talking. You will find simpler techniques for getting an individual to listen to you. You can confide in him to develop trust. You can flatter him to make him as if you. You can show understanding as well as sympathy. Acting out of a position of authority is additionally simple. Simply say you've been in the same circumstance, and you've handled it. Show just how much knowledge you've on a matter.

Make The individual Understand The Value Of Doing Everything You Want

This's the answer to exercising mind control. Think about the scenario this way. The idea you would like the individual to do will provide him a lot of advantages. The process of yours is explaining the advantages to him. This's the mindset you need to have for highly effective persuasion. The next thing is to determine the actual help the individual is going to get from doing everything you would like. These need to be unique. They've corresponding to the person's values, desires as well as beliefs.

The most effective way to make the individual understand the values he'll receive would be to make him see them and experience them in the subconscious mind of his. You've to work with the creativity of his for the purpose. The easiest brain control strategy is simply to make use of the good old word "imagine." You can conveniently say, "Imagine what it is going to be love to enjoy these benefits." You then can say, "Wouldn't you would like this? This's how you can get them."

Give The individual Confidence To Do Everything You Want

Usually, the trouble with mind control comes out of the reality that the individual believes he's incapable of doing everything you would like. He might lack trust since he feels poor, scared, insecure, or anxious, although by completing step two, you've by now inspired him. The most effective way to make the individual sure to do what you would like would be to make him think in the power of his to get it done. This typically involves replacing a belief or perhaps quite replacing it with a brand new one.

You will find a variety of mind control methods for replacing beliefs. One of them requires replacing the thinking pattern. For example, you can say, "How would you think when you are going for a stroll at the park?" You then can finish the pattern by stating, "Feeling calm and confident is the thing that you're aiming for." You can likewise make use of a good anchor to come up with the individual self-confidence. Simply ask him when he's felt confident as well as the many and make him picture the situation to elicit self-assurance. And now, you understand the way to do mind control in 3 simple steps. Continue knowing more to improve the abilities of yours and turn into a master professional.

NLP (NEURO-LINGUISTIC PROGRAMMING)

NLP has methods that have grown to be worldwide popular and profitable, and in case you discover them and make use of them correctly, it is going to break you free of the chains that are presently tying you down. NLP is a useful issue that calls for face to face interaction as well as ability practice. You can enhance the knowledge of yours of it by delving into these pages or perhaps the lots of books readily available. Still, in case you want to produce the skills for yourself you are going to want to attend a face to deal with NLP professional program? Anything you want to do, please read on. You will find extensive assistance as well as support from you on this sizable guide.

Discreet NLP, also called conversational hypnosis, is the capability to hypnotize others and speak with the subconscious brain of theirs without them knowing they've been hypnotized. Discreet NLP is a remarkable instrument that enables you to entice others for you and mix them to go by you and go out of the way of theirs to please you.

With Discreet NLP, you can secretly sway visitors to purchase from you, persuade them to do things for you, as well as stay in command of interactions. It is an amazing tool that could change the life of yours in a day that is basic daily interactions. With the thorough use of exact body language and vocabulary, you are going to enter the subject's subconscious mind bypassing the crucial conscious mind. You will substantially affect the behavior of theirs. Given that the topic isn't conscious of being affected by hypnosis, they believe they came up with the thought themselves.

Discreet NLP provides you with the crucial to growing recommendations, bringing the subject matter to a hypnotic state, and talking with the subconscious mind of theirs. When you enter the subconscious mind of theirs, you can conversationally make influence and recommendations their beliefs and views. Individuals will be engrossed with what you've to point out as well as be drawn to you, such as a magnet.

You can make use of the strength of suggestion on people without them realizing it, and they are going to believe it had been the inspiration of theirs. By changing the tone of yours of voice and the body language of yours, you can make recommendations to virtually anybody, and they are going to do something you wish them to (as long as it does not go against their ethics or maybe morals).

Discreet NLP is an incredible power when three remarkable disciplines are used collectively. Each person by itself is extremely efficient by itself; however, when you mix all three into Discreet NLP, the benefits will astonish you. Those three disciplines are hypnosis, NLP (Neurological Linguistic Programming) as well as mentalism. Hypnosis is the ability to hypnotize individuals and talking with their subconscious mind to change the conduct of theirs, beliefs, or perhaps ideas.

Neurological Linguistic Programming is the art of discussion or perhaps dialogue. NLP shows you exactly how to produce a good rapport with individuals and then simply encourage them to Need to please you. Mentalism shows you exactly how to produce false realities. With these bogus realities, subjects are going to believe all that you tell them.

If you discover as well as perform these three disciplines to the type of Discreet NLP, you've inside you an ability to alter not simply the life of yours but additionally the life of those around you. As soon as you're talking with the subconscious mind of theirs, you can utilize the strength of suggestion to make the life of yours much better, though you are able to additionally utilize it to make the lives of theirs better.

Fast induction (putting somebody in a trance state) could be created via seemingly typical discussion. After that, inside that conversation, you can make recommendations and set ideas into the subconscious mind of theirs. You can change your behavior.

Discreet NLP is merely one type of hypnosis. It's a discipline that provides you the benefit by getting total command with the life of yours, which means you are able to achieve greatness. You do not need to be a magician, psychic, or perhaps gifted in any way to perfect Discreet NLP. Once you've created the important abilities to achieve success at Discreetly hypnotizing individuals, you are going to be on a route to gaining all you might wish or perhaps need in daily life, not simply for yourself but additionally for the family.

To distract The Conscious Mind

Hypnotism is everything around us. A lot of it is hidden or perhaps discreet. Frequently we think of hypnosis as phase hypnosis, as just occurring whenever we go to a show. Though the simple truth is that hypnosis is just the distracting of the conscious mind to ensure that the subconscious brain is actually running.

This's what's meant by the trance state. Possibly you're driving down the freeway, along with every one of a sudden recognizes you're two exits passed the places you intended to get off. Or maybe you're out running as well as breakthrough the wall to that runner's high.

You get to that time in which you're not actively alert to what is taking place. For the minute you start to be conscious of just how much fun you're experiencing, you're out of the state. The kid who's playing a game plays the game isn't watching himself play the game. The musician that practices eight hours one day doesn't see it as a chore; rather, they view it as a pleasurable activity in which they become lost.

The Hypnotic Secret

This's the key to hypnosis, to bring the subject to a pleasurable status in which some objects could be brought about. And also, the goal is both the key element to the good results of the trance state as well as the kind of hypnosis getting used. There's a fantastic deal of conversation about Discreet NLP. As well as conversational hypnosis. The thing that makes hypnosis Discreet is the apparent significance of the term Discreet, concealed. The strategies of the hypnotist are actually hidden.

So the hypnotist utilizes hypnotic methods to bring about the trance state without having the subject matter knowing it. This's the appeal of mind control. It's the drive to manage another to get these to take action you need. Just before we jump to any moral conclusions, we need to comprehend that Discreet NLP is actually spent each day, all of the time by everybody.

Day To Day Hypnosis

For sure, you may think of a male seducing a female as Discreet NLP. And there are enough books, DVDs as well as courses accessible. And also, you might check it out morally reprehensible. But what if a female flirting is not that Discreet NLP?

Is not the usage of perfume, lipstick, and languid movements component of "the game"? This's the explanation that the radical wants to prohibit the behavior type. Due to the fact it works. The issue with the fanatic is they're a part of the mind control issue. They, too, need to manage you. An even better answer is usually to be conscious of mind control methods. By becoming informed of how the mind of yours is actually being worked on, by being conscious of just how you're getting sidetracked, you are going to be in control.

- Discreet NLP - Using hypnosis in typical ways is generally called Conversational Hypnosis or maybe usually Discreet NLP. It may be Discreet since you do not need consumers to understand you're performing this with them or even mainly because telling them wouldn't include a lot to the conversation.
- Hypnosis and NLP are a lot connected. A broad model for how the mind of your works is you've unconscious and conscious components on your brain. The conscious component is logical, and rational the portion of the mind of yours you believe with. The subconscious brain of yours is the part which retailers your emotions as well as memories. Additionally, it has control over the muscle movements of yours as well as automated capabilities like keeping blood pumping near your automatic, habits, and body bits of conduct which all of us have.

In case you might provide immediate recommendations to the subconscious mind of yours bypassing the critical and discerning thinking faculties of the conscious mind of yours, you might have excellent power over women. You have apparent limitations. The subconscious brain of yours is targeted for self-preservation. Therefore it wouldn't follow commands to quit breathing, for instance.

But imagine if you might make suggestions to get excited about a specific device, or even to feel attracted to certain individuals or perhaps vote a specific way in an election? It will be a lot easier to find a wavering voter to vote for a specific party compared to somebody that has voted for a different component all the lifetime of theirs. Obtaining someone associated with an alternative sexual orientation to fall in love with you is a lot harder than say someone who pretty much finds you attractive. It's possible to move folks a great distance utilizing Discreet NLP. A great NLP Practitioner Course will teach you in all of the methods that you have to have the ability to make use of these strategies.

The stage, however, is while you can avoid a person's conscious, thinking mind, rational, you can't eliminate it. What this means is at some point they are going to notice what you've done to them. They might not understand how, though they're more likely to breed resentment towards you due to the way they think. Say you're using Discreet NLP to mis-sell products.

The buyers of yours may originally disappear pleased simply because that was the hypnotic declare you induced around them...but whenever they turn out of it, they're more likely to feel cheated, manipulated as well as conned into purchasing a thing that they do not want. The net result is a complaint and returns a huge loss of reputation. Used rightly, Discreet NLP methods can help individuals to get into the strong wants of theirs as well as reasons and begin to fulfill them. In case I take the product sales illustration. At the same time, I discover a buyer with a demand for a product. If I can buy a method of linking the item to satisfy the needs of theirs during a strong mental Stage they are going to feel great about the sale, the item and about me. The net outcome is quite satisfied clients, along with an excellent track record.

I suppose you can begin to think of some excellent uses for yourself, like presenters increasing the charisma of theirs, linking enjoyment as well as fun to meeting friends or maybe work satisfaction for the people of yours. Learn to associate people's core values to the things which you would like them to do is a vital component of Discreet NLP, and it is incredibly useful.

In case you make this happen with things which aren't great them, they'll be cheated; if you are doing it in a way that moves them exactly where they wish to go, you are going to create friends for life. A good NLP Practitioner program is going to show you can make use of Discreet NLP to get individuals to do everything you like as well as thanking you for this since they will also get what they need.

Brainwashing In Dark Psychology

Brainwashing is a phrase often utilized at the popular media to relate to a phenomenon known among psychologists as coercive persuasion. The phrase describes a set of techniques utilized to forcibly change someone's belief system to ensure that they are going to adhere to a brand new range of responsibilities and beliefs. In the public mind, the phrase usually has been related to the change of abandonment and perspective of values and family usually seen in members of religious cults. Several of the methods discussed below, nonetheless, also have been typical resources of the interrogation of uncooperative prisoners across human history.

Main Elements Of Coercive Persuasion

Application Of Physical Or Maybe Emotional Stress: Physical stress would include things like deprivation of exercise, light, food, or sleep. Mental stress would include things like isolation without any stimulation, continuously repeated chanting, or perhaps sleep deprivation to the use of keying in a trancelike state. Attribution of all the person's problems to an easy reason that is repeated again and again. This particular method worked nicely for the Nazis, though it works just as well for today's economic self-help gurus as well as fringe religious organizations.

Creation of a brand new Identity: This often features a title change as well as exclusive garments, like the methods of the Hare Krishna movement, who all dress identically and feature distinct haircuts. This makes team club membership much more crucial compared to a specific identity, therefore rendering members simpler to manage.

Entrapment: also referred to as the foot-in-the-door method. The member agrees to a couple of little changes but then involves start to increase steadily. After the needs start to be unreasonable, it is way too late, and cognitive dissonance is cut back by continuing to go together with the needs.

Access To Info Is Severely Controlled: The team might call for a severing of preexisting community ties, which includes connections to family. Uncertainties about the team or maybe its leader are mocked, together with attempts at thinking that is critical. Any distress brought on by this is linked to an absence of adequate confidence of the team or maybe the leader of its.

Brainwashing Techniques

You'll find ways of brainwashing you that are very, repetitious, and Discreet valuable. You most likely are receiving brainwashing without the knowledge of yours today. These methods are the main reason you're obese, smoke, have pain, can't sleep, together with most of the shortcomings of yours.

You've been getting communications your whole life, which has caused one to question your perceptions, beliefs, and thoughts. This occurs all of the time, and it's become a simple practice of human interaction. These patterns of interaction frequently are accustomed to the gain of another party. Nevertheless, recognizing these strategies in motion, you can quit them before they hurt you more.

Many of these strategies are very successful that the recipient willingly reevaluates whatever they see. Nevertheless, these methods may additionally be extremely forceful, symbolically demanding the recipient changes the belief of theirs.

Questioning Brainwashing

One of those Discreet brainwashing methods takes place in the format of questioning. Repeated questioning organized in a precarious pattern is going to cause the topic to evaluate things about which they weren't considering. As this method proceeds, the subject unintentionally follows through until there's a state of confusion about the initial thought or perhaps experience. A brand new mind consideration or maybe an altered way of thinking maybe the outcome.

Here's what goes on when an experienced fellow examines you. Each time a question is presented, you might answer with subtle variants of a story or even memory. This competent practitioner, advertiser, the authority figure can result in one to question the thinking of yours at last.

The longer this procedure, the more it's repeated, the less you identify the pattern, the better the outcome. Just before you understand it, you don't understand what you believe or maybe have encountered as well as the more you go along with the information, ad or perhaps authority figures representation of the info. You've only been brainwashed!

Pay Attention And Recognize The Brainwashing

If perhaps you focus on the news, to advertisers, to authority figures, you are going to start to see the type of brainwashing. A lot of people are very great at these methods. They use it as a regular kind of communication. In case you're innocent, you are going to become a target. You must be on guard for these strategies. You have to understand you're under continuous assault. In the event you don't, it will not be long before you decide to don't have an original thought.

You'll not have discerning thought procedures. You'll not be in charge of the daily life of yours. You are going to think you'll do, you'll buy, you'll follow, and you'll be one of the many people who have been brainwashed. And also you won't actually know it!

You have to challenge everything. In case you're obese, in case you cannot quit smoking, in case you're riddled in pain, in case you lay awake during the night with insomnia, the brain racing of yours, stopping you from sleeping, if you've some state where another person can gain, that condition was created, and just you can overturn it.

Is Hypnosis Mind Control A form of Brainwashing?

Brainwashing has a questionable history. Commonly when we think of the expression, we are prone to picture cult leaders or perhaps CIA spies that are intent on creating others bend to their will from a kind of psychological control.

Same with Hypnosis mind control a kind of brainwashing? Essentially, I assume it might be seen as such.

All things considered, hypnosis mind management does plan to affect the brain of the subject matter, along with that's just what brainwashing does too. But generally, I believe brainwashing has a great deal more methods involved than hypnosis, and the consequences are more durable.

While several of the government agencies of ours are generally accused of practicing brainwashing, and perhaps they do, there is no question which it's cults which are so known for doing this particular type of mind control. Cults have numerous methods created to acquire long-lasting control over their methods as well as members of slowly changing them in such a manner that they no longer think independently, no matter if they're from the cult.

Methods include exploitation, negative reinforcement, guilt, love bombing, and hypnosis of any type of mental vulnerability until the cult member gradually gets completely determined by the cult for the sense of theirs of self-esteem and offers overall of the choices regarding the behavior of theirs to the cult.

In addition to mind control techniques, although, brainwashing generally also entails physical isolation and cutting individuals off from their family, that is a kind of imprisonment. The individual who's being manipulated is being put to a prolonged period of anxiety about which they've no control and from which they can't escape.

What exactly about hypnosis mind management? Right now many individuals will most likely scoff at the concept which you can, in fact, manage anybody else's mind. Still, cults are clearly in a position to achieve this and do so effectively, so in case you meet somebody that believes the concept is nonsense, then you definitely may wish to point out every one of the cults which have effectively accomplished so for a long time.

Hypnosis works, and as soon as you discover the way to utilize them, Discreet NLP strategies, you do not need to head out and build the cult of yours. That is an abuse of the abilities. It's likely to discover how you can affect individuals without causing damage. To call this particular type of influence, "mind control" may be regarded as a little hysterical at times, particularly as a result of the short-term nature of nearly all hypnotic methods since they're usually conversational.

Is Anorexia A form of Brainwashing?

I've been keen on quite a while regarding what makes folks change their attitudes, mindset, and beliefs towards things. I firmly believe that the majority of eating disorders are actually a result of people's beliefs that are incorrect as well as perceptions towards themselves and others. Inherited predisposition additionally plays the job as well.

As soon as I was reading through a book about brainwashing. Brainwashing is an attempt aimed towards instilling in the head of one various individual beliefs as well as perceptions, which ultimately create an individual behave in a particular way and have confidence in certain items.

Brainwashing was used a great deal by communists to distribute the mindset of communism. It was additionally used on war prisoners in the Korean war - when American soldiers after being shot as well as stored in Chinese camps oftentimes ended up taking the edge of the communists and considered themselves to be the supporters of theirs.

Brainwashing happens when individuals join cults or perhaps strange religious organizations. These change people's identity totally; just love anorexia changes people's identity totally. Thus, you see, brainwashing is actually something that could change the complete identity of yours. The media does it all of the moment also. But not merely just the press issues enjoy the lifestyle you reside in can brainwash you.

Us Psychiatrist Robert Jay Lipton did a specific research project on what is needed in brainwashing. Did he come up with a summary of measures on brainwashing techniques:

- Assault On Identity

- Guilt And Shame

- Self-Betrayal

- Breaking Point

- Leniency

- Compulsion To Confess

- Channeling Of Guilt

- Releasing Of Guilt

- Progress And Harmony

- Final Confession And Rebirth

I think anorexia goes through equivalent stages? I believe it does when you consider it. The one difference is the fact that when individuals get brainwashed, it's done intentionally by another person. In the situation of anorexia, individuals ordinarily perceive events in the life of theirs and what goes on to them and get it the wrong way; chances are they become prisoners of their feelings and views.

I've examined the brainwashing measures previously about eating disorders, and here's what I've come up with:

Assault On Identity

When anorexia takes place after a psychological event or maybe several occasions, the anorexic begins to believe they're not just who they must be and just who they wish to be. The individual is under continuous self-identity attacks for days, months, or weeks, to the stage that she/he gets exhausted, confused as well as disoriented. With this state, their opinions appear to be less strong. They look around for an alternative for the identity theirs.

Guilt And Shame

"You are actually terrible the strategy you are." They believe that the body of theirs is actually disgusting; they feel embarrassed about their own body of theirs. If the improvement of anorexia coincides with the time of puberty - ideas of being embarrassed by their own body are related to thoughts of disgust about intimacy and sex, which may have remarkable effects.

Associations of shame, as well as guilt regarding intimacy, are able to wind up to be a lifelong sentence for a lot of sufferers until massive neuroplastic modifications are instigated later.

Eating could additionally be connected with guilt, and this's a significant reason why anorexia turns into bulimia at a later on phase of the illness for several sufferers. Individuals start to feel a deep feeling of shame, that all they do is wrong. A lot of scientists have found that feelings of guilt are firmly connected with the improvement of eating disorders (especially bulimia as well as binge eating).

Self-Betrayal:

This's once the anorexia begins to tell her/him, "Agree with me; you're bad." And when the individual is confused as well as drowning in guilt, these ideas force them to withdraw from her/his family, peers, and friends that are usually eating and enjoying life theirs. This particular betrayal of her/ the trust of his in themselves and folks close to them raises the shame as well as the loss of identity that the individual is today experiencing.

Breaking Point

The sufferer is continually asking her/himself: "Who am I, exactly where am I, and what am I claimed to do?" At this stage, the individual has her/his identity in crisis, experiencing massive shame and guilt. Furthermore, the individual might go through a "nervous breakdown." This might entail uncontrollable sobbing, common disorientation, and severe depression and withdrawal. Not every person has the same severity of symptoms, though many individuals do have this actual reaction.

Leniency

The Anorexia then tells the sufferer:" Follow me - I will help you." Anorexics frequently think that the anorexia of theirs is the sole way of life they can follow. Exhibiting anorexic behavior - such as starving, purging, which takes them momentary relief of the thoughts of theirs, although short-lived. Then again, it demands increasingly more interest until the individual gets a hundred % ingested by the distorted anorexic thoughts of theirs and feelings.

Channeling Of Guilt

This's precisely why you are in pain. Following weeks or even weeks of suffering, confusion, moments, and breakdown of leniency, the person's guilt has lost all meaning - numbness replaces it all. This creates a thing associated with a blank slate, which allows the anorexia deeper as well as more in-depth into the soul. The anorexia attaches itself to the person's guilt as well as a belief system, opposite what people that are healthy individuals have. For instance, foods are related to shame as well as guilt.

It's the point when anorexics begin to exhibit undesirable tantrums when parents attempt to feed them or perhaps persuade them to consume as well as end the abnormal behavior of theirs. They begin to think that anorexia isn't an illness, though it's a lifestyle and connect the self of theirs with the anorexia: they get one with the illness.

Releasing Of Guilt

It is not me; it's the values of mine. With her/his complete confessions, the individual has finished his/her mental rejection of the former identity of theirs. The sufferer had slowly given up all their before enjoyable tasks, left their university or office preferably the faculty of theirs. All this's only for the benefit of doing the lifestyle anorexia offers. Individuals begin joining pro-anorexia groups, forums, searching for justification, etc.

"Progress And Harmony. In the event you like, you can decide well." - say the "thinspiration" buddies of theirs.

These "Thinspiration" buddies present a brand new belief system as the road to "good." At this particular point, the anorexia stops hurting, offering the sufferer physical comfort as well as psychological calm in conjunction with the new belief system of theirs. Individuals get a "team spirit "attitude with friends of theirs that apply the same dangerous way of living.

Final Confession And Rebirth

The brain of theirs equals the Anorexia, which directs them:" I pick kind." Sound will be the anorexia. The individual doesn't question the righteousness of her/his decision to be anorexic. Around this point, separating themself from the anorexia appears to be impossible. Many people continue doing this lethal way of living.

Thousands of them die as a consequence of this sooner than later on. Some may live longer; however, they ultimately die from serious complications or even commit suicide due to their starving as well as the reality they cannot handle daily life and cannot evaluate issues logically. This's how the anorexic brain gets programmed (brainwashed) to become the manner they're suffering from severe anorexia. Many eating disorder sufferers go through similar stages, but frequently, these stages occur otherwise for every sufferer, and it's tough to distinguish between them.

The goal of this particular publication is showing you what the brainwashing procedure is about as well as this what goes on in prisoner and cults of war camps is akin to what goes on in individuals with anorexia. Additionally, I wish to mention the phenomenon of anorexia is primarily in the reasonably small.

Individuals of the past did not have anorexia to the identical Stage we've nowadays. In the past individual cases of anorexia were discussed only in individuals who starved themselves for religious functions, the like, and cult purposes. There were no anorexic cases reported of individuals working to be tiny for beauty benefit or maybe prestige purposes. All of this points to anorexia becoming a contemporary disease: I believe caused by several beauty product advertisers and also the media which market beauty requirements, which are not possible to attain by regular human beings. You can point out it's created to make individuals fork over money for far more and more beauty and slimming merchandise, making someone incredibly high, made on the suffering of several.

The resolution to this particular issue is teaching people that are young and emphasize inner and natural beauty. To make young people strive for learning, growing and learning the brains of theirs, never to shoot for this unattainable appearance which several of the press and some portray as gorgeous. For most younger folks to get to this unattainable Stage just creates death, hardship, and suffering.

Brainwashing - Common Ways It's Used To Manipulate Others

Mind control, brainwashing is a procedure where somebody uses manipulation and unethical methods to persuade a person to abide by the desires of the individual in control. Generally, this method takes place to the detriment of the individual being brainwashed. Other common names for this include coercive persuasion, although reform, and thought control, along with some other labels. You will find many ways in which it's often used, and this particular guide will check out several of them.

One of the ways where coercive persuasion has been being used is actually through the policies of totalitarian regimes across the globe. These regimes aren't afraid at all about using pressure to getting what they need, even if that force is unethical and excessive. As a result, they've been recognized to be successful in convincing their prisoners of war with different methods about regular propaganda and torture.

One other way these head control brainwashing methods are being used is actually in new religious movements. Typically latest religious groups that pop up are led by extremely charismatic people who wield particularly convincing powers of persuasion, in addition to the capability to brainwash others through different methods, one of the main ones being remote from friends as well as a family that are not fellow team members. By being remote from others with views that are different, you are more solidly entrenched in the group's beliefs.

The last case is a less sinister one, though often when taken to extremes, it can lead to tragic outcomes. Members of sororities and fraternities in colleges are usually victimized as well as created to endure a variety of instances of physical and psychological torture and humiliation to be a part of the team.

By ruining the ego via distributing to a more celebrated expert in the team, or even through performing different actions which are usually humiliating, the person begins to produce a compelling team identity and loyalty.

Frequently, the substantial nature of several of the physical tests the aspiring members are made to conduct might result in serious physical injury as well as death. This particular technique of brainwashing leads members of particular fraternities to do stuff that they wouldn't do if not for the team dynamic pushing them advanced.

There are lots of instances of mind control brainwashing other than the three talked about in this specific guide. This's an excellent issue that even applies to sales, military service, and numerous other parts. Additionally, you must be aware that there are honest methods to affect others, which do not entail some kind of torture or perhaps sinister mental manipulation.

CHAPTER 12 THE ABCS OF BRAINWASHING

Brainwashing is probably one of the most powerful types of social control in that it involves a whole lot of brainwashed and victim involvement. Brainwashing, also known as mind control, thought reform, or coercive Persuasion, isn't a technique that can be applied with results on a one-off basis. It needs clear manipulator feedback up to the point that they can break the victim down to their desired outcomes. You've heard more likely than not someone described as brainwashed. You may have even used the term yourself to refer to someone who expressed opinions that seemed too brazen to be true, that obviously is not theirs. Although many people still use this phrase loosely in daily conversation, the full scope of this exploitation technique is something that can only be grasped after all the details surrounding it have been accepted.

First things: many methods of manipulation or methods of social influence, if you prefer, rely on specific approaches to deliver intended results. There is the compliance approach where you are making a subject do something without really caring about its underlying ideas or beliefs. Then there's the approach to Persuasion, which seems to make somebody do something by targeting their beliefs or attitudes. A manipulator may try to tell you, for example, that doing something will help you feel better or become more successful. In other words, they try to persuade you to adopt a different attitude toward yourself or your life. Finally, an approach is called the method of propaganda or the method of education, if you like. This technique aims at getting converts by showing them the error of their past ways and introducing them to better ways and values. It's similar to walking up to somebody and showing them that so far, everything they've ever believed in has been a lie, thus making them think you're the only bearer of the real truth. The explanation the brainwashing is so effective and hard to reverse is that it incorporates all three methods. To convince anyone who has been brainwashed that they are actually brainwashed is often nearly impossible.

Brainwashing is a routine thing in the modern world. As far as brainwashing is concerned, the media is a particularly nasty culprit. Media houses have been responsible for disseminating information at their own discretion, since time immemorial (or at least since the invention of the newspaper and television). The media decides on which tone to set across the board for different social, political, and economic topics. TV shows, TV personalities, marketing departments, and glossy fashion magazines have defined time and time again, which standards of beauty are acceptable and which ones are not. As a result, a large segment of society is left with the feeling of not being beautiful or worthy enough because the media have said so.

As far as brainwashing is concerned, the politicians and religious leaders are two other major culprits. Most politicians are self-serving and will do everything in the world of politics to get ahead. They mastered the art of brainwashing masses of people to get behind them, because the more brainwashed supporters they have, the more likely they are to advance. Brainwashed supporters also aren't asking their leaders for much accountability. It is through brainwashing that a whole lot of political leaders have succeeded in mobilizing their followers to commit senseless crimes that would not be committed by a sane person of normal thinking and conscience.

On the other side, religious leaders who brainwash their followers are keen to surround themselves with people who can be manipulated easily and who believe in the same values as the leaders themselves. Think about it — if you were yourself a self-serving pseudo-religious figure, you would want to have a submissive congregation that did as it was said. The last thing you would want is an outspoken crowd of people who question every single sermon you give. That is something that has been noted by many questionable religious leaders, much to the detriment of their followers. Perhaps some of the greatest reminders of the effects of brainwashing on religious spheres are the multiple mass suicides that have occurred as congregants at the instruction of their religious leaders seek to reach for the afterlife.

One example of this is the mass suicide of the religious group Heaven's Gate followers. Heaven's Gate party, led by Marshall Applewhite, believed their deaths would help them get into a spaceship that would carry them to the other planet. A man who believed himself to be the representative of Christ on Earth carried this belief on through years of brainwashing. In addition to the Gate of Heaven, there were several other incidences where groups of people were forced to end their lives because of one religious belief or another. Even when congregants are not persuaded to take their own lives, some religious leaders can brainwash their followers in other ways, which are often harmful.

Maybe one of the questions to come to mind when you learn about these events in history is this: how can a person be so gullible and confident to the degree that they follow him so blindly? The answer is simple: Brainwashing strips you of your identity and makes you unquestionably conform to the will of others. In reality, breaking down the identity of your victim and bringing them into question everything they have ever known about themselves is the very first step of brainwash

The Ten Steps of Washing the Brain

As noted earlier, brainwashing isn't an experience of one day. Often, it takes years of consistency and hard work to brainwash a person completely. It is no wonder then that some members of cults will take years to create a follow-up before eventually making their mark in the world, although infamously. While they may overlap from time to time, brainwashing steps are often distinct, and can be widely classified into three stages. The first stage includes all the steps the predator uses to break down their victim; the second stage includes showing the victim that there is a chance of salvation, and lastly, the third stage includes leading the victim to salvation, or at least their own definition of salvation.

First step: Breaking the Target

Step I: Identity Assault

To break down a predator's target, they must first target what makes the target what they are: their identity or ego. Every human being has, in his mind, a picture of himself, which is what he thinks he is. That is the way they identify themselves. You can have several identities. You could be a mother and a career woman. You could be a clever businessman and a dad. You could be a hard-fought student at the college. You just might be a Christian. You can choose between endless identities. That identity is your answer to the statement tell me about yourself a little bit.

Take a moment and think about your personal identity. What/who are you?

Suppose one day you woke up and somebody told you that you are not what you think you are. How did you manage to say that? If this were mentioned in passing, you would probably brush it off and move on with your life. Or maybe you'd think about it for a few minutes or hours, and maybe get frustrated for a bit, but eventually, move on. Now imagine someone came to your house every minute of the day to tell you that you're not the guy you think you are. How'd it made you feel? If that persisted over weeks or even months, then at the end of it all, you would probably be out of your mind. You will be disoriented and left to wonder where to draw the line between fiction and fact. If you'd thought of yourself as a good writer before, you'd start to doubt it. If you thought you were your children's biological father, you might start questioning him. If you grew up believing you were a true Christian, reading regular conflicting reports would make you start believing you might not be.

The first step of the brainwashing cycle is where all of the dirty work starts to take root. A person whose ugly seed of doubt has been planted in them is vulnerable to exploitation. As people, we want to believe the best of ourselves. They also want to make people believe in us to the full. Sure, there are people who don't care about recognition and acceptance of anyone else. It is important, and we will all fight for it. But at the end of the day,, the person who goes to bed believing he is the worst of the worst (thanks to other people's feedback) sleeps more restlessly. Having high self-esteem and a good sense of self, of course, protects you from the predators trying to prey on you, but that's a topic for another post. The outcome of brainwashing's first step is a full-blown identity crisis which the perpetrator will prey on for the purposes of the second step.

Step 2: Guilt tripping

Guilt, as it has been called, maybe a futile emotion, but it is also a very strong emotion. Guilt can make you, as a person, promise things outside of your scope. Guilt will have you stay up at night, asking why you're such a horrible human being when you're actually not. The human predators around us are continuously harnessing the power of culpability. This is how the second stage of brainwashing works: the brainwasher has already convinced its victim that they are not what they have always thought to be. Hence, the victim is in a state of confusion as they seek to answer for themselves the question of identity. That is if they aren't a decent guy, who are they then? The predator swoops in at this point and begins to take them for the entire guilt trip of their lives. When you're unsure who you are, it can be very easy to believe any lie you're being fed up with about yourself. A brainwasher will make statements convincing their victim that they are essentially a bad person, irrespective of the context this adjective is being used.

A brainwasher, for example, might try to convince a young mom that they're a bad person and a bad mom because they've agreed to vaccinate their children or prefer the breast to the bottle. A predator will take every opportunity to remind the victim that they are lacking in a particular field or in all areas of their lives, and that the only way to redemption is to listen to and accept what the predator has to offer. In their attack on the victim, the predator is merciless because the ultimate goal is to break the victim down to the point where they are helpless and completely free from their authentic self-image and identity.

Steps 3 and 4: Self-trafficking and breaking point

Most people themselves are fiercely loyal. They're going to defend themselves and their actions and fight to hear their voices. Particularly those people who are incapable of standing up for others also will stand up for themselves. A person having been brainwashed is the complete opposite. Brainwashed people have no trouble rejecting themselves and everything else attached to them after being continuously bombarded by messages of being the opposite of what they once considered themselves to be. These include their friends, belief system, relatives, and any other associations they may have that connect them to their old identity, which has been 'evaluated' by the brainwasher and found 'seriously lacking.'

There are certain reasons why a person who has been brainwashed can easily find himself in this step and can not fight back. For starters, they've already been through the first two steps and come out in confusion and remorse, feeling disoriented and sinking. Most often, they don't have the energy to fight back. Bear in mind that there is often a chance of physical harm if enforcement is not reached, and the target will be too scared to question all the messages that the abuser receives from them. Around the same time, there is a tendency for culprits to want to make up for their sins. For some people, especially those broken down by brainwashing, making up involves cutting ties with everything related to its 'sinful' history.

What is sadly always the case is that the survivor is still left in an even worse situation after their friends, relative and belief system have been disowned. They've felt the embarrassment and remorse until they broaden. They are, after all, a traitor now, and the fact that they could not be loyal to their circle is sufficient proof that they are as bad a person as the predator had supposed. It is obvious that brainwashing is psychological warfare aimed at tearing a person down to the point where they are incapable of thinking in a coherent way. It's all-consuming and exhausting, and victims often struggle to get out of their predators' jaws, especially if they do it through the other stages of the brainwashing process.

Second Stage: Dangling the Salvation Carrot

Step 5: The Olive Branch

After the first three steps of brainwashing mentioned above, a victim of brainwashing often feels so awful about themselves that they try to redeem themselves at whatever cost. The survivor is also in poor mental condition and has low self-esteem. They have lost their old sense of identity and will clutch up on any straws offered to feel something again. At this stage, a victim is likely to experience a nervous breakdown, and this is the signal for the predator to swoop in and give redemption.

The manipulator usually extends an olive branch after breaking down their target for a sustained period of time so that the target can fall into the trap of believing there is some light at the end of the tunnel. An olive branch at this point could be anything from a kind word to a gift, or perhaps even some form of physical affection. This olive branch helps to show the goal that if they are on the good side of the manipulator, there is certain leniency to gain. The manipulator is, after all, a 'fair guy' who wishes them the best. That is at least what they have heard since the start of brainwashing.

Step 6: Forced confession

Consider this: You have been subjected for a period of time to extreme psychological torment by a person. You have lost your sense of identity and feel confused and indignant. You're nearing a nervous breakdown, or you've already undergone one and can't make any aspect of your life head or tails. After denouncing your social circle, you have lived in solitary confinement and can't remember the last time you had a proper meal. Then, one day, this person shows up at your door with a steaming coffee pot and freshly baked muffins. They just say they want to talk. You are letting them into your house. You just can't believe it. This is the only kindness you've been receiving for the longest time. What do you think your former abuser will be reacting to this unexpected kindness?

You'll feel a sense of indebtedness more often than not. Human beings like being kind enough to reciprocate for kindness. If someone does something nice for you, then in return, it is human to want to do something nice. The need to pay back is even greater for a brainwashed person because they also feel they have to pay for everything (at least as per the brainwasher's gospel) they are wrong about. The brainwashed group, therefore, will be more than willing to give back some sort of kindness. This goodness will always be in the form of a confession, in their troubled minds. The rapist would usually offer the option of a confession as a way to get paid back.

Step 7: Channeling Guilt

A brainwashed victim sometimes gets filled with so much crushing remorse that after weeks and months of being told they're wrong about everything, they're just no room for any other emotions. The target has been bombarded by predators with so much psychological torment that they don't even know what they feel most culpable about. The perpetrator obviously believes he is guilty of something. During this uncertainty, the manipulator swoops in and convinces them that the blame is due to all the things that were previously considered wrong. The abuser, in other words, channels the remorse into the belief system. The victim now begins to associate their belief system with the guilt and the burden of dealing with the guilt. In essence, the predator is to make their victim learn to associate all the bad feelings with their past, while at the same time making them believe that if they choose alternative beliefs, there is a chance to be redeemed and to feel better.

Step 8: Freeing the Guilt

The victim is feeling a little relieved at this point to realize that he is not inherently wrong; rather, it is his beliefs that are wrong. He can be right again, by dissociating himself from his beliefs. He sheds his remorse by relinquishing everything and everything related to his prejudices, including those nearest to him. He confesses the errors of his old ways and is able to take on the new set of values that the brainwasher provides.

Third Phase: Brainwashed Self Rebuilding

Step 9: Progress and consistency

At this point in the process of brainwashing, the target is eager to redeem itself and look good in the brainwasher's eyes. As such, they will start rebuilding a new identity based on the manipulator's offered belief system. After passing through the suffering and torture of the earlier stages of brainwashing, the victim is convinced that only pain and guilt will come from their old belief system. They are relieved to be rid of the old self and replace it with a new self that is their safe haven from all their misery past and present.

Step 10: Last Confession and Reborn

Following acceptance of the new belief system, the survivor also feels reassured about their past and all of the associated suffering. They will stick to their new identity like the proverbial last raft on a sinking ship because this is the only peace they have experienced in a long time. At this stage, the brainwasher succeeded in obtaining a convert, and may even be conducting a ceremony to welcome the new convert into the sacred inner circle. At this point, it is common for the majority of victims to be completely isolated from their families. They're going to have it in their minds that they're different people now who don't have to associate with their past bad things. A brainwashed person who has been through these ten measures is usually almost difficult to persuade that they have been brainwashed. The damage done here is so immense that a do-over is an uphill climb. Professional support may be pursued to save a brainwashed loved one, but it is never a guarantee of success.

A simple way of describing how the process of brainwashing works shown in the table below:

Steps to Brainwash

Message to goal

Intended result

Stage one

- You're not who you claim to be
- Doubtlessness

Stage two
- You are a bad guy
- Crime

Stage 3
- You will agree with me you are poor
- Bullying and Guilt

Stage 4
- You just don't know what you are
- Confusion and misdirection

Stage Five
- I manage to save you
- Brainwasher Loyalty

Stage six
- Could you save yourself
- Conformity

Stage 7
- That's why you suffer
- To blame the belief system

Stage eight
- It is not you; it is you who believe in it
- Disclaimer

Stage nine
- Select well if you want to feel better and be better
- Indoctrination

Stage ten
- You are fine now

- Help and acceptance

The ten stages of brainwashing were attributed to experiments by Robert Jay Lifton, an American psychiatrist, and pioneer of the change of thought. Lifton interviewed prisoners of war and wrote about the psychological effects their experiences have had.

What makes a person brainwashing susceptible?

What makes one person more likely to get brainwashed than the next person? Do you ever wonder why some people appear to be more easily recruited into radical cults than others? There are grounds for that. There are some people who have a faint sense of identity through one reason or another. A person is not born with an identity; self-identity is something which develops through childhood over time; and as a baby grows into adulthood. Experiences of an individual shape self-identity, the things they do, and even the choices they make. If a person can not convincingly identify who they are, they run a greater risk of falling prey to brainwashing. This is because, in the first place, they have no identity to protect themselves.

A solid, strong sense of identity makes it more difficult for a brainwasher to root you down. For example, if you strongly believe that you are a strong, confident, capable, and caring person who is a believer and a good sister and mother, convincing you otherwise are almost impossible for anyone else. But a struggling teenager who thinks he is a loser will easily believe the misinformation he is being fed by the brainwasher. He already has extremely poor self-esteem, after all, and is most likely seeking a way out of his self-imposed psychological prison.

The absence of a support system is another factor that makes an individual more susceptible to brainwashing. The important role played by a group of supportive friends and family who rally around you in times of trouble can never be overrated. Unfortunately, that support system is absent for some people. A predator could swoop in the absence of a large circle of people looking for you and give you the community you're so keen to see. Brainwashers realize the value of a support system; thus, they will go to great lengths to separate their victims from the people they care for. It's true there's strength in numbers, and that kind of strength is exactly what a brainwashing agent doesn't want to have their target.

Some people do not seem to possess the skills required to go through life successfully. As a child, you depend entirely on your parents or guardians to keep you alive, at least to the best possible extent of their ability. As you grow older, you need to venture out to the best of your ability and make the best of your life. When you are on this road to self-actualization, those abilities come in handy. These skills include learning how to make decisions, how to make money so you can pay at least for your way through the basic needs, taking care of your body properly, maintaining a positive attitude, and even building good, beneficial relations. Some people make it to adulthood without the requisite survival skills, often through no fault of their own. They look to others for survival when this happens. The first individual who seems to know the way will be followed by a person who does not know their way through life. Look at it this way: you wouldn't care who threw in the life jacket if you drowned in the deep end of the pool; you would take it and be grateful to that person forever. This kind of debt and rescue feeling is what some brainwashed people experience when they finally get the 'life jacket.' What they don't know is that what looks like a life jacket is actually a trap to keep them floating in false waters.

The type of family establishment to which one is exposed may also make one more vulnerable to brainwashing. That can be argued in two ways. First, a neglected child would always gravitate toward the first person who shows interest in them. They are, after all, used to getting scraps and, so to speak, will do anything for a full meal. Secondly, when a child grows up in a family that is excentric in its beliefs and behaviors that a child is at a high risk of brainwashing. After all, they grew up experiencing things beyond the norm — what is one more thing?

Individuals living in harsh socioeconomic environments often run a high risk of brainwashing. Often a person who can barely afford a meal a day is not in the best frame of mind to choose well for himself. Added to that, the prospect of a better life can be used to entice them into a brainwasher's preference belief system. Some extremist groups, for example, were known to recruit young people from economically disadvantaged backgrounds, with the promise of economic rewards and recognition. For a young person who is culturally used to being invisible and otherwise such a reward is worth all the misinformation, albeit unknowingly, that they might be subject to.

How To Shield Yourself From Brainwashers

Predators who seek to control your mind walk the same streets you do, and probably also live on your block. While some brainwashing attempts may be obvious and easy to detect, others are subtler. As such, the process can be sucked in while unaware. The important thing is to stay alert to any signs of abuse and manipulation and always second-guess whatever you come across. In short, go through life with the proverbial pinch of salt in order to season all the information that you share. In addition to having a good dose of cynicism, there are other ways you can support yourself.

Hold the vulnerabilities warning

Always note that the mind is prone to making errors in the way it handles information, however smart you can consider yourself to be. Occasionally, your mind may get sloppy and make you vulnerable to external forces controlling you. Also, remember to watch out for the people that matter in your life that are particularly vulnerable based on how their minds work. For example, the elderly and the very young are ripe candidates for brainwashing due to the inexperience-induced naivete and out of touch with modern brainwashing scams.

Beware of spun stories

A person can dress up truth to the extent it turns into a blatant lie. This is particularly culpable to the media. There's a wise person who said the news is when a man bites a dog and not a man bites a dog. In a bid to show the man biting the dog, news outlets are always looking to make what they report sensational. A media company could conduct a quick poll of ten men living in Indiana and then report it as a survey of Midwest American men. It's hardly a representative sample, but this way, it packs a bigger punch. Always be mindful of the elements of exaggeration and ask for references to be cited for any story you come across in the media, whenever possible.

Don't trust the hype

Have you ever found that many things that get the most attention are overrated? Numerous marketing gurus have mastered the art of dismissing their products and services as the best on the market when they are not, in fact. Before you think that all the hype created about a person or product takes a moment to consider why that entity requires so much advertising if it is as good as it claims to be. There is no need to announce a thing of value because people will naturally flock to it.

The world today is particularly invested in the hype, especially since information, false and otherwise, has become so much easier to disseminate. A person just needs to write an article or create a video that will 'go viral.' Before you know it, there's an individual at the other end of the world who believes that a particular individual or product is the solution to all of their issues.

Watch out for group thinking

Groupthink is, in the simplest terms, the uncanny ability of otherwise intelligent people to make dumb decisions just for the sake of consensus. Groupthink is a trapdoor for people who don't like to stand out in crowds or be the voice of dissent. Brainwashers are especially pleased with the existence of group thinking because they don't like their targets to question them more often than not. Groupthink is why hundreds of followers of a questionable religious figure are going to make decisions that do not seem to everyone else normal. Whenever you are in a room with others, where you have to make a decision, don't be afraid to be the voice of reason that the room needs so desperately. You could only save yourself from being brainwashed and a few others.

Choose temporality over trends

Which phone are you on? What happened to your last phone — had it outlived its usefulness, or had you purchased it because you thought you needed to upgrade? Do you buy stuff when you need it or because you feel pressured to get it? Depending on how you answered these questions, you may start to see a pattern in your choices: either you're the sensible sort that buys for convenience or the fashion junkie who wants to get every new version of the iPhone when it's unraveled. Owning the sleekest new model of anything is nothing wrong, but if you've been brainwashed into believing you have to have the newest of all, you have a big problem on your hands.

By always choosing timelessness over trends, you will shield yourself from further descent down the slope. Most upgrades are often not even upgrades. A manufacturer could claim that something is new and improved when they only actually changed the packaging. A manufacturer like that will only prey on your desire for shiny new objects. The producer can not be blamed — that's how they remain in business. Just make sure you don't fall for their tricks.

Beware of your gut feeling

Whether you like to call it intuition or hunch, you should recognize your gut feeling as you go about your everyday life. By paying attention to that nudging inner voice that many individuals love to ignore, many people have saved themselves a whole lot of trouble and pain. Your unconscious mind will take the danger easily to itself before your conscious mind can. Listen to your gut feeling when someone sends you an idea that doesn't feel right. Your unconscious mind has gathered signals that are not sitting right and sending you red flags for your own preservation.

CHAPTER 13 HOW TO HANDLE THE MANIPULATORS IN YOUR LIFE

We all have been guilty at one time or another of resorting to manipulation to get something that we wanted. Now and then, it is almost painful to never talk without any form of agenda. Every time we need a friend's favor, we might resort to slight manipulation or persuasion in trying to get them to go along with what we need them to do. If we need a colleague at work to go along with our agenda, we might need to resort to bribery or intimidation to get them to act. Leaders, managers, and supervisors rely on some form of techniques of manipulation to either inspire (persuasion) or play on your emotions and fears to get you to listen and follow their instructions. Manipulation is all around us, despite the negative association with this term. It is either you are being manipulated, or you are the one who manipulates.

As we know by now, manipulators will always want to be in charge, to put themselves above you and everyone else around them to feel superior. To be the one who pulls all the strings and lets everyone else dance to their drumbeat. To do this, they will do whatever and whatever they can to try and rattle your faith, making you guess yourself in second place. Even if you don't necessarily see yourself as a manipulator, you might have done something like this before. Have you ever met a new friend at work who was laughing and joking as they tried to get us to learn how to take a step back and tone it down? Maybe you felt a little jealous that everyone was starting to warm up so quickly to the new colleague, and you didn't like to feel your popularity could be threatened. That colleague might have been taken aback by this sudden remark, and what you would have done is to put in their minds a little seed of doubt that their behavior may not have been as acceptable as they thought it was. Or maybe there was a friend you were in danger of losing the promotion to, so you secretly point out all the "errors" they made when playing on their insecurities to throw them off their game. You may even have done this to you, where someone made a remark that caught you off guard entirely, made you feel stupid, and doubt your abilities.

Manipulators want those around them to feel as if they never are good enough. What's worse is that to begin with, most of us already feel inadequate, and we're concerned that other people might notice it too. This feeling has now become so popular, with studies finding that 70 percent of the population is experiencing this feeling that it has its name-Imposter Syndrome. According to the California Institute of Technology, those who suffer from this syndrome are continually feeling incompetent or feeling like a failure. Many who live with Imposter Syndrome tend to feel self-doubt and believe they are intellectual frauds, no matter how much evidence there is to suggest their success. Another research found that people who regularly experienced this syndrome were often poorly performing (although they were able to do better) and were usually much more nervous than those who treated Imposter Syndrome less often. Sufferers with imposter syndrome also experienced a higher, more significant loss of self-esteem after what they perceived as a failure. This sensation often hits them harder than anyone else, and several studies have shown a strong correlation between Impostor Syndrome and feelings of shame, humiliation, and self-sabotage.

Individuals with the Imposter Syndrome are just the kind of people that manipulators want the most to try. When they can tap into this psychological fear, you become easy targets for them to prey on, and they will make your insecurities worse by continually questioning your actions in a way that makes you doubt your self-worth. They do this purposefully to keep you as unfocused and off-balanced as possible, making it easier for them to strike when the time is right and to take from you what they want.

Handling the Manipulators In Your Life

Narcissists, emotional abusers, manipulators of the Discreet-aggression. They're everywhere, and if you're sick of being a target of their mind games, it's time to put a stop to their once and for all power over you. Nobody has the right to manipulate and take advantage of your insecurities, whether their parents, siblings, uncles, aunts, friends, colleagues, bosses, supervisors, or customers. No one has the right to make you feel bad about yourself, and they should not force you to do something that you don't want to do. For years a relationship with a manipulator can continue, mainly if it is within your own family. Cutting ties with the manipulators you're not related to is more comfortable, but what do you do if they may be your parents or siblings? Or friends that you have grown up with and have known all of your life? Remembering your fundamental rights is the first step towards learning how to deal with those people. You have the right to:

- Have value.
- Emotional expressions.
- Views expressed.
- Express wishes.
- Set priorities.
- Unguilty, say no.
- Take what you paid.
- Take action to defend yourself from any form of moral, emotional, or physical harm.
- Do what suits your happiness.

Your Basic Rights

These are the fundamental rights that belong to us all, and no one has any right to disregard your rights in disrespect. Remembering those rights when dealing with manipulators will help you steel your resolve to fight off their attacks. Remember that you are responsible for your own life and your happiness, and you should never put those two things in someone else's hands, especially if that person happens to be a manipulator.

The next steps needed in your life to manage the manipulators are:

- To stay away from them-This is the only way to eliminate their power over you. If they aren't members of your immediate family, consider staying away from them altogether, even cutting ties with them if you can because unless they change their ways, it's unlikely that the relationship will ever do you any food. If the manipulators are members of your family, you may not be able to cut ties with them completely, but you can minimize the contact time you get with them. Avoid spending some time alone with them, remain "too busy" to have too long a chat, and be careful about how much time you allow yourself to spend about them. Don't forget the fundamental rights you hold.

- Start Defending Yourself Against Their Bullying-Some manipulators will resort to bullying if they know that their targets are weaker. Manipulators whose personalities fall within the Dark Triad's can even enjoy attempting to intimidate their victims mentally and emotionally, relishing the strength they feel when they realize they've struck fear in others' hearts. Defend yourself against their manipulation by recognizing that the manipulator clings to the vulnerabilities that they feel are yours. If you give in and play their game to what they want, you reinforce their belief that they are right. When you choose to stand up for yourself and instead confront them, they tend to retreat as most manipulators tend to be cowardly under all that bravado. They will never put themselves in a position that allows others to see their true colors.

- Not to let you pressure them-even if you feel pressured to make a decision, do not let them know. Be firm, stand firm, and say firmly, "I'm going to need some time to think about it." Whenever you begin to feel the pressure in you, take a deep breath, and remember that no one has the right to force you to do something you don't want to do. If you want to, you have every right to say no, and you need not feel guilty about it. People's pleasurers often struggle with this step because they have a strong desire to avoid upsetting anyone, even if they know full well that they are being exploited. Yet you have to stand your ground and let the manipulator know once and for all that they can't press and drive you around like your thoughts aren't counted for something.

- Learn How to Say No – It's not the world's most comfortable feeling to say no, but as guilty as you feel, your happiness and your needs will come first. You owe nothing to the manipulator, and they have no right to expect you to bend to their will (though that is precisely what they intend). When you learn to say no, you don't deliberately annoy others, you love yourself, and you set your limits. Knowing to say no is how you stand up for yourself, knowing that you won't be bullied around and saying no is within your rights if it doesn't fit with your happiness anymore.

- To point out the consequences-When, you see that the manipulator puts you in a situation where you feel verbally and emotionally abused, let the manipulator know that you are aware of that by pointing out the possible consequences of what they are trying to do. Putting yourself one step ahead of them by letting them know that you're completely away from the consequences will take them by surprise, and signal that you're not someone to be messed with. You'll force them to re-evaluate their strategies and think twice about trying to take advantage of you in the future when they know you don't get misled so easily.

- Do not expect anything from them-particularly when you expect them to see things from your viewpoint. This won't happen because most manipulators appear to be self-absorbed people, concerned solely with their desires and interests. They care little about other people's feelings or opinions, and they certainly won't go out of their way to try and see things from your perspective. We lack empathy and can never see past their interests, and if you expect them to change their tune, you 're only setting yourself up for disappointment. Never expect them to change their ways, persuade them to change their ways, or even attempt to fix them because that's not going to happen 99.9 percent of the time. Just because they want to mend their ways should a manipulator alter, not because someone else has asked them to.

- Diffuse and Exit-When you find yourself in a confrontational situation with a manipulator, there are only two goals to consider. The situation needs to be diffused and then exit. Even if the "exit" means to put an abrupt stop to the conversation, or to end a friendship altogether, the longer you keep engaging with the manipulator, the more they may try to rile you up by criticizing you, arguing with you, accusing you of something you've never done just to get a rise out of you, trying to make you lose your patience, and even pressing your buttons until you become overly emotional and vulnerable to doing something you might regret.

- Accept Your Skills-Dealing with a manipulator requires a certain degree of emotional intelligence to be able to fend them off successfully. Patience, maturity, discipline, self-control and self-regulation, and the tools you need to keep you from losing your temper or reacting in a manner you might regret (some people will push your buttons far enough and enjoy seeing you fly off your handle). Having an awareness of your skills and what you can do can help you stand your ground and keep things out of control from escalating. For instance, if you think you might not be emotionally resilient or confident enough just yet to stand your ground against a manipulator, enlist a trusted friend's help as the mediator in the situation. If you're more comfortable sending a professional email than confronting the person head-on (assuming it's something that can be solved by email), then sending an email too is fine if that gives you more confidence.

- In some cases, it might be a good idea to have black and white proof of your correspondence, as some manipulators will try to disarm you and cause you to doubt yourself by denying what you said if they know that there is no way you can prove it. Do not feel bad about having to ask for help if you need it, can take time to build the resilience and emotional intelligence necessary to stand up to a dominant personality. Finally, you will get there, and before then, understanding your strengths and the current Stage of ability will help you make the most of what you have.

- Determine Your Boundaries-The next best thing you can do is to reframe your boundary Stages for the relationships you can't eliminate from your life. As hard as acknowledging that your loved one may be able to do such a thing, you need to come to terms with it so that you can then start working on adjusting your standards and setting the limits you need to start protecting yourself. Take small steps to enforce these boundaries slowly, allowing it to happen gradually over time while building your confidence in the process. If they were someone you've been to for advice before, start phasing that out by instead turning to someone else for advice. If they were someone you've been to for validation before, stop actively seeking it out or ask them for their opinion. They may still be providing it because they are so used to doing it, and when they do, just thank them and leave it at that. You no longer have to take their counsel; let it be a case of getting in one ear and out the other. If you want to avoid a confrontation or have to deal with the manipulator demanding why you set boundaries against them, be subtle about setting your boundaries by doing so in smaller steps.

How to invalidate a conversation you won't deal with

You are validating the other person when you sit down there listening to a conversation; you don't necessarily want to be a part of it. You tell them it is important enough to demand your time and attention. That they're important enough for you to see, hear, understand, and care about them. It's refreshing when it's someone you care for, but if the conversation takes place with a manipulator, then the last thing you want to do is to endorse them. Invalidation is considered a form of emotional abuse and how subtle and even unintentional this type of abuse can be is what's dangerous about it. Manipulators are regularly using invalidation to their targets by denying their emotions and feelings, making them feel frustrated in the process. This is what you are going to do with a manipulator now. Not to invalidate the conversation to abuse them mentally but to invalidate the conversation so that they have no control over you.

Let's get a bit of clarity about what "invalidate" means here. Whenever you invalidate a person, what you're doing is basically making them feel like you either don't understand them and their feelings, or you simply don't care about them anyway. It is the same kind of tactics that a manipulator is trying to use on you. Invalidating a conversation can occur in several subtle ways, including:

- Being Coercive-Manipulators who use coercive invalidation are those who are sure (in fact very sure) that theirs is the best way to do things. They would have no trouble butting themselves in, attempting to interfere and forcing others to see the "error of their ways." They might even tell you outright that this is how things should be done (according to their way, of course), and it can be seen controlling invalidation in several everyday scenarios, including parenting. Here's what invalidation controls might look like:

Manipulator: This is NOT the way you do it because I told you that it was incorrect. The best way to solve this problem is to solve it my way.

How to invalidate them: I respect that, but I am confident that my solution will work just as well, so anyway, I will go ahead with it. Nothing drives a manipulator up the wall to see you go against what they want, especially as they expect you to listen anyway because "they said that to you."

• Being inattentive-not paying attention to the conversation makes the speaker feel like they don't matter-you guess it. Feel like what they've got to suggest isn't enough to make your time worth it. An example of how you could use this technique against a manipulator is here:

Manipulator: I'm so frustrated that NOBODY helps me around the office when all I do is go out of my way to try and help everyone else when they need it (they try to guilt you of taking on their workload).

How would you invalidate them: The progress on the group project is going great, don't you think?

You're invalidating their tactics by not acknowledging what they're trying to do and letting them know you're aware of what they're trying to do, and you're choosing not to go along with it anyway.

• Being Belligerent-By refuting instead of listening, you invalidate the efforts of the manipulator are trying to get you to see things their way (so you are more inclined to do what they want). Here's an example of how this technique could look:

Manipulator: I feel like you're rude to dismiss my idea when I've told you this is how to do it.

How would you invalidate them: Your idea was an inappropriate solution to this situation with all due respect when we both know there are more effective ways to handle it.

Being belligerent lets them know that you are not afraid to make your opinions known and that if it is the right thing to do, you are willing to refute them.

• Being Judgmental — The manipulator of judgment will minimize or downplay what you think is important because they don't feel it's important or beneficial. Being judgmental is a relationship, and invalidating the feelings of your partner can cause you to disconnect, making you feel as if your interests are taking a back seat to your partners'. Somehow, while they hardly ever tolerate what you want to do, you still find yourself doing what they want.

You: Why not go out this weekend for a hike? I haven't done this in a while, and I thought it could be fun for us to spend some time outdoors together.

Manipulator: Nope, I don't care. I'll stay over this weekend and watch my favorite Netflix series binge. You can join me, that's a lot better than taking a boring hike. You almost ever spend time watching my (guilt trip) favorite series with me.

How to invalidate them: That's okay, then I'll go for a hike. See you later. They will fully expect you to feel guilty enough to do what they want to do, and they will be frustrated at your invalidation of their manipulative tactics when you do exactly the opposite.

• Being emotional-A classic manipulative move is to invalidate the emotions of someone else because it is less important than yours. If you've ever dealt with someone who feels entitled to disagree with you or tell you what the "appropriate" way of reacting should be, that person might be a manipulator.

You: I feel down that I didn't get the promotion that I was hoping for.

Manipulator: Why are you THAT sad? You ought to be happy you even got a job. As usual, you're overreacting, and you need to get over it.

How to invalidate them: Because I worked hard for it and my efforts and commitment, I deserved to be remembered. I have a right to be upset about it; I was looking forward to this.

By standing up for yourself, and recognizing that your feelings matter, you take control of the manipulator away. Instead of allowing them to invalidate your thoughts and emotions, you take a stand for yourself and invalidate their views by letting them know just as much about how you feel as about how they feel.

Practical tips to keep manipulation at Bay every day

Toxic relationships are never easy to deal with, even more so when the relationship that drags you down is almost impossible to completely cut ties. It can be harder for others to embrace the fact that you have been a victim of abuse and open their eyes to how harmful this toxic person has been to their lives, as hard as it is to break ties with the one who manipulates you. It can initially be challenging to decide whether or not you are being taken advantage of. Still, if the same pattern of actions appears to happen over and over again, it is a sure sign that manipulation is taking place.

To let go of individual relationships can be heart-breaking. We hurt more than most, and even though we know we shouldn't, we continue to find excuses to hang onto it. If you're struggling to let go, ask yourself this one, easy question-Does this person KNOW they're profiting from you? The answer will most of the time be yes, they knew it, and they did it anyway because they chose to. It can be difficult to pry yourself away from the hands of the manipulator, but it can be achieved if you take the appropriate measures to defend yourself. As with the practical tips below, you could use to keep your mind and emotions safe every day.

- Keeping Close Connections You Can Trust-Keeping close contact with family and friends you can trust will keep the mind-control efforts of the manipulator on you to a minimum. The family and friends you can trust can give you the support you need and strengthen your self-confidence, so the manipulator has no room to plant their seeds of doubt or shake your faith.
- Speak to Your Friends and Family-Another reason the manipulator never allows you to detach from those you love and trust is that you can still trust them to have your best heart interest. Those who love you (in a non-manipulative fashion) will always look to your safety. If you're ever unsure if you're subjected to manipulation (though you may have your suspicions), talk to them about what's going on and see how they're reacting. Their immediate response-if it is shock and anger-should serve the wake-up call you need something that may not be entirely correct.
- Choosing Not to Tolerate Your Moods — Relationship manipulators sometimes sulk or resort to temperatures to get things done. If you allow them, the only one that takes an emotional toll on this kind of conduct is you. Choose not to tolerate it by walking away from the situation every time they resort to such behavior. Explain why you should not put up with this, and if they fail to change their ways, it might be time to doubt whether there is any need to hold on to this relationship for a long time.

- Ignore them-It is the best practical advice that you can find on your own. Ignore them because your time, effort, and emotions are not worth wasting on. Ignore them when they are trying to give you "advice." Ignore them as they try and tell you what to do, just go ahead and do what you wanted to do anyway. Manipulators can never be trusted, and they are always going to try to get you to do their dirty work. When you seek to hold them to account, they are going to refuse all accountability. They flip flop, go back and forth, and change their minds as often as they change clothes. Ignore them and forget everything they say; this is the only thing you can do.
- Don't try to correct them when you do, you just sink deeper into their trap. Remember, they're trying to confuse you enough so you can't see what they're up to when you're an emotional wreck and whenever you're trying to "fix" the situation, it's too easy for them to twist you around their little finger. These little traps are often set to see how you respond so they can figure out your triggers and use them to their advantage. Do not communicate, do not answer, and do not seek to correct them. It is a never-winning game.
- Don't doubt yourself-the the manipulator needs you to do just that. Why is that exactly what you shouldn't be doing. You know yourself better than anyone else might ever have, and you shouldn't have to depend on affirmation from someone to let you know you 're good enough just the way you 're. What separates the successful individuals from all the others is the fact that they don't base their self-worth on the opinions of someone else. We depend on their judgment, and that's perfect if we make mistakes along the way. They are learning from it and coming back up again. Believing in yourself can be among your most potent defenses against an attack by a manipulator.
- Quit Trying So Hard to Fit in The Wrong Crowd-If you 've got to work too hard to fit in with a group of people, they 're not the right group for you. Manipulators are charming and popular enough to make you feel like you're part of their crowd, and they love feeling in control by making

you work hard to earn their approval. They know that keeping you in this state enables them to get away with more "favor" because you are going to be more than willing to do what they just want to feel accepted. Don't let yourself be subjected to their manipulative ways any longer unless they can accept you for who you are; don't worry, there are plenty of other people who will. Each time you've had to work so hard to feel welcomed, that means you're working hard for the wrong people.

- Turn Tables-Manipulators always try to work against you. They are going to be buddies with your neighbors, then try to turn them against you. They will persuade you to do most of the work, and then take equivalent or more credit behind your back. They will entice you with the same reward and watch as you try to chase it all the time. They will remember and never miss an opportunity to make you feel bad about all your past mistakes. If the manipulator you are trying to get rid of keeps working even harder to make your life a living nightmare, you have to turn the tables on them and strike back. Find what their support is giving them, then weaken it so that the manipulator no longer has a strong enough foothold. This support might be their followers, supporters, subordinates, a skill they possess, or some resources they may be in control of. Know their supporters, and make them your allies. Make connections to others with similar skills so that the manipulator is not the only one in control. Turning the tables on them and weakening the hold they have will end up throwing them off balance so that they no longer focus on trying to dominate your life but on trying to reclaim their position in their circle instead.

- Don't compromise-Undermining your own beliefs and principles is one of the many significant mistakes you might make when dealing with a manipulator. When you go against everything you believe in just to do what they want, you play right into their hands. It's all right if they make you feel bad or guilty (just another one of their tricks), let them do whatever they want. What's important is that you don't compromise your happiness, emotions, time, and energy in circles that try to accommodate them anymore. Ask yourself this: If the roles were reversed, would they be willing to do the same for you? Go back to basic rules once again, where you have the right to put your happiness and your needs first.

- Don't ask for permission-It's a hard habit to ask for permission to break. Ever since we were children, we have been taught to do that, asking our parents for permission whenever we wanted to do something. We had to ask the teachers in school for permission for the things we needed. As adults, we ask our supervisors or managers for permission before taking action. We ask permission from our partners in a relationship to get their approval before we make a move. Asking for permission can be a tough habit to break because of this. When you allow the manipulator to be in charge, you are continually seeking consent and demanding permission, rather than taking control and making your own decisions. Isn't it time to end this? This is your life, after all, and not theirs. Why are you waiting around to get their permission to tell you what to do?

- Choose Your Own Intent-You certainly don't want to do what the manipulator wants you to do. Those operating without a sense of purpose make it easier for the ones with a stronger will and agenda to control themselves. That is why manipulators continue to be influential to this day, because so many people go around without a sense of purpose, leaving themselves open to being exploited. If you don't have a good sense of your own identity, you're more likely to believe what you're told, and to do what you're ordered to do. Because you don't have that bigger purpose of focusing on, of basing your choices on. The bigger purpose that dictates what you are ready to do and what you are not. It is easy to spot other people around you who may not even have a strong sense of purpose. They're the ones who often flit without any real rhyme or reason throughout their lives. They are the ones who work useless jobs that either inspire or fill them with happiness, yet they do not have any real desire to change the situation. They are the ones who spend far too much time concentrating on negative gossip and other meaningless information that does not serve any real purpose. This lack of focus is what manipulators are just waiting to pounce on, so it's time to start thinking long and hard about what your goal will be if you haven't found your sense of purpose yet. Give yourself something specific to concentrate on, and you're less likely to fall victim to temptation and deceit.

- Take on New Challenges-there are new possibilities all around you; all you need to do is be bold enough to take a risk and a leap of faith. Manipulators tend to stop you from taking on new opportunities, and in the same process, they want to tie you down. They want you to live in the same loop that you are because this makes it much easier for them to retain control. That's why they are sowing seeds of self-doubt in your mind, and why they're working hard to discourage you from improving yourself or seizing new chances. Every time you grow more durable and more comfortable, you lose their grip over you, which is what they work hard to prevent. They're going to try too hard to keep you in your place; they're going to even resort to making you feel ashamed even to entertain the thought of taking on new opportunities to improve yourself. Don't let them stop you, and don't let go of self-doubt. Even successful people made a lot of mistakes along the way to get to where they are right now; all they did was have the courage to take the leap and make a change for the better.
- Stop Being a Punching Bag-Manipulators will only continue to treat you as a punching bag if you allow them to do so. Respect yourself enough to stand up and say you're not worthy of this type of treatment. Because, you are not. Once again, go back to your fundamental rights, where you have the right to be respected. Any time someone takes advantage of you, they don't appreciate you. The choice of whether or not to stand up to it rests entirely in your hands. People are going to try to use you, abuse you, and take advantage of you, but you have a choice of saying no to it all. Nobody has any power to manipulate you unless you allow

them to. Stop being a punching bag, start taking responsibility for your decisions, and remember that there's no reason to feel guilty about standing up to someone who doesn't treat you fairly.

Manipulators will always seek to do whatever they can to undermine your faith and weaken you enough for them to take control over you. They will claim to be concerned about you, or that they just have the best interest in mind (funny, because they try to get you to do things that favor them more most of the time). They will convince you they want to "help," when the truth is, they will be the only person they want to help, and if they have to step on their toes to do so, they will. They can be hard to get rid of once you bring them into your life, but it can be done now that your know-how. The final key is never to stop working to build your self-confidence, the healthier you are, the less control they have over you.

CHAPTER 14 HOW TO PROTECT YOURSELF AGAINST DARK PSYCHOLOGY

Anyway, much you should have confidence in the best of everybody; the reality of the situation is that we are, for the most part, obvious targets the extent that control goes. There are individuals in this world who leave their homes with just the most noticeably terrible of goals. They will likely damage others and to get the most they can out of others without giving anything consequently. The information on dim brain science introduced in this book isn't proposed to be utilized to make hurt others. Or maybe, the primary goal is to assist you with seeing the truth about control in its different structures and, if need be, to reverse the situation to ensure yourself. In the event that you can control a controller before they outdo you, at that point, that is a success for you and the remainder of humankind.

Variables that Make You Easier to Manipulate

Other than realizing how to recognize a predator, it additionally assists with understanding what makes an individual progressively defenseless against mental assaults. Basically, there are obvious targets that are nearer to the line of fire than others. In Chapter 3: The ABCs of Brainwashing, we investigated a portion of the variables that make an individual progressively vulnerable to indoctrinating. In any case, we presently realize that conditioning is only one of the routes through which individuals are controlled. All in all, what makes an individual powerless against the entirety of the sorts of brain control and control that exist?

You are Intelligent

You are most likely befuddled by this one since you have consistently accepted that more intelligent individuals are more enthusiastically to outmaneuver, isn't that so? Stop and think for a minute; however: savvy individuals like to utilize rationale to help their dynamic procedure. The rationale is simpler to control. Henceforth, canny individuals are bound to controlled when you corner them with coherent contentions. Less astute individuals are more enthusiastically to persuade with rationale and will, in general, be increasingly difficult notwithstanding realities and logical contentions. It is no big surprise that a ton of individuals who have been misled by extortionists and Ponzi plans happen to be individuals who are generally brilliant and who you'd not hope to be effortlessly tricked. The motivation behind why this is regularly the situation is on the grounds that tricksters know to speak to this sort of individuals with realities and insights. Individuals who are less savvy will be effectively pompous of anything that seems like turmoil since they don't get it.

- **You are trusting and like to accept the best about everybody**

In all honesty, there are awful individuals in this world. There are individuals who leave their homes each morning with the aim of hurting others. There are individuals who have no second thoughts about exacting sorrow and strife upon others. While you might be situated in your home stressing over super-rich organizations who take from poor people, there is a meeting room brimming with corporate hotshots who are going to take from the poor that you are stressed over. Basically, not every person partakes in your soul and your compassion. Individuals are wired in an unexpected way. Individuals on the dull group of three are wired significantly more, not the same as you would ever envision. At the point when you meet a renewed individual, it is honorable to need to accept the best of them; however, it is savvy to hope to be astounded in a not very good way. Downplaying your desires for individuals is an extraordinary method to secure yourself against everybody that is attempting to get a bit of you.

- **You are continually looking for outer approval**

With regards to control, an individual that is continually looking for approval from others is similar to a sheep strolling inside a lion's lair. It is just only minutes before the sheep is totally obliterated from the essence of the earth. Controllers are profoundly equipped for seeing escape clauses and misusing them to their advantage. A major, glaring proviso for a controller is a desolate or shaky individual who needs some friendship at whatever cost.

Everyone is inclined to feeling desolate occasionally. We are social creatures, and without organization, we can frequently feel disliked and sad. Try not to look for outside approval to where you make yourself an exposed target for approval. It is alright for individuals to like you, and it is likewise alright If they don't care for you. Preferring yourself is sufficient. At the point when you have put on the covering of self-esteem and acknowledgment, you make it somewhat harder for predators to crawl through your guards. This isn't to imply that any individual who has been controlled doesn't adore themselves enough. In any case, in sentimental connections, you can truly secure yourself in the event that you have as of now inside approved yourself before going out there to the wolves.

You have secluded yourself from family or companions

You've likely heard this story previously - an old individual who lives alone meets an enchanting youngster on the Internet. This online colleague rapidly turns into a sentimental intrigue. A couple of months down the line, the youngster is stating quite a few things and getting cash wired into their ledger consistently. A year down the line, the old lady or man has depleted all their retirement investment funds and reeling from the revelation that their online love premium was only a con. While the casualty flounders in humiliation and cleared out accounts, you can just think about how the configured out how to pull off a trick that is so straightforward and evident that it is bizarre. In what manner can an individual be so artless, you wonder? It truly is basic. It is simpler to trick one individual than it is to trick many.

One individual who clearly had some insight in him put it along these lines: You can trick all the individuals a portion of the time, and a portion of the individuals constantly, yet you can't trick all the individuals constantly. This is a reality that predators know- - it is a lot simpler to chase the solitary pronghorn as it meanders in the savannah, alone and unprotected against all the perils of the world. At the point when you are encircled by cherishing loved ones, you have a divider around you that keeps the predators out. In any event, when you are sure that you are infatuated, and your accomplice is the best thing that transpired, there will be that one individual in your circle whose basic reasoning has not been weakened by the enthusiasm of another relationship. That one individual will be your support against control. It is nothing unexpected that numerous individuals who control and misuse their accomplices attempt to get them far from their families. These controllers and abusers realize that if another gathering comes in with the general mish-mash, their whole gig will be up.

You are exceptionally enthusiastic

Feelings are extraordinary. The capacity to encounter satisfaction, euphoria, shock, love, misery, and each feeling of the human experience is a blessing. For certain individuals, this blessing was given in spades. In the event that you are the sort of individual who experiences life feeling things more than deduction things, you are exceptionally defenseless against control. Controllers can counterfeit feelings while saying and doing all that you have to hear. They don't need to bode well - they simply need to verbalize the things that you long for, and you are sold. Presently, in the event that you are exceptionally enthusiastic, there is definitely not a ton of things you can do to change yourself. You are brought into the world that way, and you can just figure out how to adapt to being so exceptionally enthusiastic. That being stated, you can generally ensure that you remain aware of your feelings with the goal that they are not continually directing your choices for you.

You don't teach yourself

You don't have to return to class to get familiar with all the manners in which that individuals are attempting to exploit you. Something to be thankful for about living in this day and age is that information is openly accessible right at the fingertips. You just should be eager to learn. A mess of individuals is exploited on the grounds that they don't have the foggiest idea about the strategies utilized by controllers. If you don't realize that manipulators have a thing known as the reflecting procedure, you may believe that you and your date just have stunning science when this is unquestionably not the situation. Something to be thankful for about controllers is that the vast majority of their methods are as of now in the books, and you should simply get yourself a book and get to peruse. Along these lines, you will have the option to leave any predator speechless before he gets excessively near purpose you any mischief.

At the same time, the free accessibility of information implies that you can generally look into somebody with the goal that you validate their character before they get an opportunity to get anything from you. Gone are the days when you needed to employ a private agent to do a personal investigation on somebody. In this day and age, it is conceivable to run a record verification on somebody on the Internet and have the outcomes prepared in no time. This could either be a paid personal investigation or a brisk careless check of their online life pages. Luckily, nearly the whole world is via web-based networking media these days, and a larger part of us love to overshare.

Straightforward Strategies You Can Adopt to Protect Yourself

Regardless of whether you view yourself as exceptionally defenseless or impervious to control, it generally assists with being protected as opposed to sorry. Fortunately, it is conceivable to keep the narcissists, insane people, and high Machs at a sheltered separation in your life. In what capacity?

Insane people are available in our working environments, in business exchanges, in our own connections, and even in our families. Some of the time, you just can't stay away from a maniac by uprightness of the idea of the relationship that exists among you. For example, it may be difficult to disregard or maintain a strategic distance from your psychopathic manager since you have to carry out your responsibility, get paid, and advance in your profession, or if nothing else, take care of your tabs. If your supervisor is a maniac, you simply need to manage him some way or another. You may, for example, need to make sense of a method of downplaying your collaborations all things considered. Be that as it may, if you ever have the decision not to manage an insane person, get it and run. For example, in the event that you are beginning to become more acquainted with a renewed individual with the goal of dating them and begin to understand a few propensities that coordinate the insane person rules, run and don't think back. You don't have to stay a person or thing that isn't beneficial for you.

Try not to fall into the snare of reasoning. You can change a mental case, sociopath, or narcissist into being a superior individual. Not exclusively is this not your occupation; however, it is likewise for all intents and purposes incomprehensible. First off, the things that make individuals dim and manipulative are so profoundly installed in their minds that they can't simply be expelled and supplanted with sugar and flavor freely. Also, change is an individual decision that is made by a person. An individual that changes does so in light of the fact that they need to change and not on the grounds that someone else asked them to. To wrap things up, in the event that you are managing a mental case and believing that you can transform them, you are basically taking up arms against science and hereditary qualities. Who do you believe is going to win?

Focus on activities more than you do words. Predators are excellent with their words since words are their most amazing assets. Rather than concentrating on what an individual says, take a gander at what they do. Did they satisfy the guarantee they made to you about doing a specific thing? Do they treat everybody just as they need to make it sound? A basic method to check whether an individual's activities coordinate their words is by using something that is alluded to as the standard of threes.

Here are the means by which it works: If an individual appears to lie or makes a guarantee that they don't keep on one event, you might be managing a basic misconception. If this happens a subsequent time, there is probably going to be a genuine misstep that requires tending to. In any case, in the event that there is a third event, at that point, you are most likely managing a liar. Falsehoods are regularly the main indication of manipulative conduct. In the event that you can distinguish this common example in your relationship or connection, at that point, you realize you have yourself a circumstance on your hands. How you choose to deal with this circumstance will mean the distinction between liberating yourself from the jaws and dramatization of a controller or remaining on for the most overpowering ride of your life.

At whatever point conceivable, let the insane person win yet not to your detriment. The characters that affection to win are frequently forceful and will make a huge effort to guarantee that they trump every one of their rivals. In the event that you ever end up confronting an insane person on an exchange table, consistently go for the recommendation that ensures success for both of you. This is a compelling method for guaranteeing that you don't exhaust all your vitality, attempting to ward off a maniac who is attempting to complete you.

When managing individuals, be they holy people or heathens, consistently tune in to what your gut needs to state. Researchers who have attempted to clarify gut intuition state that it is the body's response to an intraspecies predator. This bodes well when you consider how in some cases, you'll feel uncomfortable around somebody you don't realize just to discover later that that individual was not a decent individual. Try not to release your gut sense disregarded when it is endeavoring to keep you from committing an error. In numerous cases, sociopaths expect jobs, for example, guide, chief, boss, church pioneer, watchman, or even parent. While these jobs are without a doubt honorable, your premonition may be shouting that the congregation chief isn't as dependable as he should cause you to accept. If so, consistently offer the need for the hunch. What your gut says is consistently a superior wagered than what you might suspect, you know.

Try not to permit yourself to get brought into the games that mental cases, sociopaths, narcissists, and other dull characters play. Of course, you've perused this book and are feeling especially certain about your insight on the dim set of three characters. At the rear of your brain, you accept that you have the stuff to take on an insane person and win. What you can be sure of is that while you have quite recently perused this book, a mental case has had as long as he can remember to rehearse on his casualties. Try not to be brought into their controls. It isn't your business to engage the insane person. Your main employment when managing a maniac is to secure yourself against their stunts.

CHAPTER 15 MYTHS AND MISCONCEPTIONS ABOUT DARK PSYCHOLOGY

There are various themes that are alright for supper discussion. Dim brain research isn't one of them. The exact opposite thing you need to ask during Thanksgiving is the means by which Uncle Joe scores most definitely. In view of the noxiousness encompassing dim brain science, there are normally not many open conversations with respect to the subject. How about we take the dark psychology test, for example. It is safe to say that you want to take it? If truly, do you intend to impart your outcomes to anybody? The high possibilities are that If you addressed yes to the main inquiry, you are likely going to answer no to the subsequent one. Most individuals like to consider themselves great individuals. Likewise, they like others to consider them great individuals. Putting your dim group of three tests in plain view for anyone passing by to view may not actually fill this need. As a result of the entirety of this secretive encompassing dull brain research, there is, in this way, a ton of misguided judgments and fantasies about the character characteristics that are key vessels for dim brain research. This section investigates these fantasies and misinterpretations while revealing some insight into the equivalent.

Fantasy #1: Psychopaths and sociopaths are very much the same things

Truth: Psychopathy and sociopathy are two distinct sorts of standoffish character issue

The term mental case and sociopath are utilized reciprocally in regular discussion. In any case, the two attributes are fundamentally unique in relation to one another. That being stated, these two character issues do share a few likenesses. Specialists consider sociopathy to be a less extreme issue than psychopathy. The table underneath shows a portion of the attributes that recognize a mental case from a sociopath.

- Maniac

- Sociopath
- Has no still, small voice
- Has a frail still, small voice
- Can mix in by being beguiling and are in this way harder to spot
- Have no expectation of mixing in and are regularly simple to spot. Will fundamentally be keen on themselves as it were
- Relentless
- Hot-headed and jump without looking

Fantasy #2: Psychopaths are made and not conceived

Truth: Psychopaths are brought into the world that way

Psychopathy is an exceptionally convoluted character issue in that sociopaths are more regularly conceived as opposed to made. A sociopath comes out of the belly wired uniquely in contrast to the vast majority. Subsequently, they go astray from the digression of what is typical and frequently end up in places that some other 'ordinary' individual would not really wind up in. The research attempted has to be sure indicated that the minds of mental case's capacity are diversely when contrasted with the cerebrums of others who don't have any recorded character issue. Things being what they are, what happens when a mental case is conceived?

Contingent upon the kind of condition the insane person experiences childhood in, the mental case will get one of a few things. If the little youngster who gives indications of psychopathy experiences childhood in a supporting domain, he will probably turn into a business or political pioneer of much impact. In the event that the youngster experiences childhood in a brutal or horrible condition, they are probably going to become sequential executioners or killers. Insane people who are supported in a domain that is someplace in the middle of the first two situations end up in quite a while of intensity in fields, for example, law implementation and the board.

Fantasy #3: Sociopaths are conceived

Truth: Sociopaths are chiefly a result of their surroundings

As a rule, sociopaths are because of the condition that they are raised in. It regularly begins with a natural or hereditary aura to sociopathy, which is then declined by the sort of support that they get. For example, a youngster who experiences childhood in a situation where no one appears to think about him will likely convey a similar absence of sympathy in his adulthood. If they grew up with grown-ups who had no feeling of respectability and came up short on an ethical compass, their heart would be profoundly weakened thus.

Fantasy #4: Females can't be maniacs

Truth: There are recorded instances of insane female people

Almost certainly, when you know about the term maniac, you consequently think about a male character. All things considered, Hollywood has put forth a valiant effort to depict insane people as hatchet employing guys on a homicide binge. In any case, note that mental cases can be female as well. In contrast to their male partners, in any case, female mental cases are more averse to be truly forceful or savage. Or maybe, they resort to utilizing their sexuality and womanliness to control others. Female mental cases are likewise liable to have a high number of sexual accomplices.

Fantasy #5: Psychopaths are fixated on murder.

Truth: Psychopaths are daredevil.

Murder is only one of the routes through which mental cases extinguish their craving for the rush. At the point when the vast majority consider insane people, they naturally considering murders left, right, and focus. Nonetheless, while the facts demonstrate that an executioner is bound to be an insane person than not, it is likewise obvious that mental cases are not considering submitting murder anything else than the remainder of the populace. Numerous sociopaths experience their lives looking for thrills and never truly causing anyone brutal mischief. Indeed, they may break a couple of hearts as they hop, starting with one sexual accomplice then onto the next and toss a few people under the transport in a mean to ascend the company pecking order; however that is the extent that a large portion of them go. In the event that you are searching for a mental case in your life, you won't almost certainly discover one in the event that you are just searching for savagery and bloodlust.

Fantasy #6: Psychopathy is a psychological sickness that can be relieved.

Truth: Psychopathy is a character issue that has no fix.

If psychopathy were a psychological sickness, there would be a possibility for medicines. Rather, psychopathy is a character issue, and this implies no fix exists that would transform insane people into typical, feeling, and compassionate individuals. Since they truly don't accept that anything isn't right with them at any rate, sociopaths would not be keen on treatment regardless of whether it existed. In occasions where insane people have been persuaded to get into treatment for motivations behind patching existing connections, it isn't remarkable to discover them attempting to control the specialist into believing that the treatment is working or has just worked. Keep in mind; these people are exceptionally manipulative and fit for using whatever implies important to get themselves out of troublesome circumstances. On account of their intense absence of dread and nonappearance of compassion, an insane person will have no issue burning through a friend or family member's time in treatment if just to cause it to appear as though they are putting forth an attempt.

Fantasy #7: You can change an individual on the dim set of three by cherishing them effectively.

Truth: Most individuals who score profoundly on the dim ternion test remain so for the remainder of their lives.

Love is a weird thing in that it causes individuals to accept that they are equipped for the unthinkable, in any event, when the fact of the matter is uncovered before their eyes. If you are involved with an individual who scores profoundly on the dim set of three tests, the initial not many months of your relationship are probably going to be joyful. Manipulative individuals have a method of affection bombarding you into accepting that they are the ideal match that you have been sitting tight for from the start. Lamentably, this is typically only an endeavor to draw and ensnare you into a relationship that is simply purposeful misdirection. When you have sunk into this sort of relationship, the controller's genuine nature becomes visible. Much of the time, you will discover a relationship accomplice staying with the expectation that things will change. That affection will be sufficient to make something happen. Sadly, this regularly never occurs.

First of all, the way that psychopathy is, for the most part, hereditary implies that it is extraordinarily hard to vanquish. Best case scenario, the insane person can just channel their absence of affectability towards accomplishing objectives that are not adverse to the general society. With respect to Machiavellianism and narcissism, these frequently come from a profound mental injury that may require a ton of weapons store to survive. Numerous individuals will float towards Machiavellianism and narcissism as a resistance instrument. Any endeavor to get them out of this will just appear to be an assault hence making them dispatch their own safeguard. In that capacity, intercession as affection might be unfathomably counterproductive. It is additionally important to recognize that affection and other nervy feelings are not actually a dull set of threesome tea. They may not see it for what it is. Accordingly, should you wind up involved with an individual who shows the attributes of the dull group of three, you may need to reevaluate whether that is the thing that you truly need.

Fantasy #8: People who score exceptionally on the dull set of three are progressively alluring.

Truth: This has been set up to be false.

How can it be that individuals regularly float towards the narcissists and the mental cases of this world? Is it in light of the fact that the dull set of three characters are more appealing than all of us? In an offer to decide if a dim group of three characters are better-looking, scholarly specialists took to considering a few subjects who had a dull high set of three scores. The aftereffects of these examinations recommended that the motivation behind why these subjects seemed appealing was on the grounds that they spruced up and introduced themselves truly in a way that was organized. At the point when dressed down in exhausting garments, these subjects didn't show up as appealing as in the past. In that capacity, it is practically protected to accept that the consideration and exertion that goes into preparing and the certainty from there on are what causes a narcissist or insane person to appear to be more alluring than they truly are.

Fantasy #9: Psychopaths change when they have youngsters.

Truth: Psychopaths can't have feelings of compassion or caring even towards their own youngsters.

Insane people start their own families, and when this occurs, they, as a rule, have a difficult time sustaining their posterity. Not at all like typical guardians who are not on the dim group of three scales, mental cases make some hard memories recognizing their youngsters as independent elements. Or maybe, they believe them to be devices or expansion of themselves which are accessible for their utilization; however, they see fit.

Mental cases are bound to see their youngsters as trophies that make them look great then as youthful, susceptible people who are searching for somebody to manage them through life. All things considered, an average insane person will push their children to exceed expectations in something they have no enthusiasm for despite the fact that this is to the detriment of the children's emotional wellbeing and prosperity. They may mightily select the children in swimming classes; for example, since they accept their child turning into a specialist swimmer and contender will improve their social remaining in the network. Obviously, maniac guardians are extremely difficult to please observing that they are accustomed to exceeding expectations themselves and won't comprehend why their children won't take the necessary steps to get to the top.

Fantasy #10: You are either on the dull set of three or not

Truth: The dull group of three is a continuum on which some score exceptionally while others score modest

The characteristics of narcissism, psychopathy, and Machiavellianism are inborn in each one of us. The main distinction is that in certain individuals, these characteristics are amplified to where they regularly become damaging to the individuals around them. Take narcissism, for example. Everyone has a way that they consider themselves. Probably, you like to ponder yourself. You like to accept that you are attractive and skilled and simple to adore. For a narcissist, this mental self-view is made a huge deal about to the degree where their whole life spins around. It isn't sufficient for them to accept these things about themselves- - they additionally need every other person to accept they are great and pious and everything great.

Psychopathy, then again, is likewise a range. Everyone has their place in this range. Consider it along these lines: have you at any point accomplished something that was not all that pleasant but then didn't feel regretful about it? Have you, at any point, acted in a way to propose that you are not actually sympathetic towards somebody? If you have addressed yes to any of these inquiries, at that point, you showed psychopathic qualities at any rate once in your life. This doesn't imply that you will proceed to kill somebody later in your life. It possibly implies that there are occurrences when the maniac in you comes out, and different cases when you may have the option to get yourself in the nick of time. The manner in which you were raised affects whether you can prevent yourself from releasing your full insane person.

Fantasy #11: Your manager is an insane person

Truth: Your supervisor could conceivably be an insane person

The facts confirm that numerous insane people who don't become professional lawbreakers proceed to turn out to be profoundly fruitful in business, legislative issues, and different fields. In any case, this isn't reason enough to blame your manager for being a mental case. A few people are basically determined and requested on the grounds that it is the thing that they know and comprehend to be the necessity for progress. Regardless, not a ton of individuals have sleepovers and informal breakfasts with their supervisors. There is a sure powerful anticipated from a manager representative relationship. Your extreme talking, the barbarous supervisor, might be a totally unique individual when they are not wearing their manager cap. Try not to go imagining that everybody in power positions is a sociopath or mental case. It doesn't generally work that way.

Fantasy #12: Your ex is a psycho

Truth: A relationship finished on a harsh note. This doesn't make any of you a psycho.

Many individuals are attached to alluding to their exes as psychos. Sometimes, a relationship will finish strong where the two gatherings proceed to become extraordinary companions for the remainder of their lives. Sadly, this isn't the means by which most connections play out. Numerous romances end in tears and allegations and ridiculing. Before you consider your ex, an insane person, assess the signs expounded in this book and see if your ex's conduct coordinates any of these. Obviously, this ought not to make any difference If you are finished with the relationship; however, it may assist you with abstaining from falling into a similar snare of dating somebody who shows similar signs. If you are right now associated with somebody who gives any of the indications talked about here, you should think about leaving them for your own wellbeing. Acknowledge that the way toward leaving a mental case or narcissist is unique in relation to that of leaving an ordinary individual who doesn't accept the flight as an attack against their own individual. There are various assets that are accessible to people who are hoping to leave oppressive and manipulative connections. These assets can be found through a straightforward online hunt.

CHAPTER 16 FAMOUS DARK TRIAD PERSONALITIES

It isn't sufficient to find out about the qualities that a dim group of three characters exemplifies; it should likewise be recognized that a dim set of three people have names and have lived among us either presently or previously. In the entirety of history, there have been people who have acted so absurdly in the entirety of their dim group of three greatness for all to see. This part is committed to those people who have left, or keep on leaving, their dim imprint on the planet.

Alexander the Great

Child of Philip II of Macedon and Olympias, Alexander the Great, was a lord of the antiquated Greek realm known as Macedon and a furious narcissist too. Alexander accepted that he was bound for the enormity and that anything that existed inside his creative mind was achievable, in actuality, paying little heed to the cost. His mom didn't make things any better for him- - she had grand aspirations for him. He tried to realize these desires for his entire life, and it is no big surprise that he wound up being named 'the Great' in acknowledgment of his wild accomplishment as an unparalleled military leader.

Maybe the best sign that Alexander was a narcissist is simply the way that he thought as a divinity. At the end of the day, he believed himself to be a divine being. Once more, his mom had persuaded that he was the child of Zeus, the ruler of the Greek divine beings. Further, Alexander was enamored with making light of his own dad's accomplishments to his companions. In his eyes, these accomplishments didn't make a difference, and the main successes that tallied were those that had his name on them. He was continually stressed that his dad didn't leave him any inheritance that tallied.

Accordingly, he made it his business to win the same number of fights as he could. He took his military on unlimited fights on a journey for his very own brilliance. It didn't make a difference who lost their lives or got harmed. Alexander was determined to make his own inheritance, and any person or thing who held him up was the foe.

Napoleon Bonaparte

Harassed as a little youngster, Bonaparte rose through the positions to turn into a general in the French Revolution at 24 years old. Tragically, Bonaparte conveyed with him the impacts of his tormenting and low confidence, in any case, alluded to as a feeling of inadequacy. While he had the option to accomplish an inheritance that numerous men of his time didn't, Napoleon conveyed with him the mental scars of his past. It is accepted that Napoleon lashed out and acted forcefully to compensate for his inadequacies. Which deficiencies, you may ponder.

First off, Napoleon was shorter than the normal man. Remaining at five feet and two inches, it is anything but difficult to perceive any reason why Napoleon may have been shaky about his stature. His height regardless, Napoleon accepted that he was something uncommon and even expounded on it in his book, appropriately named Thoughts. In the book, Napoleon discusses how he had come to accept that he was uncommon and could go forward to accomplish things that he had just recently accepted to be a dream. By the day's end, it's most likely out of line to blame Napoleon for going to narcissism to perk himself up. He was most likely just attempting to compensate for the sentiments of insufficiency that he had become acquainted with gratitude to his youth insults from his cohorts and classmates.

Adolf Hitler

Who is simply the most retained individual that you at present know about? Take that individual's considerations, practices, and activities and afterward duplicate them one million times. What do you get? Adolf Hitler that is the thing that. Adolf Hitler lived in the mid-1900s, so he is more likely than not done some quite awful things to be despite everything discussed today. Furthermore, for sure, he did.

In addition to the fact that Adolf believed that his race was better than every other person, however, he likewise needed to get every other person on the promulgation machine as well. Therefore, a large number of Jews lost their lives because of the computations and maneuvers of a small-time whose narcissism and hunger for power turned crazy. Hitler's initiative style was organized with the end goal that he was at the top, and no one else could address him. His inferiors were to take these orders unquestioningly in light of the fact that he accepted he knew better than every other person.

While his officers were executing the Jews left, right, and focused, Hitler had no compassion for those withering and languishing. Truth be told, he needed this homicide binge to proceed for as long as possible, or if nothing else, until he had the option to clear out the second rate race.

Hitler will perpetually be recognized as the explanation behind probably the greatest war at any point saw on earth, and all since he accepted that he and white Germans were better than every other person.

Charles Manson

Charles Manson is one of the most notable clique pioneers of present-day American history. Manson was a jobless ex-convict who used psychopathic control to make himself an after which he named the Manson Family. Manson had a capacity to persuade youngsters to join his family by going after their shortcomings and causing them to feel as though he was their sheltered spot and savior. In the wake of attracting them, Manson, at that point, persuaded them to perpetrate wrongdoings for his sake. In the mid-year of 1969, for example, Manson's Family executed nine individuals on his order.

Much in the wake of being captured, Manson indicated no regret or blame for the enduring he had perpetrated on others. He had negligence for humankind that must be portrayed as insensitive. That being stated, Manson was likewise profoundly beguiling, and this made individuals float towards him. Indeed, even while in jail, Manson was as yet ready to utilize his psychopathic appeal to bait ladies, even to the point of getting drawn into one.

Albert DeSalvo

Nicknamed The Boston Strangler, Albert DeSalvo was a criminal who admitted to murdering thirteen ladies in the Boston territory, by the method of strangulation. DeSalvo was a run of the mill mental case. Directly from adolescence, he displayed the indications of an insane person. For example, he tormented creatures. This is an average admonition sign that you may have a youthful mental case on your hands. Children who torment creatures frequently proceed to perpetrate different intolerable violations later on. Numerous killers and sequential executioners have a background marked by creature maltreatment from before.

What's generally remarkable about DeSalvo's killings was that the greater part of his casualties was older and alone at the hour of the assaults. While the vast majority are fit for demonstrating compassion, kindness, and in general sympathy on the older, DeSalvo was a remarkable inverse. He realized this was a defenseless gathering that could be effortlessly curbed to satisfy his dull wants.

It is accounted for that DeSalvo had a phenomenal sex drive, which is another indication of an individual that might be inclined to psychopathic propensities. DeSalvo likewise preferred to boast incredibly about his victories, sexual and others. His inclination for embellishment drove a few people to accept that he was not so much the Boston Stranger significantly after he admitted to the killings.

Jeffrey Dahmer

Jeffrey Dahmer was an American sequential executioner who was seen as liable for the assault, murder, and dismantling of seventeen young men between the time of 1978 to 1991. Dahmer's violations were too frightful that it is hard to envision that a person really dedicated them. In addition to the fact that he killed his casualties, however, he likewise performed necrophilia and barbarianism on their carcasses.

Dahmer's adolescence was no more astounding than the run of the mill youth of a child experiencing childhood in America during his time. That being stated, a few sources private that Dahmer was disregarded by his folks as a baby. Absence of consideration and friendship, and generally speaking disregard, can make a child form into an all-out insane person later on in his life. Dahmer's mom had a horde of issues that she had not worked through, and his dad was inaccessible more often than not. Subsequently, Dahmer was left to battle for himself and discover approaches to possess his time.

Growing up, Dahmer was, to a great extent, held. He, be that as it may, had a sensible number of companions that he could converse with and play with. His companions revealed Dahmer had an enthusiasm for creatures. That in itself will not be an issue if that is all it was. Rather, the intrigue spiraled into something darker and vile. As a youngster, Dahmer gathered huge bugs and roadkill and proceeded to eviscerate this at his home or in the forested areas close to his home. This ought to have been his folks' first sign that something wasn't right, yet reports have it that the guardians were engrossed with different issues that did exclude sustaining their child.

Later on, as Dahmer's interest with creature cadavers and bones developed, he connected with his dad and requested to be instructed how to blanch creature bones. His dad, glad that his in any case held child was connecting, exhibited the best possible approach to dye bones. Dahmer would utilize this information to clean the remains he kept on gathering.

Dahmer was eighteen years of age when he began focusing on human casualties. His first casualty was a youngster by the name of Steven Hicks, who was a drifter that he got and baited to his home on the guise of partaking in some mixed beverages together. After this first homicide, Dahmer analyzed his casualty's body and covered it in a shallow grave in his yard. At that point, he kept on carrying on with his life as though nothing had occurred - no blame and no regret. Over an incredible span up until when he got captured, Dahmer proceeded to take the lives of twelve increasingly shocking casualties.

Amy Bishop

Amy Bishop was a science teacher who worked at the University of Alabama in Huntsville up until February 2010 when she strolled into the college complex and slaughtered three of her partners. Three others supported extreme yet non-lethal wounds from this assault. There are a few reasons why Amy Bishop makes this rundown. To start with, Amy displayed away from narcissism when she circumvented telling everybody that she had earned her Ph.D. from Harvard. It was nearly the absolute first thing that she let you know after gathering. By the goodness of having a degree from Harvard, Amy trusted herself to be better than every other person. She thought of herself as a competent educator who was meriting residency, notwithstanding the way that her understudies had grumbled about her capacities and showing strategies on various events.

A lot prior, before she slaughtered her partners, Amy had shot her sibling in what was later governed as a mishap. A few sources insinuated that Amy might have executed her sibling intentionally on the grounds that he was getting the consideration that she thought she merited. Upon the arrival of the killings, Amy went to a workforce meeting and sat unobtrusively as it advanced. She seemed, by all accounts, to be quiet and simply to be her typical self. Around forty minutes after the fact, Amy tranquility pulled out a handgun and began firing. She was repressed in the wake of murdering three employees and harming three others. It is intriguing to take note of that Amy wanted to slaughter her associates in the wake of getting denied residency at the University. In spite of her, in any case, terrible showing as a teacher, Amy accepted that she merited residency. In her psyche, she was the most elite, and no one else had a more prominent option to be at the college.

Amy lost her residency in 2009, and it was not until 2010 that she murdered her partners. It is obvious to see that she was cold and ascertaining and set aside the effort to think of the perfect intend to dispose of her 'foes' — Amy's activities for an amazing duration point to an individual that was exceptionally narcissistic and psychopathic also. An individual from a composing bunch that Amy had a place with is referred to as saying that Amy appeared to be an individual who felt qualified for acclaim. She is likewise said to have been rough in her connections with others.

Almost certainly, these people are only a drop in the expanse of a dull group of three characters that have strolled on this planet. With analysts recommending that maniacs make up around one percent of everybody, it's a given that making a rundown of all insane people ever to exist would be a deeply-rooted task.

The Most Effective Method To Talk To Your Child About Dark Psychology

Other than the situations where there are exemplary notice indications of psychopathy, for example, the maltreatment of creatures, you may have seen that a mess of the characters recorded in the past segments experienced a typical youth. In the event that you are a parent, the wellbeing of your kids is vital. The sort of concern you feel towards your youngsters reaches out from their association with others to their own inside discourse occurring without any other person's notification. At the end of the day, you need to realize that your kid is protected when with others and when alone too.

It is particularly perplexing to realize that there are individuals in this world who utilize their time, considerations, and endeavors to hurt kids. While there isn't particularly much that you can do to change that sort of individuals, you can set up your youngster to manage the sort of individuals who are almost certainly to utilize dull brain science to exploit others.

Make your home your kid's place of refuge

Your home ought to be the place your youngster feels most secure. The outside world isn't the most amiable spot there is out there. There are menaces in school, pedophiles sneaking in parks and play areas, and youngster executioners who have no misgivings about consummation youthful lives. At the point when your youngster is finished managing all the perils introduced by the cutting edge world, they ought to consistently have a sheltered spot to come to. This implies you should be cautious about who you welcome into your home consistently. Commonly, the individuals who exploit kids are individuals who are not able to them. Accordingly, it assists with screening who makes it into your kid's life and who doesn't. Other than making the home truly safe by making it unavailable to predators, you should likewise be your kid's sheltered spot inwardly. Kids who realize that they can depend on their folks have a simpler time opening up about the difficulties they are confronting, which will incorporate that troubling discussion they had with the dreadful uncle during the last family get-together.

Be cautious about what your kid is watching and tuning in to

At the point when predators can't get to youngsters genuinely, they utilize other virtual channels to accomplish their detestable work. Guardians of twenty to thirty-year-old and other more established ages had a simpler time similarly as warding the predators off. Predators in those days moved toward kids while they strolled to class, at the play area, in shopping centers, and indifferent spots that were anything but difficult to screen. Predators of today have gotten more intelligent and will enter your home in any event, when you have bolted all entryways. Because of cell phones and the Internet, there is most likely somebody keeping an eye on your child or attempting to take care of your child's information that they are in an ideal situation without. If you should purchase a cell phone for your adolescent, ensure you give them a long, hard discussion about the perils that hide on the inward web. Screen the kind of substance that your child is watching and utilize parental controls that are offered by most video stages. Try not to permit your youngster to warm up to odd individuals on the Internet. A portion of these outsiders who contact kids on the Internet has the most exceedingly terrible of aims, incorporating being associated with youngster dealing rings.

Try not to gloss over facts

At the point when your youngster is youthful and unequipped for understanding brutal truth, you'll in all probability put forth a valiant effort to gloss over reality with the goal that you don't give them long stretches of unlimited bad dreams. For instance, you'll not tell your child that their goldfish passed on; rather, you'll lie to them that little Mr. Bean went to live in another fish tank with his best fish companions. This is an ordinary piece of child-rearing that includes needing to shield your young one from the real pitiless factors of the world. As your youngster becomes more established, be that as it may, it is essential to let them hear reality from you before they begin hearing misleading statements from others. Children are truly susceptible and will, in general, accept what grown-ups let them know. You should guarantee that your youngster's first purpose of contact is yourself. Try not to let a predator creep into your kid's life under the appearance of being their go-to individual. In the event that something terrible occurs in the network, disclose this delicately to your kid and let them realize those awful individuals who need to hurt others exist, and they live among you, and there are sure signs that she should pay special mind to.

Be the parent

Truly, you need to ensure that your kid likes you. No one needs to be detested by their child. Simultaneously, you should recognize that triumphant a ubiquity challenge isn't your main goal as a parent. Your kid is allowed to consider you a gathering pooper as long as you are centered around guarding them. In the event that something doesn't agree with you, utilize your power as a parent to address it until your gut sense affirms. Your moping young person won't be in their adolescents everlastingly, and once they are more seasoned, they will be thankful that you paid special mind to them when they required it most.

Remain on top of things

Predators are continually changing the guidelines of the game since they know the remainder of the populace is making up for the lost time. For example, a few predators have taken to setting unsafe messages in apparently innocuous children's recordings and other substances. Internet games and steady online life challenges are additionally now and again used to control, and impact youngsters do participate in rehearses that are unsafe to them. As a parent, you should guarantee that you know about the stunt and injustice being utilized to control your child and afterward stop this from the beginning before it is past the point of no return.

Imagine a scenario in which Your Child is the Problem.

No one needs to accept that their kid may be anyplace close being a maniac, sociopath, or narcissist. But, grown-ups, who score profoundly on the dim set of three, were once kids. We need to accept the best of our youngsters; however, maybe this is the disavowal that makes guardians pass up chances of helping the children find support before it is past the point of no return. Initially, note that analysts are not enamored with calling kids mental cases in any event when these youngsters display practices that are stressing and anomalous.

This is just in light of the fact that the term itself conveys an excess of disgrace and conclusiveness. When is a kid known as a mental case at age six, who isn't to state that they won't seek to develop to satisfy the name? Additionally, kids are only that-- they might be inconvenient as children and afterward ended up being something very surprising when they are more seasoned. Rather than reserved character issue, accordingly, kids are frequently determined to have direct turmoil. All together for this determination to be given, a child must meet certain standards that have been settled upon and carry on in a way to show these models for at any rate a half year. This means a youngster who carries on forcefully on a couple of occasions isn't actually a contender for the lead issue. Probably, they are simply having a terrible day. Things being what they are, who meets all requirements for the direct issue range?

A youngster that has a high possibility of turning into a mental case in their later life shows the accompanying attributes:

- They incredibly need sympathy. This is the kind of youngster who won't recoil when their companion gets injured on the play area. Truth be told, you may even find them giggling at the torment of others.
- They need regret and blame. A kid who doesn't have regret or blame will foul up and not want to apologize for it. They may hit their younger sibling or throw the family pet against the divider and grin about it. When requested to apologize, they will be difficult and may even totally decline to coordinate.
- They are apathetic regarding discipline. Most youngsters get exceptionally sensational when rebuffed. They wail their little hearts out and even attempt to cause you to feel terrible about rebuffing them. Not so for kids with the lead issues. As a general rule, such kids won't like the discipline. They won't be moved the slightest bit and will guarantee that you realize they are not moved. This is just in light of the fact that they don't encounter torment and feel like every other person.

Ultimately, grown-ups who proceeded to turn out to be all out sociopaths displayed indications of hostility and pitilessness in their adolescence. Since a kid is a little person who doesn't have a lot of solidarity to take on greater casualties, youngsters will regularly target defenseless creatures to take out their animosity and cold-bloodedness. If one day your youngster awakens and kills the family feline, you ought to be concerned.

What do you do when you are confronted with a kid who shows every one of these signs? The principal thing you have to do is comprehend that only one out of every odd insane person is set out toward fate and decimation. As referenced before in this book, a few insane people proceed to turn out to be extremely fruitful in their fields as a result of their hazard taking, laser-sharp core interest. A kid that is apparently dangerous and eager can be formed to become something extraordinary in their life. Rather than stressing that your youngster will turn into a sequential executioner, consider how you can transform them into the following scene acclaimed CEO. Something to be thankful for about children is that they are anything but difficult to divert. Keep your youngster occupied, and they won't have the opportunity to consider all the unfeeling things they could be doing with their rush looking for selves.

Contingent upon the idea of the turmoil that is available in the kid, there may be a requirement for proficient mediation. Experts who work with kids that display psychopathic practices don't attempt to transform them since they realize that it is all in the cerebrum, and there's very little that you can do. Rather than changing the children, the experts rather pick to work with what is left of the 'great mind' to push the children towards great conduct. For example, despite the fact that an insane person's cerebrum probably won't be fit for compassion and feeling, they are as yet ready to perceive reward and the energy of getting that reward. What clinicians do in this manner is to prepare the child to do great in return for a prize. Maniacs love winning, and the equivalent is valid for kids who show psychopathic inclinations. This prize methodology is likewise utilized in penitentiaries where the number of inhabitants in mental cases will, in general, be higher.

In the event that you have a kid who is giving indications of being an issue youngster to the extent the recorded signs go, you should be extremely cautious about how you get out of the issue. The messages that kids catch wind of themselves are what they grow up to accept. If a youngster grows up being called moronic, they will experience they're dumb as well as could be expected. A youngster, paying little heed to their psychopathic attitude, will develop into something incredible If they hear fortifying messages about themselves. Sustain may not generally prevail upon nature unfailingly. However, it is consistently worth a shot. It may be considering something enabling the state to a youngster who slaughters little creatures, yet naming them as an incredible will just give them something to yearn for.

CHAPTER 17 THE WAY WE THINK AND MIND CONTROL

Another concentration in the field of dim brain research is mind control. This can be a piece of both control and influence as the two strategies reach within your psyche and attempt to get you to accomplish something, think something, or tail another person's way for you. For some individuals, mind control can mean various things, for example, control, influence, impact, and indoctrinating. For the reasons for this book, we will see mind control as an approach to change an individual's contemplations, convictions, and to control their activities. One of the most well-known analysts of the 1970s, Philip Zimbardo, expressed that brain control "is a procedure by which individual or aggregate opportunity of decision and activity is undermined by specialists or organizations that change or contort recognition, inspiration, influence, perception or potentially social results" ("Mind control clarified - the perils and how to secure yourself," n.d.).

Numerous individuals accept that brain control is one of the most all-around shrouded types of impact in light of the fact that the vast majority are not even mindful; it is occurring. It is additionally a moderate procedure, which makes it harder for individuals to take note. Individuals who are under psyche control will feel that they are settling on their choice, yet these choices are really being made by another person. You additionally should know that the time allotment it takes to control somebody's brain relies upon the strategies that are utilized, their character, individual elements, and social elements. Now and then, mind control can happen in light of physical power.

Like control and influence, mind control is utilized in our regular day to day existence. We, for the most part, are unconscious that the strategies publicizing organizations use are a type of brain control. In any case, when they can get us to accept that their item is the best, this is actually what they are doing. This doesn't imply that you have to know about what the promotion organizations are doing consistently; however, it may assist you with setting aside cash. The psyche control you should know about is the sort that is dim in nature. The sort that follows individuals like Adolph Hitler or Charles Manson. You should know about psyche control when it can hurt you in a negative manner. Obviously, focusing on promotions is an incredible method to rehearse how to monitor yourself against mind control and to get what kind of procedures are being utilized.

Ways You Can Control People or Be Controlled

Individuals who need to control their brain can utilize any of the accompanying methods or systems that fall under control or influence. One of the most significant variables to recollect is individuals who control others are incredible at understanding individuals. They can ordinarily determine what sort of individual they are managing before long. This encourages them to recognize what sort of system they can utilize and which one they can't. This additionally encourages them to comprehend what kind of individual you are. They have to know whether you have a ton of enthusiastic and mental quality, as this can make their activity harder. They additionally need to know whether you have high confidence or are effectively impacted.

Conduct Molding and Conditioning

Conduct molding, otherwise called alteration, is the way to get individuals to do what you need. You do this through a progression of remunerations and disciplines. It is regularly utilized in child-rearing classes and brain research courses in school. Before I go any farther, you have to comprehend that conduct adjustment is the demonstration of changing somebody's conduct. At the point when the individual reliably follows the conduct they were instructed, it is known as social molding. Social alteration will consistently precede conduct molding.

Individuals who need to assume responsibility for your psyche exceed expectations at conduct change. This is on the grounds that they have to change your conduct so as to condition you, which is the point at which they completely have control. The conduct mind controllers will decide to change, and the condition initially will be little. They will, at that point, keep on searching for little qualities; however, step by step increment the practices. They have to ensure that opposition towards the changing practices is negligible, else they will wind up battling with molding. You may likewise get on to their brain control inclinations and do what you can to end it.

The stunt for any psyche controller is they have to understand that social alteration just attempts to change the conduct. It doesn't work to change to the thought process. Subsequently, they ordinarily need to utilize methods so as to progress in the direction of changing an individual's rationale in the conduct. If your thought processes don't change, at that point, you are bound to remove a portion of the conduct once more, regardless of whether they conditioned you not to.

Conviction Change Processes

Perhaps the greatest key to altering somebody's perspective is you have to concentrate on changing their conviction forms. This implies you not just change their conviction; you change the thinking behind it. What caused them to accept that weapon control was significant? You have to take a gander at the means their brain took when they chose to settle on that choice.

Probably the greatest subject that mind controllers are acceptable at is brain research. A brain controller will consider the manner in which their objective thinks so that they can deal with their points of view. This causes them to open an entryway into controlling their objective's brain. Obviously, this makes specialists probably the best model with regards to mind control. In any case, advisors are attempting to enable their customers to change practices so that they can better their lives. Psyche controllers need to change their objective's practices so that they can acquire control and control over the individual.

This is a case of how brain control can be utilized decidedly and adversely. You can change an individual's convictions by giving them different models or pictures. This is frequently how advisors work to transform somebody's conviction process. For example, if you believe you can't return to school to get your degree since you are excessively old, you will be approached to envision your conviction. Put you in your too old state. At that point, you will be approached to envision a positive result in the event that you do choose to return to school. Do you see yourself landing the position you had always wanted? Do you see yourself making the Dean's rundown? There is a lot of inquiries you could be posed so as to envision the positives.

You will, at that point, center around something that isn't correct any longer. You may feel that your past too old state is what isn't correct. Since you have envisioned yourself in your fantasy work, you are beginning to accept that you can achieve returning to school, regardless of what your age is. This is the conviction that they can learn at any age. Next, you will need to compose the pictures. You will put the I am too old picture into the classification, which is not, at this point, valid. You will, at that point, put your picture of you prevailing in school and your vocation into you can learn at any age class.

Undercover Belief Changes

You don't have to utilize pictures so as to get somebody to change their convictions. Most brain controllers, who are attempting to control you so they can pick up the high ground, won't center around pictures. This is on the grounds that you will get on too effectively, particularly from the outset. This doesn't mean they will never place certain pictures in your mind. It just implies that they will, in general, spotlight more on clandestine conviction changes.

Psyche controllers should ensure that they have your trust, regard, and an association with them. Without these variables, they won't have the option to effective change your convictions. They are additionally talented at tying down. This is on the grounds that they understand that feelings are regularly a solid guide for individuals, particularly when they don't have a clue how to control their feelings. For individuals who can keep up their feelings well, mind controllers will battle to get effective through this technique.

The initial step for the psyche controller is to draw in you in a discussion that will lead you to the conduct they need to change. At the point when they do this, they will attempt to be inconspicuous in their endeavors. They won't act like they need to change your conduct straightforwardly. Nonetheless, they could make reference to how it affected them as this will evoke an enthusiastic reaction from you.

When you give them a feeling, they will pull out the mooring method. Whatever conduct they need you to transform, they will quietly give you what you ought to do. While this probably won't work quickly, you will begin to change your conduct. Each time you do what your life partner feels isn't right, you will recall how you felt when you were talking. After some time, you will quit partaking in this conduct increasingly more since it gives you a negative inclination.

Rewards and Consequences

It is now and then difficult for grown-ups to get a handle on the possibility that they get prizes and ramifications for their activities, however, they do. Actually, this happens a few times each day, yet we once in a while pay heed to it. For instance, if you complete an undertaking, your manager will compliment you. In the event that you can't finish the assignment by the cutoff time and need to request an expansion, you will hear the failure in their voice. This will make a negative outcome, which will make you increasingly mindful of time on the board. In this manner, you will be bound to make cutoff times later on.

Brain controllers will likewise follow the prizes and result framework. Now and then, they are not as unobtrusive when they do this since they need you to get enthusiastic. For instance, if you go out with your companions when your loved one disclosed to you they didn't generally need you to, they will give you the quiet treatment for two or three days. This will cause you to understand that they are baffled in you, which will make you disillusioned in yourself. While you probably won't comprehend why they are doing this as you just went out with a few companions, your feelings will manage you more than your considerations. Whenever your better half discloses to you, they would prefer you to remain at home than go out; you are bound to consider remaining at home. Obviously, this doesn't mean you will.

Psyche controllers will regularly utilize rewards when you participate in the conduct that they need. For instance, if you do remain at home as opposed to going out, they may make it worth your time and energy. They may choose to get you supper and a film. They may likewise venture into your feelings by disclosing to you how cheerful they are that you picked them over your companions. They may state something like, "You cause me to feel so cherished." This prize will stick in your psyche, particularly the remark made by your loved one, as you need them to feel adored and thought about, not relinquished.

The I to You Shift

This is something that is basic in the normal discussion, which implies it very well may be difficult to spot. Nonetheless, individuals who are attempting to control their brain will regularly move their story onto you. This implies as opposed to stating "I" they will say "you."

There are a few explanations behind this. One reason is on the grounds that it gives both of you a feeling of association. This is something that scholars frequently use to interface with their crowd in a positive way. In any case, with regards to mind control, this is utilized in a progressively negative way. Psyche controllers who need to work on your self-assurance will utilize "you" when they are examining a negative story, one which can place you in an awful light. Despite the fact that you realize you didn't do this, and you are not very of the story, it goes into your psyche mind and can cause you to accept that you accomplished something comparable in your life. Subsequently, what you are emotions toward the individual in the story is really what you are feeling toward yourself.

Following

Psyche controllers and controllers regularly discover their objectives through perception. They regularly have a sort; for example, individuals do when they are searching for a noteworthy other. Their sort maybe somebody who is sitting unobtrusively in a corner or somebody who is attempting to shroud their body since they are hesitant. When they discover their objective, they will invest more energy watching them as it gives them leads on what systems and procedures to utilize.

While a great many people would look at this as a type of following, it is all piece of their impulse. Actually, it does by and large fall under the class of following. This is on the grounds that numerous individuals are known to discover where the individual lives and add any information they can about the individual's life. They will likewise not be bashful that they know these things about you. For instance, they may appear close to home since they are experiencing vehicle difficulty, and their telephone is dead. They may likewise send you rose to your home or business locale. They may begin to get some information about how your children are getting along or in the event that you make the most of your activity.

While a great many people begin to discover this concerning, they will, in general, answer the inquiries since they are found napping. This implies they may address the inquiries without truly considering it, or they may come to accept that the individual cares about them since they are making a special effort to become more acquainted with them. While there are a few romantic tales that begin this way, there are likewise a few terrible connections that begin along these lines.

The main concern is, you generally need to be cautious about what addresses your answer and what information you give out. If you begin to feel that you are being followed, told somebody. You can tell your loved ones alongside the police. You generally need to do what you can to secure yourself since wellbeing is number one.

They Will Think for You

Individuals who need to control you intellectually will have no difficult beginning to think for you. Their stunt is regularly; they will initially begin to settle on a choice for you where it truly doesn't make a difference. You may be examining something and let them know, "I don't know what I think. Let me consider it." This is an open way for somebody who needs to control your brain. This discloses to them that you need assistance settling on a choice. Subsequently, in the event that they step in to settle on the choice for you unobtrusively, it won't trouble you.

They will, for the most part, reveal to you something like, "I realize you are worried about everything else, so why not let me settle on the choice, and we will discuss it." Then, to appear as though they set aside an effort to settle on the choice, they will come to you somewhat later with their answer. Obviously, they will act like you have a decision or act as they care about your opinion of their choice. Be that as it may, you truly don't have a decision. They are simply attempting to get you to believe that they can settle on choices for you.

They will, at that point, begin settling on more choices for you, without your authorization. Be that as it may, you won't give a lot of consideration to these choices since they truly aren't excessively significant. At that point, they will quit getting some information about anything. This is regularly when they begin to restrict your choices, notwithstanding, you, despite everything, probably won't notice quickly in light of the fact that you have begun to get used to them thinking for you.

They won't start with exceptional choices, for example, what you are going to wear or what you will eat. They will begin by giving you decisions or accomplishing something decent for you, so you didn't need to think to do it. For instance, they may choose to pick the cafés you eat at, however, every so often, they will pick your top pick. They may choose to begin taking care of the garments for you. This is the point at which a portion of your garments may disappear, or you begin taking care of garments their direction.

Inserted Commands

Inserted orders are messages that are sent to our inner mind. We don't frequently understand this is going on, despite the fact that we hear the orders. This is on the grounds that they regularly occur in unobtrusive manners. They can likewise happen through a customary discussion you are having with your life partner. One of the key stunts of inserted orders is the manner of speaking you use. Individuals will inform a great deal concerning how you feel through your manner of speaking. They will have the option to know whether you are furious, being wry, or in the event that you are tragic. This feeling will be inserted with the message and will tell the individual how something affects you. If something drives you crazy, they will recollect this and be less inclined to make some portion of the move.

You can likewise utilize installed orders through-composed words. At the point when you underscore states through italics, intense, or by utilizing every single capital letter, you make an impression on the individual that what they are perusing is significant. For instance, if you need your kids to ensure they do their errands, you may make a note that says, "You need to stack the dishwasher and flush out the sink before you begin playing on your Xbox."

Meta Programs

Meta writing computer programs are the means by which individuals take in the information they are given. Because you state something a specific way, doesn't mean the individual will see the message a similar way. Individuals frequently rate information they are given by significance. Accordingly, if you give your youngsters an extensive rundown of errands, they will take a gander at the rundown and choose what should be done first. They may likewise rate the rundown through what they appreciate accomplishing more to what they don't care to do.

There are a few meta programs that individuals use in their psyche mind.

1. Towards the Meta Program

Individuals who utilize the meta program are persuaded to get an undertaking finished. For instance, if you give them a rundown of errands, they will need to finish each task on the rundown. They will have an explanation behind getting resolved to finish the errand. This could be anything from they need to play on their Xbox to regarding their folks by tuning in to them. Obviously, grown-ups will work similarly. At the point when individuals are in a sentimental relationship, they will need to demonstrate their regard to their life partner by doing what satisfies them. This consistently gives a brain controller a stage up, particularly when their life partner is an individual loaded earnestly.

2. Away from the Meta Program

Away from is the inverse of towards. At the point when individuals utilize the away from, they don't have the inspiration to finish the assignment. Consider them moving endlessly from what they have been advised to do. At the point when a brain controller is hoping to check whether they should utilize the away from or towards strategy, they will frequently ask the individual what is critical to them. This will offer them an immediate response to the method without watching the individual. It is anything but difficult to tell when somebody has a ton of inspiration, and when somebody is inadequate with regards to drive.

3. Methods Meta Program

Individuals who follow the methods meta program as of now have the inspiration they need. They likewise have a set method of doing errands. A case of somebody who utilizes the methods meta program would be a stickler. They need things to be done a specific way since this permits them to realize that they were done impeccably. This sort of program can be intense for a brain controller to dominate, just on the grounds that individuals are increasingly wary about what they are doing. Since they need to complete something a specific way, they don't regularly prefer to offer control to another person.

4. Alternatives Meta Program

Individuals who follow the alternatives meta program are inventive. They like to develop thoughts, and they are continually ready to take a stab at something new.

This frequently leaves them open for somebody who is a brain controller. Since they need to hear another person's thoughts, they will tune in to the controller. At the point when the controller utilizes types of influence and control, they will like the thought the controller brings more.

They Believe They Are Doing You a Favor

Individuals who are settling on choices for you and attempting to control your psyche will accept, and cause you to accept that they are helping you out. This is simple toward the start since they do regularly discover ways that help you. For instance, they will attempt to restrain the measure of pressure or choices; you have to make during the day. While you feel they are useful, you may likewise begin to scrutinize their fundamental thought process when they begin to settle on more choices for you. Notwithstanding, they will continue disclosing to you that they are helping you out. They will likewise begin scowling or turning out to be aggravated when you don't accept that they are attempting to support you.

Enthusiastic and Mental Discomfort

Individuals who need to control somebody's psyche will intellectually and sincerely cause them a torment or distress so as to take control and stay in charge. For instance, when police examine somebody for wrongdoing, they will regularly cause them distress intellectually and inwardly. They are attempting to get the individual to concede what occurred and any bad behavior.

Psyche controllers can utilize any sort of enthusiastic or mental inconvenience they see fit. They will regularly pick something deliberately on the grounds that they need to ensure that it will give them the advantage. Some may attempt to back you in a corner while others will utilize your past to cause you to feel awful or useless. The fact of the matter is to cause you to torment, however, not genuinely.

Some will utilize this as a type of control. This implies when they begin to see that you are feeling the manner in which they need, they will attempt to cause you to feel better. In your psyche, this will give you an association with the individual. You will begin to confide in them more, give them more information about yourself, and accept that they are attempting to support you. Sadly, any information you give a brain controller is something that they can use against you.

Social Pressure

Social weight is all over the place, which implies it is simple for a psyche controller to utilize it. They will do this deliberately, as they will do with some other procedure. You have to recollect that one of the most significant elements of a procedure is the system that the controller employments. If they don't have a decent procedure, or simply utilize a method with technique, they won't have the option to assume responsibility for somebody's psyche without any problem.

Many psyche controllers will play up their game with regards to social weight. The primary purpose behind this is most grown-ups are past the mindset that they need to follow social weight, or they will lose their companions. In any case, controllers additionally understand that the more individuals who pressure any individual, the almost certain they are to surrender to the weight. Along these lines, numerous controllers will utilize the procedure of a horde so as to get into your psyche.

Probably the best case of a social horde are social fights. These gatherings are a lot of individuals who need something very similar. It doesn't make a difference what a number of individuals are in the gathering, what makes a difference is the means by which incredible the gathering is. It is not necessarily the case that individuals who are fighting in bunches are awful; a considerable lot of them are improving the lives of others. Notwithstanding, consider how you are all the more effortlessly impacted when there are many individuals disclosing to you something very similar.

Because something is commonly utilized for good, it doesn't imply that you can't utilize it in a negative manner. Individuals who control your psyche get this. They additionally comprehend the intensity of social impact. They couldn't care less in the event that they are taking something that is regularly useful for society and utilizing it in a negative manner. They will probably control your brain, however much as could reasonably be expected, particularly If they are a narcissist, mental case, and controller.

So as to utilize social horde control, they will accumulate an assortment of individuals who need to pressure you. This is regularly what happens when individuals are in religions. The individuals comprehend there are sure advances that should be taken so as to make the crowd control work.

1. They have a reasonable result. They are ordinarily not recounted this result excessively far ahead of time. Be that as it may, when they are educated, they consent to the arrangement.
2. Ensure everybody is accumulated in one spot and comprehends there is a mutual encounter. If individuals from the crowd don't totally concur, this circumstance could undoubtedly reverse discharge.
3. Ensure the gathering gets enthusiastic. A great many people use outrage to increase a reaction from the gathering and make a feeling of solidarity. In any case, any forceful feeling will work.
4. Ensure they all consent to the arrangement, again. In the event that you discover individuals who don't know about it, disconnect them from the remainder of the gathering.
5. Keep on raising the horde as this is a definitive advance in increasing more individuals.

Self-Defense Against Mind Control

Since mind control happens gradually, you are likely to face control for a time before you start realizing and attempting to escape from this environment. It can take you time to escape, depending on how strong the influence over you is. For instance, if your significant other has people checking you in during the day, you'll be trying to find an escape. Before you escape, you must get to the right mindset too. You have to want to escape and want a better life for yourself in order to take the escape through and stay away.

This means you might need to use various tactics of self-defense to protect yourself against more control of your mind. Such strategies are, of course, perfect for people who are concerned about mind control and the need for self-defense. The best advice is to be cautious when trying to escape someone who is in control of you. Most people will do whatever they can to make sure you don't escape their hold. You may potentially have a war on your side, which can quickly become both violent and legal. Also, you'll want to be cautious about what sort of technique you're using to fight off mind control. You certainly won't try to get your significant other to catch on to the fact that you're working on an escape plan to realize how they've handled you.

- **Always remain in close contact with family and friends**

You are really aware of those people who really care for you. You'll want to make sure you do whatever you can to stay in close contact with them. Although you might not always like hearing what they're telling you about your significant other, you need to note that they want the best for you, rather than the one who dominates you. Your closest friends and family should never be afraid to warn you if they think that someone is potentially damaging you, spiritually, psychologically, or physically.

They 're not good for you if you start to realize that your significant other is trying to separate you from the ones you love and who love you. You need to stand firm when telling the person you 're refusing to let them push you away from your family and friends. When they don't go back down or pursue other methods of mind control, you have to walk out of the connection.

Be mindful that if you walk away, then the person will try to come back for you. Individuals who use mind control don't easily give up on their significant others, particularly if they've been training you to follow their instructions for a long time. Each time they contact you, you'll need to stand firm. Do what you can to avoid meeting them by yourself anywhere and always keep your safety in mind.

- **Refusing to recognize the Sulky behavior**

Another way to protect yourself against mind control is to continue to submit to sulky behavior. If you tell your significant other that this conduct is beyond you and them, stand firm. Let them know it's immature and childish, and you're not going to let them deal around you this way.

- **See how many rules you are forced to follow**

While you should take advice from your close family and friends on the rules that your significant other sets down for you if it feels wrong, it is probably wrong. Nobody will tell you exactly what clothes you should or shouldn't wear, not even your significant other. They shouldn't tell you when you can or won't be able to use the bathroom, what job you can have, or even work at all. Above all, you should not take away any sort of identification from your significant others. If that's what they're trying to do with the rules, you need to get out of the relationship because it's only going to be detrimental to you.

- **Note when someone looks at you**

One of the first signs you 're a mind controller candidate is that they can mimic your behavior. It's important to note we 're just different individuals. And when someone wants to behave the same way that you are, they have a motive. If you're unsure they will truly mirror you, try them out. You can do this with a few hand motions, or by jumping on your feet back and forth. They 're not going to think you've caught on to the mirroring, so they're going to keep acting the way you do. When you note that they are making almost every step the same way, you 're going to want to get back away from them. You can do so by saying that you will go there or come up with another reason.

You should also note that if a person has more ability with mind control, they 're not going to copy every moment you make as they know it's too noticeable. They may also realize you 're moving more than normal and start going back as they feel you 're catching their way. You want to try and be as skilled as they are, therefore. And not a lot of moves at once. Wave your hands a certain way while you say a certain word or phrase if you sing. If you notice that they were doing this when they weren't before, then you're probably reflecting.

- **Adjust your eye movement patterns**

As people perceive new knowledge, a certain way, their eyes move. People who engage in control of mind, particularly the professional ones, know this so they will pay careful attention to your eyes. They usually can do that quickly, of course, because most people believe they are interested in what they say when someone is staring directly into their eyes. While mind controllers note your words and phrases because this helps them understand your mind a little better, they are more interested in the movement of your pupils. When they understand what your eyes are saying about the knowledge that you are storing in your head, they will be able to understand your mind better.

Although it's still hard to tell at first, you'll want to turn your eyes differently if you start seeing someone paying close attention to your eyes, and they have other signs of a mind controller. At first, this may be hard for you because we typically do not know how our eyes shift as we process information. The best advice you can give is just to switch your eyes around. Look right, look up to the left, and even look down. Sometimes, move your head while you move your eyes. This will make it more difficult for them to learn what happens inside your brain.

- **Don't let somebody touch you**

Some people are not going to have a problem with this one, as they do not like being touched. Others will feel the human touch, as they don't mind, even if it's from someone they really don't know. However, it's also better for general protection that you don't let anyone contact you unless you meet them. There are, of course, exceptions to this law, such as shaking hands with someone you just met or giving someone a hug at a funeral to console them during their loss period.

What you need to be vigilant of is when you are talking to others, and your feelings are elevated. You're in a conversation, for example, and you start to feel angry about a social issue that you're passionate about. As you get deep into the discussion, and your frustration grows, the person taps you gently on the shoulder. While they can use the excuse that it was a way to try and get you to relax or feel better, when they feel angry, people typically don't touch someone. This is a sign they can anchor the emotion to the touch.

- **Always Pay Attention to Language and Tone of Voice**

Mind regulators, along with manipulators and manipulative men, can use such words and sounds as they attempt to convey messages to you. You'll want to pay attention to this as they'll let you see how their minds work, just as they're trying to see how your mind is working.

If you realize that someone is being ambiguous about what they're doing, they may try to get you into a trance, allowing them to take control of your mind. This trick works because it is difficult for you to respond or form an argument when the message is ambiguous, which leaves you open to a mind controller.

They'll give you permission to do stuff too. Although this seems to be contradictory to what a mind controller desires, it is something they want you to do. For instance, if they want you to watch a movie, they may say, "Watch this movie if you want" or "You have to watch this movie over and over again." Both statements give you permission and allow them to be in charge because you are more than likely to watch the film.

While you'll want to watch the words and phrases they're using, you'll also want to hear their tone. Many individuals, even mind controllers, are not always aware of the tone of voice that they communicate. Therefore, if you notice they speak slyly or think carefully about their words, they may be distracted by your actions, eye movements, and how you speak. If the sound does not make you feel confident, you should generally do what you can to keep them at a distance.

- **Holding people a distance**

This is a tactic that some people find simpler, as it will rely on the type of personality you have. For instance, if you're an introvert, you'll feel you need to keep people closer to you because you enjoy people's company. If you are an introvert, though, you'd rather naturally keep people at a distance. It is important to note that many mind controllers are gravitating toward extroverts because they are more outgoing, and this gives them the upper hand in learning the personality of their target. Some, however, like to gravitate towards introverts because they think introverts have less self-esteem. That is not exactly the case. Just because someone would like to spend more time alone does not mean that their confidence is lower than someone who likes to be around people.

No matter what type of personality you are, however, you should always be aware of the people that you meet. This is only normal precautions for protection because you don't want to put yourself or someone else in the way of harm. So, keeping people that you don't really know at a distance is always smart. When you've just met someone at the club, for example, they don't need to know how many kids you have, whether you're in school, what you're doing, or what your hobbies are. Mind controllers are going to try to get you to open up quickly as that makes their process go a bit faster. If you believe the questions violate your privacy or do not ask, you don't have to answer their questions. You can either push the conversation to another topic or decline to reply.

- **Trust Your Intuition**

Everyone has intuition. The problem is we're not always listening to what our intuition tells us. For instance, if you're talking to someone you've just met and you get the feeling of being awkward or that something's gone, you just can't put your finger on it, something's wrong. Your intuition tries to warn you this person isn't your friend, they want something you shouldn't give them to. The problem with our society is that we often feel that this is overdramatic or that it doesn't give anybody a chance. The reality is, our intuition is a powerful force that works deep inside us to help us make the right choice. No, 100 percent of the time, it won't always be right. But being safe is better than being sorry too.

CONCLUSION

Now that you can recognize who the manipulators may be in your life (or whether you've been guilty of using these techniques as well), identify signs of being manipulated and learn how to handle them, you can better evaluate the relationships around you to make the educated choices you need in your own life. Through a more realistic view of life, without feeling guilty, you may share your thoughts, opinions, and wishes, realizing that they are indeed your own.

You can detect and understand the signals of persuasion and manipulation by evaluating and examining the contact signs in your relationships. When that is evident, you will exercise your right to be treated with dignity. In a contact exchange, you regain the power and right to be equal individuals to yourself. In a relationship with an equal balance of control, you CAN say 'no' without feeling guilty and CAN set your goals to build a better life or world for yourself and others you care for.

The ability to interpret the body language of people and see beyond misleading phrases stops you from being extorted or abused unknowingly. You are more open to opportunities around you, and less likely to be affected by others' purpose and motivated by it. But being able to identify those tactics means that you too can manipulate these tricks. Be sure to consult with your moral compass and be always mindful of treating each person as an equal citizen, worthy of the right to be treated and free to choose.

The principle of Dark Psychology assumes possibly you're ignorant of previous devious actions or just do not care. Here's an opportunity to change the trajectory of yours and start anew. Whatever predatory actions you've engaged in, criminal and sociopathic, there's usually a decision to cease, desist, and part from the abyss of getting sociopathic.

The capability of the head might be said to be very vast, and this might be said that the individuals that see how the mind of theirs functions might tend to get much more out of life. Additionally, learning how you can take control of the mind of yours might enable you to be in charge of the points that occur in daily life. Thus, rather than allowing life to come about for you, you can decide what goes on in the life of yours. The survivalist mentality is the norm of ours, and this what society tries to do is manage the wild beast in every man by teaching them out of an early age to obey the laws, morals, and rules of the controlling team, typically the rich, who dominate our institutions and governments.

Thus, must we condemn the ones that think society isn't providing them a good offer - which they need to take whatever they have to endure an often hostile atmosphere in which privilege relies on the school of yours, wealth, or loved ones? Dark Psychology Secret itself needs to come out of the closet and acknowledge that the typical human action is opposing rules and societies strict.

The individuals resent society, but since they're powerless against people who control law-making and morality, they think specific helplessness in looking to live amongst the sheep. Could it be any wonder then sometimes a private person takes it and create their own hands to change society or maybe the environment of theirs to live a freer self-controlled existence from the rigors of communities which as we've seen all eventually breakdown and reinvent themselves as the powerful and wealthy newly retake control?

All empires can't see the demise of theirs! Exactly how will Dark Psychology Secret then contend with this particular question of human behavior like a simple survivalist mechanism, which humans are obviously brutal, harsh, and dominating of others that are weaker than themselves?

Psychiatry in mental hospitals is frequently viewed as the elements of societal control - in case you don't go along with society as well as the rules of it is you then should be insane - for that reason, you need to be dedicated as well as managed for the security as well as the advantage of all.

Dark Psychology, on the additional hand, is actually viewed as the liberating part of psychological health - the place we help those out of synch with the society of finding the place of theirs and fit back into what's regarded behavior that is ordinary for that team.

Anywhere will the solution be for individuals who rebel against the society they live in and would like another method of presence without the interference of the effective as well as the independence to live a life they select as suiting themselves. Or perhaps do we wait - for the films to come true the disaster that awaits a return, as well as all humans to a dog, called survivalism - the genuine cultural majority!

Around this junction, it's some time to determine from these observations which societal norms, laws, and morals are, in fact, "not normal" for man, and this society typically forces group conduct depending on what the highly effective want with the powerless.

Book 2: Manipulation

INTRODUCTION

Have you ever gone into a confident conversation and then walk out feeling confused? Have you ever come out of a discussion and decided to do something for someone, but couldn't find out why you first decided? Odds are, you exploited. If you were playing with your feelings or using convincing words, you were brought to believe in or act on something you originally were not wholly comfortable with. Before you started the conversation, you could be totally convinced and so sure of yourself, but midway, you found yourself losing words, confused, frazzled, and disoriented.

Manipulation may feel like you are being controlled, and leave your own abilities in question. Being continually manipulated will leave you angry, demoralized, despondent and wonder how you have not seen this coming. Nonetheless, might you have stopped it, if you knew how to identify the indications that mean that someone may not be good? Manipulators exercise their power by taking advantage of your feelings and distorting your mental experiences to manipulate and achieve advantages. They are preying on your vulnerabilities and taking advantage of you by communication tactics designed to confuse you so that before it's too late, you don't see what they are. Identifying whether you are being manipulated to protect yourself from being abused is critical, and promoting a healthy balance of power in relationships. And it begins with learning how to evaluate people.

Another way of knowing whether you're being fooled is by body language. The sturdy, non-speakable, and subtle signs that speak volumes when you know what to look for. Through identifying the transmitted movements, postures, and facial expressions, one can recognize and understand the full meaning of what someone is trying to say -or not trying to say. Understanding how to evaluate someone will provide some exciting discoveries, and more importantly, open your eyes to the signs that you might be taking advantage of so that you can take action to avoid or entirely stop the advances. Thank you for picking out our work. Know that we know there are plenty of reading materials for the same subject, so we're trying to get you the best details you can use each day.

CHAPTER 1 THE MANIPULATION ETHICS - COULD MANIPULATION BE GOOD AND BAD?

At the mention of the word 'manipulation,' negative connotations associated with this term is what immediately springs to mind. Manipulation means taking advantage of someone else by unscrupulous and underhanded tactics. Manipulation means theft and lying outright. Manipulation is unethical. Through the years, the word has definitely had a poor reputation, and even the phrases used to characterize deception in play depict an image that is quite nasty or negative. "She's got him absolutely wrapped around her little finger," "I told my boss exactly what he wanted to hear," "He's got a reputation for being a heartbreaker," "I spoke to my buddy about doing what I wanted." These traditional manipulative scenarios definitely don't make a positive difference to the situation for the parties involved in the transaction. It makes the manipulator become someone who is greedy, self-serving, deceitful, and unconcerned about manipulating someone else for their own gain, and it makes the one being manipulated seem stupid, ignorant, and maybe even weak in character to "allow" himself to be so easily fooled.

Manipulation has always been seen as a cruel, smart, yet cunning act and always where one person ends up being manipulated or manipulated. Manipulation is seen even more negatively when it is clear that the conniving person has a heartless presence disregarded the other's feelings, placing their own selfish needs above all others. Even worse than the manipulator, he exploited the other by pretending to be his friend and then using trustfully shared information against them. There is one fact that remains in our personal or professional lives. No-one wants to learn that they were abused. Nobody. For such uncertainty associated with this hard, it is almost painful to imagine that a possibility might be used to exploit a positive, or even that it could bring about change for the better. Manipulation isn't all evil; however, shocking it might sound. There is manipulation all around us, and often you don't have to look very far to find evidence of it. Take, for example, marketers and advertisers, with their constant messages telling us to buy this, buy it, stop doing it, and stop doing it. They all try to influence our decisions one way or the other. However, what kinds of manipulation are really trying to make us change for the better?

Ads that advise us to stop smoking and eat better are trying to exploit our choices, but they're trying to do so in this case to promote positive change. Quitting smoking is in your own best interests. And it feeds well. Would this not make it a constructive way of manipulation, if it is for your own good? Governments around the world are exploiting people around them. Religion does, likewise. Yet, sometimes we choose to ignore it because it comes, so to speak, from a more "authoritative" source. Businesses are actively exploiting their customers by producing goods to raise their sales figures and then telling consumers, "without them, they can not survive."

Whether it's utilized for "good" or "bad," manipulation is still manipulation, at the end of the day. Does any of us really have any right to dictate the decisions or actions of another, even if we believe this is to their advantage? What makes the thought of manipulation so upsetting is maybe the fact that we don't like the thought of anyone else trying to decide what we can do, or forcing us to do anything we wouldn't be inclined to do ourselves otherwise. Working managers try to manipulate their staff all the time, even if the good leaders do it to try and keep their staff motivated or performing at their best. Active managers have mastered the art of motivational reinforcement skillfully and have turned it into an important method used to influence the success of their workers, driving them to achieve their objectives. That distinctive detail is the defining difference between what is classified as manipulation and what is called Persuasion. Persuasion is a form of manipulation, but what distinguishes it from the negative image of manipulation lies in three things:

• Aim.

• Honesty.

• Which gain or positive effect the person you 're trying to convince would have.

Manipulation vs. Personalization

These three key points are being made to be the decisive factor as to whether you are trying to manipulate or convince. When it comes to your manipulation, you are selfish intention. Usually, when you persuade, it is well-meaning for the other person's good. When you manipulate, you lie, you deceive, and you try to hide what is really happening. When you convince, you should be frank and upfront with what you're trying to do, and if it's not done for personal gain, you have no excuse to hide it. When you exploit, the other person, just yourself, is not having a positive effect or profit. The other party you are trying to influence when you persuade is the one that reaps the most benefit from the situation. All the time, non-profit organizations resort to Persuasion, trying to get others to act and change for the better in order to have a positive impact on the world. They are persuading donors, raising the necessary funding, and trying to raise awareness among others about important issues that need to be addressed or changed.

Evidence And Manipulation Of These Laws In Our Routine

Manipulators are the puppet masters who sit behind the scenes pulling strings, playing so subtle mind games, and convincing you to do their dirty work for them. If you are in a problem and you don't know how it happened, the manipulator might have had something to do with that. In a work environment, the evidence of manipulation is more evident as this is where you spend much of your time, Monday through Friday, coming into contact with all kinds of people. A few signs you could have a manipulator in your middle to watch out for that signal include any of the following:

- Too much flattery seems insincere to the point.
- Down with artificial appeal.
- Misgivings.
- Negotiations that end up being one-sided, and you are the ones who usually don't profit from it.
- Tries to intimidate you physically.
- Team projects in which you take on more responsibility than others who are just as able to share the workload but somehow don't.
- Exposure to acts of passive violence.
- Feeling wrong or left in the dark on What is going on right up to the very last minute.
- Feeling the essential decisions that are made out of the loop, realizing too late that you were not privy to certain information.
- Rumors or rumors circulated through the office, trying to turn one employee against another.
- When you spoke with them, there still seems to be more uncertainty than answers.
- Coworkers who fail to accept their faults and seek to cover them up by transferring the blame to someone else, even though they were obviously incorrect.

That makes such manipulators so risky is that even at the workplace alone, these techniques don't end. You may even be surrounded within your immediate circle of friends or family by such individuals, except that it's much harder to see them for who they are and what they're doing because, at some level, you don't want to believe these people you care about might resort to such behavior. Unfortunately, these people exist all around us, and it is only when we wake up and pay attention to the following facts that we begin to realize that our lives might be surrounded by more manipulators than we would like to accept, and this minute the 13 laws of manipulation may happen to you.

- Build Your Trust-Only to tear you down when it works in their favor. When you meet someone for the first time, and they instantly start showering you with praise and flattery, be warned that if they tell you what you want to hear, this may be one of the 13 laws of manipulation at play. They could treat you like a fiddle by telling you what you want to hear, and if you think they could put it on just a little too thick, you're probably right. They could build your trust, coerce you into believing you can trust them enough to reveal information, only to tear you down at a later time when it's convenient to them.
- You Question Your Reality- The friend who tells you "you just imagine it" or "you're making a big deal out of it" is not doing it to be a good friend. It's okay to allay your fears once in a while, but if your concerns are discarded or ridiculed whenever you bring it up, that could be a sign of manipulation at work. One of the classic tactics that a narcissist or manipulator resorts to is trying to shift your perspective or reality by calling your own judgment into question. They make you think you're overreacting, or you're the only one feeling this way, so maybe there's something wrong with you. It sounds innocent enough, but if it goes on for too long, it can make you begin to doubt everything, making it difficult for you to trust your own judgment.
- Start Digress – A classic sign that you're dealing with a potentially manipulative character on your hands is when they're going entirely off the topic and steering the conversation in a different direction. There's a reason they're doing this, and that's often because they leave you feeling confused and frustrated. Many politicians favor this strategy, using digression as a means of diversion.
- They Belittle You-By telling you that your opinion doesn't matter, or you're far too emotional to make a rational choice. They berate you for your thoughts and even send you a derogatory mark to start thinking twice before elevating your views. Social media has made it much more comfortable than ever for

manipulators to sit comfortably behind their keyboards or screens and make grand, general statements aimed at causing their targets maximum emotional damage. Pay close attention, and you will notice that, in fact, many of their statements have no rational basis for those claims. Their sole purpose is merely to belittle their goal.

- Love Extreme Labelling-Who do you know in your life who likes to make you feel bad by exaggerating statements that show how biased you can be? A friend who makes negative comments about your dress and plays it off as "just kidding around" will turn around really well and make you the bad guy if you point out how much you do not like getting comments on the way you dress. You can't put on a joke, can you? Or honestly, are you that sensitive? Are examples of exaggerated statements designed to make you the bad guy.
- They never thank you- it's never going to be food enough, no matter what you do for them. It'll never be satisfactory enough to warrant any gratitude, no matter what you do. Say you can dance to them, and they'll ask you if you can do math while you dance. Tell them that you're happy to be single, and they're going to ask that it's not a fight to be lonely. Tell them that you've been happily married for a while now, and if it's just you and your spouse, they 're going to ask what you're waiting for and why you're not already starting a family. We are just going to find some kind of fault in it, no matter what you tell them.
  - They 're making you feel wrong — about everything. Everything really literally. They will make you feel unfortunate not to have them invited if you go out with another group of friends. If you don't live up to their expectations the manipulative partner can make you feel bad in a relationship. If you're telling them you can't afford both dinner and a movie because you need to work late and ask if it's okay to have dinner alone, you could get an answer like "Yeah, I guess so. I was really looking forward to both of them, but if you're happy with that, I guess it's okay.

Such harmful individuals may even be members of your own family, and this is one of the most challenging truths to acknowledge. To think your own family can exploit you is a concept that nobody wants to be faced with, but it does happen. If you suspect that you in your household could be dealing with manipulative family members, keep an eye out for the following signs:

- Every encounter leaves you feel drained, because it's always about them and involves, almost always, high-strung emotions.
  - Whenever they are around, they make you feel bad about yourself.
- They push your buttons and continuously try to find fault with you, either continue playing the victim or refusing to admit their errors.
- You 're making excuses to avoid their company because you don't want to be around them.
- You must always put aside your own desires to suit their needs.
- You have to watch what you're doing about them because this isn't the first time they've tried using what you're doing to threaten you personally.
- They make you feel bad for not wanting to spend time with them.
- Once you're in their company, you feel like you have to pretend to be someone you're not.

KNOWING YOUR PERSONALITY

When we first understand how others can manipulate us, and how we can affect ourselves, we have to find out what makes up various types of personality. There are the exploited people and the ones who control, or so it appears. A person can be both, and it is up to you to find a way to be mindful of your actions and make sure your behaviors and emotions are in control.

Some manipulators don't know what they're doing, and some are professional, living in a delusional universe where everything is like a string puppet, and they're the master. If you want to make sure you are free from this kind of influence, then it is important to understand the personalities that make up these interactions.

Many dishonest people have similar qualities, no matter how different they can look. It is always difficult to say since their behavior is discreet. They know how to play it to their benefit, behind the scenes. Many dishonest individuals just enjoy the fact that they can speak to others behind your back about your positive and bad qualities. The distinguishing trait of these manipulators is that when they speak to someone about you, they appear to place everything about you in a bad light. If someone regularly gossips about those around you, then you can be certain that they will only gossip about you the same thing. They could even play both sides in certain cases, using you both on either end of the gossip as a pawn of their exciting game. They will address you regularly with others, even though the two of you seem to have any unique confidence when conversing about others with you.

Manipulative people do not understand the concept of limitations. For them, there is no limit to what they can accomplish. They will stop at nothing, no matter who they will end up hurting along the way, to get the things they want. The only thing that interests some manipulators is to fill in their wants so they can feel strong. They are going to disregard your boundaries and drive you beyond the stage you feel safe at. They'll still drive you back, no matter how resistant you may be. They're interested in seeing how far they can take things, meaning they'll stop at nothing to satisfy their curiosities.

Manipulative people do not like to be asked what to do. It is they who want to be in full charge. Even when figures of authority are not reaching out to them directly and attempting to tell them what to do, they may still feel very uncomfortable by their power. They can take the slightest comment when someone tries to assault their character, and they will stop at nothing to make sure they feel strong every day, all the time. They don't care about what to hurt and make sure they don't get told what to do. It could cause just a minor suggestion and end up setting them off.

Manipulative people will say that they understand you, but never really do. Some are professional actors who might make you believe they are emotional beings. This may simply be their effort to make you fall even harder for them. They can make you feel like they want to interact with you, just to be able to get closer and have a stronger grip. Manipulative people want the things they can't get, and sometimes that means pretending to be someone else. For the right environment, some individuals will put different faces on. Others would know how to exploit the environment so that it aligns with their current personality. They're going to pretend to listen to you, try to relate, and practice having empathy, but deep down, that's not really who they are. They will end up being both aggressive and manipulating and, at one point, may even use some of the knowledge exchanged with them against you. Such men may be narcissists, psychopaths, and other deeply deceptive individuals who want to take control of you and hold it for themselves. There are three variables in manipulative behavior: fear, remorse, and blame. When anyone manipulates you, you are potentially emotionally manipulated to do something you would rather not do. You may feel scared to do it, committed to it, or blameful not to do it.

Some are excellent at bullying you when it comes to manipulating people. In contrast, others can end up making themselves the victim in the end. Anyone who is more inclined to control you would feel afraid, using anger, intimidation, and other fear as a way of manipulating you. They might also end up causing you to feel the responsibility for the problem as they do so. In other instances, the controller may be the one who appears to be the victim. They that act hurt by what you've said, elevating their emotions to make you look like the bad guy. They're usually the ones that initially caused the problem. By managing the situation, they are the person in charge to match their needs, conveniently manipulating the situation to suit their own needs better.

Popular Handlers

Following are some of the deceptive individuals' personality traits, so you'll know what to look for when one comes your way. Understanding these basic characteristics will help you not get fooled into a deceptive relationship. Staying vigilant, staying in touch with what you know is the truth for yourself — not just a perspective — and knowing your worth will help you stay away from these men. Narcissists, psychopaths, and sociopaths are among the most common forms of manipulators. The biggest difference between the three is how they want to share their feelings with each other, and the persona they put up to protect who they are.

Of these types of people, narcissists are possibly the most common. They do not have much regard for others and will just think about defending themselves and their identities. Instead of genuinely listening and thinking about who you are and what you may have to say, then they'll just be worried about how they feel, doing their best to ensure that their needs are met.

A psychopath does much tougher research. They will make sure you are under their full influence, and they will find a way to make you feel bad about yourself even while they have a smile on their faces. Such types of individuals will never reveal their true colors and put up a false image of who they are, instead. They will not show when they are upset and will do their best to protect their reputation, even if it means behaving in an unreasonable or humiliating manner.

A sociopath is the one with the least concern for its image. They will deliberately freak out in front of everyone, and they will never care if other people may be affected by their angry outbursts. These are rising manipulators, and have similar qualities for all. They 're just going to concentrate on the things that matter to them, and they're showing no disrespect for you. It's important to remember that they're not careless about others because they don't like those people. A narcissist is not going to neglect your needs because they are despising you. They simply lack the requisite skills to understand what a person is going through. In the search for what they need, they persevere and have no respect for who gets hurt along the way. They don't care about jamming into your space — physically, inwardly, emotionally, or deep down. One may equate them to a parasite. This is regularly an acceptable partnership in our country. But to take advantage of others to their detriment is exhausting, painful, damaging, and frustrating.

It is not so much that dishonest individuals in any given relationship do not realize what their duty is. They do; a dishonest person merely finds nothing wrong with shirking responsibility for their actions, while at the same time making you take responsibility for yours. They also pose double standards for this purpose, which can be frustrating, confusing, and exhausting. What they think is Good action is unacceptable to you, and vice versa. Those forms of people are almost difficult to compromise with.

Highly Sensitive People

Individuals who exploit imitate our values, desires, and beliefs. Manipulative people can pick the vulnerabilities quickly. They'll see if you've got anything that could annoy you, a subject you'd like to avoid, or a certain place that makes you uncomfortable. They will take advantage of this weakness to tap into your insecurity and find a way to take advantage of that. Then they'll strike the passions. They can see that you are a loving and empathetic person, and they will exploit that as well, on both a conscious and subconscious level. Finally, they'll destroy your character, morality, and other values that make up your life, so you don't have a unique identity anymore and represent their agendas instead.

Each emotion, whether positive or negative, fills a need in our journeys. And every one of us needs to be mindful of people who use the persuasive strength of emotions to exploit you. When you identify as empathy, this will primarily apply to you, since this type of individual is most defenseless against other people's negativity. Next time you feel badly misused, use the tips that we have to protect yourself in this book. A highly sensitive person is known as one who can sense other people's emotions more readily and who may feel more irritated when thinking that others have a negative feeling. The intuition may have the same meaning, but this word is often used in a more abstract context and can be compared to a psychic at times.

For example, people who enjoy playing with the emotions of others will use all kinds of strategies, perplexity, blame, and cross-examination to make you feel uncomfortable indeed. We know that they have a good chance to lead you into a relationship because you are a caring person who likes to support others. At first, they may take your honesty and respect into account, always praising you for the great person that you are. Nonetheless, after some time, knowledge of these traits would be restricted, because someone who doesn't care about you, what you do, or what happens to you is using you. What they think about is what you can do for them. Highly reactive people are the ones who suffer the most against manipulators, or others who can often be referred to simply as empathies. It's almost as if manipulators see empathies with so much love to offer that they're trying to kill their inner demons with it; they're just going about it in the worst way possible.

When you need to treat these kinds of individuals daily, as in your professional world, ignore them or amaze them by saying something nice as opposed to approaching them with a confrontational attitude, compulsive controllers are growing to aggravate you, so make sure you don't give them what they need — after a few fizzled attempts, they might start ignoring you.

Positive People in Manipulation

Not all coercion is harmful or necessarily toxic. The distinctions between coercion, persuasion, and control are important to understand. Although this first chapter can be intense, it is a warning about the risks of coercion, and what may happen if others are not as careful about how to use this critical instrument. We will help you to understand deception in the remainder of the text, as we now know it. This is also used in more manipulative and harmful forms that can take over other people's lives. This can destroy relationships if not used correctly and can place a burden on several individual lives. It can be used to cruel ends and satisfy selfish desires. However, it is seen in the context of power and persuasion as coercion is used for the good of others. It all starts with persuasion. You will inspire people to do positive things by explaining the various advantages of the result you are leading them toward. Even for ourselves, motivation needs to be used, because it can be difficult to continue doing the things we think are better for us.

When an individual achieves a high degree of persuasion, they can become an influencer. They are the individuals who will help shape the environment, improve lives, and be conscious of a more optimistic and healthier outlook. This can make for a happier life and a better world when exploitation can be noticed, understood, and turned to a more positive light. Negative is easy to exploit. Often, our minds can even do it without knowing us. If someone gives you good news, but you respond badly because the good news might damage you, then it can be very subtle deception against the other. For example, a mother learning that her child has been accepted several states away from a university may respond poorly because of her anxiety about losing her child. It's still good news, and rationally, the mother should know that. So then the child knows that mom is not pleased with this decision and would prefer not to go to this school because of the negative, angry response from mom.

Perhaps the mother didn't want to respond like that and only rely on feelings, but it was still something that affected her daughter negatively. There would be a more optimistic influence on that situation if the mother told her daughter how happy she was for her, and then had a more serious conversation later on about the obstacles that a first-year college student might face while living many states away from your parents. It also helps the daughter to make her own choice regardless of what other people want. She might also want to stay home, but if she does, it is a significant choice she made by herself without being coerced.

The more we can understand what coercion is, the simpler it would be to live a life in peace with others, and how we can use it for ourselves. You will be able to grasp the things you want for yourself better, and you will know how to get those outcomes better. Rather than driving people away or straining relationships because of the difficulty of having what you want, for constructive and healthier power, you can draw people together and make them rely upon you.

CHAPTER 2 THE ART OF MANIPULATION

If you can understand individuals through their actions, then their words will never deceive you. Keep in mind that what someone says and does is two different items. Because deceptive individuals can "woo" you with their kind words, make sure that they live up to their words and that a trap is not just an empty shell. If a dishonest person puts as much work into being a good person as they do in professing to be one, they may be a trustworthy individual. Also, even though we share the warnings in the novel, deception doesn't always have to be evil. Don't misinterpret someone's effort to affect favorably as they are attempting to exploit you.

If we understood from the earliest point of departure that a person is not who they seem to be and merely takes cover behind an exterior of what appears to be socially acceptable actions by all accounts, then we should be careful to engage with them at that point. Constantly test what you are accepting. Perhaps we're not doing enough. Our beliefs and frames of mind will change as life progresses, and we need to know how these shifting thoughts affect us. The only way to know what it is and how it can influence you is to consider the nature of coercion. It's easy to believe people who are manipulators are all poor and egotistical. You can dismiss these people and keep them out of your life, but we have to note that we also have to accept the facts about these people. We may seem evil, but in our lives, we will always be there, and knowing their nuances will eventually benefit us the most.

Purposes and Aim

Manipulation starts with aim and encouragement. Any coercion is a result of someone trying to get what they want. The problem is that there is a more concentrated emphasis on getting it at all costs, rather than simply getting it. Often we have a sense of urgency and feel like if we don't force people to give us what we want, our needs will not be met. We all have different expectations and aspirations, and a manipulator is someone who goes in the wrong direction to get certain things. Manipulation may often begin in infancy. When you weren't taught properly to express your emotions or share the things you want, so it can be difficult to know how to get them, or to fulfill those emotions. Beginning from an early age, we will try to change the truth to shape it to help us fulfill our needs. Often it is a fast fix to force someone else to do what you want, rather than to do things yourself the hard way. For wanting to manipulate them, we can confuse wanting to be close to others, and we'll take wrong acts trying to fulfill that inner need.

There is an essential distinction that we need to make ourselves aware of between coercion, inspiration, and motivation. For someone on the road to being convincing, it is necessary to consider the distinction between the motivations of those who want to convince or control, and the motivations of the people who attempt to exploit deliberately. Persuasive motivation happens when a person is considerate of the work that must be performed, as well as the individual. Manipulation comes in when only the actual work that needs to be done is concerned with the client, not the person who should be doing it. She acts deceptively when a person is concerned with just making money for her company, not caring how she might manipulate her employees, using fear tactics to keep them working and underpaid.

Persuasive motivation happens when the person they are affecting is sympathetic toward. Manipulation stems from a need to have pride and power over someone else. If someone is trying to convince you to stop drinking because you have an alcohol addiction, they're inspired to help. If a husband asks his wife to stop drinking because he doesn't like it when his wife goes out with friends for wine tasting, then that's coercion. Persuasive motivation is truth-based and genuine, substantive honesty. Manipulation is for external appearances only. If someone tries to encourage you to lose weight following a heart attack, that's motivation. If someone is trying to persuade you to lose weight because in a bikini, your stomach doesn't look flat, but your health is good, that will be coercion. Persuasive motivation cares about the other person and is concerned with their needs and desires. Manipulation is only rooted in self-fulfillment and can be achieved with or without hurting people – it is not about others. Leaders should regularly rely on themselves to assess their moves and ensure they are truly convincing — not manipulating. If you're guilty of manipulating, seeking to manipulate individuals, or not caring about those you're leading, then you're not driving success.

Our opinions and feelings

Manipulators are people who are regularly engaged in intelligent, assertive, and cunning behavior. Those master manipulators are also referred to as Machiavellians or High Machs. In comparison, the Low Mach mark means that one's strategic inclinations fall within the normal range. Although Low Machs may be able to engage in deceptive behavior, they prefer not to defraud and exploit, except when they see that such activity is appropriate or significant. Why are people wired into being Big Machs for what? Does the conduct cause a fundamental identity issue? If that is the case, is the problem at hand discussed possible? To put it simply, no.

Issues of identity don't turn people into High Machs. Machiavellianism is an inherited trait, presumably then exacerbated by the social and family conditions of an individual. Cunning predispositions occur independently from any issue of identity a person may have. We shouldn't disregard identity issues, though. Different issues of identity can cause anxiety, panic, melancholy, alienation, craziness, joy, and other mental states that can trigger violent responses. When someone consistently deludes and uses others to prove his or her points, that person may develop a manipulator's label — self-assigned or otherwise. Being under constant stress from the issue of identity doesn't offer a free pass to terrible behavior. Before we do act, we have a decision to make, and we are responsible for our behavior. Despite this, certain individuals with serious identity problems may be likely to rely on deceptive actions as a way to persevere and cope with stress.

Apart from such underlying psychiatric disorders, such as antisocial personality disorder, borderline personality disorder, bipolar disorder, and obsessive-compulsive disorder, some certain thoughts and emotions can generally cause anyone to become a master manipulator. The first emotion that could push exploitation is fear. As soon as our brains feel we do not get the exact thing we like, then we do end up being highly dependent on manipulating others to satisfy that desire. Fear of being alone can lead someone to exploit several people in their lives to make sure that person sticks to it. It can cause us to cheat, especially in the workplace, to get what we want and ensure that we remain in a higher position because we are afraid of losing the things we have, like money and material objects.

The sense of uncertainty and the overwhelming need to relieve that insecurity is compounded by the belief that we are not good enough to be able to get what we want. Manipulators and those who struggle to manipulate others do so because they typically have low self-esteem, which tells them they are not good enough. They need to look to others to gain power and motivation. Manipulators can have intense desire feelings too. They would want some things badly and believe that if they exploit others, the only way they can get these is. One may actively crave other people's approval, so they can exploit perceptions to make them appear more attractive than they do. The reason a lot of manipulators have this behavior is that they are ignorant of the actual things they want and allow their feelings to be the main factor in their life-round decisions.

Instead of being aware of the things they really want and how to do these things effectively without harming others, they will behave from one moment to the next without making any clear ideas for the best way to get what they want.

The Manipulative Engineering

We are most concerned, as people, with maintaining ourselves. Whether it's by having shelter, food, rest, or something else that fulfills our most primal impulses, that's what drives our mind at the very root of all. Some people will understand this and practice self-control, even when in the driver's seat, their animal behavior is in. Others, though, won't know this and then believe the solution to all their problems is the thing they want the most. We are all beginning to build such standards of the environment. You may have an idea of what you want in the future in your mind, and this seems like the ideal solution to it all. Because most of us know, when we expect it, nothing will ever work out the way we imagine, and nothing ever feels the way we believe it should.

Also, there are days you 're hoping to have a flawless idea on what the day looks like. It can lead to manipulative tactics when things go wrong to try and achieve that desired result. Our brains will start to worry when things don't go the way we expected. We 're afraid that if one thing doesn't happen, it means all the other things we've wished for won't come, and we can take some drastic action to try to satisfy those desires. It's not like we are manipulating because our brains give us what's needed. Manipulation comes from simply believing that doing so would give us what we feel we need, not what in the long run would benefit us. At that moment, when you're hungry, you 're hungry, even though you know you'll eat in an hour. You 're not only getting to turn off the hunger sensation. Your body has little time to think about it. At that moment, it cares for what it needs.

At the moment, manipulators are trying to satisfy their needs. If we all sat down and thought about all the difficult feelings we've had, then the majority of relationships will be much better. Rather, our animalistic brains make us behave in ways that push us to attain just what we want at that moment. While it is a scientific phenomenon that is occurring at the moment, long-term exploitation is a continuation in this sort in the cycle of thought. For certain people, it is a normal way of thinking, and our brains embrace that as a way to get the things we want, regardless of who may get harmed along the way.

How To Phase In Manipulators

That can all sound basic. You can start thinking of a manipulator as an evil villain who doesn't care if he hurts others to get what they want. You start talking about monsters, like Cruella de Ville, who will murder puppies only to get a fancy fur coat. So how do manipulators walk into our lives, then? The consequences of this problem are fantastic because this form of exploitation often happens at both an individual and a societal level. So it's grown used to our culture. The definition of what deception is may seem evil and simple, but what happens is that it starts small and spreads into a complex web of distorted myths, misunderstandings, and other people doing everything they can to persuade you of the things they want you to believe.

Manipulation starts with the person who wants to take advantage of others. They'll first go through what they've been told that influencing others is the way they get the things they want. They'll find their target next. Generally, this would be a more caring person and one who has given them respect and empathy. Rarely does a manipulator start a relationship with another manipulator right away? From there, they form a close bond, making the other person feel unique and different. First, they 're going to start showing signs of influence slowly, but that is generally out of "respect," or so they make it look. Then, they'll start watching what you're doing, and the manipulator will try much harder to make you think you can't trust yourself when resistance shows up. The other person usually is conscious of the deception and leaves after that, or they won't know what's happening and fall deeper into the lies that build up around them.

It's hard to break this loop, but it needs to be done. Taking advantage of another is unfair to one human. We all help each other, and there are some things we need from others, such as affection, financial assistance, or even emotional support.

These are all things to be simply and consensually granted, not anything to be coerced from them.

CHAPTER 3 LAWS OF MANIPULATION

Will you believe your mind is being manipulated or influenced in one way or another at every waking moment of your life? Not even by someone who you know either. Social networking, online news material, things that you see and hear in mainstream media, advertisement, conversations that we see and hear at work or in our personal lives. They are all some form of manipulation or mental control, and it happens most of the time without you even realizing it. Also, what you're about to read in this book in the next chapters may be a form of "manipulation" that somehow influences your thoughts. And why is the human mind so prone to manipulation? Could it be that your active mind is full of the so-called "loopholes"? Let's take a look at the experiment conducted by Solomon Asch in 1957. Asch carried out this experiment on conformity in a series of psychological experiments to show the degree to which an individual's views may be affected by those of a group of individuals. The results, Asch discovered, were that people were willing to ignore the facts or reality that were before them with the right amount of peer pressure, and resort to giving a false or incorrect response just to conform to the rest of the group.

Here's a short question before that...

Do you consider yourself a non-conformist? But is he a conformist? Many people say they can be just the right amount of non-conformist when they know they 're right about anything to stand up to others. However, a conformist would prefer to blend in with the group. While most people tend to think they 're non-conformist, research would suggest otherwise, and people might be more inclined to conform than they initially thought. Here's a short study. Imagine that you are now part of a psychology project with a group of a few people. Everyone takes the same test where a series of oddly shaped images are shown, and they ask what you can see when you look at the image. Many participants unanimously announce on some occasions that they can see the very same image, but when you look at the photo, you see something entirely different. You are the only one to see that too. Every other in-room participant has the same unified answer. Which is it you should do?

Were you standing by what you see? Or do you go ahead and declare that the other participants give the same answer?

That is precisely what the experiments on conformity with Asch aimed to discover. Conformity, which is the propensity of an individual to go along with the unspoken actions or laws of a social group of which they are a member. Asch set out to discover if people could be pressured into conforming with his experiments, even though they knew everyone else in the group was wrong. His experiment's primary purpose was to demonstrate just how powerful conformity within a group might be.

Once Asch performed his experiment, there were participants "in" on what was going on and pretending to be like all the other participants, along with others who still were unaware of what was going on. Those who knew what was going on would react in some ways, and the aim was to see if their behavior would affect the other participants. There would be one naive participant in each experiment that was carried out, who was placed with a group of "aware" participants. There were 50 participants in the study, and all were told they would engage in some sort of "vision check." Many who were aware of what was going on were already told in the "vision check" what their responses were going to be for the mission that was posed. The naive participant had no clue they were the only ones blissfully unconscious. All the participants had a line challenge, and each had to verbally announce which line (A, B, or C) was the closest match to the target line they were assigned. A total of 18 separate trials were performed, and 12 out of the 18 trials had incorrect responses for the participants who were conscious. Asch wanted to determine whether the naive participants would change their responses in order to conform to how everyone else (the conscious group) reacted. During the first half of the trials, everything went well, with the conscious responding to the questions being asked correctly. We then, however, began giving incorrect responses, just as experimenters told them to.

The Outcomes?

Interestingly enough, it was revealed at the end of the Asch experiment that at least once 75 percent of those who participated in the conformity experiment went along with the answers from the rest of the group. When all the trials were studied, Asch discovered that roughly one-third of the time, the naive participants conformed to the incorrect answer from the group. Each participant was asked to pen down the correct match individually to decide whether the participants could actually gage the correct length of these lines they were given during the vision check. Based on the tests, the decisions of the participants were right, with 98 percent of the time being chosen for the correct answer.

Asch 's experiment also explored how much impact the number of individuals present within a group could have on conformity. When only one other participant was present, it had no effect on the response of a participant. If two participants (the aware group) were present, their responses had a small effect on the response of the naive participant. There was a significant difference in the responses received by the naive participant in the presence of three or more participants (aware). Asch also found that only one knowledgeable participant given the right answer while the majority of the knowledgeable participants gave incorrect answers significantly decreased the degree of conformity encountered, with just 5 to 10 percent of the participants going along with the other group members. Studies that were later carried out have confirmed the results of Asch, which then indicates that social reinforcement was an essential factor that needed to be present when it comes to conformity.

When the participants were later questioned as to why they wanted to go along with the rest of the party, when they knew the responses were wrong, most replied, even though they knew that everyone else was wrong, they didn't want to risk being mocked. A few of the participants believed the majority of the group had the right answers, and they were the wrong ones. Asch's experiment results show the truth about conformity, which is that it is ultimately motivated by both a perception that other people may be smarter or better educated and a willingness to fit in with the rest of the band. Therefore, this "loophole" is where the human mind becomes sensitive to manipulation.

Why Do We Comply?

Then it is too convenient for those who understand how the human mind works to take full advantage of the power they have. With only a few well-placed words or basic instructions, they can easily manipulate all the other naive individuals using this information to their advantage. Manipulation quickly puts you in a position of control when you are playing the most straightforward goal on someone else's emotions. If you could convince someone else, and make them believe they'll be happy to do what you want them to do, they'll be more than ready to bend to your rules. If you make them feel guilty enough, they'll try to "fix" the situation and do what they can. Even playing on another person's fear makes them an easy target. Let them think they're in danger of losing something they can't afford to lose, and they'll run at any chance they'll get. If your supervisor were to hang the possibility that you might lose your job in front of you, wouldn't that fear spur you on to do whatever they ask of you? Emotions are so easy to manipulate.

Asch performed more studies and found out the reasons we are more likely to adopt when:

• More people are in attendance

• If the job becomes harder and we face confusion. Then we tend to confirm when we believe that others may be better informed than we are on the matter.

• If we see others as having more "power" or "influence" in a community.

Nevertheless, Asch discovered that the power of conformity decreased when the participants were able to react independently or privately from others. Further research indicates that less conformity occurs when the person concerned has at least one other person inside the community who shares their point of view.

The 13 Rules to Exploit

Manipulators can come in all forms and dimensions. There are some things that manipulators have in common with each other as different as they might be as individuals, and that's the fact that they're manipulative, dishonest, and underhanded and will resort to using whatever methods if it means they get what they want at the end of the day. For that matter, they care little about your feelings or anybody else's, even the people they love. The only thing that matters is to them; they have their own agenda to get what they want. Manipulators turn to one, two, or more tactics to achieve their goals, often at the detriment of someone else. While the tactics may vary from manipulator to manipulator, there are 13 manipulative laws each manipulator will use at one time or another:

• **Rule # 1-Cover your feelings.**

Lying is perhaps the most powerful and oldest form of deception around. Manipulators often resort to this tactic when attempting to avoid responsibility or to twist the truth to their advantage. Many manipulators also turn to lie when there is no particular reason to do so, only living on the joy of causing confusion or the awareness that they play with the emotions of someone else. A professional manipulator knows how to work so subtly with the angle you don't even recognize the lie they're spinning until it's too late. There can be many reasons why a manipulator resorts to lying. It could be for another to take advantage of. To hide their real motives, so that you don't know what they are up to. Or maybe even to level out the playing field so they can stay one step ahead of you. An employee interested in their job could approach the boss and ask about the possibility of being laid off or fired. In an effort to hide what is really going on, the manager may convince the employee there's nothing to worry about when in reality, arrangements were already being made to replace him once he's finished work on the project to which he was assigned. A colleague who has seen the same promotion that you are can withhold potential information in order to be able to put themselves before you.

• **Rule # 2-Seeking attention.**

A little excitement in life makes things exciting, but excitement happens all too much for a manipulator. Why? For what? Since they set it up intentionally. Manipulators want to be the center of attention for validating themselves and giving their egos the boost of trust they feel they need. A colleague at work could have recourse to creating conflict between colleague A and colleague B by telling tales about each other. This ensures that while colleagues A and B are at odds with each other, they then turn to the manipulator for "comfort," making the manipulator feel important afterward. One partner could continuously pick a fight in a relationship to ensure that the other's attention is continually focused on them and trying to solve a problem that may not exist.

- **Rule # 3-Emotional behavior.**

Manipulators may be people who are highly emotional, prone to dramatic, or even psychotic outbursts when they want things done their way. Melodramatic, loud, obnoxious, over-the-top, a manipulator will resort to emotional behavior even at the slightest provocation, which is, most of the time, inappropriate in a social setting. A couple arguing loudly in the restaurant because one partner is acting unreasonably when things are not done their way resorts to this action, hoping that their spouse will be humiliated enough to cede to their demands makes this a hugely successful manipulation tactic when used correctly.

- **Rule # 4- Playing the victim.**

Everybody just feels terrible. They do appear to have the world's worst luck. Any problem you might have, they find a way to make you feel bad for even thinking about it by pointing out how "10 times worse" their problem is than yours. Every now and then, we all suffer from a stroke of bad luck, but the manipulator has managed to use that unfortunate streak skillfully to elevate their own "victim" status and to place themselves above all others. A buddy who is continually playing up all the negative aspects of his life while ignoring the problems is resorting to this manipulative technique to get the attention they want. Inform them you've had a rough day because you've got a flat tire on the way to work this morning, and they'll inform you how lucky you could still have a car to talk about because they have to suffer the public transport difficulties. This emotionally exhausting technique is used by manipulators to obtain support from others, which is another form of gaining publicity and ensuring that everyone is concentrated on them.

- **Rule # 5-Credit When Not Due.**

Manipulators don't hesitate to get you to do much of the legwork, and then come in at the last minute to take credit as they did the job of the lion. A common tactic that is often used in a professional setting, especially in group or team-work projects. These crafty manipulators are fluttering around delegating jobs, seemingly "busy" when they don't actually do anything at all, but when it comes to taking credit, they have no trouble pushing you aside and taking credit for the ideas and the work you've put into it.

- **Rule #6-It depends on Me.**

Manipulators want you, in your life, to feel like you need them. That you just can't live without them. They are the "famous" ones in a social setting to which everyone else seems to flock, making you desperate to want to be a part of that party. They could be the partner in a relationship that continually reminds you, "what would you do without me" or "how would you survive without me." They do you a favor and help you out at a time when you need it most, making you feel indebted to them so that at a later date, they can come and cash in on those favors (with a manipulator, no favorite ever comes free). Manipulators build this false impression that you need them in your life, and the more you depend on them, the more control they have over you, which is precisely what they want. They are preying on the vulnerable and becoming the "indispensable friend" they created in their lives, basking in this special status. The more support you lean on them, the more opportunities they have to take advantage of your emotions, and exploit you for their own benefit.

- **Rule # 7- Being Selectively Honest.**

Did you ever feel so disarmed by how suddenly a generous person you know can turn around and stab you in the back? Or felt so unrooted, knowing that you just knew half of what had happened? That's because the person who provided you with information was a manipulator, and the reason you feel stabbed in the back or wrong-footed is that they only fed you information that they wanted you to know whilst purposefully withholding the rest. Selective honesty, an effective psychological technique for disarming an innocent "victim." A technique that is particularly common today within professional settings. Working manipulators use it all the time to make headway. If there are five people at work for the same promotion, the manipulator will attempt to give itself the upper hand by hiding vital information they know and, at the same time, assuring everyone else that "this is exactly What is going on." They lead you to believe they're generous by hinting at What is going on, but in reality, they make sure you're at least two steps behind each step of the way.

• **Rule # 8- Don't be misled**

A "friend" claiming to be the exceptionally lovely guy you just met at the workplace on the first day. They could pretend to be your friend while gathering information about you, which they could use to their advantage later on. While some people may be genuinely friendly, if this person is a bit too friendly, start raising the red flag by asking very personal or inquiring questions, especially if you've just met them. Within a professional setting, this tactic is prominent, and if your gut tells you something is off, it's probably off. The manipulator may even reside inside your own friends' circle. By being clearly the one in charge of the discussion, we believe we are your "friend." The conversation will always be what they dictate it should be, and it will only happen when they determine it should be. This "friend" may also put pressure on you to make decisions by giving you very little time to think. Phrases like "if I am really your mate, you're going to do this for me" roll out the manipulator's tongue too quickly and usually to their benefit.

• **Rule # 9-No Compromise.**

Would you know someone has a hard time committing to something in your life? Even after you told them how important it is and just now, you could use their support? The non-committal person is not your friend; that person is a manipulator. They take pleasure in withholding their approval or support even if it means they have an opportunity to give themselves the upper hand to take advantage of the situation. We just look out for themselves, and will especially refrain from committing to something if it means taking responsibility. Being non-committal is a tactic of manipulation which is often used in romantic relations. When a romantic partner is non-committal, it keeps the other on their toes and keeps them coming back for more, thus giving the upper hand to the manipulator. The longer they withhold their commitment, the more willing you are to bend backwards, just to get their endorsement.

- **Rule # 10-Silly Play.**

Is that colleague you really do not know What is going on? And will they feign innocence to prevent shouldering extra responsibility? Playing dumb is a deceptive technique that is frequently ignored, but if you pay close attention, in a lot of professional settings, you can find it evident. If you were a group project leader at work, would you delegate extra responsibility to the one member of the team who "wasn't as sure of anything?" Or assign that extra responsibility to someone else? The employee who was then "playing stupid" get away with doing far less but receiving the same amount of recognition in the group as everyone else. If there is a disagreement between a group of friends, could a friend who "does not know what's going on" tell the truth? Or should they feign innocence, knowing full well that they were solely responsible for initiating the conflict? In a romantic relationship, could your friend, who "does not know what you're talking about," say the truth when you're faced with a problem? Or could they be "playing dumb" to avoid getting caught up in a lie? At times, after all, the "innocent party" might not be so innocent.

- **Rule # 11-Point Everyone to the Paw.**

In the first place, a manipulator will always want to keep their hands clean, never take responsibility, and in the second place by always attempting to point the finger at someone else, so they get off scot-free if a problem occurs. Especially when the issue could endanger their reputation and reveal them for who they are. You could be dealing with a manipulator if you know someone in your family, friends, or even among your colleagues who always blames the problem on anything and anyone other than themselves. Keep an eye out for anyone who's behavior pattern always involves making someone else the scapegoat.

- **Rule # 12-Tell you what you want to hear.**

If you're flattered, it's hard not to feel beautiful, and you're more likely to like the person who does all the flattering more than others. If there is one person who continually tells you all the things you want to hear in your life, wouldn't you be more likely to pursue them or spend more time with them? It's hard not to feel good about such people, but telling you all the things you want to hear is not necessarily a good friend's sign. They could be buttering you so that at a later date, they can cash in on a significant favor that you would feel "guilty" to support them with "because they were so good to you."

- **Rule # 13-Oversight of the actions.**

An ideal environment is inside a romantic relationship where there is manipulation in the process of manipulating another's decision. While it is perfectly normal for your partner to base or change your decisions, is it because there is a genuine desire within you to make them happy? Or do you do it because you don't want them to risk getting angry? There is a beautiful line in one relationship about what constitutes exploitation. If you find yourself with friends canceling plans far too often because your partner expresses their disappointment or makes you feel bad, that is manipulation in the play. It's a subtle type of manipulation if you refrain from wearing clothes that your partner dislikes (even though you love it) or avoid getting a haircut because your partner said, "they don't like short hair" They are manipulating the choices without actually making it clear they are. It could start innocently enough with a remark or two, anything so simple as explaining whether the clothes you 're wearing don't look good on you or the kind of dress you 're wearing should be something else, and then you find your life transformed into nothing but choices that don't make you happy because they're decided by someone who supposedly loves you.

CHAPTER 4 I THINK I'M BEING MANIPULATED!

There are certain people in your life that just make it too difficult for everyone to get along with them. We may be violent, bossy, angry, dominant, volatile, arrogant, rude, and a host of other intimidating traits of personality. While many of these behaviors can be neutralized if you handle them carefully, some characteristics and traits can be more harmful than others to the point that no amount of management can neutralize the toxic effects of their behavior. Such people, in general, are the manipulators.

Manipulation, Persuasion and Dark Psychology Explained

As bad as this behavior can be, we often do not want to go straight out and call manipulative someone. To be called a manipulator is a criticism of the character of yours or of someone else. If manipulation and Persuasion are nearly similar (separated by intention only), why is manipulation seen as immoral and plainly wrong? Human beings often seek to influence one another in one way or another, but specific characteristics associated with manipulation make this type of influence much worse than all the others. We're always vulnerable to exploitation. We are only on the receiving end, and sometimes we are the ones who do the abuse. Gaslighting, a common manipulative word, is when you seek to persuade someone else to doubt their own choices in favor of just going along with yours. This is a type of bullying when you make someone feel bad (whether directly or indirectly) about not being able to follow through or pulling out of a commitment. One type of manipulation is to be forced to go along with the group just to gain acceptance or approval. It's happening all the time around us and within society.

What separates manipulation from all the other convincing techniques that we use is that manipulation appears to affect the manipulated one directly. Take advertisements, for example, on cigarettes. They trick you into believing it's "good," but it has a detrimental impact directly on your health. Phishing or schemes that trick you into believing you have a chance to win a large sum of money are directly harmful to you as they contribute to fraud or theft of identity. In some countries, politicians rely on manipulative tactics to weaken the notion of democracy. The necessary effect of deception, and more often than not, is what sets it apart from all the other convincing techniques out there. That's why, instead, it is not called Persuasion, although the two approaches depend on more or less the same strategy.

Ultimately all comes down to your goal. The purpose behind your actions is that which distinguishes Persuasion from manipulation. If your intentions are good, and you really want to create a situation that benefits the other Party, persuasion. It is encouragement if your goal is to do well. If you're truthful about what you're trying to do right from the start, then it is Persuasion. If you can say wholeheartedly, you have the other person's best interest in heart, this is Persuasion. Needless to say, manipulation yields a far less desirable result. This is deception if your purpose is to confuse, mock, blame, instill guilt, and use it for your own gain, regardless of whether they get hurt by your acts along the way. If you deliberately indulge in actions that you know may cause someone else to get upset or look bad, but you are doing it anyway, this is manipulation. It's manipulation if you don't care about the consequences of your actions and what they might do to someone else as long as your own agenda is served. At the end of the day, it is the motive that decides whether the actions make you a manipulator or not.

The Triad Of Dark Psychology

Just when you felt the deceit was bad enough, an even darker side of psychology arrives here, known as the Dark Triad. The triad consists of three very distinct but interrelated forms of personality, namely narcissism, psychopathy, and Machiavellianism. Why is the Dark Triad, or the darker side of human psychology, called these three? It is because these three terms define the very tactics that some people resort to in order to get what they want-manipulation, Persuasion, and manipulation. Yes, the term Dark Triad has a sinister ring to it, and it's a term that many psychologists and criminologists use as a defining predictor that signals an individual's criminal behavior. Let's look at the three personality characteristics that make up this trifecta more closely:

- Narcissism-The word comes from the Greek mythology of Narcissus, the hunter who fell in love with his own reflection when he saw it in a pool of water where he drowned. He was so consumed by himself that he could not concentrate on anything else. Those with characteristics of narcissistic personality also show signs that include being boastful, greedy, and rude, caring more for themselves and nothing else. Also, narcissistic individuals lack empathy and are highly sensitive (one may even say hypersensitive) to any sort of criticism, since they can not bear the incomplete or false thought.

- Machiavellianism-This word comes from the famous diplomat and politician Niccolò Machiavelli who lived in Italy in the 16th century. Machiavelli became famous with the publication of his book, The Prince, in 1513. This publication has been interpreted as the recognition by Machiavelli of the deception and ruse that takes place in diplomacy. Those who tend to exhibit Machiavellianistic tendencies are often only concerned with their own self-interest and are manipulative and duplicate. Some people lack both morals and conscience, so they're not into anything else but what's going to help them.

- Psychopathy — Antisocial behavior, manipulative, aggressive, violent, lack of guilt, or empathy are characteristics associated with a psychopathic character. Psychopathic and being a psychopath are two very different features, the latter generally associated with or explicitly associated with crime.

The Dark Triad

In 2010, Dr. Peter Jonason, who was an assistant psychology professor at the time-based at the University of Western Florida and Gregory Webster, his co-author and assistant psychology professor based at the University of Florida, came up with what is now called the Dirty Dozen Scale. Jonason and Webster developed this scale as a method of measuring the traits that comprised the Dark Triad. In the triad, at some stage, these three personality traits tend to converge and are usually characterized by the degree of self-centeredness, aggression, discord, and manipulation that exists. Jonason, Webster, and their research team were trying to decide if sadism could possibly be identified inside the laboratory. They were also trying to find out if these sadistic measures of personality could be used to predict behaviors beyond the measures already established in the Dark Triad.

In a second and related study that was conducted, the results interestingly revealed how people who exhibited a high tendency of sadism, narcissism, and (or) psychopathy were willing to act aggressively against an innocent party when aggression proved to be the more comfortable choice. It was only a sadist who showed a tendency towards higher levels of aggression when it became apparent that their "victim" could not fight back, and that unlike other "darker personalities," it was the sadists who were willing to spend the extra energy and time needed if that meant that extra effort would give them a chance to hurt someone else. It was a major surprise, given that other scientific findings in the past showed that while psychopaths had no problem inflicting harm on others, they were much more likely to do so even if it served a particular purpose. On the other hand, narcissists were far less likely to engage in aggression unless they felt their ego was being threatened, whereas Machiavellians only resorted to aggression if they felt the benefits were sufficient to warrant such action, and only if it involved acceptably low risks to themselves. A study by Jonason and Webster measures the reactions people gave when asked to rate themselves against the following statements:

- I appear to be short of guilt

- If it means getting my way, I have resorted to manipulating others, and I still tend to do it.

- I tend to rely on trickery to get my way.

- In the past, I used flattery to achieve my goals.

- I have taken advantage of others as a means to an end, and I still tend to.

- I prefer to expect "special care or preference."

- I do not care about morals, nor do I care about morals or the consequences of my decisions and acts.

- I tend to be insensitive and, at times, callous toward others.

- I tend to exhibit cynicism.

- I like trying to get status or prestige.
- I want to have others to admire.
- I just want to be careful.

The individuals who participated in this study were rated from a scale of 1 to 7, and a score ranging from 12 to 84 was given to them. The higher the score of a participant was, the higher the probability they were individuals with one of the traits of the Dark Triad personality. Covert marketing strategies are everywhere we look, from the social media to the ads we are subjected to, and when we try to make purchases in person, the sales techniques were bombarded with. Even children occasionally resort to manipulative tactics as they begin experimenting with the various ways that work to give them the autonomy they are seeking. Also, the people you love and trust most use these techniques, and here are some examples of ordinary people in daily life who may succumb to dark psychology more so than others:

- Real Narcissists-Of course this one. In particular, people who are clinically identified as narcissists appear to bring with them an exaggerated sense of their own self-worth, meaning they still seek to justify this conviction by being superior to those around them. Narcissists harbor fantasies of being worshipped and worshipped by the public and will resort to all sorts of coercive and immoral actions to receive the respect they crave.
- Real Sociopaths — Those clinically identified as sociopaths often seem witty and charming, but their downfall is impulsiveness. Since sociopaths appear to lack the capacity to feel some sort of guilt, they take advantage of these dark strategies of personality to create relationships that are shallow and not real, because they do so for their own benefit only.
- The Selfish People-Someone with a secret agenda that favors itself before anyone has the ability to return to those dark, deceptive tactics if the result is a win for them.

- Politicians – To get the votes they need to get the people to vote in the way they want them, politicians are guilty of using dark methods of manipulation as a means of serving their purpose.
- Lawyers-Some lawyers will stop at nothing if it means winning their case, even if it means they have to resort to shady tactics.
- Salespeople – Much like attorneys and politicians, specific salespeople may be so focused on doing nothing but selling that they have no shame in using deceptive techniques to convince a customer to do what they want.
- Leaders-Not every leader is there to inspire, and some rely on manipulation to get us to meet their demands.
- Public Speakers – Not all public speakers can be trusted, and there are some out there who would resort to bribery if it means selling more goods to do so.

There are just two of the many instances of people out there who would turn to the more malevolent side of the continuum of human nature, and often for the benefit of none else than their own. German-Danish research recently revealed that while the Dark Triad is composed of psychopathy, Machiavellianism, and narcissism, other personality traits may fall within a similar spectrum. Examples of these include selfishness, despitefulness, and sadism, just to name a few, and as the research showed, these malevolent traits all share one common aspect, namely that they have a "dark heart." It's quite likely that if you possess any of these traits, you may also have a propensity for the others.

Sadists have been mentioned a few times throughout this chapter as those with Dark Triad tendencies have the potential to overlap with sadistic behavior within them. You may have also known one sadist once or twice in your life. They're probably still in your life now. If you know anyone who is deliberately causing another emotional harm and deriving great pleasure from it, that is a sadist. What makes a sadist this dangerous is that their acts can be anywhere from petty to severe. Some common examples of what could look like sadistic behavior include:

- Deliberately depicting someone else in an unflattering or misleading way with the intention of undermining their image.
- Sharing secrets that they know intentionally were meant to be private.

- Purposefully trying to get a fired colleague behind their back.
- Obviously jeopardizing the reputation of a colleague in their absence.
- Its aim is to marginalize a boss, family member, neighbor, or even a neighbor.
- Deliberately attempting to hurt the relationship with someone else.
- Recourse to bullying and cyberbullying.
- Recourse to intellectual, physical, or financial theft.

A Sadist 's Characteristics

A professional sadist can so deliberately set these conditions up that it is impossible to prove that they were involved in the guilty party. What makes it far worse is that they will never be held responsible or feel any sort of regret for the harm they caused. People can also be hesitant to assume that the sadist 's charming and likable personalities are behind the chaos. A sadist will attempt to harm someone else intentionally because they believe that doing so will benefit them. They may resort to such underhanded tactics if they feel envious or threatened by others or even if they perceive someone else as weaker and less likely to retaliate against them. In some instances, it might not be obvious why the sadist opted to conduct a victim attack. We don't often think-or want to believe-that the sadist might exist within our own immediate circle of connections, but they do, and they could be your parents, siblings, extended family members, spouse, friends, and the people with whom you work.

Here's an example of a situation where a sadist may be hiding in your midst among your relatives. Let's say that person - John Smith - lost his job not too long ago, and he was struggling with frustration and anxiety because he was struggling to find another one.

John seeks comfort and support by talking about it with his brother but asks explicitly his brother to keep the information to himself. Brother John accepts. John gets an invitation to his brother's house for a casual get-together after some time. When several guests offer their sympathies over the fact that he had lost his job and couldn't land another, John is then taken aback by thinking nothing of it.

Embarrassed, hurt, and angry, John knows immediately that he was his brother who leaked his secret because he had not trusted anybody else in his troubles. When John confronts his brother, his brother later denies any knowledge, and "does not have any idea" of what John is talking about. John's brother appears to refute the allegations steadfastly, making him feel bad for suspecting him as the guilty party. It takes a while for John to realize that this is not the first time in the past that he and his brother have been engaged in the same situation, where John's brother has been responsible for several incidences that either hurt or embarrass John while denying any responsibility. The sadist maybe anyone, anywhere, and they're always hiding undercover that makes you doubt your own wellbeing while they intentionally injure and ruin your life and then take any blame for it.

Clues Indicating You Can Be Manipulated

Have you ever had that impression in one of the relationships you have that something was not quite right? Even with a casual gathering with someone you just met. Something just didn't feel quite right, and you left feeling far more anxious, irritated, or confused than you were when you began. That could be a sign you have been in a manipulator's presence. The reason manipulators use the tactics they do is because they are often unable to simply ask what they need or be able to express their needs in a healthy, straightforward manner. The resort to this emotionally abusive tactic in an effort to try to manipulate the other people around them and compel them to bend to their will, as they lack these skills.

Manipulation comes in various forms, and it can range from abusive to just being around a bossy personality anywhere. Some deceptive habits are much easier to spot than others, and if you believe you may be a psychological bully's target, these are the tell-tale signs for which you want to keep an eye out:

- You're still expected to forget-if you don't go along with what they want, then they'll make you feel guilty. Even if you did have every right to say no. If you feel pressured continuously or compelled to do something you don't want to do, you are being manipulated. If you're afraid to say no, then you're manipulated. If you feel bothered to go along with the demands of someone else, you will be manipulated. Manipulators are experts in playing the victim card, and they're going to play it to make you feel as guilty as possible as you're doing something wrong because you've chosen to tell them no.

- Doubt, Your Own Judgment-You, still find yourself questioning your own judgment every time you are around a particular person. Suddenly, after having a conversation with a manipulator, something you were so sure of a minute ago fills you with doubt and makes you second guess your own decisions. Present them with an idea or an opinion, and they will somehow find a way to twist and turn it around, making you uncertain and uncomfortable. Spend enough time with them, and they will make you feel unworthy as if you were a complete failure, and nothing you could ever do is the right choice.

- No Favor Comes for Free-You can guarantee the strings will still be added to the offer if they do you a favor. Nothing that a manipulator ever does is a "genuine favor," there is always going to be an ulterior motive for why they help you out. If accepting somebody's help or favor makes you feel uncomfortable because you know you will later owe them for it, you are dealing with a manipulator. There's an obligation to be repaid when the manipulator gives you a favor. They are going to be the first to tell you that you owe me this, and you're going to feel obliged to go out of your way to help because you feel guilty of saying no. Say no, and they'll make you feel like the world's most ungrateful person.

- You 're just blaming yourself-even though you 've done nothing wrong, you 're blaming yourself somehow. That one dishonest friend who always has an explanation for their bad conduct or poor judgment is not his friend who always makes you the scapegoat. This one is a manipulator. It's your fault; you made me believe I should, if you thought it was a bad idea, I wouldn't have done it. A dishonest "friend" 's trademark is when you're in the mix somewhere, and the one who made you feel like you're wrong.

- They 're not really a listening-Another indication that you might deceive is when you're not listening while you're talking. They may stare at you while you're talking, but they twist the conversation back to something that involves them at the first chance they get. Everything is about them. In fact, the only time they appear to be engaged in is when they gather the information they can use against you later when the time is right. Beware of what you are saying when you are around them, and never trust confidential or essential information to them.

- They come to you when they need something-do you have the one friend who seems to only ever get in touch with you when they need a favor? That friend could exploit you, particularly if you're the one who's always doing those favors, but they're never around when you need the most support. Or they always have an excuse for why they can't help you up to their sleeve. However, when they need something from you, they will behave like you are their best friend in the world.

Clues To Indicate That Your Partner Is A Lying Manipulator

One of the worst sinking feeling you might feel is knowing that all this time, your partner, the person you love and who supposedly loves you, turns out to be using you to their own advantage. A partnership is supposed to be the one place we believe we can get the sincere inside support, love, dedication and care we all yearn for. In return, to be wholeheartedly loved and respected. Sadly, there are those out there who have broken their hearts because they know there's not just someone who's dishonest about their partner but someone who's manipulated their strings like a puppet all along.

We all have particular aspirations and romantic ideas of what we think love is due to the way we do it in which love was portrayed in society through the films we watch, articles we read, and social media posts scrolling through almost every day. When we see on-screen jealousy, we believe it's a sign of intense love because the two people in the film are afraid to lose their loved one to another. The popular literature and Twilight movies lead us to believe that true love and relationships are about obsession. That love is an omnipresent emotion. That when there are two people in love, nothing else matters, and there are no boundaries. This romanticized notion blinds to the fact that this isn't what life is at all, and that kind of love occurs only in movies and between the pages of books because they make for a good storyline. Such behavior is an indication of manipulation in real life. It is not about love to be controlling, and it is manipulation. It is not being passionate about being obsessed, and it is manipulative.

On some level, we know that we should be able to recognize in a relationship the signs of an abusive partner. We know we can, but it is said easier than done. When we love, we prefer to blind ourselves to a fault with our mate. We are making excuses for the actions that should set off warning bells in our heads as we try to avoid facing the facts. We don't want our hearts to be broken that way, and we're trying to convince ourselves they aren't really like that at all. There is cause for concern when a relationship escalates from controlling to being purely abusive, but being in a manipulative relationship can also be harmful and damaging.

Getting in a manipulator relationship can be as detrimental to you both physically and psychologically. Manipulative partners will try to dominate you, minimizing your freedom. They try to manipulate every decision you make, to belittle you, and to destroy your self-esteem so that you begin to doubt yourself and think you are the "lucky" one, and no one can love you as much as possible. They make you scared of losing this relationship and make you scared to enter into any future relationships because this past experience has traumatized you, scared of getting into another relationship with someone who manipulates you. Being in a manipulator relationship will leave you with emotional wounds and scars that, if they ever do, will take a very, very long time to heal.

Any of the more common signs you're in a manipulator relationship is when your partner continually pressures you to look or act in a way that they only approve of or decide who you can and can't spend your time with. The love and support that would come from genuine relationships is not something you will note when you're in a relationship with manipulators. Lying to try to manipulate you and the situation in their favor, when your partner is a manipulative person, is something that will be a regular occurrence in your relationship and these are the signs to look out for:

- Lying to Make You Feel Guilty About Spending Time with Others-Because the manipulator needs to be in charge, they will try to cut you off as far as possible from your support network by trying to minimize the amount of time you spend with your family and friends. They'll turn to lies and sob stories about how to hurt they feel you've abandoned them when they really need you (although that may not be true), and tell you they believe you 're still placing the needs of others before theirs when you say you love them. Their aim is to try to isolate you from other people in your life so that you become totally dependent on them, and the more you rely on them, the more power they have over you to control. They may not tell you to stop spending time with other people, but they're trying to subtly nudge you off your social circle inch by inch through the lies that spin to make you feel guilty about your actions.

- They lie and criticize-When you 're with someone who's manipulative, every little thing you do is subject to criticism. The worst part of all this is that they lie so convincingly when they say they do it because "they love you" or "it's for your own good." They'll continually criticize just about everything you're doing, the longer you remain in a relationship with them. They 're going to criticize everything from the way you dress, the way you 're talking, the things you 're doing, the way you 're spending your money, your excitement, your hobbies, your interests, the choices you 're making, even if you're putting forward fun ways to spend quality time together if it's not something they want to do, they 're going to find a way to criticize that. They will judge you so much that you feel so inept and insecure that you no longer feel confident making decisions without first running it through them. They 're not here to help you. They 're trying to get you underway.

- You may be the most trustworthy and truthful person, but a manipulator will make you feel different. They are still individuals in their own right, as deeply in love as two people are, and all have the right to privacy. Unless you are in a manipulator relationship, that's because they 're going to totally disregard this fact because they're never satisfied unless they can control every aspect of your life, a deceptive partner does not recognize your right to privacy and will have no difficulty spreading lies and guilt in attempting to defend your privacy. They make you feel like you have something to hide if you want to keep your emails or text messages private. Even if you have one to protect your diary, they'll try to make you feel bad. The manipulator thirsts for control, and when they can't get it, they resort to any means necessary to try and invade your privacy. Your privacy is your privilege, and you should never feel obligated to disclose anything you do not want.

- Manipulators may demand access to your passwords, social media accounts, and even more private information by spinning some tale about how they're "fearing" you might break their hearts by cheating on them. They might even tell you tales of how they've been cheated on in the past and how much it hurts them to break their hearts that way (although it might not be exact). The point is, they will tell you whatever story it takes to get you to feel guilty enough to share your private details, even going so far as to say that there should never be secrets from each other for two people who are in love. But there's a big difference between being secretive and having a privacy right, and being in a relationship doesn't mean you have to sacrifice the latter one.
- They 're talking a lot about "protecting you," which, of course, is just another lie when the manipulator comes along. They 're not protecting you; they 're not even talking about it, because all they care about is their own self-interest. Deep down, who wouldn't love the idea to know there's somebody out there who loves them enough to protect them from the big evil world? That person exists, alas not with a manipulator. There's a natural desire to protect them when you love someone and to keep them from feeling hurt. You 're willing to do whatever it takes to keep them safe when you love someone, and there's no way you want to see them hurt, frustrated, or sad. The deceptive partner can lead you to believe they want this for you, but when "protecting" on their terms means they can make all the decisions on how to live your life for you, the red flags will start to increase. They 're going to tell lies about wanting to "protect" your finances, "protect" you from friends who aren't a good influence in you, "protect" you by keeping tabs always on where you are going and what you are doing. When you tell them that you are uncomfortable with this kind of control, they turn around and lie again by convincing you they do it out of love and because they want to "protect" you, when the truth is they try to do the opposite. They want

you to depend on someone other than them, and they'll still have the upper hand. If you were indeed in a healthy relationship, your partner would be protective, but they would be realistic too. They know they can't shield you from anything, and by dictating how every part of your life should be handled, they definitely won't try. They'll find constructive ways to help you when you're in trouble, instead of making you feel bad for not listening to them. In the name of "protecting" you, they will not demand that you hand over your password or any other private information.

- They provoke you with lies-Sometimes a manipulator might resort to provoking you into an argument by lying and exaggerating, blowing things out of proportion just because they know that when they do, they push your buttons. They deliberately say things that are aimed at triggering negative emotions within you, even going so far as to lie just to make their argument more persuasive. The nagging question of why they do things the way they do is left to you. And sometimes they just want to push your buttons just to get you mad enough to say something they will later use against you. When you tell them their argument doesn't make sense, they 're going to put on an Oscar-worthy show about how deeply you hurt them. They 're going to keep pushing and pushing, and if you let them, they 're going to drive you right off the edge, and at the next chance they get, anything you say can and will be used against you.

- They 're going to tell you they 're going to die without you-maybe one of the biggest lies a manipulator spins his lies telling you they can't just live without you. That if you leave them, they will die. They 're not going to, and they're sure never going to do anything to harm themselves. It is just a lie they tell to make you feel inadequate even for considering the notion of ending the relationship when you see them for who they really are. There's a name for this behavior, and it's called emotional manipulation, and it's probably one of the most narcissistic aspects of being in a manipulative interpersonal relationship. No one should make you feel afraid or guilty about doing What is best for you, and they should certainly not shoot your life 's responsibility in such a way. Telling you that if you ever abandon them, they will die is nothing but a hollow threat, and once you know for sure that you want to break ties with the manipulator, never let them make you feel bad for this decision. You have a responsibility for your own health, and they are responsible for what they want to do with their lives.

- Twisting Lies with Even More Lies — Manipulators will spin lies almost as intricately as spinning their website. They're going to lie, twist those lies, and then twist those lies even more till you don't know What is real and what isn't. Twisting the truth and distorting them, tangling lies on top of more lies is the manipulator's favorite technique to confuse and frustrate you. They're going to drive you nuts and make you doubt your own sanity, and they're doing it so skillfully that you think something is wrong with you rather than them. Keeping tabs on the convoluted web of lies of a manipulator can be hard, but you have to learn to trust your intuition and rely on your own judgment, even though they are trying hard to persuade you that you are wrong. Learn to trust your instincts if anything doesn't sit right with you, because you're probably right, mainly if you know you've caught them in a lie more than once. Before you entered into a relationship with them, you trusted your own judgment, and now more than ever, you have to trust your own judgment. Don't let them embarrass you with their lies.

Manipulation and self-defense

- **Keep a Conversations Journal**

There are usually some kinds of signs that send hints somebody is trying to manipulate them. Those aren't always easy to find, of course, unless you've been in the situation before or recognize coercion. One strategy that you can do if you feel you are being manipulated by someone is to keep a journal of what's said. You can write down your conversations or stuff they say to you, randomly. You should even write down what they are doing, at the same time. Although this may sound like an unusual thing to do, it will help you understand what is really happening, since manipulators are operating on an emotional level. This is sometimes hard to notice, notably if you are already lacking in self-confidence. You may also include how the mentioned circumstance or words made you feel. You may find a connection between what is stated by the manipulator and how you feel. You might find, for example, that your self-image is starting to diminish. It is a sign when you notice this that you have to stay away from the person or get out of the relationship as quickly as possible.

- **Confronting manipulators about their conduct**

With some people, that will be easier than others. For example, if your supervisor is the manipulator, and you need your job, you may not be able to confront them directly. You might also have a hard time confronting your significant other, especially if they've lowered your self-esteem. Confronting the manipulator, however, is a perfect way to let them know you understand their actions and you're not going to stand for it. When you are following this path, you want to be aware of the other tactics that they may be using against you. They might try to create a distraction for example, or try to play the victim. They might also blame someone else for their behavior, or tell you that you imagine it all. You need to be firm when confronting a manipulator. You need to be fully persuaded and understand that they are going to try and exploit you because they don't want other people to catch on to their actions. You also need to be careful, as some manipulators can become passive aggressive or violent.

- **Put Manipulators Focus**

You can also focus on them, in addition to confronting the manipulator. You can do this by asking a range of questions regarding their motive. You want to try and find out why they act the way they do, which is the foundation of dark psychology. Some of the questions you may ask are: "Do you feel reasonable? "What will I get out of this? "Is this really helpful? "That's what you want from me (state their request)." You show the manipulator what they are doing by asking questions like these. They would be remorseful or alter their request if they are not a master manipulator and did not intend to take part in that action. If they're a master manipulator, however, they'll think of other tactics to turn it back on you. They're going to try to act like the victim, like ask "Why are you attacking me?" Or by saying 'I'm just trying to help, I don't appreciate being attacked like this.'

- **Start Driving Your Agenda**

Manipulators don't want to win over other people. This puts them in a threat. The more you succeed, though, the more you drive a manipulator backward. Your ability to believe in and continue to succeed in yourself will depend on how long you know the manipulator and how close you are to them. For example, if you have been emotionally beaten down by the manipulator it will be much harder to remain motivated and work hard to succeed. If you've just met them, without too much trouble you'll be able to continue pushing towards your success. Of course, having the mindset of believing that you can fulfill your dreams, and supporting people will help eliminate the manipulator through your success. And if you need to speak to someone to get better mentally and emotionally, this is what you do.

- **Don't get physically tied up**

While sometimes we get trapped by a manipulator because we didn't know their personality, other times we know they're manipulators but they still need to keep in touch because they're colleagues or family. You need to protect yourself in a different way when this is the situation, because you can not simply ignore them. A lot of people also recommend you do your best not to get emotionally attached. For some people this will be tougher than others. If you're a more emotional person, you'll be struggling to avoid becoming emotionally attached as your relationships are emotionally based.

One way to do this is to ensure that they know the boundaries. You'll also need to make sure that you stick to your limits. If you cross your boundaries, manipulators don't care, so you need to protect yourself. Tell them if you think they're jumping a fence. Don't fall back for any of their techniques and don't turn back.

- **Don't Feed The Drama**

One of the most essential things a manipulator thrives on is suspense. For this reason they often disagree with someone or something that will cause people to respond. So one of the best ways to stop a manipulator in their tracks is to tell them "you are right." Manipulators aren't used to having people to agree with them, and when you do, they'll be left speechless. This also creates a threat that could make them want to leave you alone. They may feel that they can't trap you with their techniques, especially if you do so right away. This is not to say that they will not try. Manipulators also aim to bring people into the network. Letting them win the argument, though, even if it upsets your ego a little bit, is much better than falling victim to their pitfalls.

- **Say that you would "think about it" to the manipulator**

They want to know the answer immediately when the manipulator has a request. So when you say something like "I'm going to think about it" or "maybe we're going to see," they're not going to be happy with that answer. They may be walking away in anger, wondering why you need to think about it or trying to persuade you to do what they want you to do. What this tactic does is buy time for you. This lets you distance yourself from the manipulator. This means you will not need to deal with the client or manipulator again, or at least until they return. This will also give you the opportunity to really think about what you were asked to do. You should weigh the pros and cons and determine which decision would be the best one for you.

- **Have a healthy attitude**

Having a healthy mindset is another way of eliminating a manipulator from your life. You want to make sure you feel confident that you can stop them from using techniques against you. You will want to make sure you feel good about your self-esteem and self-image. At the same time, you want to understand the manner in which they manipulate you. To battle them, you need to grasp their techniques. You have to understand they're probably not going to stop with just one technique. More than likely they will use a few in hopes they can start breaking you down. The more strong you remain, the more likely the manipulator will leave you alone. If you always push them away, call them out on their behavior, and continue to believe in yourself, manipulators won't spend a lot of time trying to use different techniques.

- **Meditation**

Many people don't realize how helpful meditation can be. Meditation is not just about keeping you relaxed but also about keeping you optimistic and feeling good about yourself. When you feel this way, it's easier to remove the negativity from your life, which means manipulators. Meditation is easy, so you don't have to put too much time aside. You can schedule meditation in around ten minutes out of your day. Find a time and place where you can be on your own and without interruption. You also want to keep it quiet, so you can concentrate on eliminating your body and mind from the negativity. Many people would be using relaxation exercises to help them remain focused when meditating. This is when you close your eyes and start to normal breathing. You want to concentrate on the breath. Notice feeling on your body on your clothes or put one hand on your chest and the other on your stomach. Feel how your hands move in and out as you breathe. Then you focus on the deep breaths. Take a deep breath in, then slowly exhale. Finish the exercise until you feel smooth.

In addition to helping you eliminate manipulators who have not become a close person in your life, meditation will also help you manage your life with a manipulator. Of course, if your significant other is a manipulator for your own mental health and safety, you want to leave but meditation can help give you strength. It will give you the strength to concentrate on your attitude and find ways to defend yourself against the tactics of coercion. It may give you the strength to leave as well, once you're ready.

CHAPTER 5 IDENTIFYING MANIPULATION TECHNIQUES

Emotional or secret coercion may be defined as having a distinct effect by emotional violence, to manipulate or gain benefits at the detriment of the victim. Recognizing the major social effects of mental violence resulting from coercion is key. One person is exploited with coercion to benefit another. Intentionally the controller does whatever it must to represent its interests and only its interests better. This chapter will discuss ways of distinguishing which techniques deceptive individuals use regularly to manipulate others into a position of hurt. Many of these things are going to be very clear indicators of coercion you may already have widely known. Others would be more subtle and aspects we need to be mindful of as we speak to people we might not necessarily consider coercion. Remember that not every person who acts according to those behaviors attempts to manipulate you intentionally. Yet perceiving such activities is crucial in situations where the freedoms, interests, and protection are in doubt.

Signs of Manipulation of the Emotions

Manipulators will seek to get you to their "home turf," or at least to a position they're comfortable with. This will ultimately facilitate their control of you. A manipulative person may require you to engage with them at a particular location, such as an office, home, or public setting. This gives them a sense of control as they most probably scoped the area out before asking you there. This way, though you might not know much about the place yet, they are familiar with their surroundings. Cunning, but a simple means for manipulators to gain control access. Manipulators should give you the chance to have the first day and build up your confidence before they tackle your vulnerabilities. This is what numerous sales reps do when they decide if you will be the perfect candidate to buy what they are about to offer. They build up a benchmark about your logic and behavior by asking general questions and analyzing them, from which they can then determine your strengths and shortcomings. This kind of hidden program addressing may also occur in the work environment or with personal relations.

Manipulators know how to twist the truth, and they're going to get away with it because they don't always think they 're lying. We find a way to so much twist the facts that we assume it to be real to 100 percent. This may take place in the forms of deceit, making an argument, double-dealing, censoring the injured person for causing their abuse, manipulation of fact, disclosure or holding of vital data, misrepresentation, minimal portrayal of the facts and seeing only the facts of their narrative.

Often manipulators can confuse you by providing you with a great deal of information, often in a confusing way. We trick you by presenting yourself with false statements, measurements, and other facts that you do not want to worry about or investigate. It can happen in transactions and financial situations, in meetings at an expert stage, or in social interactions. The manipulator creates the perfect opportunity to trap you by assuming control of you. A few people make use of this method to provide a sense of scholarly predominance.

Manipulators also come up with ways to overwhelm you with formality. It means they are going to blame their acts on laws or legislation, and events that are clearly outside their control. Some people use administration — desk work, strategies, rules, advisory boards, and various types of red tape to advance their policy of trying to make you fall for their deception scheme. Similarly, this approach can be used to delay the discovery of truth, conceal imperfections and deficiencies, and sidestep test. Your boss might make you work on a holiday and explain that he couldn't do anything, even though he might have taken that same shift himself. This strategy is like saying, "I would if I could," given the fact that the manipulator can alter the situation. A manipulator will sometimes raise his voice and exhibit negative feelings. This can be a forceful means of control. If they complain loudly enough or express negative emotions that seem out of proportion for a situation, most rational people would yield to their threats and give them what they need, if for no other reason, to keep the peace. The powerful voice is typically accompanied by strong non-verbal contact, such as standing or vigorous gestures to enhance conflict.

Surprise is another growing technique a manipulator could choose to use. They could use an outrageous statement when telling a story, such as "you'll never believe what the other person has done to me.' They also use incredible assertions, such as, "I was the only one doing any work today." These paint a surprising situation that can catch off guard the other person, more likely to fall for the increased truths that the manipulator shares. Regularly, the sudden negative information comes unexpectedly, so you have only a brief period to plan and counter. The controller may request extra concessions from you to keep working with you. A manipulator might also **not even allow you to choose in some situations.** This is a typical deal and arrangement strategy, where the controller leans on you to settle on a choice before you are prepared.

A manipulator will have high expectations of you and demand high requests, ignoring that you might not be able to do what they are asking. They will make it seem like it's not even an option to say "no," even though what they are asking of you might be unreasonable in the first place. By applying **pressure and control**, manipulators expect that you will split and yield to the manipulator's demands. Instead of saying, "Do you think you can do this?" they will simply ask, "When can you have this done?" never allowing you to agree to do something in the first place. This makes it hard for you to be able to say "no" to whatever it is that they might be requesting.

Manipulators will enjoy negative cleverness intended to jab at your shortcomings and weaken you. They will make sarcastic jokes to belittle you, and when you show hurt from these words, they will say, "I was just kidding," or "No big deal." Manipulators like to make simple comments, frequently shrouded in wittiness or collegiality, to portray victims as second rate or deficient. These remarks can relate to appearance, traits, experience, and qualifications, and the way that you strolled in two minutes late and exhausted.

By making you look bad, and getting one to feel terrible, the manipulator wishes to establish dominance over you. Additionally, they do this to point things out about you that could alter how others view you. While you may enjoy a specific musician that others believe nothing of, a manipulator may say something such as, How could any person that way band? The silent treatment is a widely used device used by manipulators. They understand that ignoring you can be often the very best way to get under the skin of yours. By deliberately not responding to your calls, requests, or messages, the manipulator presumes control by making you pause, as well as means to place vulnerability and anxiety in the brain of yours. Silence will often be by far the most effective of weapons.

They may not provide you with the silent treatment of a person, though they can pretend to dismiss you, so you are not mindful of the intentions of theirs. By pretending she does not realize what you want or even what you require her to do, the manipulator causes you to take on what's the duty of her and also can make you sweat with strain and energy. Children use that method to defer duties, delay demands after them, and manipulate grown-ups into completing for them what the kid would rather not to do. Several adults make use of this method also when they have a job they wish to ignore, or maybe a commitment they would like to evade. For instance, deliberately cleaning the floor badly could trick the individual in charge, so they choose not to assign that process for you once again.

On a bigger scale, this could imply somebody in a relationship pretends they're not aware of that which you may need on a psychological level. They will point out such things as, I do not realize what you need, although they well understand what you need & just are not prepared to invest the job to do this goal. This leads to the way manipulators will usually guilt trip you. Some examples can include blaming others rather than him or maybe herself, concentrating on the own weakness of theirs, acting as though another person holds the crucial ingredient to their achievement and pleasure, or maybe disappointment and despair. By focusing on guilt-tripping others, the controller pressures the recipient into surrender.

Manipulators will likely then be sure to play the target regardless of how incorrect it may be. Many examples of this particular behavior type include overstated or even imagined specific problems, misrepresented or even fabricated health issues, codependency, reliance, calculated fragility to motivate support, as well as compassion along with playing weak or frail.

The reason behind manipulators playing the victim is often to misuse the victim's goodwill, thoughts of remorse, feelings of commitment and obligation, or maybe eagerness to protect and assistance, to extricate preposterous benefits & concessions. The phrase gaslighting is often utilized to refer to manipulation, which will get people to deal with themselves, the existence of theirs, memories, or perhaps musings. Gaslighting is essentially when somebody will attempt to allow you to think insane to ensure that they can get away with the manipulative behavior of theirs. A manipulative person might twist everything you condition and allow it to be all about them, record the conversation, or even make you have an inclination that you have achieved something bad when you have done absolutely nothing wrong.

When you're being gaslighted, you might feel a misguided sensation of blame that you've done something bad, flat when that's not the circumstances. Manipulators blame; they don't recognize some liability in a scenario. Whenever you allow a manipulator know they hurt the feelings of yours, they're rather going to point out exactly how you're insane, remembering things bad, or perhaps being overly sensitive about the circumstances.

Once somebody does you a favor, not for the benefit of simply because, however, with concealed motives, you can be certain you're being manipulated nearly. One important kind of manipulator may be named Mr. Nice Guy. This person might be useful and finish a lot of favors for others. Nevertheless, with each terrific deed, there's a string attached - a desire. If you do not meet up with the manipulator's motive or desire, you'll be referred to as unreasonable.

A sales rep, for example, might affect the decision of yours on buying a clothing item. However, they do not believe the product fits you. In a relationship, a manipulator might get you flowers directly before asking you for a favor. These techniques do the job since they misuse community standards. It's common to react to favors, but when someone offers one deceitfully, we still are constrained to accept as well as go along.

An additional technique of manipulation is inspiring fear to somebody, just to provide them a lot of help later. An individual could frighten you in to going someplace new, developing the fear of yours within the school. Next, they are going to strive to shield you and allow you to feel secure, although the worries they warned you about in the very first place were not serious.

This may be done whenever you could be making a crucial decision. The manipulator will, in the beginning, let you know all of the factors that you need to be scared. They are going to tell you about the negative things that are happening and can do whatever they've to be able to make sure that you're afraid. Afterward, they are going to come up with a fix to ensure that they can ensure you're determined by them and look up to them as a "savior" sort.

A variety of businesses may make use of this tactic to be able to market you the item of theirs. For instance, someone could make an elbow cream and all over their commercial, tell you about just how in case you do not put it to use, you run the danger of obtaining a specific illness. After that, you are going to start to make certain to purchase the product of theirs since you're afraid of this particular disease, although you do not ever hear of it, or perhaps thought about this, before seeing the business.

Bribery is a good tool for manipulators in a few instances. They can do it in clear ways, saying a thing about precisely how they will provide you with cash or maybe a particular incentive in case you're competent to make the point for these people. In the event you refuse, next, they are going to start to make use of different manipulative tactics until they get what they would like, often actually taking out the bribe in the task, so you wind up walking away without any benefits at all.

To mirror the target is a way that manipulators will manipulate. They can begin to act just like the other individual to ensure that the one being manipulated feels a closer relationship to them. They may discuss the same struggles as well as tricky lifestyle problems they went through, which are much like the individual who's being manipulated. For instance, someone speaking about the way they have difficulty with grief after losing a couple of friends may discover that the manipulator of theirs can make up or perhaps exaggerates an alternative death to be able to attempt to connect to this particular individual. They'll, after that, discover it's much easier to regulate the individual when they're feeling empathetic.

Storytelling is a very common manipulation strategy. Manipulators are going to be professionals at twisting a story to make certain it fits the ends of theirs. They will not always totally make up original and new lies. However, they'll surely twist the fact so it may sound much better for these people, which makes them look like a hero, or maybe the victim, whichever fits the needs of theirs during the specified time that they're sharing the story.

Manipulators are going to learn the right way to set the mood of the victims of theirs. Although they're strict in getting what they need, they can be extremely adaptable in case it means having much more control with a particular person. in case they understand that a person wants a particular restaurant, they are going to take them there, or even in case they choose to be by yourself and quiet at home, next they'll do that. It's not bad to take individuals to places they love. Still, in case you're doing so to mentally fool them into providing you with a thing you would like, then that's when it turns into manipulation.

Managing your speech is vital for manipulators, and the gestures as well as touch they use. They may be excellent actors, in a position to turn their gestures as well as a speech at the drop of a hat. All of us have various moods, which may result in us to act varied with regards to the circumstance. However, a genuine manipulator will use numerous faces they can change when they need. Manipulators usually understand the potential of silence. Although they may have limitless techniques as well as interactions they can easily use on other people, after the day, they'll continue to understand that being quiet may often be by far the most effective issue that they do.

Less Common Manipulation Tactics

Sustaining an intent gaze could make people feel as they're truly listened to. Manipulative people are going to make exceptional eye contact and get it a step further and improve the eye contact of theirs with an interest as well as invested facial expression. A mesmerizing appearance is constantly offered testing limits. Manipulators might do or even say something awkward simply before or perhaps after the mesmerizing appear to look at the way you respond. The appearance may feel as an enticement or even love. If somebody's mesmerizing appearance makes you feel off in any capacity, it's ideal for getting up and take a rest from the scenario you end up in. Check the sentiments of yours and also remind yourself of your values and character when things get extreme.

Manipulators do not care about various other people's body language. They can instead overstep boundaries with no a lot of notice. People who, usually, overstep boundaries enjoy a certain appeal about them. Manipulative people are going to endeavor to break the rules in modest and, at times, playful methods. For instance, they might step in front of you on the sidewalk simply to check out whether you will permit it. Manipulative people may well lift you off of the soil amid embraces, and they will discover ways to attack the private space of yours.

Narcissists, as well as manipulative people, most of the time, stand nearer to others compared to other individuals do. They normally use room intrusion to threaten, show management, test limits, and to tempt. Manipulative people love making use of this strategy to market power over you and entice one to provide directly into their demands or even needs.

Occasionally a manipulator may discuss secrets along with you with no hesitation. They are going to do this as a strategy to keep you keen on them as well as to make them appear to be much more approachable, relatable, and reliable. They may additionally do this since they're wanting one to reciprocate, sharing secrets which they can easily make use of against you. Next, whenever you face the manipulator regarding the betrayal down the road, the manipulator will deny having said something, causing you to think insane and defeated.

Manipulative people understand how to sweet talk the victims of theirs. Additionally, they understand how to keep you keen on what they're thinking on all occasions. Manipulative people, in addition to narcissists, are spinners of accounts. If they get going about anything, it tends to be tough to stop them. Manipulative personalities are going to make you feel special by how often they trust in you. If they stop disclosing items for you, you might feel as you did something wrong and can do your very best to have once more people and create their awesome graces. Producing that kind of insecurity is tied in with controlling your concentration as well as time, to secure the focus of yours at the manipulator's whim. If you notice somebody manipulating you by selectively sharing as well as withholding, have a stride again and set some area between yourself and that person.

Often manipulators make use of pet names rather compared to the real name of yours. It may seem to be cute when someone starts calling you by a pet title. Be that as it might, manipulative identities will make use of text as "dear" or "baby" to belittle you. Next, whenever they stop calling you by a pet name, it can produce feelings of abandonment and leave you wanting to know what you fouled up. It's just yet another little bit of the strategic maneuvers of theirs. If such labels bother you, reveal to them you do not value being known as pet names and would rather love to be called by the actual name of yours.

When someone compliments you a good deal, naturally, you're about to feel very good with regards to yourself. It's crucial to distinguish what the real intentions of theirs are. Several of the time, people will utilize compliments to get something out of you. If perhaps you possess expert at the work of yours, school, and any other advanced setting, people with less authority or perhaps at a lower position than you might make use of compliments with expectations of advancement. In case the person complimenting you is actually at an equal level, it might be a reputable compliment without any manipulative thought procedures. Naturally, male-female relationships complicate these matters even more. Even in a situation between equals in the work environment, a compliment might be utilized as manipulation to advance a social agenda.

Not everybody that offers compliments means to manipulate you. It is a good idea to be conscious of individuals' real expectations. Trust the instinct of yours. If something feels off about someone, it can be advantageous to discover exactly why. To keep yourself from falling for manipulative approaches might have some instruction. A traditional technique to make sure whether you're in a relationship, or just having a chat with a person who is attempting to manipulate you, is focusing on the place they bring the conversation. In case they're endeavoring to allow you to feel also exceptionally fortunate or perhaps unfortunate about yourself, that is a crucial warning sign.

It's crucial, nonetheless, to be aware that the explanations as mentioned above don't assure you're working with a manipulative individual. Using pet names, for instance, doesn't imply you or maybe an associate is manipulative. To evaluate manipulators, you have to draw the whole character of theirs into consideration and not only distinct characteristics of the behavior of theirs.

CHAPTER 6 THE DARK PSYCHOLOGY OF MANIPULATION

We know there are manipulators, and they're all around us, but who exactly are these people? What kind of persona do they have? They are the partner who is abusive and controlling in a romantic relationship, damaging not only the relationship that the two of you have built but taking down your self-esteem right along with it. They're the family member in a family dynamic that continuously causes disharmony and confusion or the one who always needs to be the center of attention. They might be the sister, brother, aunt, uncle, cousin, mother, or father, who makes subtle remarks to make everyone else around them feel insufficient or unsafe.

The manipulator could be your neighbor or friend next door who spreads rumors and gossip, the one who enjoys pitting one person against another and then standing back and watching the fight. The manipulator at work might be that colleague who has a track record for being dishonest and unethical, willing to stoop as low as they can to get what they want and stepping on the toes of everyone else on their way up to the top. The manipulators on the streets are the criminals and con-artists who rely on deception and distraction to swallow you out of your hard-earned cash, rob you in broad daylight without you knowing it, and stealthily cover their tracks to avoid detection.

The manipulator can come in any form or shape, sometimes in the form of a person you least expect, and among the many things that many of these manipulators have in common is the fact that they suffer from some form of personality disorder which makes them who they are. In 1835, the word "religious insanity" was coined by physician Dr. James Cowles Prichard to describe certain persons who, while not objectively insane by today's standards, had severe and noticeable variations in their attitudes and behavior when it came to morals, ethics and their emotional reactions or responses to individual circumstances. Yet, despite these apparent differences, those classified under moral insanity showed very little social or emotional distress over their behavior.

These individuals who had some sort of personality disorder had a long history of emotional, personality, relationship, and behavioral difficulties that differed significantly from those of their families or even culture. The behavior patterns displayed were unstable and intruded into just about every aspect of their lives, which generated difficulties with their emotional and personal capacity to work, which undoubtedly leads to their manipulative tendencies. Among the forms of personality, most likely to resort to manipulation are:

- Histrionic Personality Type-Individuals with this omnipresent behavior tend to seek attention and resort to excessive emotional displays, often referred to as dramatic. They can resort to highly manipulative behavior when engaged in a relationship to obtain what they want.
- Types of Antisocial Personality-These individuals are capable of being manipulative because they have little regard for the unspoken social rules that are followed by everyone else. These antisocial traits may consist of many behavioral behaviors, like being unsupportive, chronically incompetent and irresponsible, bullying others. For those who do not value the human rights of another person, they may also turn to illegal activity and display no remorse. Clinically, these individuals are highly selfish, with deceit, manipulation, manipulation, and even physical attack being one of the many behavioral behaviors that they may potentially exhibit.
- Borderline Personality Disorder-In terms of self-perception, moods, and relationships, these people may be severe, unpredictable, and dysfunctional. They have little or no capacity to control their impulses. The common features associated with this type of behavior include fear of abandonment, being unstable when it comes to their self-image, social relationships, displaying inappropriate but intense feelings of anger and paranoia, and even resorting to impulsive or self-damaging acts that include substance and alcohol abuse. This uncertainty may then lead them to commit manipulative acts.
- Narcissistic Personality Disorder —Having a narcissistic personality is a condition that leaves us with a sense of superiority, a desire to be respected, and a sense of self-worth inflated. It's not uncommon for these people to have an enormous

ego, and they care little about anyone else but themselves. This lack of empathy for others, pride, inflated self-esteem, sense of entitlement that makes them believe they deserve special privileges and attention can lead to feelings of resentment or envy when their needs are not met. This strong sense of entitlement often causes them to believe they have the right to punish or inflict vengeance on those they view as not giving them the attention, due respect or recognition they feel they deserve. Psychologically, narcissism is not capable of true self-love, because those dealing with narcissism are more in love with their grandiose and idealized, unrealistic self-image. Such illusions of grandeur that they harbor inside them are precisely what leads to such dysfunctional behavior, and why they are portrayed more often than not as demanding, greedy, patronizing and manipulative. Their friendships, family life, romantic relationships, and even professional relationships are not safe from their narcissistic tendencies, and what makes it harder is that those with this personality disorder are reluctant to change, preferring to expect others to comply with their needs rather than being exploited by individuals.

What Makes The Manipulator A Dangerous Narcissist

It is not only arrogance and vanity that contribute to the delusion of the superiority of a narcissist, but the grandiose idea that they are more important than anybody else around them, which leads the narcissist to believe that they are special enough to warrant getting anything they want. They see themselves as being better than anybody else, and they want to associate only with those they consider to be on the same level as they are. What makes the narcissist such a dangerous form of narcissistic personality (which is why it's part of the Dark Triad), is that they don't just think they deserve respect and appreciation, they demand it.

We have produced in their minds a distorted view of fact in which they are the star of their show, and everyone else is merely a supporting player. Anything and anyone perceived as a threat that is just waiting to burst the bubble of their fantasy world will be met with extreme reactions that could include defensiveness, threats and even outright rage. Since they have a constant need to be praised, admired, and acknowledged (although they may have done nothing outstanding), maintaining a healthy relationship with a narcissist becomes almost impossible. The relationship is doomed to be unilateral from the outset, a relationship in which there is no mutual benefit as the narcissist is the only one who stands to gain anything.

Since they genuinely believe they deserve to get anything they want because they are better around them than anyone else, they expect everyone to bend backwards and fulfill their every demand without question automatically. To the narcissist, it's considered unnecessary and necessary for someone who doesn't meet their expectations or accompanies what they want. If you're brave enough to refuse their demands, or even daring enough to ask for a favor in exchange for all the support you've given them in the past, it won't take much for them to fly off their handle and react aggressively in frustration, resentment or even emotionally torment by subjecting you to the silent treatment.

The narcissist is a danger to your mental and emotional well-being for the simple reason that they have no regrets and will be more than willing to make the most of exploiting you for their gain without shame or remorse for their actions. This inflated sense of self-worth leads them to believe that they are entitled to treat you in any manner they see fit, and they will never consider their acts as incorrect or immoral in any manner. In many ways, the narcissist has almost won his place in the Dark Triad, and one of the main reasons for this is that they see all else around them as objects to be used. To the narcissist, you do exist, and that is it, for no other reason than to serve their needs. They will never stop worrying twice about taking advantage of you, just to give up if you no longer serve any useful purpose for them.

At the same time, they can be both malicious and oblivious, mostly blinded by their entitlement themselves. They are unable to think about how their actions could have consequences for everyone else; even if you pointed it out to them, they will simply reject you and refuse to believe you.

The narcissist would be demeaning you, threatening you, and belittling you if it means they'll get their way. They resort to putting you down to inflate their already expanded ego if they feel threatened by you or perceive you as trying to "push back" upon them. This is how they neutralize their "enemies" in their minds, by stomping on them until they feel too insecure about rising and challenging them in any way. Threats, bullying, insults, shame, dismissiveness, and ridicule are just a few of the many tactics they will employ to try to get you back in line and put you in your place.

Their covert-aggressive personalities and manipulators

Two categories could fall into when it comes to aggression. We turn to either overt-aggression or covert-aggression. That is over-aggression when someone is obvious, direct, and open in the way they choose to stand up or fight back with. It is unlikely that this is a category the manipulator will fall into since they never want anyone to know what they are up to. No, a manipulator tends to go for the second strategy, which is covert-aggression. This tactic enables them to be manipulative, discreet, and sufficiently underhanded to mask their true intent. A very good manipulator, however, must know how to use both characteristics and manipulate the combined strength of both, avoiding any blatant shows of overt-aggression while also being able to threaten another sufficient to get them to do what you want. When it comes to interpersonal interaction, covert-aggression is the preferred mode of operation for a manipulator.

Covert-aggression is not necessarily an act reserved exclusively for manipulators. Practically everyone has engaged in some sort of covertly aggressive behavior now and then. Occasionally, having to turn to covert-aggressive behavior for one reason or another doesn't mean you have a covert-aggressive sort of personality. When you habitually repeat this type of behavior, the way a manipulator does, it becomes part of your personality.

To keep them going, covert-aggressive personality manipulators rely on a steady diet of control, deception and manipulation. That technique has become a part of who they are, and their favorite way of coping with those around them to do it the way they want it to be done. For those who have never witnessed it first-hand, they may have a hard time recognizing why it is difficult for deceptive victims to know what is going on and why they fail to recognize that they are being abused. It may be tempting to brush the victims off and conclude that they are stupid to allow themselves to be exploited in this way. That's when you come to understand that before it's too late the victims don't know they're being abused. Especially when the manipulator is relying on covert-aggression to hoodwink its objectives. Covert-aggression is as effective in a manipulator's hands since:

- Aggression by the manipulator is well concealed. It makes it difficult for the victims to fight back against something that they can't identify or find evidence against. Even if their intestinal feeling tells them something is off. Maybe this person is trying to take advantage of it, the manipulator does it in such a stealthy way that it becomes difficult for the victim to identify their true motives.
- It gives the manipulator the appearance of resorting to any tactics other than combat. Covert-aggression permits the manipulator to cover their tracks by making it appear as if they are defending their victim, maybe even looking after them and standing up for them. It's hard to say for sure that these strategies are nothing more than a clever trick because the manipulator does it in such a way that it makes some sense to be convincing enough that the victim starts to question their intestinal intuition to warn them that they might be fooled. In addition to being a clever tactic that keeps the fact that the manipulator is actively battling the victim well concealed, covert violence makes the victim deliberately defensive at the same time, making it very difficult for them to think straight when they feel exhausted from running emotionally. That's why manipulators love covert-aggression because it's a psychological tool so powerful.
- Gives the manipulator the ability to know exactly which buttons to push the victim. Everybody has their insecurities and vulnerabilities that they're struggling with. If the manipulator has been around you for long enough, they'll know those

vulnerabilities better than you would think, using subtle manipulation to manipulate you correctly and make it easier and forget that you're being manipulated. Taking a parent who knows one of their weaknesses, for example, is that they can easily be made to feel guilty. When their manipulative child, who has been able to detect this weakness, pushes on the right buttons to get what they want, it becomes easy for the parent to forget what happens when they want to give in to their child and make them happy.

- The manipulator is the proverbial wolf in sheep's clothing. Manipulators working closely with these forms of covert-aggressive personalities keep their violent actions well and truly concealed under a mask that prevents us from seeing what is happening. They hide their less than honorable intentions behind the guise of being charming and a likable personality so hard to believe that underneath that layer is an aggressive and ruthless personality just waiting to take you down. We know how to target just the right victims too, always aiming for those that are more overtly vulnerable than others, cautious or someone with a weaker, more fragile disposition that is harder to manipulate and less likely to fight back. Here is an example of what the covert-aggression would look like in a scenario for a husband and wife. Let's say that one day the wife (the victim) decides to have a conversation with her husband (the manipulator) about the fact that he doesn't spend enough time with her and the children she'd like him to have. She's worried that he's missing out on quality family time with the children. The husband immediately reacts by becoming the victim in this situation by pointing out how he feels abused by the wife. She "constantly" makes unfair demands. He then goes on to portray himself as the one who is suffering and undervalued because "nobody" seems to feel grateful or acknowledge how hard he is working to support the family.

The husband then finishes it off by delivering the knockout punch that entails embarrassment and makes the wife feel bad by claiming that all she seems to do is complain. Nothing he does is ever good enough. The wife, who started with a very different objective in mind, one where she tried to solve what she felt was a question, is now being made to look like the inhuman, heartless, and unrecognizable bad guy, when in fact that was not what she was attempting to do at all. If the wife does not see this assault coming, she may be easily tricked into thinking that she is the one in the wrong, unable to see what the husband has just done there, as this pattern of action has replicated itself many times in the past. In this scenario, the wife will most likely apologize and give in to the husband's dominance, totally unaware that she had just been fooled into feeling like the guilty party. The louder a person makes claims about sainthood, the larger the horns they try to hide, as the American author Steve Maraboli so succinctly puts it.

- Only the manipulator will know exactly why they want to choose the people they do. Still, when they pick a choice, it is because they either need something from that person or want something from it. It may be a financial requirement, an emotional or even a physical need, so you're a priority for them because you have it, and they need it. In this cat and mouse game, manipulators enjoy playing with their victims, revealing that they are the ones in a position of power all the time since the victim has no idea what is going on. They use the connection and bond they have built with their victims in order to keep them hostage, and sometimes they make the poor victim feel they have no choice but to comply. And that is why people with personality disorders are so dangerous and manipulative.

Mind Control- Could It Happen To You?

It may sound like something straight out of a science fiction film, but it's possible to control the mind. Okay, sort of. Not the sort of mind control where you have the power to turn someone into a robot you want to manipulate, but close enough to that. The kind of mind control that goes largely unnoticed, much of the time, is the type of mind control that takes place around us every day.

- Persuasion: The Persuasion Psychology, a book written by researcher Dr. Robert Cialdini in the 1980s, discusses several different scientifically validated techniques and concepts that are used to manipulate others, along with some tips about how to do it. It has become one of the most important books in the marketing world since it was written, and businesses are constantly using those tactics to try to sell their products to consumers. Mind control is not about the power of magic or any kind of supernatural knowledge. In fact, mind control exists in the form of marketing and advertising in its most basic form, something that we are all exposed to every day. On a more personal level, manipulators tap into mind control techniques to control everyone else around them when they try to dictate results in their favor.

Once we open our eyes and begin to look around, there are techniques of mind control all around us. Publicity and marketing are nothing more than one form of subtle mind control. Another big one that has every day become addicted to much of the planet is social media. Facebook has effectively built up its global empire that boasts 1.6 billion users who are actively participating and counting on this site, and hardly any of the users are likely to know how Facebook has acquired that kind of power through subtle mind control strategies, and one such technique is through inducing fear of losing out on what's happening inside its users. Human beings have always longed for contact with other people, and we have never coped with isolation, traditionally. Each and every one of us has a deep desire to be accepted, to have a group we can relate to or associate with, and it is precisely the fear of losing contact with friends and followers of your social media accounts (not just Facebook) that keeps you coming back for more.

Social media aren't the whole story yet, because mental control techniques don't stop there either. What do you think happens every time you type a fast search into your Google browser? Do you truly believe that you have complete autonomy when carrying out your online research? According to Robert Epstein, a psychologist, this is not what is happening at all. What really happens is what Epstein calls the Search Engine Manipulation (SEME) effect. The SEME impact is rooted in the fact that the first two results found on

Google's first page are half the time we end up clicking on it each time a user hopes online to search for something. Inside the top 10 results, Google has shown in front of you, over 90 percent of the clicks that happen to happen. There are other pages and pages of results, other websites, and links that also contain the keywords you're searching for, but it's Google that ends up "deciding" what you're reading. Most of which one is, What's on the first page? And we thought we had full control over our search options here too.

Dr. Robert Hare, a researcher, and specialist in the field of criminal psychology states that simple mental control strategies are often used by psychopaths who want to develop a relationship with someone who wants to manipulate and conquer them. The narcissist is another category of individuals who often resort to mind control techniques to compel their victims to make their offering. Mind control is nothing more than another extreme form of manipulation, and it's just as dangerous as all the other manipulative techniques employed because we don't see mind control as something present in our daily lives. We tend to think about brainwashing as something that only cult or religious groups resort to, or something that advertisers and politicians are more likely to resort to than the average person. It can be hard to understand that in the next cubicle, the colleague who works with you is more than capable of applying subtle mind control techniques as a means of exercising control over you. Popular examples of mind control tactics that occur right in front of us through the manipulator we know include:

- Several choices being offered without realizing that all of those choices lead to the same conclusion. This is how the manipulator leads you to believe that you have a "choice" and that you are making your own "decisions" when they have already made the decision for you in reality.
- Have you heard the same idea or word so frequently that it now sticks in your head?
- Letting the manipulator perform an intelligence-dampening tactic on you. It is here that they will provide you with a series of brief snippets of information on several different topics, train your brain indirectly for short-term memory, and make you

feel overwhelmed by the amount of information you receive on several topics. This overwhelming feeling is exactly what they want you to feel as it has you turning to them for answers and making you more susceptible to what they want to go along. Have you ever had a colleague who came to you and shot off a series of instructions before you had time to process it? So then propose options easily (which they've required anyway), so you feel so relaxed that you accept without a second thought? Controlling the mind at work.

- Manipulate your emotions by placing you in a situation where your emotions are heightened to the point that you have trouble thinking straight. The more difficult it is for you to concentrate, the easier it is for them to control you by putting ideas into your mind. Mind control techniques are effective in the psychopaths' hands because they know how to read the people around them effectively. They worked hard to turn this into an art form, primarily inspired by a deep desire to regulate and conquer their goals. Psychopaths have learned how to quickly size their goals, perform a quick but accurate assessment of what their weaknesses and strengths may be, and as they go along, they continue to gather more information about their goals that will give them more leverage and control. Watch out for the following red flags if you think someone you know could use subtle mind control techniques against you:
- You feel isolated-one day you look around, and you realize that you've managed to isolate all of your friends somehow and that you're suddenly feeling extremely lonely. You 're not quite sure how it happened, and the only "friend" left to whom you can turn is the one that first caused the isolation.
- Change your actions for them-When did you last do something that really made you happy in your romantic relationship? Something that was about you without worrying or thinking about what your partner would say or how they'd respond. Sulking, being moody, and getting you to change your behavior for them just to prevent an argument from happening is a tell-tale sign that mind control techniques are beginning to make themselves known in your relationship. You are being controlled when you start to change your actions because of what someone else wants.

- Non-verbal Signals to Manipulate — Based on a strategy known as metacommunication, the manipulator can seek to control you by relying on nonverbal signs to change your mind. For example, if you and your partner go out to get dinner from that pizza place you like, but they don't, they might agree but follow that "yes" with a loud, dramatic sigh and a slump of their shoulders that leaves no room for doubt that they'd rather say "no" instead.
- Neuro-Linguistic Programming (NLP)-The more skilled manipulators use NLP as one of their many methods of mind control. NLP is a major technique in which the manipulator uses language to layer certain thoughts that, without you knowing it, they want to plant into your subconscious mind. NLP works by observing an individual's different aspects and then using language to implant a suggestion. For e.g., if Person A was someone with a more visual orientation, then might the manipulator use NLP by turning to language via visual indications like you see what I mean? If Person B was someone more inclined towards auditory signals, the vocabulary used in the NLP might be along the lines of I completely HEAR what you are saying.

Signs You Are Controlled Mind

Not all mind checks are bad. Yes, mind-control can be a bad thing in a manipulator's hands. But mind-control is not all bad on its own. There are actually several forms of mind control techniques being practiced today that have significant advantages in helping us improve our lives for the better. These techniques cover:

- Meditation-A practice that has existed for centuries, meditation is one of today's world's oldest and most effective mind control techniques. It literally encourages you to control your mind intentionally by calming your thoughts and emptying it of all the noisy chatter so that peace and serenity can flow through you instead and help you relax when you need it most. Science has even been able to prove successfully that the alpha waves produced in mind tend to peak after a good meditative session, and the alpha waves are responsible for enriching our creative minds and for strengthening positive thinking.

- Imagination-A technique that many successful individuals have long used to help them psychologically prepare themselves for success. Visualization is a training technique used to prepare the mind for performance, regardless of how insurmountable or unlikely the set target is. All the time, sports trainers and athletes rely on visualization strategies to get them to perform at their best. Lebanese-American writer and poet Khalil Gibran has famously penned the couplet that reads that the universe will deliver everything you ask for in a single-minded way. Rhonda Byrne later took the same idea to the masses in her book The Code.
- Mirror Technique – An approach that has long been recognized as an effective means of increasing self-confidence, talking to yourself in the mirror, is another example of mind control technique at work. Every day giving yourself a positive pep talk strengthens your belief in your own abilities, just like positive affirmations do. In each sentence, you say you're feeding your mind to concentrate on your good qualities, which will then give you the energy you need to work towards your goals.
- Hypnosis-Another type of meditation is hypnosis, which is also a form of mind control because you have to consciously erase all other thoughts from your mind and focus on nothing but one target. Hypnosis, or self-hypnosis, requires one single mantra to be repeated and repeated often enough that it sticks within your mind. This technique is often used to free those who struggle with self-destructive habits and behaviors, such as alcoholics.
- Aim Writing-Nothing ever seems true enough unless you see it right in front of you. The act of writing down your goals might not have occurred to you as yet another form of mind control, but it is. When you write down your goals, you give them a specific shape. Having a piece of paper written down in front of you makes it more tangible than it ever was when it was just an image floating through your head. Seeing it before you shift your mindset and gives you something concrete to focus on, and that sense of purpose will spur you into the success you want to accomplish.

Positive Forms Of Mind Control

When used the right way, mind control techniques can make a substantial change in your life for the better. Mind control can teach you how to do this:

- Remain in Check- If you 'd let your mind wander freely, who knows where it might lead you. One of the most distracting and dangerous thoughts to which everyone tends to be leading us down a dark and negative path. Without mind control to compel you to take over and drive your thoughts in the direction you want them to go, the concentration you need to remain on top of your game may be difficult to sustain.
- Protect yourself-With proper mental control training; you can teach yourself how to become more resilient and protect yourself from the manipulator's willful ways. Mind control will improve your self-confidence and reaffirm your self-confidence by reminding you that you are a strong, positive, and capable person, and no one will ever make you doubt your own abilities.

Manipulation Evidence Taking Place In Society

Nearly 30 years ago, Noam Chomsky presented an interesting take on manipulation to the world and how it is used in the media. This was perhaps the greatest evidence of manipulation taking place in our culture back then, but in the past 30 years, things have changed very dramatically. Now, there's evidence of bullying not just in the ads we 're subjected to every day but on the internet and on social networking sites like Facebook, Twitter, Instagram, and more. This is perhaps the strongest proof that there is deception all around us.

All you see, hear, watch, and read online and on social media now is manipulating you in one way or another. We 'd had far fewer manipulative threats to contend with before the social media days. Today, with a simple click of a mouse, news spreads around the world in mere seconds, and because the power of the internet is one that anyone who can string multiple sentences together can take advantage of, we are now more susceptible than ever to content that has been manufactured, exaggerated, distorted, simplified and presented in such a way that it is intended to skew our perception. It's almost as if today's media exists to make you do stuff you would not otherwise be saying or doing.

When you go online to the website of a company and read the product reviews on the internet, who is going to say that the company's marketing department has not written such reviews in an attempt to make their goods look good? It's almost too good to be true that the product reviews of a company would be nothing but 5-star ratings and praise about how the customers were "blown away" because the product worked wonders for them. If you've ever purchased an online product based on these "reviews" just to be let down because it didn't live up to the hype and expectations, there's probably a good reason for that. The sole purpose of a business is to sell, and if it means that those tactics will boost their sales figures up a notch, they are not above fabricating the truth.

Both traditional and social media have a long history of pulling strings behind the curtains, and they've been able to get away with it for so long because many of us still fail to see What is going on right in front of our eyes. We know it's happening on some level, yet we keep allowing it to influence our thoughts, and sometimes the decisions we make. How many times have you changed your perception of a certain group of people due to something you read about or watched online or on social media? How many times have your choices and lifestyle choices changed as you "saw something on Facebook that says you shouldn't do it"?

Social media is like an addictive drug that keeps you coming back for more, and the fact that it begins to rewire the way our brains start thinking is what makes it such a dangerous, manipulative force to the reckoned with. Scientists have confirmed that our brains are now being activated in a way that they have never been before in human history, with MRI scans showing that social media has begun to cause the release of dopamine-the very chemical that makes us feel good-into our minds. When that form of manipulation begins to feel good, it is when we know it has a stronger hold on us than we would admit.

CHAPTER 7 HOW TO RECOGNIZE A MANIPULATIVE RELATIONSHIP

When thinking of love, the society of ours romanticizes manipulative connections a great deal that it might be tough to identify them for what they're. We've lots of literature hinting to us that authentic relationships are around fixation, that love that is pure is all expending, and that people that are captivated have individual lives or no limits. While a lot of individuals romanticize the thought of a manipulative connection, we've to learn this the truth is, it's not genuine like. At times it may make for a remarkable plot as well as a conflict, which keeps the audience invested. Still, there's no enjoyment in actually living by way of a romantically manipulative relationship.

You might have been warned about the fact and manipulative individuals that command, as well as maltreatment, is one thing to be concerned about; the facts are actually that being in a manipulative relationship and a controlling which never grows into ill-treatment could be frightful and harm also. Simply because somebody is not harming you does not imply that you cannot feel soreness from the actions of theirs. To be managed or even place down by a companion can damage the confidence of ours, help make us feel fear about interactions down the road, and leave us feeling abandoned rather than comforted, with an assortment of emotional and mental injuries which we shouldn't be burdened with.

You may be familiar with indications of a harmful connection. For example, you might have encountered a mate that compelled one to put on just particular things of clothing or perhaps didn't wish one to see your family as well as friends. This particular individual may constantly wish to find out exactly where you're going, what you're doing, and the reason why you're just a couple of minutes late. Manipulators are usually rather nervous individuals; therefore, they are going to allow anxious feelings to pass through their influence as well as brains the actions of theirs. They'll spiral the too much emotion of theirs as well as strain into fantasies about what you might be performing when you're not near them. They are going to think about the worst fears of theirs and what you might be performing to harm them, then when you're not available, they're going to believe you're doing these things.

This could result in them disliking when you're not all over. It can seem to be complementary sometimes to have somebody be so worried about you. You may think, "It is very cute they usually want to find out exactly where I'm and that I am safe." Still, when somebody is going to great steps to manage you, this is not the purpose of theirs. Regrettably, the concern of theirs is not for the wellbeing of yours. Rather, they're thinking, "I need to ensure I know exactly where this particular individual is at all times, and so they are not doing something I do not approve of." The existence of yours is the guarantee of theirs; you are not satisfying the worst fears of theirs about the negative stuff you're performing to them once the 2 of you are not jointly. They will not be considerate of the needs of yours in this particular circumstance. The manipulator is just acting to deliver their interests theirs.

A manipulator won't ever tell you this and can instead merely feint problems to enhance the manner they seem to you. They'll additionally make use of this strategy to make certain you're feeling guilty. If you do not respond for twenty minutes, instead of them admitting it's appropriate for an individual not constantly to copy back instantly, they are going to make you feel guilty. They are going to treat you as in case you've done something wrong or perhaps selfish to them, without considering the reality that you just were not around the phone of yours at the time or perhaps had been way too busy to reply in the very first spot.

Love must feel good, but not confining, terrifying, or perhaps distressing, along with developing an accomplice must make you much more joyful, not sadder. You can find going to be times that are hard in love. You may not realize the mate of yours, and they may not realize you. These issues must be simple obstacles on the means of making you stronger. A proper relationship should not be one that's always draining you and breaking you apart, causing you to think continually exhausted.

Signs of a Manipulative Relationship

An excellent deal of us has had terrible material take place in the lives of ours - adequate awful material that the chance of a hero sweeping us off the feet of ours and shielding us from any problems for whatever remains of the life of ours can seem extremely enticing. Because of this, we occasionally look for care, compassion, and protection in the wrong places.

Reconsider whether your partner's thoughts of assistance include stopping you from making your own choices of yours and carrying on with your own life of yours. A partner that secures you by assuming responsibility for the maxed-out accounts of yours, or possibly speaking with a companion you have been fighting with is not paying particular brain to you; they're trying to make you've no other option but to place all the trust of yours in them and no one better.

A genuine partner realizes that they cannot protect you from daily life and just what it holds - they can just aid if you want them to. Must you, at some point, run right into a money related problem, a reliable partner might help you in praying an overabundance of unopened bills - assisting, however, not taking control of the circumstances. They will not take your demand or maybe passwords. You simply are permitted a restricted sum of money every month until you've paid off all the current debt of yours. A true partner is going to offer assistance yet will recognize you have to handle your problems of yours. One typical manipulative relationship tactic is making us feel guilty for seeing close friends as well as family members. Whenever we envision someone trying to reduce the companion of theirs off from their psychologically supportive network, we envision something much like the contemptible husband in a made-for-television movie telling the better half of his, which she will certainly not chat with her closest companion once again. Be that as it might, manipulative partners also can separate you from the support network of yours in an inconspicuous manner.

A shrewdly manipulative individual is not going to outwardly forbid you from seeing the family of yours simply because that may be a clear indicator you need to run in the various other paths. They're planning to come up with the manipulation subtler, rather pulling you from the family of yours gradually instead of an outright forbiddance. In the event that the partner of yours is able to persuade you to apologize for an action you realize you didn't do wrongfully, and also you do, the manipulative partner of yours will see he or maybe she is able to compel one to do something they need one to do.

Maybe your partner sulks every time you go out with the companions of yours until you blow off some other friends simply in order to save yourself the pressure. Perhaps the partner of yours makes negative remarks about your family until you begin to believe in that the feelings, they've about these individuals are actually legitimate. You may often have an exercise or a pastime that you like that the manipulator of yours will attempt to help you to quit doing. They are going to make certain you understand they believe the interest of yours is actually idiotic and ridicule you for this till you surrender it.

A controlling partner's scrutiny may not constantly show up as a result. It might be framed within the rational and reasonable language, which suggests the partner of yours is just trying to assist you. They might actually let you know they're merely attempting to assist you.

They might study the options of yours at the office. Several of the phrases of theirs might include: Why could it be you decided to make use of that for the business presentation of yours? Are you not concerned about what the boss will believe? They are going to question the spending habits of yours and just how you decide to buy things with questions like Did you truly have to purchase yet another shirt? Manipulators will spin the words of theirs. Therefore it is not clear they feel the selections you are making are actually incorrect, but a seed of doubt, as well as insecurity, is actually planted.

Nevertheless, all partners occasionally scrutinize each other. Our family must really appear out for us, and quite often, we want others to assist us in making choices or even point out undesirable habits. Remember to constantly check out the real goal of this particular individual as well as figure out the reason they'd really like you to change the behavior of yours. At times, a manipulator in a relationship may ask to have access to the personal belongings of yours, though they will not provide you with the exact same privileges. They may understand all of the secrets of yours; however, they hardly ever confide in you. They are not just less prone to discuss, and they definitely are not protecting you.

This particular behavior type shows that the various other individual is now being domineering. The partner of yours does not reserve the opportunity to browse your messages or email or even ask for the passwords of yours since they state they're apprehensive of whether you might cheat. There is a distinction between having insider specifics and getting proper independence from the partner of yours, and also, you do not have to surrender that when you're in a relationship with somebody.

Every so often, authentic couples that are recuperating from an occurrence of betrayal will permit the undermined partner access to each other's mail messages as a kind of accountability. Nevertheless, in the event this is not an arrangement that you've explicitly worked out with the partner of yours, it is not correct. Manipulation is about impacting the way another person believes, as well as behaves, all through mental command. This's hidden with passion, or even what appears to be a kind of empathy, at least. The majority of the time, this's a calculated effort at relating to the victim by the manipulator in question.

To be able to overcome this manipulation completely, it is crucial that people are able to acknowledge the effect that it's had on us. In the event that you would like to enjoy a proper connection with someone, it is essential that we're taking a look at all of the ways the relationship of theirs has impacted us. If its effect is negative, it may be the very first hint that a manipulative connection is available. Many manipulative individuals have four standard attributes:

- They understand how to understand the shortcomings of yours.
- They utilize the shortcomings of yours against you.
- Through the fast plots of theirs, they persuade you to surrender a thing of yourself to deliver them.
- When a controller triumphs in exploiting you, he'll most likely repeat the offense until you put a stop to the mistreatment.

They are going to have several diverse reasons for exactly why they wish to keep you around and influence you. One could be mere since they are pushed out of a previous connection. They may have trust issues that have led to them having issues in being open and accepting of some other partners. This could result in them to really feel as they have to manage you to help keep you faithful to them.

Several partners may just be lonely people that are eager for attention and love. If they feel as if you could take in that way, or perhaps are afraid that you are going to leave them, they'll stop at absolutely nothing to make sure you stay around, even if it involves manipulation. They may additionally just wish useful items coming from you, like financial assistance, perhaps your shared house, an automobile, along with other privileges that are not connected to you as an individual whom they love, but only the life that you decide to live. These're several of the most dangerous manipulators, and they're equally common as the others.

Understand Your Right

When somebody is in the midst of a manipulative connection, it could be very difficult to be aware of how you can get out. Manipulators are very good at producing confusion so that they can frequently stay away from quick blame for looking to manage others. The right way to make sure you're being protected is by remembering the rights of yours. These are the things which you're definitely entitled to and should not let an additional person take away. When you are able to recall these constantly, it is going to be simpler to confront manipulation as it is going on and more quickly identify when a conversation may be deadly.

On the other hand, in case you convey vulnerability to various other individuals, you might relinquish these rights. The following are our frequent, principal human rights: You deserve respect from others, particularly those to whom you offer respect. You are permitted to voice your emotions, feelings, and thoughts. You reserve the best to understand the own needs of yours, share those with other people, and do what you've to be able to fulfill those requirements, so very long as you do not take something away from others. You reserve the opportunity to state "no" with no looking regretful. You reserve the opportunity to get everything you buy, work for, and place effort toward. You have the proper to safeguard yourself against others in case they're harming you. You have the proper to create your own personal cheerful and awesome lifestyle.

The general public of ours is full of people who do not respect these rights. Psychological controllers, particularly, have to deny you of the rights of yours, so they are able to try out the manipulative tactics of theirs on you. Nevertheless, you are able to push back once again such attempts at control whenever you voice the self-confidence as well as the authority to announce it's you, not the controller, who is liable for the daily life of yours. These people have probably bossed around others for such a great deal of time and also have never been stood up too because of it. Remember to stand up for yourself and allow them to recognize they allow you to feel tough and exploited.

Regardless if they deny their effort or conduct to change it back around on you, in any case, you are able to relax, realizing you safeguarded yourself and took a stand for truth. Maybe they are going to start to change the tune of theirs in case they think you hit a nerve with them; all things considered, whenever they frighten everyone off, they'll have nobody to adjust any greater. Maintaining a strategic distance from their website is much easier said than accomplished in case they do not demonstrate their real nature instantly. Remember to heed the very first indication of them steamrolling the feelings of yours, steadily move in the exact opposite direction from the relationship, as well as create the effort to tell them the limitations of yours.

Manipulators require someone else to influence, and that is the reason they go to this kind of frantic lengths to find individuals that they are able to affect. If perhaps you've been a part of a manipulative connection of the past, they may be in a position to see several of that prior trauma as a method to make you much more vulnerable to the developments of theirs. When you see that a person is regularly interested in the history of yours and also the negative experiences you have been through, consider they're searching for your triggers and weaknesses. Some people may simply want to connect to you on a far more human level, but be conscious of the techniques which manipulators use trying as well as get a much better influence on the victims of theirs.

Several manipulators will regularly shift the individual they could be through one situation to the subsequent, becoming extremely courteous to a unique also completely inconsiderate to the next or perhaps definitely defenseless one minute and extremely forceful the following. If you notice this sort of conduct from an individual often, keep a proper distance and then refrain from engaging with the single aside from the most immediate needs. Regardless of what the demand, you will find a number of manipulators who'll make an effort to make use of the pressure of force and time one to make decisions fast, so you do not have an opportunity to think about what they're asking truly. On such events, instead of responding to the controller's request right away, consider using some time to market the wellbeing of yours and removing yourself out of this manipulative grip. You are able to exert experts over the circumstance by creating an easy declaration like "I'll think about it."

Consider just how incredible these couple of words are able to seem to a manipulator. You haven't dedicated to the demands of theirs; however, you don't refute them often. That provides a manipulator the sense that they currently have power over you, though you know normally. Take the amount of time you've to evaluate the pros and cons of a circumstance & consider whether you have to set up a far more fair game plan or even take control and set yourself in the ideal scenario.

The essential human rights of yours include the opportunity to determine the own needs of yours, the privilege to state "no" with no guilt, as well as the privilege to decide on what a fulfilling and life that is healthy is like. Doing the action of thinking "no" out obnoxious allows you to rehearse assertive and clear communication. And to then say "no" to a manipulator, doing so with hygiene, however immovably, provides you with a feeling of self-control while trying to keep the door ready to accept the connection. A manipulator turns into a domineering jerk whenever the person in question scares or maybe damages another person. Nothing is able to help expose a genuine manipulator's intentions as well as thoughts a lot more than in case they're pressured to face themselves and truly appear heavy into the ways they're dealing with others.

Probably the essential point to keep in mind about oppressive jerks is they are inclined to scope out the people that might seem prone to give in to manipulation. Hence, in case you continue confident, you will not fall as high on a manipulator's prospect summary as others might. Be that as it might, some harassers are actually defeatists on the inside. At the stage when their victims begin to exhibit the authority to stand up for themselves, the domineering jerk will frequently withdraw. This's legitimate in social and school scenarios at the same time as in business conditions.

On a caring note, investigation proves that many harassers are actually casualties of brutality themselves. Still, this shouldn't in any manner pardon harassing conduct. Knowing that harassers have usually been victimized could allow you to consider the domineering jerk in a far more empathetic light. But keep in mind that someone who's hurt should not be harming others. When you've been manipulated, does that necessarily mean you are going to go as well as perform the exact same to somebody else?

While heading up against menaces, ensure to apply a brave face and stand the ground of yours while having others present to look at as well as a stand along with you if you require extra help. In instances of physical, verbal, or maybe mental mistreatment, do not be scared to notify or even consult appropriate legitimate online resources, law enforcement, and wellness specialists. It may seem to be remarkable to get an entourage along with you, and on occasion, even a police officer, when doing something such as picking up outdated belongings from an ex-manipulator's house or even meeting up with them. Nevertheless, it's usually well worth guarding yourself. Although we are able to predict several of the thinking patterns of a manipulator, we never ever can really understand how they're going to respond in any situation.

Do not Allow the Self-Guilt to Take Over

Since the controller's inspiration is actually searching for and abuse the weaknesses of yours, it's clear that you might feel lacking, or perhaps scorn yourself for not fulfilling the manipulator's motives.

In these conditions, recollect that you're not the issue; you're being manipulated to feel bad with regards to yourself, with the aim which you're certain to surrender your rights as well as capacity. Think of the connection of yours with the controller, and get the following questions:

- Is this individual considerate of the fundamental human rights of mine?
- Is exactly what they're asking me to do something fair and reasonable that I can do without harming myself?
- Can they be asking this of me since they cannot do it, or even since they do not wish to do it?
- Are both parties in that relationship giving, or perhaps could it be just coming from one end?
- Do I love the individual that I'm when I'm near them? Can they be their best edition when they're near me?

The responses of yours to these inquiries provide you with crucial hints regarding if the "issue" you end up in is a consequence of something you're doing or maybe something the partner of yours is doing. Yet another idea you are able to do to defend yourself from manipulators is actually to place a target on the back of theirs by asking questions. Never fail to make them answer their own concerns of theirs and pressure them to self-reflect on the behavior of theirs.

If they are saying or even recommend something which appears unfair, makes you uncomfortable, or perhaps is actually unreasonable, it's essential to return the focus to the controller by asking a few of questions to check out whether they've plenty of mindfulness to perceive the imbalance of the plan of theirs.

When you're asking the above-mentioned issues, you're establishing a silhouette of what the manipulator expected of you. The way, the manipulator is able to see precisely what the behaviors of theirs are masking. In the event that the controller has a degree of mindfulness, the person will most likely excuse the offensive behavior of theirs as well as express what they need in a far more positive manner. On the other hand, pro manipulators are going to dispel the questions of yours as well as demand getting the way of theirs. When this occurs, take note of the following suggestions, which we discuss to go out of a manipulative scenario.

Set the Consequences

At the stage every time a manipulator demands one thing that transgresses the limitations of yours, make the effects of the actions of theirs acknowledged. Make sure you're constantly sharing the thoughts of yours since these they can't deny. They may not realize the feelings of yours. Neither will they generally be ready to listen. And do not count on them to provide up sympathy.

Nevertheless, they cannot state that the thoughts yours are not correct. In case they do. Next, they're gaslighting you, that is an abusive strategy you should not stand for. When you're forcing them to truly think about the way in which that they made you think, it is able to assist in showing the consequence. Even in case you forgive them internally, do not show it instantly. Wait for these people to display the changed behavior that you've been asking for.

Let us look at an example. Let us say your partner manipulated you within skipping the family party of yours since they did not wish to go, and they did not need one to go without them. Allow them to know they hurt the feelings of yours, and they made you feel bad about missing the family members of yours. They may say, "No, I didn't," though they do not get to determine that. You are able to allow them to know you comprehend may not have been the purpose of theirs (even though it probably was), but that you still harm either way. In case they are not prepared to recognize this, why do you think you're prepared to admit these were hurt whenever you had been thinking about going to the party without them? Ask this question. Assuming they're unwilling to listen to the thoughts of yours, why must you be happy to listen to theirs?

Don't offer into them, regardless of how difficult they try until they identify they hurt the feelings of yours. It is as easy as that. They may attempt to stay away from it, make you laugh, or perhaps distract you, so you are not mad, but don't offer in before they confess they damage you and apologize for it.

The ability to distinguish as well as declare effects is among the most crucial aptitudes you are able to utilize to cope with a troublesome person. A direct result is actually a feature that's going to harm them, not you. Think about what you are able to take away from their website to genuinely get them to begin considering you, and not only themselves in any situation.

Yet another example of manipulation maybe your partner is providing you with the silent treatment after you've disregarded them for an hour. Let us say you are at the office and also you got very busy, so of course, you missed their message asking what you needed to look at on television later that night. This's a really easy point and a sensible situation. You cannot be anticipated to reply to the phone of yours every minute of the day, particularly when you're tending to work obligations.

If you get home, the partner of yours is actually locked to the bedroom, not speaking to you at all. They're ignoring you and are not prepared to tune in to you. This will make you feel terrible, and also you begin to challenge whether a thing is actually wrong with you. In case they're lying in bed, then you think they must've been upset each night, and also, you may begin to feel truly guilty about everything you did, despite the fact that you did certainly nothing wrong.

Instead of providing into them and apologizing, again and again, they need actually to be the one apologizing for you! With this circumstance, it is best to sit down on the bed and tell them you are busy at the office, that is the reason you were not in a position to react. Allow them to realize you'd still enjoy seeing something. In case they do not quickly change the spirits of theirs and continue to throw a pity party for themselves, just walk away. They're searching for a psychological reaction. They wish to realize that they effectively controlled you. Do not offer into this. They have to reflect as well as recognize that the sole person responsible for that terrible spirit was themselves. In case they were legally worried about expanding along with you.

Next, they will agree to you were not in a position to answer as well as discuss the thoughts of theirs along with you. The silent treatment is actually a manipulative strategy targeted at making you feel guilty. Therefore you are going to submit to the power of theirs. Seize the control of the evening of yours in this particular situation. To view a film by yourself, giving them in bed to be angry.

CHAPTER 8 MIND CONTROL

For several years now, there has been about the theory of mind control. People were both fascinated and afraid of what would happen if someone could control their minds and make them do things contrary to their will. There are countless conspiracy theories about government leaders and other influential individuals who use their abilities to monitor what small groups of people do. Even some court cases were brought up using the brainwashing excuse as an explanation of why they committed the crime they are accused of. Despite the play-up of mental control depicted in the media and films, little is understood about the various forms of mental control and how each of the functions. This chapter will discuss the most popular types of mind control a little bit as an introduction to explain more about this fascinating topic.

Although there are many different types of mind control that can be used to control the intended victim, the most commonly thought of are five. That involves hypnosis, brainwashing, coercion, persuasion, and deceit. These are all to be discussed in the following.

Brainwash

Brainwashing is the first kind of mind control to be debated. Brainwashing is essentially the process where someone would be connived to give up convictions they had in the past and take on new principles and ideals. There are many ways this can be achieved, but not all of them are considered evil.

For instance, if you're from an African nation and then moving to America, you are always forced to change your beliefs and principles to fit in with the new community and climate in which you live. On the other hand, people in concentration camps, or when a new dictatorial regime takes over, will also go through the process of brainwashing to convince citizens to obey in peace. Many people get misunderstandings about what brainwashing is. Many people have more cynical ideas about the procedure like mind-control systems that are funded by the government and thought to be quickly turned on like a remote control. On the other side of things, there are skeptics who don't believe brainwashing is possible at all and whoever says it has occurred lies. In the center of these two theories, the form of brainwashing will probably fall somewhere.

During brainwashing practice, the target can be convinced by a mixture of various techniques to change their views about something. In this method, there is not just one technique that can be used, and it can be difficult to bring the practice into a tidy little package. The subject will also be disconnected from all the things they learn. From there, they are broken down into an emotional state, which makes them fragile before new concepts are implemented. As this new knowledge is absorbed by the subject, they will be rewarded for sharing ideas and thoughts that go with these new ideas. This should be used to justify the brainwashing that is taking place is rewarding.

Brainwashing is nothing new to the society. For a long time, people have been using such techniques. For example, those who were prisoners of war were sometimes broken down in a historical context, before being convinced to change sides. Some of those most successful cases would result in the inmate becoming a very fervent convert to the new side. In the beginning, such activities were very new and would always be applied based on who was in command. The concept of brainwashing was developed over time, and a few more methods were added to make the practice more widespread. The newer techniques will focus on the field of psychology because many of those concepts were used to show how people, by persuasion, could change their minds.

There are several steps that go along with the process of brainwashing. It's not something that can happen to you just as you walk down the street and talk to someone you just met. First of all, one of the main demands that come with successful brainwashing is that the subject should be kept in isolation. If the subject is around other people and experiences, they can learn how to behave like an adult, and there will be no brainwashing at all.

They can undergo a process designed to break down their own selves if the subject is removed. They 're told all the facts they know are wrong, and they're made to feel like they're wrong with everything they do. The subject will feel like they're bad after months of going through all of this and will be overwhelmed by the guilt. Once they have reached this point, the manipulator will begin to lead them to the desired new system of beliefs and identity. The topic would be led to believe that all of the new options are their own, and therefore, they are more likely to last. The entire brainwashing cycle can take months or even years or complete. It's not something that's going to happen in just a conversation, and it won't be able to happen outside of detention camps and a few isolated situations for the most part. Chapter 2 will go into more depth on what happens during the three primary phases of brainwashing and how the whole process takes place.

For the most part, when someone is simply trying to convince them from a different point of view, those who experience brainwashing do. For example, if you're in an argument with a friend, and they're telling you their ideas make sense, you've been through brainwashing technically. Sure, it may not be bad, and you might objectively think about it all, but you were also persuaded to alter the previously held convictions. This is really unlikely that someone undergoes real brainwashing where they would have changed their whole belief system. It will usually occur during the process of getting around to a new point of view, irrespective of whether or not the tactics used were forceful.

Hypnosis

The next, well-known form of mind control is hypnosis. The meanings of what hypnosis is are several different. Hypnosis is a mutual activity, according to the American Psychological Association, in which the hypnotist will provide suggestions that the patient will respond. Many people have become familiar with the hypnosis techniques thanks to popular performances, in which participants are told to perform ridiculous or unusual tasks. Another form of hypnosis that is gaining in popularity is the type that uses this practice for its therapeutic and medical advantages, especially when it comes to reducing anxiety and pain. In some cases, hypnosis has been able to reduce dementia symptoms in a few patients. There are, as you can see, several different explications that can be used for hypnosis.

If the hypnotist will give solutions that may be detrimental or alter the way the client behaves in their situation, the point where it starts to become mind control.

When they hear about hypnosis, they think of a person on stage who swings a watch back and forth to put the participant in a trance, for most people. If you got to a stage show for amusement, you might have some pictures of the absurd actions performed by the participants in your mind. In fact, those who are going through what is considered to be real hypnosis are going through a very different process from this picture. "The individual is not hypnotized by the hypnotist. The hypnotist then acts as a sort of coach or mentor whose task is to help the person become hypnotized, "John Kihlstrom said. This means the hypnotist is trying to bring the client into a relaxed state of mind, so they are more open to suggestions offered.

Most of the hypnosis sufferers claim they are in a kind of sleeplike dream state. Notwithstanding these feelings, while the patient is in a state under hypnosis, which includes vivid hallucinations, increased suggestibility, and concentrated attention. This new condition makes them more responsive to suggestions offered by the hypnotist. The effects that hypnosis can have on subjects are difficult to describe since the experiences can differ quite a bit for each person who undergoes it. Some participants will describe the feeling as though they are disconnected from the whole process, some will feel highly comfortable during the hypnosis, and even others will believe like their acts will take place beyond their conscious choices. On the other hand, individuals will claim to be fully aware of their surroundings and will even be able to conduct conversations during their hypnotic state.

Several studies done by Ernest Hilgard show that hypnosis can be used to alter the beliefs of the subject. Hilgard's experiment included a warning from the subject that they should not experience any pain in their head. The subject had their arm stuck in some ice water after they were told this. Those who did this experiment and did not get hypnotized had to take their arms out of the water in just a few seconds because they felt pain. Many who had been hypnotized could leave their arms in the water without experiencing any pain for a few minutes. Though more research is required, this study shows how powerful mind control can be when using the technique of hypnosis.

Hypnosis can be used to include: There are several different uses illustrated by studies that:

- Treatment of chronic pain like the one associated with rheumatoid arthritis. Treatment and avoidance of the suffering that comes from childbirth.
- Reducing the symptoms related to dementia.
- Since using hypnotherapy, some ADHD patients have reported a reduction in their symptoms.
- To reduce cases of vomiting and nausea in patients with chemotherapy.
- Pain control during a dental procedure. Eliminating and reducing skin disorders, such as psoriasis and warts, alleviating symptoms linked to Irritable Bowel Syndrome.

These are only a few of the uses of which hypnosis has become popular. While many people believe that using hypnosis is used to manipulate the subject and make it perform cruel actions or reject their own values, the most popular applications are those to enhance individuals' safety.

Most experts believe that hypnosis as a method of mind control is not really a fact. Although it may be possible to convince the mind to make a few changes in the subject's behaviors and behavior, it is impossible that the subject will change their whole belief system even by this process. Many of the people who are trained in this field would use it to assist the subject in handling self-improvement and discomfort rather than attempting to take their minds over.

Manipulation

Manipulation is another type of mind control, which can be used in various ways to decide how the person thinks. Manipulation is referred to in this guidebook as psychological manipulation. It is a sort of social power that serves to alter other people's actions or understanding. It is done using methods that are hostile, insulting, and underhanded. This form of mind control is used, often to the detriment of others, to advance the one controlling desires. The approaches employed are also perceived as manipulative, devious, coercive, and exploitative. Most people can understand when controlled or controlled around them, but they don't identify that as a form of mind control. It can also be a difficult method of mind control to resist as the coercion generally takes place between the subject and someone they know well. Manipulation leaves the subject feeling as if they have no choice. We would have been fed lies or half-truths outright, and we did not know the full severity of the case until it was too late. When they find out ahead of time about the situation, the manipulator would be able to threaten and use the topic to achieve the final target. By fact, the subject gets lost, and the manipulator will have worked it out in such a way that they won't fall into trouble, the subject will take the blame or get hurt when it comes to it, and the manipulator can make it to their final target.

The worst thing about this is that the manipulator is unable to sense their subject 's needs or any other person's needs; they won't know whether the subject gets harmed in the process if it's emotional or physical damage. Although the subject will be involved emotionally in the situation, the manipulator will be able to walk away (as long as they achieve their ultimate goal) without feeling any guilt or regret for what happened along the way. This can be a dangerous type of mind control because the manipulator will be an expert at it, capable of blackmailing, threatening, and doing whatever else is needed; often, they will even be able to turn it around, so the target feels like they're going insane.

Persuasion

Persuasion is another type of mind control similar to persuasion in that it acts to manipulate the subject 's actions, emotions, thoughts, attitudes, and beliefs. There are many different reasons why persuasion could be used in everyday life, and it's often a necessary form of communication to get people on the same page with different ideas. For business, for example, the persuasion mechanism can be used to shift the attitude of a person about anything, concept, or event that is happening. During the process, either written or spoken words are used to pass reasoning, feelings, or information on to the other person. Convincing another time may be used to satisfy a personal gain. This may include encouraging trials, when delivering a sales pitch, or during an election campaign. Although none of these are considered negative or bad, they are all used to convince the listener to act or think in some way. One definition of persuasion is that one uses one's own personal or professional power to alter others' attitudes or behaviors. There are also many different forms of persuasion known; the process of changing beliefs or attitudes by appealing to reason and reasoning is known as systemic persuasion; the process of changing beliefs and attitudes by appealing to feelings or behaviors is known as heuristic persuasion.

Persuasion is a form of control of the mind that is used all the time in society. When you talk about politics to someone, you can try to convince them to think the same way you do. If you listen to a political advertisement, you are motivated to vote in one direction or another. If anyone wants to sell you a new product, there's a lot of persuasion going on there. This form of mind control is so widespread that most people don't even know it's actually happening to them. The problem will occur when someone takes the time to convince you to believe in beliefs and principles that do not suit your own belief system. There are several different kinds of persuasion on sale. Maybe all of them have negative intent, but they will all try to get the target to change their minds about something. When a political candidate appears on television, on election day, they try to get the subject, or the voter, to vote on the ballot a certain way. The company that produced the advertising is trying to get the audience to purchase this product when you see a commercial on television or online. They are all forms of persuasion bent on trying to get the target to change the way they think.

Deception

Finally, deception is often considered a form of mind control because of its potential effect on the subject. Deception is used to spread assumptions in events and things in the subject, which are actually not real, whether they are full lies or just partial lies. Deception may include several different items like hand sleight, deception, and concealment, disguise, diversion. This kind of mind control is so dangerous because the subject sometimes does not know that there is any kind of mind control at all. We were persuaded that when the complete opposite is right, one thing is real. It can become dangerous when the deception hides details that would keep the subject secure. Often during relationships, deception is seen and will usually lead to feelings of distrust and betrayal between the two partners. There has been a violation of the relationship rules when deceit happens, and it may make it impossible for the partner to trust the other one for a long time. It can be particularly dangerous because most people are used to trust those around them, especially relationship partners and friends, and often expect them to be true to them. When they find out they're being misled by someone they're close to, they may have problems with trusting people, and they won't have the sense of security they 're used to.

Deception can trigger several problems in a relationship, or in the manipulator and subject. Once they find out about the deception, the subject will have a lot of issues trusting the manipulator in the future. There will be occasions where the lie is made to help the partnership out. This may involve things like not asking a partner when someone says they mean something. Other times the deception is of a more spiteful or harmful nature, such as when the manipulator hides important information from the subject or even deceives the person they really are. All people believe that deceit is unethical and should not be performed, no matter what form of deceit is deployed.

CHAPTER 9 BRAINWASHING

This chapter will focus on the brainwashing process and all the components that come with it. Through the media and films were shown, many people see brainwashing as a sinister activity performed by those who try to manipulate, control and obtain power. Some who really believe in the power of brainwashing believe that people around them are trying to control their minds and behaviors. The process of brainwashing occurs mostly in a much more subtle way and does not involve the sinister practices most people associate with it. This chapter will go into much more depth about what is brainwashing and how it could affect the subject's way of thinking.

What is Brainwashing?

Brainwashing is usually discussed around topics on human psychology. Brainwashing is referred to in this connection as a method of transforming thinking through social control. This sort of social impact happens to any person during the day, regardless of whether or not they know it. Social influence is the collection of methods used to change the behaviors, beliefs, and attitudes of other people. For example, enforcement procedures that are used in the workplace may potentially be considered a form of brainwashing because while you are on the job, they force you to behave and think a certain way. In its most extreme form, brainwashing can become more of a social problem, as such methods work to transform the way someone thinks without the subject consenting to it.

For brainwashing to function effectively, due to its intrusive impact on the subject, the subject would need to go through total isolation and dependence. It is one of the reasons that many of the brainwashing events that are written about arise in totalistic cults or detention camps. The brainwasher, or the handler, must have full power over their subject matter. This means they have to control the eating habits, sleeping patterns, and fulfill the subject's other human needs, and none of these actions can occur without the manipulator's will. The manipulator will work during this process to systematically break down the entire identity of the subject to basically make it no longer work properly. After losing the identity, the manipulator must seek to substitute it with the desired values, attitudes, and actions.

The brainwashing mechanism is still up for discussion as to whether it would succeed or not. Most psychologists hold the belief that a subject can be brainwashed as long as there are proper conditions. The entire thing isn't as serious as it is portrayed in the media, even then. There are also different definitions of brainwashing that make the determination of the brainwashing effects on the subject more difficult. Some of those definitions require some sort of threat to the subject's physical body to be considered brainwashing. If you follow this description, then no physical violence can be regarded as true brainwashing, except for the activities performed by many radical cults.

Other definitions of brainwashing will rely on control and coercion to bring about a change in the beliefs of the subjects without physical strength. Either way, experts think the brainwashing effect is just a short-term phenomenon, even under the perfect circumstances. Through practice, the subject 's identity is not completely eradicated; instead, until the new identity is no longer strengthened, it is concealed and returned.

In the 1950s, Robert Jay Lifton came up with some interesting thoughts about brainwashing after studying prisoners from the Chinese and Korean War camps. During his research, he concluded that the brainwashing of these prisoners was undergoing a multistep phase. This process started with attacks on the prisoner's sense of self and ended with a supposed change in the subject 's beliefs. In the subjects he studied, there are ten steps that Lifton defined for the brainwashing process. These encompassed:

1. An attack on the subject's character

2. Forcing responsibility on the matter

3. Driving the subject through self-indulgence

4. Achieving a breakpoint

5. Providing leniency for the subject if they alter

6. Manipulated to confess

7. Channeling culpability in the path expected

8. Setting off the subject of alleged guilt

9. Progress toward harmony

10. The final confession leading to a rebirth

All of these stages must occur in a completely isolated area. This means that all the usual social references in which the subject is being used to come into touch are not available. Furthermore, mind clouding strategies are used to intensify the cycle, such as malnutrition and sleep deprivation. Although this may not be true in all cases in brainwashing, there is often a presence of some kind of physical harm which contributes to making it difficult for the subject to think independently and critically as they would normally.

Important Steps

Although Lifton divided the steps of the brainwashing cycle into 10 phases, it is structured in three stages by modern psychologists to understand better What is going on with the subject during this phase. These three stages include breaking up the self, introducing the idea of salvation to the subject matter, and rebuilding the subject 's self. Knowing each of these stages, and the process that occurs in each of them will help you understand what occurs in this process to the subject 's identity.

Self-destruction

The first step of the brainwashing cycle is self-destruction. During this process, the manipulator wishes to break up the subject's old identity to make them feel more vulnerable and open to the new identity they desire. This step is necessary to carry on the process manipulator will not be very effective with their efforts if the topic is still firmly fixed in their resolve and old identity. Breaking the identity and making the person wonder about the stuff around them would make a change of identity simpler in the later stages. This is achieved through multiple phases, including assault on the identity of the subject, bringing about shame, self-treatment, and eventually reaching the point of breakdown.

Identity Assault

The assault on the subject's identity is simply the systematic attack on the sense of self of the subjects, or their ego or personality along with their core belief system. It raises the question of who they are by making them believe that everything they have ever learned is incorrect. The manipulator will spend a lot of time denying all this is the subject matter. For example, in prison camps, the manipulator will say things like "You're not defending liberty," "You're not a man," and "You're not a soldier." The subject will constantly be under attacks like these for days to months. This is done to exhaust the subjects into becoming disoriented, confused, and exhausted. Once the subject enters this sort of state, their convictions may begin to become less strong, and they may begin to accept the things they are told.

Crisis

Once the subject has passed through their identity assault, they will enter the stage of guilt. The topic is continually being told they are poor as they go through this current identity crisis that has been brought on. This is done to carry the topic a great sense of guilt. The subject is constantly under attack for any of the things they have done, no matter how big or small the acts might be. The nature of the attacks will also vary; the target may be attacked in the way they dress for their belief systems, and also because they eat too slowly. Over time, the subject will start feeling guilt all the time around them, and they'll feel that the things they're doing are wrong. This can help make them feel more comfortable and will possibly go along with the new image that the manipulator wants to establish.

Self-tragedy

Now that the subject is led to believe that they are bad, and all of their actions are unwanted, the manipulator will work to force the subject to admit that they are bad.

The subject drowns in its own guilt at this point and feels very disoriented. The manipulator may force the subject to denounce his old identity by continuing the mental assaults, by threatening any great physical damage, or by combining the two. This can include a wide array of issues like getting the topic to criticize their own colleagues, relatives, and family who share the same belief system as they do. Although this cycle may take a while to occur, until it does, the subject may feel like he has deceived everybody he feels close to. That will also increase both the shame and the loss of identity already felt by the target, further breaking down the identity of the subject.

Breakdown point

The subject is feeling really broken up and disoriented by this point. They could ask questions like, where am I? Who am I, then? And what do I do? The subject is at this point in an identity crisis and is going through some deep disgrace. Since they have betrayed all the values and the people he has always known, a nervous breakdown is going to occur on the subject. In psychology, this simply means a collection of severe symptoms, which often indicate a large number of supposed psychological disorders. Some of the symptoms may include general disorientation, profound depression, and uncontrolled sobbing. The subject may feel completely lost alongside having a loose grip on reality. Once the subject hits this stage of breakdown, they will have lost their sense of self, and at that stage, the manipulator will be able to do pretty much whatever they want because the subject has lost their grasp of what is going on around them and who they are. Even at this point, the manipulator will set up the different temptations needed to convert the subject into a new system of beliefs. The new system will be established in such a way that it will offer the subject salvation from the misery they feel.

Chance of redemption

It is time to proceed to the next step after the manipulator succeeded in breaking down the self of the subject. This step involves offering the subject the possibility of salvation only if they are willing to turn away from their former belief system and embrace the new one offered instead. The topic has the opportunity to realize what's around them; they 're told they 're going to be healthy again, and they'd feel better if they just followed the right new course. This stage of the brainwashing process includes four steps; leniency, confessional compulsion, guilt channeling, and the release of guilt.

Compassion

Leniency is the scene of "I'm going to help you." The subject has been broken down and forced to turn away from the people and the values they have upheld for so long. They've been told they 're bad and they're wrong with everything they do. The topic is going to feel lost in the world and all alone, ashamed about all the poor stuff they've done and wondered if they can turn around. Once the manipulator reaches this stage, it can offer them some form of release by offering help. This will often be in the form of relief from the abuse or some other little kindness incurred by the subject. For example, the manipulator may give the subject a little extra food or a drink of water, or just take a few moments to ask the family and loved one's questions about the specific subject matter. These little acts of kindness in the present state of the subject can seem like a big deal, resulting in the subject feeling a great sense of appreciation and relief towards the handler. These emotions are often out of proportion vis-à-vis the bid made. The subject may feel, in some instances, that the manipulator has done the act of saving their lives instead of simply offering a small service. This distortion of events works in the manipulator's favor, as the subject will now gain loyalty ties with the manipulator rather than past things.

Confession

Once the manipulator is in a position to gain the confidence of their subject, they will try to get a confession out of the process. This stage is often referred to as the "You can help yourself." During this stage of the brainwashing cycle, the subject starts to see the similarities between the pain and remorse they felt during the attack of identity and the relief they experience from the sudden leniency that is offered. If the process of brainwashing is successful, the subject may even begin to feel a desire to reciprocate some of the kindness the manipulator has offered to them. Once this happens, the manipulator will be able to present the idea of confession as a possible means of relieving the subject from the pain and guilt they feel. Then, the subject will be led through a process of confessing all the wrongs and sins they have committed in the past. Such errors and sins would, of course, be in relation to how they affect the new identity being formed. For instance, if the subject is a prisoner of war, this step will allow them to confess the wrongs that they have done by defending freedom or fighting the other country's regime. Also, if these are not actually wrongs or crimes, they go against the current philosophy that the government is always right and must be admitted as such.

Channeling Guilt

When the subject enters the channeling of the guilt process, they have undergone their own self-assault for many months. By the time the subject reaches this point in the brainwashing process, they may feel the guilt and shame that has been placed on them, but it has lost a lot of its meaning. They can not tell you exactly what they have done wrong in order to make them feel this way; they just think they are wrong. The manipulator should be able to use the subject's blank canvas to describe why they find themselves in the pain they experience. The manipulator will be able to attach to whatever they wish the sense of guilt that the subject feels. If the manipulator attempts to replace a belief system, they will take on the old system and convince the subject that that belief is what makes them feel the guilt. This is the stage where the contract is established between the old beliefs and the new beliefs; basically, the old belief system has been established to correspond with the psychological agony that the subject felt while the new belief system has been established to match the ability to escape that agony. The choice is going to be the subjects, but it's pretty easy to see that they're going to select the new system to get better.

Delivering Guilt

In this step, the subject has come to realize that their old values and beliefs make them pained. By this time, they're worn down and tired of feeling the guilt and shame that has been put on them for months to come. They often realize that they did not necessarily do something that would make them feel this way; instead, it is their beliefs that cause guilt. The subject being embattled can feel some relief from the fact that they can do something about guilt. They're also going to feel relieved because they've come to understand that they're not the bad person, they're the people they've been around, and their belief system is the real culprit that causes the discomfort they can fix to get good again. The subject has learned that they have a way of escape simply by escaping from the wrong belief system they have held and embracing the new one that is being offered. All that the subject would have to do to remove the remorse that they feel is to condemn the institutions and individuals associated with the old belief system and then free them from remorse. At this point, there is some control on the subject now. They should be able to understand that their relief from guilt is solely their responsibility. All the subjects would have to do for this stage to be freed from the wrongdoing is to confess to all of the crimes they have performed that are connected with the old belief system. Once a complete confession has been made, the subject will have completed the psychological rejection of its former identity completely. The manipulator would need to step in and give the subject a new identity at this point, and help them to rebuild their identity into the desired one.

Self-rebuilding

The subject has gone through many steps and emotional turmoil by this step. They've been placed through an ordeal that's meant to strip them of their old identity, tell them they're bad and need to be fixed, and slowly come to realize that their belief system is the cause of their wrongdoing and that it needs to change. Once all of this is reached, the subject will need to learn, with the help of the manipulator, how to rebuild themselves. This stage allows the manipulator the freedom to implant the ideas of the new system as the subject is a clean slate and very keen on learning how to be better and feel better. During this stage, there are two steps that are seen, including harmony and the final confession before starting.

Coincidence

The manipulator should use that move to convince the subject than making a change in their decision. They could tell the subject they have the choice of choosing what is good and making a change that will help them feel better. The manipulator must then implement and present the new belief system in a way that makes it the right option or the right one.

The manipulator should stop the abuse at this stage, and then make a point of offering mental calm and physical support to the subject. The point of doing so is to reconcile the old beliefs with the pain and misery while giving the new beliefs, joy and relaxation. This stage is set up in such a way that the subject has to choose which route to take even though it is not really their responsibility. The topic must use this stage to choose between old beliefs and new beliefs to effectively decide how they will feel for the remainder of their life. The subject has already gone through the process of rejecting their old convictions at this point due to the leniency and suffering they have endured. Despite this, they are fairly likely to make their guilt relief the alternative for the new belief system. The new identity introduced is attractive and safe, as it is completely different from the old identity, which contributed to the breakdown in earlier measures. Using reasoning and taking into account the state of mind in which the subject is, it is easier to see that the new one is the only identity the subject would want for its own peace of mind and security.

Final Confession and Starting Over

Because the option is not really theirs at all, the manipulator has worked all the time carefully to make the subject feel like they have the free will to choose the new identity. When the process of brainwashing is performed right, the subject will objectively think about the new options and decide that the best one is to take on the new identity. They have been conditioned to think this way, and it is the one that makes the most sense in their new state of mind. There are no other choices; they can be relieved from the guilt they feel and lead to happiness while choosing the old identity leads to pain and guilt. If the subject had rejected the new identity for whatever reason, there would be backtracking in the whole cycle of brainwashing, and they would be forced to experience it all over again in order to end up with the desired results.

During this stage of the cycle, the subject gets to decide they're going to choose nice, meaning they're going to choose to go with the new identity. When the subject contrasts their old identity's agony and pain with the peacefulness which comes with the new, they will choose the new identity. This new identification is something of a sort of redemption. It's the thing that helps them feel good and no longer have to deal with guilt and unhappiness. As this stage draws to a close, the subject will reject their old identity and go through a process of pledging loyalty to their new one, knowing it will work to make their lives better.

There are lots of ceremonies and rituals happening during this final stage. The conversion from the old identity to the new identity is a big deal since both sides have had a lot of time and energy. During these ceremonies, the subject will be introduced into the new culture and will be welcomed with the new name. There's a sense of rebirth for certain victims of brainwashing during this time. You are encouraged to embrace your new identity and are now accepted with open arms into the new world. Instead of being lonely and alone, a lot of new friends and group members are on your side. Instead of feeling the remorse and suffering that has plagued you for several months, with everything that is around you, you will feel joy and peace. The new identity is yours now, and complete transition from brainwashing.

It can occur over a span of months or even years. Most people are fixed in their identity and their beliefs; all of this can not be changed in only a few days unless the individual is already willing to change, and brainwashing strategies are unnecessary. Isolation will also be required, as external factors prevent the subject from relying on the manipulator during this process. That's why most forms of brainwashing occur in concentration camps and other isolated instances; the vast majority of people don't have the chance to undergo brainwashing because they are often surrounded by people and technology that can hamper the whole brainwashing process. Because of the many steps that need to be taken to change the values held by the individual for many years, the transition takes a long time to accept the new identity as their own while still thinking that the choice has always been theirs.

As can be seen, quite a few steps are needed to go through the brainwashing process. It's not something that is going to happen by simply running into someone on the street and exchanging a few words. It takes time and distance to convince the subject that everything they know is incorrect and that they are a bad person. It then goes on to try to force out a confession that the subject is bad and that they want to give up all the bad stuff they have done because of their old past. Finally, the subject will be led to believe that, if they only abandon their old values and instead embrace the peacefulness and reason that comes with the proposed new identity, they would change for the better. To be successful in brainwashing, and to create a new identity, both of these measures must occur.

Brainwashing as a defense at court

People have been saying throughout history that they committed horrible wrongs because they had been brainwashed. This became an excuse for others to pretend to be trying to save their own lives or to get away with mass murder or some other human crime. It might also be anything as easy as stealing from someone else. Whatever the action was, brainwashing was an easy defense because it took away the accused's responsibility for the action, and it was hard to prove whether or not someone had been brainwashed.

Whether pleas for brainwashing can be used in court as a defense is up to some debate. Many experts feel that allowing this defense into the courtroom would overwhelm the courts with false brainwashing claims, and it would be more than the courts could handle the resources to prove or disprove that defense. Despite this, some cases have been brought before the court, which can demonstrate the validity of brainwashing as a defense for crimes committed.

The first such example occurred in 1976. Patty Hearst, the heiress of a large publishing fortune, used brainwashing defense when she was standing trial for a bank robbery. In the early 1970s, the SLA, the Symbionese Liberation Army, kidnapped Hearst and ended up joining this group. During the trial, Hearst reported being locked in a closet for at least a couple of days after she was kidnapped. While in the closet, Hearst said she feared her life was brutalized, tired, and unfed, while SLA members bombarded her with their ideology against a capitalist country. Within two months of her kidnapping, Patty had changed her name while also issuing a statement saying her family was "pigHearsts" and then appeared on a bank's security tape, robbing it along with those who kidnapped her.

Patty Hearst stood for this bank robbery trial in 1976 and was defended by F. Bailey Lee. It was claimed in the defense that the SLA had brainwashed Hearst. The brainwashing had forced Hearst to commit a crime she would never have committed in any other circumstances. She was unable to tell the difference between right and wrong in the mental state that she was under with the brainwashing, and therefore should not be found guilty of bank robbery. The court disagreed with this analysis and instead found her guilty and put her seven years in prison. A few years later, President Carter commuted her sentence so that she only ended up serving a total of two years in jail.

Case Lee Boyd Malvo

The case Lee Boyd Malvo is another well-known brainwashing defense. This case used brainwashing to defend insanity, and it wound up about 30 years after the Patty Hearst case in the courtrooms. Lee Boyd Malvo was on trial in 2002 for the role he played in the sniper attacks that took place around and in Washington D.C. Malvo, who was 17 at the time, and John Allen Muhammad, 42, ended up killing ten people and wounding three during the spree of killing. The defense used for this case was that Muhammad had brainwashed the teenage Malvo so he could commit the crimes. Just as in the Hearst case, the defense claimed that if he had not been under Muhammad's control, Malvo would not have committed those crimes.

Malvo was abandoned in the Caribbean by his mother on Antigua Island at the age of 15, according to the background story used by the defense. Muhammad met the boy and brought him to the United States in 2001. Muhammad was a veteran of the army at the time and was trying to fill the teen's head with hallucinations of an impending race war. For this purpose, Malvo was trained as an expert marksman. Besides sharing these ideas with Malvo, Muhammad has separated Malvo from others when steeped in the vitriolic and idiosyncratic form of Islam that Muhammad adopted along with a strict regime of diet and exercise. It's thought all this was part of the brainwashing process on young Malvo.

The defense argued that Malvo had been brainwashed because of his time with Muhammad, and because of that, he was unable to tell what was right out of what was wrong. Malvo was found guilty amid the defense efforts and was sentenced to life in prison without any chance to take the air. In a separate proceeding, Muhammad was sentenced to capital punishment. So far, brainwashing does not seem to gain much ground in the courts as a means of defense. To begin with, arguing a defendant was brainwashed in the first place is far too complicated. Next, it's very unlikely someone will have been brainwashed, and instead, the defense will just use it as a means to get a lighter sentence or their client's actions forgiven. Additionally, the notion of brainwashing appears to be utterly ludicrous to other juries. Overall, in the courtroom, this defense probably won't see much power rising.

Popular Brainwashing Tactics

Brainwashing isn't always as serious as what was mentioned in this chapter so far. The described methods are used for "true brainwashing" and are rarely done for the subject. There are also other forms of brainwashing that do occur on a regular basis. They might not work to make you give up your old identity completely in favor of a new one, but they do work to help you change your thoughts and ideas about what is going on around you. This segment would concentrate on some of the techniques that are frequently used during brainwashing, regardless of whether the brainwashing is real or not.

- Hypnosis-hypnosis, to be discussed in greater detail in the next chapter, is, in some circumstances, a form of brainwashing. Hypnosis is fundamentally the induction of a high suggestibility state. This state is often disguised thinly as meditation or relaxation. The manipulator is able to propose things to the subject during the hypnosis process in hopes of getting them to act or react in some way. Many people are familiar with the hypnosis from the shows they've seen on stage. It is also used as a way of enhancing safety, too.
- Peer Pressure-All have an innate need to belong. This might be with a specific group, their family, friends, and the community. With peer pressure tactics, the doubt that the subject feels along with getting rid of their resistance to new ideas by leveraging this intense desire to belong is suppressed. If done correctly, the subject might be more willing to try new things, be less shy about new people, and make new friends easier.
- Love Bombing-the sense of family in people is very strong. This is the group in which you were born, and which you were supposed to have been around for your entire life. They know you better than anyone else, and those who miss this kind of relationship may find they feel alone and unwanted. Through love bombing, with the use of emotional bonding, feeling and sharing, and physical contact, the manipulator can build a sense of family. This allows for the family bonding of the manipulator and the subject, making it easier for the new to trade in the old identity.

Rejecting Old Values-As Mentioned

A little earlier in this chapter, the manipulator works to persuade the subject to denounce all his own values. This cycle is intensified by intimidation, physical threat, and other means. In the end, the subject would abandon the ideals and principles they once kept close and start embracing the new lifestyle that the manipulator introduces to them.

- Confusing doctrine — there will be an incentive in this tactic to blindly accept the new identity while rejecting the other logic the subject will have. To do so, the manipulator must go through a complicated series of lectures on a theory that will be incomprehensible. Through this phase, the subject must learn to blindly believe what the manipulator is saying, be it about the ideology or the new identity is created.
- Metacommunication — this tactic is used when the manipulator works to instill subliminal messages into the subject 's mind. It can be achieved when other terms or phrases that are crucial to the new identity are emphasized by the handler. These phrases and keywords are implanted into confusing long lectures, which will force the subject to sit through.
- No Privacy — privacy is a privilege that will be lost by many subjects until they have converted to the new identity that they are given. Not only is this removed as a method to make the subject 's guilt and wrongdoing more apparent, but it also removes the ability the subject has to evaluate the things they are told logically. If the subject is permitted to have privacy, they will have time to consider the information given to them privately and may find that it is untrue or does not hold up to what they already believe. Removing this anonymity means the manipulator or manipulators are always present, and the subject is always guided to the new identity.
- Disinhibition — the manipulator urges the subject to offer childlike obedience during this technique. That makes it easier for the manipulator to shape the subject 's mind.
- Unbending Rules — the rules that the manipulator puts in place are often strict and never will change. Such guidelines are supposed to make it impossible for the subject to think and behave on its own; instead, they'll spend their time doing just what the manipulator wants them to do. There are many different rules that might fit into this category, such as the rules that will be followed for the process of disorientation and regression all the way to how the subject is allowed to use medicines, take breaks in the bathroom, and eat meals. These rules are put in place to control the subject in full during the process of brainwashing.

- Verbal abuse — verbal violence is one of the techniques used during the process of breaking down. And when bombarded with a violent and offensive language all the time, the subject will become desensitized. Physical abuse can, at times, supplement or replace verbal abuse.
- Sleep deprivation — when a person doesn't get the amount of sleep they need, they sometimes become vulnerable and disoriented. This will help create the perfect atmosphere the manipulator is searching for during the stages of brainwashing breakdown and confession. Moreover, the subject will be required many times to do prolonged physical and mental activities on top of the inadequate sleep in order to hurry the process even further.
- Dress codes — the enforcement of a dress code further removes any individuality the subject may have, as well as the choice they are used to picking out their own clothing. Often, the subject will be required to wear the dress code held by the rest of the group during the brainwashing process.
- Chanting — the manipulator will work to eliminate any uncultivated ideas that may be present in the subject's mind. One way to do this is by singing or repetition of the phrases used by those who adopt the new identification.
- Confession — confession is strongly welcomed in those who are transforming the new identity from their old identity. During this process, the subject must destroy their own individual ego by confessing all of their innermost feelings of doubt and personal vulnerabilities to the manipulator. Once they can let go of these things, there can be the introduction of the new identity.

Financial engagement

In cases, financial contributions will be made, which must be met. This can be of some support to the handler. First, the financial commitment allows the subject to become more dependent on the group because the subject may be bridging bridges to their past. They will donate different properties in the hopes that they will be able to conquer their shame and remorse, whether it be their car, home, money, or some other financial contribution. They are now linked financially to the new name. The manipulator will also be able to take advantage of these financial contributions to further their own needs.

- Pointing the finger — you'll feel a sense of righteousness when you're able to point the finger at another. That's your way of showing the world that you're perfect simply by pointing out some of the world's shortcomings. The manipulator may point out all the killing, racism, and covetousness in the world before contrasting it with the good of the new identity to which the subject is being brought.
- Isolation — if you're isolated from all that's around you, it's hard to get outside of opinions that could change your mind. This is what the manipulator will strive for because they don't want to go away from all their work. Many that are being brainwashed would be isolated from society, friends, family, and all other logical influences that would alter their way of thinking.
- Managed approval — The manipulator must work to preserve the subject's uncertainty and insecurity throughout the breakdown phase. One way to do that is by regulated approval. The manipulator will punish and reward similar actions, in turn, making it difficult for the subject to know what is correct and what is wrong.
- Change in diet — changing the amount of food that the subject is permitted to consume is another technique used to establish disorientation while increasing the subject 's susceptibility to emotional excitement. When the manipulator dramatically decreases the amount of food the subject is allowed to eat, they deprive the subject's nervous system of the nutrients required to thrive. It is possible to add drugs to the mix in this category too.
- Games — games are sometimes used to induce greater group dependence. Games will be introduced, and most of them will have obscure rules that the subject doesn't understand. In some instances, the subject will not be told about the rules, and they will have to figure them out, or the rules will constantly change. This technique allows the handler to be more in control.

In the process of brainwashing, the subject is not allowed to ask questions. Questions encourage abstract thought, and this is harmful to the practice of brainwashing. If no questions are allowed, this will help the manipulator achieve an automatic acceptance from the subject to the new identity.

- Guilt — the victim was told that they are evil and that all they do is evil. Guilt is a typical technique the manipulator uses to challenge the subject's convictions and what happens around them. The sins of the former lifestyle of the subject will be exaggerated to bring about the guilt and strengthen the need for salvation within the subject.
- Fear — fear is a powerful motivator and can do much more than the other tactics listed above. Manipulators can use fear to maintain obedience and loyalty, which the group desires. To do this, the manipulator may threaten the subject's limb, life, or soul for anything that is against the newly presented identity.

These are just a few of the tactics which can be used in brainwashing. Each of them has the purpose of instilling the belief that the old identity of the subject is false and to convince them that the new identity is preferable. There are several different ways this can be achieved, and several will be more successful when used as a combination. Although brainwashing can alter the way, someone thinks and acts, most experts agree that real brainwashing is misunderstood and can not be accomplished. While there may be little examples of brainwashing in everyday life, most people will not find that this process has altered their entire belief systems.

CHAPTER 10 BRAINWASHING AND DARK PSYCHOLOGY

Brainwashing is a term widely used in the mass media to refer to a phenomenon known as manipulative manipulation by psychologists. In general, the term refers to a collection of tactics that are used to forcibly alter someone's belief system in order to adhere to a new set of values and responsibilities. The concept has also been identified in the public mind with the shift in outlook and the rejection of family and traditions frequently seen in religious cult leaders. However, some of the techniques outlined below have also been standard tools throughout human history in interrogating uncooperative prisoners.

Significant Motivational Elements of Persuasion Include:

- Application of physical or emotional stress: Lack of sleep, food, light, or exercise may involve physical stress. Isolation without relaxation, excessive repetitive chanting, or sleep deprivation to the point of entering a trancelike state will cause emotional tension. Attribution of all the problems of the person to a straightforward explanation, which is repeated time and again. This technique worked well for the Nazis, but for today's financial self-help gurus and religious fringe groups, it works equally well. The group leader offers unconditional affection, support and consideration, who will disregard any flaws when the issue comes to him.
- Creation of a New Identity: This also involves a name change and different clothing, as with the Hare Krishna movement's rituals, where all dress identically and sport distinctive haircuts. This makes group membership far more important than individual identity, making it easier to control the members.
- Entrapment: also known as the strategy of stand-in-the-door. The member agrees with a few small changes, but then the demands start to increase gradually. Once the demands become unreasonable, it is

too late, and by continuing to go along with the demands, cognitive dissonance is reduced.
- Access to Knowledge Is Severe Controlled: The community can require those pre-existing social relations, including family links, be removed. Doubts about the group, or its leader, and attempts at critical thinking are mocked. Any distress this causes is attributed to a lack of faith in the group or its leader.

Techniques for brainwashing

There are ways to brainwash you, which are hidden, repeated, and very successful. You 're probably getting brainwashing right now, without your knowledge. Such strategies, along with most of your shortcomings, are the reason you 're overweight, smoke, have pain, can not sleep. You got messages all of your life that made you doubt your feelings, values, and perceptions. This is happening all the time, and it's become a simple human communication mechanism. These behavioral habits are most commonly used for the advantage of a particular group. Recognizing these strategies in practice, however, you can avoid them before they further damage you. Most of these strategies are so successful that the receiver readily reassesses their expectations. However, these strategies may also be symbolically very persuasive in requesting that the target alter their view.

Brainwashing Questioning Styles

One of those hidden brainwashing tactics exists in questioning style. Repeated questioning structured according to a precarious pattern may lead the subject to examine issues they were not even thinking about. As this cycle goes on, the topic goes unknowingly until there is a state of uncertainty about the initial thought or experience. The effect might be a fresh idea about memory or a modified way of thinking. Here is what happens when you're asked by an expert person. You may respond with subtle variations of a story or memory every time a question one is asked. This professional practitioner, advertiser, and figure of authority will eventually cause you to doubt your thinking.

The longer this cycle, the more it is replicated, the less you recognize the trend, the more successful the outcome. You do not know what you think or have seen until you know it, and the more you identify with the information representation post, ads, or authority figures. I have been brainwashed!

Be Careful of Accepting Brainwashing

If you pay attention to the news, advertisements, figures of authority, you'll begin to note this form of brainwashing. Some people are so expert in these techniques that they use it as a normal form of communication. If you're innocent, then you'll be a suspect. Being on guard over these strategies is vitally necessary. You need to know you are constantly under attack. If you don't, it won't be long before you don't have any more creative thinking. You won't have mechanisms of discerning thought anymore. You won't take care of your life anymore. You're going to think you're going to do it, you're going to buy it, you're going to follow it, and you're going to be one of those who've been brainwashed. And you won't even know it!

You have to doubt all of that. If you're overweight, if you can't quit smoking, if you're filled with discomfort, if you're lying up with insomnia at night, your brain spinning, stopping you from sleeping, if you're in any situation that anyone else can benefit from, the situation has been developed, and you can only fix it.

Is Hypnosis Mind Control a Brainwashing Form?

Brainwashing has a dark past. Commonly when we think of the word, we are likely to imagine cult leaders, or even CIA spies, who plan to make us bend to their will through a sort of mental control. So is mind control through hypnosis a form of brainwashing? I suppose that could be considered as such, in essence. After all, the power of the hypnosis mind aims to manipulate the subject's mind, and this is just what brainwashing always does. Yet, generally speaking, I believe there are a lot of strategies involved in brainwashing than just hypnosis, and its results are longer lasting.

While some of our government entities are frequently accused of brainwashing, and maybe do so, there is no denying that it is a cult that is better known for performing this type of mind control. Cults have several strategies designed to obtain long-term influence over their members and ways to slowly transform them in such a way that even though they are away from the church, they no longer think independently. Techniques include hypnosis, love bombing, shame, negative reinforcement, and manipulation of any kind of emotional vulnerability until the cult member finally becomes wholly dependent on the group for their sense of self-esteem and gives cults overall decisions about their behavior.

However, alongside mind control methods, brainwashing often typically includes physical isolation and cutting off people from their loved ones, which is basically a form of imprisonment. The person being exploited is forced into a prolonged period of stress that they have no control over and from which they can not escape.

And what about the power of the mind over hypnosis? There are plenty of people who are likely to laugh at the notion that you can actually manipulate the mind of someone else, but the cult is obviously capable of accomplishing this and doing it effectively, so if you find someone who thinks the notion is nonsense, then you may want to point out all the cult that has done it successfully for years.

Hypnosis works, and if you know how to use the Discreet NLP methods, you don't need to go out and set up the cults. This is a misuse of those skills. Learning how to influence people can be done without causing harm. Calling this type of manipulation "mind control" may, at times, be considered a bit irrational, especially because of the transient nature of most hypnotic methods, as they are mostly conversational.

Is Anorexia a Form of Brainwashing?

I've been interested in a long time in what affects people's values, mindsets, and attitudes to issues. I strongly believe that most eating disorders are triggered by the prejudices and perceptions that people have about themselves and others.

Genetic predisposition plays a role as well. I had read a book on brainwashing once. Brainwashing is an effort aimed at instilling different beliefs and attitudes in one person's mind, which ultimately makes a person act in a certain way and believe in certain things. Communists used Brainwashing a lot to spread the communist mindset. It was also used in the Korean War on prisoners of war-when American soldiers often ended up taking the side of the communists after being captured and held in Chinese prisons, and found themselves their supporters.

Brainwashing occurs when people enter cult or odd religious groupings. These fully transform the identity of men, just like anorexia completely changes the identity of people. So, you see, brainwashing can alter your personality entirely. But the newspapers do it all the time. And not just media things like the society in which you live will brainwash you too. American psychiatrist Robert Jay Lipton has done a special research study into what the brainwashing entails. He developed a number of measures related to brainwashing techniques:

- Identity Attack
- Shame and Integrity
- Autopathy
- Breakpoint
- Leniency
- Asked to confess
- Guilt channeling
- Feeling Guilty
- Advances and making peace
- Final Confession and regeneration

I guess anyone suffering from anorexia goes through similar stages? When you think about it, I think it does. The only difference is that when people are brainwashed, someone else is doing it intentionally. People usually view events in their lives in the case of anorexia and what happens to them and take it the wrong way; instead, they become prisoners of their thoughts and emotions.

I studied the following steps of brainwashing about eating disorders, and here's what I came up with:

- **Identity Attack**

If anorexia starts after a traumatic incident or multiple events, the anorexic begins to believe that it is not who it should be and who it needs to be. For days, weeks, or months the person is under relentless attacks of self-identity, to the point where he/she is tired, confused, and disoriented. Its values seem less stable in this state. They are searching around to find a replacement for their name.

- **Remorse and Sincerity**

Constant thoughts: "You are poor the way you are." They feel shameful about their bodies; they feel embarrassed about their own bodies. If the onset of anorexia coincides with the time of puberty-thoughts of being ashamed of one's own body are correlated with feelings of embarrassment for sex and intimacy, and this can have drastic consequences. Guilt and guilt beliefs about sexuality will end up being a life sentence for many sufferers unless there are significant neuroplastic improvements instigated later in life. Eating may also be related to shame, and this is a big explanation that for some sufferers, anorexia progresses into bulimia at a later stage of the disease. People start feeling a general sense of guilt, that everything they do is wrong. Many studies have shown that eating disorders (especially bulimia and binge eating) are closely associated with feelings of guilt.

- **Self-Betrayal**

This is when the anorexia starts to tell her/him: "Convince me you are evil." And as soon as the person is depressed and drowns in shame, these thoughts cause them to withdraw from their families, friends, and peers who eat normally and enjoy their lives. This betrayal of her / his trust in themselves and those close to her/him increases the shame and loss of identity already felt by the individual.

- **Breakpoint**

The sufferer is continually asking her / himself: "Who am I, where am I, and what am I supposed to do?" At this point, the person has her / his identity in crisis, feeling deep shame and guilt. The person may also experience a "nervous breakdown," which may include uncontrollable sobbing, deep depression, and general disorientation and withdrawal. Not everybody has the same severity of symptoms, but it is this same reaction that other people do.

- **Leniency**

Then, the anorexia asks the sufferer: "Follow me-I will help you." Anorexics also feel that their anorexia is the only way they will survive. Doing anorexic behavior-like starvation, purging that gives them temporary relief from their emotions, but they are short-lived. But then it demands more and more focus until their distorted anorexic thoughts and feelings overtake the person 100 percent.

- **Channelling Guilt**

And you are in pain. After weeks or months of pain, frustration, breakdown, and moments of leniency, all sense has been lost to the person's guilt-numbness replaces it all. This produces something of a blank canvas that brings the anorexia deeper into the psyche. The anorexia is attached to the framework of guilt and confidence in the individual, contrary to what healthy people have. For example, food is associated with guilt and shame. It is the stage where anorexics start to show bad tantrums as parents attempt to feed them or convince them to eat and stop their erratic behavior. They tend to believe that anorexia is not a disease, rather it is a lifestyle, and they align themselves with anorexia: they are one with the disorder.

- **Psychological Rejection**

This is not me; it is my convictions. The person has completed his / her psychological rejection of their former identity with her / his full confessions. The sufferer has slowly abandoned all their previously enjoyable interests, left their work or college pretty much their life. And that is just for the sake of pursuing anorexia in the lifestyle. Individuals tend to join pro-anorexia communities, blogs, seek justification, etc.

- **Future and Peace**

You can choose well if you like.-inform "friends of their" thinspiration. Such "Thinspiration" friends implement a new system of belief as to the road to "good." At this point, anorexia ceases to harm, providing physical support and mental stability to the sufferer in accordance with their new system of belief. People are having an attitude of "gang spirit" with their mates who practice the same risky way of living.

- **Final Confession and Regeneration**

A mind is similar to the anorexia that says: "I chose kind." The anorexia is sweet. The person does not doubt her / his choice of righteousness for being anorexic. Separating them from the anorexia seems unlikely at this point. Citizens are continuing to follow the unhealthy way of living. Sooner than later, thousands of them die as a result of that. Others can live longer but ultimately die from serious complications or commit suicide due to their hunger and the fact that they are unable to cope with life and cannot objectively assess issues.

That is how the anorexic mind is conditioned to be the way they suffer from extreme anorexia (brainwashing). Many eating disorder sufferers go through similar stages, but for each sufferer, these stages also happen differently, and distinguishing between them is difficult.

The aim of this book is to show you what the cycle of brainwashing is all about, and what happens in cult camps and prisoners of war camps is identical to what happens in anorexic individuals. I would also like to point out that the anorexia epidemic occurs primarily in the relatively young. Those in the past have not had the same degree of anorexia as we have now. In the past, single cases of anorexia were only identified in people who hungered for religious reasons, cults, and the like. There were no recorded anorexic cases of people trying to be slim for the sake of appearance or reputation.

This all points to the fact that anorexia is a modern disease: I believe it is triggered by certain marketers of beauty products and the media that encourage beauty ideals that are difficult for normal human beings to meet. You might argue it's intended to make people buy beauty and slimming items more and more, making someone incredibly wealthy, based on the misery of others.

Teaching young people and stressing natural and inner beauty are the solution to this issue. To make young people aspire to learn, research, and develop their minds, not to aim for this unattainable look that is presented as glamorous by some media and by others. To achieve the unattainable amount for many young people brings only pain, misery, and death.

Mind control brainwashing – More ways to exploit others

Mind control brainwashing is a method where someone uses coercion and unethical tactics to convince someone to abide by the controlled person's wishes. This phase usually occurs to the detriment of the brainwashed individual. Many common names for that include, among other terms, coercive coercion, through change, and control of thought. There are different ways it's widely used, and some of them will be discussed in this book. One way to use authoritarian coercion is by totalitarian government policies around the world. When it comes to using force to get what they want, these governments are not timid at all, even if the force is disproportionate and immoral. As such, they were known to successfully indoctrinate their prisoners of war using various methods involving relentless propaganda and torture.

Another way to use these brainwashing methods for mind control is with modern religious movements. Many new religious movements that emerge are led by very charismatic individuals who possess especially persuasive powers of persuasion, as well as the ability to brainwash others by various strategies, one of the most important being isolated from family and friends who are not fellow members of the community. By isolating yourself from people with different opinions, you are more deeply rooted in the values of the party. A final example is a less dangerous one, but it can sometimes lead to disastrous consequences when taken to extremes. Members of the college fraternities and sororities are often abused and forced to suffer numerous forms of psychological and physical abuse and humiliation in order to become a member of the community. The person begins to establish a very strong group identity and loyalty by destroying the ego by submitting to a higher authority in the group, or by performing various actions which are sometimes humiliating.

The extreme nature of some of the physical tasks required to perform by the aspiring participants can sometimes lead to serious bodily injury and even death. This brainwashing strategy causes leaders of certain fraternities to do things they wouldn't do if not for the social dynamic, driving them forward. Aside from the three listed in this book, there are several examples of mind control brainwashing. This is a large subject which is also important for sales, military service, and many other fields. It is also important to remember that there are rational ways of manipulating others that do not require any form of violence or dark manipulation of the psyche.

CHAPTER 11 HYPNOSIS

Although brainwashing is a well-known form of mind control which many people have learned about, hypnosis is also an important type to consider. For the most part, those familiar with hypnosis learn about it by watching the actors perform stage shows with insane acts. Though this is a form of hypnosis, it has a lot more to do. This chapter focuses more on hypnosis as a form of mind control.

What is Hypnosis?

First of all, is the definition of hypnosis. Hypnosis is considered, according to scholars, to be a state of consciousness that includes concentrated attention along with a reduced peripheral awareness that is defined by the increased capacity of the patient to respond to suggestions given. This means the client will reach a new state of mind and will be far more open to following the hypnotist's suggestions.

It is widely recognized that there are two groups of a theory that help explains what is happening during the time of hypnosis. The first one is known as the theory of changed states. Those who follow this theory see that hypnosis is like a trance or an altered state of mind if the participant sees that their awareness is somewhat different from what they would notice in their ordinary state of consciousness. The other hypothesis is the hypotheses that are non-state. Those who follow this theory do not think those who undergo hypnosis enter various states of consciousness. Then, the client works with the hypnotist to enter into a kind of creative role enactment.

While in hypnosis, the participant is thought to have more concentration and focus that couples along with a new ability to concentrate intensely on a particular memory or thought. The participant is also able to block other sources during this process, which might distract them. It is thought that the hypnotized subjects display an increased ability to respond to suggestions given to them, particularly when those suggestions come from the hypnotizer. The process used to place the participant in hypnosis is known as hypnotic induction and will include a series of suggestions and instructions used as a type of heating up.

There are several different thoughts that the experts present on what the hypnosis concept is. The wide variety of these definitions stems from the fact that there are just so many different circumstances that come with hypnosis, and when they go through it, nobody has the same experience. Some of the expert's different definitions of hypnosis include:

1. "Psychological regression is a special case," Michael Nash said.
2. Ernest Hilgard and Janet Hilgard have written about hypnosis in great detail and describe it as having a way of dissociating the body from itself in another plane of consciousness.
3. Two well-known social psychologists, Sarbin and Coe, have used the term role theory to explain the hypnosis. Under this definition, the participant plays the role of being hypnotized; they act as if they were being hypnotized, rather than being in that state.
4. According to T.X. Barber, hypnosis is defined according to the various nonhypnotic parameters of behavior. Under this description, the individual will describe the purpose of the mission and will mark the condition in which they are in as hypnosis because they have nothing else to name it.
5. Weitzenhoffer has written about the hypnosis in some of his earlier essays. He conceptualized that hypnosis is an improved state of suggestibility. In more recent scriptures, he described the act of hypnosis as "a form of control by one individual exercised suggestion on another through the medium or organization.
6. To better explain what hypnosis was all about, Brenman and Gill used the psychoanalytic idea of "regression in the service of the ego." Under this concept, the person is able to go into the altered state and under hypnosis, as it boosts their ego and makes them feel better.
7. A person who has suffered hypnosis is simply in a deep state of relaxation, according to Edmonston.
8. Spiegel and Spiegel have stated that hypnosis is simply something that happens due to the participant's biological ability.

9. Erickson says hypnosis is an altered, inner-directed, and special functioning state. The participant still has the capacity to function and is aware of things around them, but they are in an altered state compared to their normal condition.

There's a lot of different opinions and claims on hypnosis. Many people believe that hypnosis is very real, and are afraid that their minds will be manipulated by the government and those around them. Others really don't believe in hypnosis and think it's just a sleight of hand. The definition of hypnosis as mental stimulation is most likely to fall somewhere in the center. The psychological community recognizes three stages of hypnosis. These three stages comprise induction, suggestion, and sensitivity. Each is important for the process of hypnosis and will be discussed further below.

Induction

Induction is the first stage of hypnosis. They will be introduced to the hypnotic induction technique before the participant undergoes the full hypnosis. For many years this was thought to be the method used to put the subject into their hypnotic trance, but in modern times that definition has changed some. Some of the non-state theorists took a somewhat different view of this point. They see this stage instead, as a method to increase participants' expectations of what will happen, define the role they will play, focus their attention in the right direction, and any of the other steps needed to guide the participant in the right direction for hypnosis.

There are many methods of induction that can be used during the hypnosis. Braid's "head fixation" technique or "Braidism" is the most well-known and popular form. There are quite a few variants to this approach, including the Stanford Hypnotic Susceptibility Scale (SHSS). This scale is the most-used tool in hypnosis research. You'll need to take a few steps to use the Braid induction techniques. The first is to take any object you may find bright, such as a watch case, and hold it between the left fingers of the middle, fore, and thumb. You'll want to hold that object from the participant's eyes about 8-15 inches. Hold the object somewhere above the forehead so that during the process, it causes a lot of strain on the eyelids and eyes so that the participant can maintain a fixed stare on the object at any time. The hypnotizer then has to explain to the participant that they should always keep their eyes fixed on the object. Also, the patient will need to focus their mind entirely on the idea of that particular object. They shouldn't be allowed to think about other things or let their minds and eyes wander, or the process won't work.

The participant's eyes will begin to dilate after a short period of time. With a little bit longer, the participant will start assuming a wavy motion. If the participant closes their eyelids involuntarily when the right-hand middle and forefingers are carried from the eyes to the object, then they are in a trance. If not, then the participant will have to start again; make sure that the participant is informed that they will allow their eyes to close once the fingers are brought back to the eyes in a similar motion. This will induce the patient to enter the altered state of mind, known as hypnosis.

While Braid stood by his own method, he did realize that the use of hypnosis induction techniques is not always appropriate in every situation. In fact, modern-day researchers have typically found that the technique of induction is not as important to the effects of hypnotic suggestion as previously thought. Over time, the original hypnotic induction technique has developed other alternatives and variations, although the Braid method is still considered the best.

Suggestion

The next stage of hypnosis is known as the step of suggestion. The term suggestion was not used when hypnosis was first described by James Braid. Braid instead referred to this stage as the act of having the participant's conscious mind focus on one central and dominant idea. The way Braid did this was to stimulate or diminish the physiological functioning of the participant 's body of the various regions. Later on, Braid began to put increasing emphasis on the use of various non-verbal and verbal suggestion forms to get the participant into the hypnotic state of mind. This will require the use of both "waking tips" and self-hypnosis.

Another notable hypnotist, Hippolyte Bernheim continued to shift the focus of the physical state of the hypnosis process to the psychological process containing verbal suggestions. According to Bernheim, hypnotism is the induction of a particular psychological condition which will increase the participant's susceptibility to suggestion. Often, he said, the hypnotic state induced will help facilitate the suggestion, though this may not be necessary in the first place to start the susceptibility.

Modern hypnotism uses many different forms of suggestion to be successful, such as metaphors, insinuations, indirect or non-verbal suggestions, direct oral suggestions, and other non-verbal figures of speech and suggestions. Some of the non-verbal suggestions that can be used during the suggestion stage would include physical manipulation, the tonality of the voice, and mental imaging. One of the distinctions made in suggestion types that can be offered to the participant includes suggestions that are given with permission and suggestions that are more authoritarian.

One of the things to consider concerning hypnosis is the difference between the unconscious and the conscious mind. There are several hypnotists who view the suggestion stage as a way to communicate, which is mostly directed to the subject's conscious mind. Those in the sector will see things in the opposite direction; they see the contact that takes place between the manipulator and the subconscious or unconscious mind.

First-class advocates of thought included Bernheim, Braid, and other Victorian-age pioneers. They believed the suggestions were addressed directly to the conscious part of the mind of the subjects, not to the unconscious part. Braid actually goes further and describes the hypnotism act as the concentrated attention on the suggestion or the dominant idea. According to those who follow this train of thought, the fear of most people that hypnotists will be able to get into their unconscious and make them do and believe things beyond their control is simply impossible.

The nature of the mind was also the determinant of the various suggestion conceptions. Those who believed the answers given are through the unconscious mind, as in the case of Milton Erickson, bring up the cases of indirect suggestions being used. Many of these indirect suggestions, such as stories or metaphors, will mask their intended meaning so as to shield it from the subject's conscious mind. A subliminal suggestion is a form of hypnosis, which relies entirely on the unconscious mind theory. This kind of suggestion would not be possible if the unconscious mind were not used in hypnosis. The differences between the two groups are fairly easy to recognize; those who believe that the suggestions will go primarily to the conscious mind will use direct verbal instructions and suggestions while those who believe the suggestions will go primarily to the unconscious mind will use stories and metaphors with hidden meanings.

In any of these theories of thought, the subject would need to be able to concentrate on one object or concept. This allows them to be led in the direction necessary to get into the hypnotic state. Once the suggestion stage is successfully completed, the participant will then be able to move into the third stage, which is susceptibility.

Likelihood

It has been observed over time that people will react to hypnosis in a different way. Some people find they can fall fairly easily into a hypnotic trance and don't have to put a lot of effort into the process at all. Others might find they can get into the hypnotic trance, but only after an extended period of time and with some effort. Many will still find that they are unable to get into the hypnotic trance and will not achieve their targets even after continuous efforts. One thing researchers found fascinating about the sensitivity of various participants is that this element appears to be constant. If you were able to reach a hypnotic state of mind quickly, you are likely to be the same way for the rest of your life. On the other hand, if you have always had trouble getting to the hypnotic state and have never been hypnotized, then you probably never will.

Several different models have been established over time to try to assess the participants' susceptibility to hypnosis. Some of the older depth scales worked on inferring what level of trance the participant was in through the available observable signs. These would encompass things like spontaneous amnesia. Some of the more modern scales work to calculate the degree of self-evaluated or observed sensitivity to the specific suggestion tests provided, such as the direct suggestions of arm rigidity. According to Deirdre Barrett's research, there are two types of subjects that are considered highly susceptible to hypnotic effects. Those two groups include fantasizers and dissociators. The fantasizers will score high on the absorption scales, will be able to block the real world's stimuli without using hypnosis easily, spend a lot of their daydreaming time, have imaginary friends when they were a child, and also grow up in an atmosphere where imaginary play was encouraged.

The dissociates on the other side of things. This group will also come from a history of trauma or childhood violence, will find ways to ignore the traumatic things in their past, and will be able to withdraw into a numbness. If a person in this group does daydream, it's more about going blank, rather than creating fantasies. Both of these classes scored high on the hypnotic sensitivity tests. The two groups which have the highest hypnotizability rates include those with posttraumatic stress disorder and dissociative identity disorder.

Requirements

Hypnosis has long been around as a discipline and as a concept. Because of this, different applications have started to emerge that help to put the hypnosis process to good use. In fact, the various applications of using hypnosis cross many fields such as entertainment, self-improvement, military uses, and medical uses. Many fields that have been using hypnotism lately include rehabilitation, physical therapy, education, athletics, and forensics. Even artists have started using hypnotism to achieve certain creative ends. This is illustrated most by the surrealist artist Andre Breton, who used hypnosis for his own artistic purposes, among other techniques. In the field of self-improvement, one of the growing uses of hypnosis is; many people have chosen to do self-hypnosis to help them lose weight, reduce stress, and quit smoking.

The following sections will discuss some different fields where hypnosis has grown, as well as how the hypnosis process works in those areas.

Hypnotherapy

Hypnotherapy is a type of psychotherapy, using hypnosis. It is used as a tool to support the patient or subject through troublesome problems that plague them, particularly when other self-control methods are not successful. In order to help them overcome posttraumatic stress, compulsive gambling, sleep disorders, eating disorders, anxiety, and depression, licensed psychologists and physicians may conduct some form of hypnotherapy on willing patients.

You may also meet with a registered hypnotherapist to help you handle problems such as weight loss and smoking cessation. If you're going to a licensed hypnotherapist, it's important to note that they're not psychiatrists or physicians because they'll only be able to help you get to the hypnotic state and not cure any more serious illnesses. It's best to make sure whoever you work with is certified to provide these services, whether you're choosing a hypnotherapist or a doctor.

In modern history, the hypnotherapy process has been seen in many different forms. They all had varying degrees of success, depending on the issue, and the participants faced. Some of the forms employed include:

Cognitive-behavioral hypnotherapy — this is a mixture of therapeutic hypnosis along with different Cognitive-Behavioral Therapy components.

- Hypnoanalysis — it's also known as hypnotherapy for age regression.
- Hypnosis to help tackle phobias and fears.
- Ericksonian Hypnotherapy. Hypnotherapy for helping addictions.
- Hypnotherapy, to help controlling habit.
- Hypnotherapy to help manage pain in those suffering from chronic pain.
- Hypnotherapy to assist the patient is already dealing with psychological therapy.
- Hypnotherapy to help you relax.
- Hypnotherapy to help with a skin condition.

- Hypnotherapy to help patients who are anxious about having to undergo surgery.
- Hypnotherapy to help athletes succeed before a game. Hypnotherapy for weight loss help.

Military Petitions

In addition to helping individuals who struggle with different health problems and addiction, people have long been asking if military and government leaders have used hypnosis to transform the way civilians think about things. There has been no evidence so far that the American military is capable or has used hypnosis to achieve their goals. Nonetheless, a newly released declassified document from the Freedom of Information Act archive reveals that the hypnosis technique was tested for use in military applications. Given the work that has been carried out, the report concluded that there was still no proof that the hypnosis technique would be effective in a military application. Moreover, there was no proof that explicitly demonstrated that hypnosis truly occurs beyond the subject's belief, high motivation, and ordinary suggestion as an empirical phenomenon.

The document further goes on to explain how the use of hypnosis in a military application would be almost impossible. It states: "The use of intelligence hypnosis would present certain technical problems that have not been encountered in the clinic or laboratory. For example, hypnotizing the source under essentially hostile circumstances would be necessary to obtain compliance from a resistant source. There is no good clinical or experimental evidence for this to be possible. The document goes on to explain that the effects and application of hypnosis to be used in the military have been difficult to study because no one can say with certainty whether hypnosis is a unique state with some conditioned responses or just a form of suggestion that has been induced as a result of the positive relationship between the subject and the hypnotist.

Autohypnosis

There are some instances, such as when there is no certified hypnotherapist or other professional available when you might decide to use the self-hypnosis process. This process happens when a person can hypnotize himself, often using the autosuggestion tactics. The primary use for this technique is self-improvement, and it will be performed by many people to lower their stress levels, quit smoking, or get the motivation they need to go on a diet. Although some people might be able to hypnotize themselves, others feel that they need some sort of support in getting to the altered state. This could include hypnotic recordings or even devices with mind machines to help them get to that state. Other areas you might use for self-hypnosis include your overall physical well-being, relaxing, and overcoming the fright of the stage.

Phase Hypnosis

When most people are thinking about hypnosis, they think about stage hypnosis. This is a form of entertainment going to happen in front of an audience in a theater or club. The hypnotist is often shown as a great showman, and this helps foster the idea that hypnosis is entirely about control of the mind. The hypnotist would try to place the entire crowd into the altered condition at the beginning of the act before choosing those individuals that meet the requirements to come up on stage and go through different humiliating activities while the rest of the group watches.

Why stage hypnosis is so effective is unclear, although it is widely believed to be a mixture of Deception, stagecraft, physical coercion, suggestibility, selection of participants, and psychological factors. Experts believe, for the most part, that the participant is just playing along with the hypnotist in a way and offering a good show. These people may be willing to do this because they want to be in the middle of all the attention, the pressure to please others and the excuse to go against their own suppressors of fear makes it easy for the participants to perform. Some of the books written by former stage hypnotists perpetuate the idea of deception, and some are made entirely of false hypnosis where private whispers have been used all the time.

Types of Hypnosis

There are several different forms of hypnosis which the subject may undergo. Each one of them will work in slightly different ways, and some of them will work to help with various problems. Some may be more apt to help relax the subject while others may be more helpful with weight loss or pain control. This section will discuss the various types of hypnosis available in more detail.

Conventional hypnosis

During this process, the manipulator merely makes suggestions directly to the unconscious mind of the subject. This form of hypnosis would work best on a subject that is known to believe the things they are told, so they don't ask many questions. If you go and visit a certified hypnotist or buy a tape to do the self-hypnosis process, you'll go through the traditional hypnosis process. The reason this type of hypnosis is so popular is that learning how to do it doesn't take that much experience or training. The hypnotist will just have to write a simple script, telling the subject what to do. While this technique will work very well on those who accept What is going on around them, for those who think critically and analytically, it's inefficient.

Ericksonian Hypnotization

The next type of hypnosis to talk about is Ericksonian Hypnosis. This one is a little deeper because it will require metaphors and little stories to be used. These are used to pose the ideas and suggestions which the unconscious mind needs. While a little more practice and preparation will be needed to do this process, it is a very efficient and strong process to use. The reason it works so well is that it can remove the resistance and blockage that the subject may have at the suggestions.

There are two main types of metaphors that are often used in the hypnosis of this kind; isomorphic and interspersal. The order that is clarified has been inserted into the story for the metaphor that is interspersal in nature, which will not be easily found by the subject outside of their unconscious mind. The other form, isomorphic metaphor, is a little more popular and provides guidance to the unconscious mind simply by providing the subject with a tale that will eventually provide a moral. The unconscious mind will be able to draw a one-to-one relationship that connects the elements that come from the story and the elements that come with the situation of behavior or problem.

The story "Boy Who Cried Wolf" is an example of an isomorphic metaphor. Many parents will use this story to teach their children about lying, especially if their kid tells a lot of lies. After listening to the story, the subject's unconscious mind would see a connection between the tale of lies and the boy in the novel. They would see that telling lies could lead to a disaster, and the child might be more willing to stop lying in the process to avoid that disaster.

Built-in Methodology

Another type of embedded technique is called hypnosis. The hypnotist can tell a fascinating story to the subject during the process. This story is intended to help the subject's conscious mind get distracted and engaged. It may also contain indirect suggestions that are hidden within the narrative but are embraced into the subject's unconscious mind. Through this story, the hypnotist will use process instructions to guide the subject's unconscious mind to locate the required memory. Typically this recollection is about the learning experience that's suitable from the past. Then, the hypnotist can apply that learning experience to help them make changes to their present.

Neuro-linguistic Programming

Hypnotists have a great selection of methods with neuro-linguistic programming, or NLP, that they can use in the hypnosis procedure. The hypnotist would be able to use the same thinking patterns while using the NLP process to generate the problem in the subject. This can save a great deal of time as compared to the suggestion process. For example, the patterns of thought that are used with stress or excessive appetite will be used to help eliminate the issue that the subject is addressing. NLP has been shown to be very effective when used with a certified hypnotist or psychologist. There are several different types of NLP programming that hypnotists used. Some of the NLP forms that are most commonly used include NLP Anchoring, NLP Flash, and NLP Reframe.

Anchoring the NLP

NLP Anchoring is the first form of NLP that will be discussed. A good way to ponder how anchoring works is to think of an old song, you know. Ever sat in a car and heard a song you didn't hear in a long time? Did that song trigger a kind of feeling that came from the past within you? You were going through those feelings the first time you heard that song, or sometime down the road when you heard it, and the unconscious mind attached these feelings to that particular song. The song would become the anchor for those feelings through this process. Now, every time you listen to this particular song, you'll trigger the brain to have those feelings over and over again. That is a good anchoring example.

Many hypnotists have found anchoring to be a useful technique for using it to hypnotize their subjects. For instance, if you have a memory of being rewarded for having done something right in the past, the hypnotist will be able to get into that particular memory and help you recreate the feelings you were going through at the time. At the same time, the hypnotist will have you do some kind of action, like touching your two fingers together during process recreation. Now every time you touch your fingers together, you can feel those same happy feelings again.

The anchoring process can work to motivate you to accomplish something by associating good feelings with it. This method, for example, is also used to help people find the inspiration they need to stick to weight loss and to sustain a diet. The hypnotist will work with the subject to create a positive anchor associated with the subject's mental image — in this case, it will be the subject in a thin and sexy body thinking about itself. When the subject pictures this image again, the anchor will be activated, and they will get the optimistic reinforcement they need. In addition, among those who undergo hypnosis, there is a significant increase in the motivation for weight loss compared with those who do not. The anchoring process can be used in a variety of different instances to assist in individual self-improvement.

Switch NLP

NLP Flash is another form of hypnosis considered by a certified professional to be extremely powerful and only done. It's also used in the subject's unconscious mind to shift thoughts and emotions around. It can be a good way to help those who are addicted to a substance or who feel chronic stress. In this process, the hypnotist will switch the subject 's feelings around, instead of a certain act bringing pleasure, that act will begin to bring pain or will bring relaxation to the subject instead of some act bringing stress. For example, when they consume that substance, someone who is addicted to a substance, such as cigarettes or alcohol, will find a sense of pleasure and happiness. These feelings will be switched around through the NLP flash technique resulting in the subject feeling discomfort or pain when consuming the substance. That's it.

Can Help Them More Effectively Get Over Their Addiction.

Those who suffer a lot of stress also found the NLP Flash technique to work well for them. When a person experiences constant stress, they can have difficulty regulating their blood pressure and tempers and may feel uncomfortable a lot of the time. Given that stress is so severe on the body, many patients are willing to undergo the NLP Flash hypnosis to help them relax. With this technique, the subject will learn and redirect their stress triggers so that those triggers instead start releasing relaxing feelings in their minds.

This technique has also proven successful in extinguishing the conditioned responses in the subject 's mind. An example of that is smoking. When you're a smoker who loves a cigarette while enjoying a morning cup of coffee, your unconscious brain will start mixing these two behaviors. That means the subject gets a craving to get a cigarette whenever they enjoy a cup of coffee, especially in the morning. When the subject goes through the technique of NLP Flash, they will learn how to dissociate the two events from one another. This helps the smoker to have a cup of coffee, without necessarily having the urge to smoke. This makes use of the technique even more effective when attempting to quit smoking.

NLP Reframe

The third form of NLP used in the hypnosis is called NLP Reframe. This approach is very powerful because it works so well to help the subject improve the way they behave. To do so, the hypnotist must recognize that there is a secondary benefit, or a beneficial result, achieved by each of the behaviors a person performs. The result that comes from the behavior is important, as that is why the subject acts first. Despite the significance of the outcome, the behavior chosen to achieve the outcome isn't really that important.

During the reframing process, the hypnotist works with the subject's unconscious mind to negotiate and reason. The goal is to get it to take over the burden of having the subject substitute in some new conduct that is possible and successful in achieving the secondary benefit necessarily. While all of this happens in the subconscious, the new behavior in their conscious mind will be more acceptable to the subject. For instance, if the person is in the habit of eating when he is sad to make himself feel better, the hypnotist will perform this method to teach the unconscious to do some other activities. The eating act could be replaced by exercise or reading a nice book, helping the subject lose weight, eat healthier, and feel better all around.

Hypnosis Video

While the other forms of hypnosis have been extremely popular in helping subjects overcome obstacles and change the way they think in order to live better lives, there are always new forms of hypnosis developing. Video hypnosis is one of the newer forms of hypnotherapy developed. This method is sold by commercial means so that people can purchase and use it at their own convenience. The techniques used in some of the video hypnosis brands are also based on the previously discussed neuro-linguistic programming technology. This suggests that the technique of video hypnosis can operate on the basis of using the same cognitive patterns the subject has, rather than using hypnotic suggestions like conventional methods.

The reason why video hypnosis has grown so rapidly is that more than 70 percent of people have found that when they see things, they learn things easier and faster compared to when they only hear the information. The mind of the subject will automatically learn to change the feelings it is having on the conscious level as well as its visual associations while watching the visual films that are presented. While there are many different types of video hypnosis programs available, Neuro-VISION is one of the most popular, since it was developed using some of the industry's best techniques. This type of video method works to train the subject's unconscious mind through digital optics, which is a process of high-tech computer simulation. This will free the subject from their tensions, compulsions, and urges. Through this process, the smoker will find that it is easy to stop smoking, the dieter will lose their appetite, and those who feel stress will start relaxing more. Often it will take at least a few video hypnosis sessions to see results, though there are those who find that just one viewing will begin to show some of the results they want.

Subliminal Hypnosis

The final form of hypnosis to be discussed here is subliminal hypnosis. The subliminal messages of hypnosis will often be placed on a record for the subject to listen to. The recording will have two tracks, each conversing with a different part of the mind. One track will contain a cover-sound to be heard through the subject's conscious mind. Often the cover sound is something that's easy for the brain to listen to, like sounds of nature or music. The other track will include direct feedback, which will be heard from the subject's unconscious mind. Throughout the entire session, these suggestions present on the second track will be repeated over and over.

Subliminal programs have the ability to play anywhere, at any time. You might listen to these messages when you're working, or even watching television. The best part is that you won't have to stop the task you're doing and sit down and relax like the NLP or traditional hypnosis that's required. In certain cases, you will be adding subliminal exercises to your daily hypnotic programs.

The use of subliminal programming is not so prevalent. Most people don't want this approach to alter their attitudes and habits. Research has shown that the subliminal programs are not really so effective and will therefore be

It cannot replace NLP or Hypnosis. It might take more than 80 hours of listening to the subliminal message by some accounts before it has an effect, and many times that will not be enough for most people. According to Joel Weinberger, an Adelphi University professor and a psychologist, regular subliminal audiotapes that can be purchased in stores or online just don't work out. Subliminal psychodynamics can work for as long as some form of visuals is present. The popular available options contain only audible components. The auditory is not adequate to make the process work on its own. Subliminal suggestions will need to be paired with other forms of hypnotherapy to have the desired efficacy.

Despite the media portrayal of hypnosis, it is not a malicious plot intended to take over the minds of unwilling subjects. Indeed, if the subject is unwilling to undergo hypnosis, it is virtually impossible to get them to enter the altered state. Hypnosis is often employed to help others improve their lives. This could be in the form of weight management; smoking can be stopped, other health conditions improved, and chronic pain management helped. Also, each of the techniques is important in helping the subject reach its overall objective. While all of them can be effective, the professional you choose to work with and the issue you are dealing with will be used to determine which of these methods will best fit your needs and help improve your life.

CHAPTER 12 PRACTICAL USES OF HYPNOSIS TECHNIQUES

Hypnosis is actually a state of mind that people fall under exactly where they're not in the influence of the actions of theirs. This's usually done in therapeutic circumstances to assist people in discovering the peace they need inside themselves to confront their darkest and deepest traumas. Hypnosis additionally provides a way to persuade and influence others. Hypnosis, as well as mind control, might look like the same task since they include exerting control over somebody different. Nevertheless, there are actually glaring contrasts between the 2. In order to realize the distinctions, it's crucial you get more familiar with whatever they depend on.

Hypnosis is actually an artificially induced state in which the individual responds to inquiries or perhaps prompts from the hypnotist. The course of action may be utilized on a gathering or a person of individuals for a certain reason. At the time when this's used for therapeutic functions, the task is recognized as hypnotherapy. At any rate, when it's being utilized as a kind of diversion for a crowd of individuals, it tends to be alluded to as organized hypnosis.

On the other hand, character management is the way to using a couple of traps in obtaining the perfect effect you need to have with others. You are able to make use of the key to get fractional or aggregate command over what's taking place around another person's psyche. When it's used amid reflection, it is able to allow you to center around the topic of the examination of yours.

You are able to cope with your contemplations as well as thoughts if you take part in this kind of reflection. Being a rule, amazing individuals who completed remarkable achievements in daily life might have the best command over the psyches of theirs through everyday reflection. To have noticed the important meanings of hypnosis as well as mind control, it's apparent to pinpoint the disparities of theirs. The actual contrast you will see in between these two is the fact that hypnosis must be used on others. It's doubtful that there's some technique by which you are able to hypnotize yourself. A subliminal specialist is essential to induce hypnosis.

On the other hand, character management reflection could be used on oneself just as on others. You are able to while not a lot of a stretch engage in this kind of contemplation whenever. Everything you will need is finding a tranquil area and then take a seat and after believe. You are able to affect others to concur with you on certain concentrates utilizing brain control traps. Once more, another difference is observed in the fashion where hypnosis is associated with mind management. If you're having a concern of appetite, smoking, or fear, a trance specialist is able to allow you to opt-out whether the hypnosis was carried out with the right mindset at heart.

At times, the hypnosis specialist might use a couple of techniques in reflection to get people to be at ease with capturing the response they require at a certain point in time. It's extremely unlikely you are able to make use of mind management traps to spellbind someone. It's designed for strategic functions. It's apparent that hypnosis, as well as mind control have crystal clear contrasts. A number of elements used in one could similarly be utilized on the other hand, though they're not the same. All relies upon just how you're prepared to bring in the important standards provided.

What is Hypnosis?

Hypnosis consists of two principal components: proposals as well as acceptance. Trancelike acceptance is actually the main proposal conveyed amid the process of hypnosis; however, just what it must comprise of is actually a situation of debate. Proposals are usually communicated as recommendations that inspire automated reactions from the members, who do not believe in they have a lot or maybe any control with the circumstance. A couple of individuals are the same, much more vulnerable compared to others, and experts have found out that these people tend to be more apt to use a reduced sensation of an expert while under hypnosis.

Susceptibility to hypnosis has been recognized as the capability to encounter recommended modifications in physiology, sensations, feelings, conduct, or musings. Neuroimaging methods have demonstrated that these people show higher activity levels in the prefrontal cortex, primary cingulate cortex as well as parietal devices of the head amid different periods of hypnosis.

There are areas of the brain associated with a scope of complicated capacities, which includes observation and mind, thoughts as well as assignment learning. Be that as it might, the specific cerebrum pieces connected with hypnosis areas but hazy. Nevertheless, scientists are actually beginning to sort out the neurocognitive profile of this particular process.

Would you realize if someone has been hypnotized? Different modifications suggest that the topic is actually in a hypnotic trance. NLP calls these deep daze markers, and they're a set of highly detailed observations one could make of the topic. Recognizing these kinds of markers requires focus as well as practice. And only some of those markers have to be existing to be able to create that a topic is under hypnosis.

Hypnotic Strategies

The initial step in placing somebody in a hypnotic status is actually opening the individual's thought process to suggestion. The hypnosis specialized makes use of a great assortment of methods along with, based on the ability of the susceptibility and also the specialist of the subject matter, the outcome might differ. Hypnosis by rest is among the most typical techniques of hypnosis. Have you read a hypnosis specialist consult a person to make him or maybe herself as comfy as they can? By doing this, the individual actually being hypnotized falls right into a calming state in which the head is likely to shut down on immediate surroundings. Here are a few fundamental methods for unwinding:

- Relax your mind as well as body
- Settle down
- Count in receding order in the mind of yours
- Control what the body of yours as well as mind is thinking as well as doing
- Feel your muscle mass give in to rest

- Tone down your voice to a whisper

The handshake program for hypnotism calls for a hypnosis specialist shaking an individual's hand. Nevertheless, in which you may feel this's a typical method for the general public to greet and welcome one another, hypnosis specialists make use of this for one more edge. Rather than simply shaking the hand of yours, they are going to grab, twist the wrist of yours or even take you ahead towards them. Therefore you start to be unstable. It's in this split second when you're unstable that the best opportunity arises for hypnosis specialized in taking control of the brain of yours.

Eye prompts can certainly additionally be essential in hypnosis. Speaking to somebody, it's just natural for one's eyes to wander to surroundings or perhaps maybe a glimpse of something of the distance. A hypnosis specialist is going to take note of this and, within a quick time, discover what prompts one to move your eyes left, right, down, or up. With this, they gain a chance to access the strategy you believe, feel as well as react to things that are certain surrounding you.

Realizing the eye moves of a market is a regular approach. Did you recognize this as the speaker, you are able to play out a sleep-inducing appeal on the market with the eye movements of yours? This particular brand new technique was developed as well as tried by Stephen Rivulets.

Perception may be worn both in order to initiate stupor and also to make suggestions. For example, request that your subject comment on an area they're acquainted with. Envision almost everything about this room: the floor, the state of the windows, the decor, the odor, as well as the light. At that time, move onto an area they're less familiar with. As they battle to go through the cautious subtleties, they open the brain to a suggestion. Certain experts make use of representation to talk about good recollections to alter one's opinion of a bad photo.

- Positive photos as well as encounters (wedding, birthday, kid, graduation)
- Dispose of dreadful photos (perhaps toss them in the garbage) Another technique to use will be the arm levitation program. Due to this typical

method, the subject starts by shutting the eyes of his. He's approached to find out the distinction in inclination involving the arms of theirs. The trance specialist can make ideas with respect to the sensations in each arm.

For example, they might point out the arm feels light or heavy, cold, or hot. The buyer enters a daze and might actually lift the arm of his, or maybe he might not move since he's already convinced in the brain of his that his arm is actually raised. At any rate, the suggestion proved fruitful. Perhaps you have, at any point, gotten yourself "daydreaming" and gazing at a fascinating point with respect to the kitchen while someone is actually speaking? Did you miss what they have stated? You might have been in a stupor.

Any object of the center could be used to begin daze. The most known designs are the pendulum or maybe a swinging pocket watch even although these two things are presently associated with hokey stage hypnosis. You're certain to fall flat and encounter opposition utilizing these things due to the notoriety of theirs. You will find two primary specifics behind staring eyes. Which said, the writer keeps the cognizant character required, opening the subliminal to a recommendation. In addition, the eyes of yours get actually worn out whenever they concentrate or even move backward and forward.

When hypnotizing others, it's vital that you realize that you are able to distract them with objects very easily. Maybe you have a pendulum in the office of yours as a salesperson, or maybe you choose to have a crucial discussion next to a mesmerizing fountain. When a woman can easily be sidetracked by outside stimuli, it's a lot easier to break through the barriers they hold up as firmly.

Additionally, there are means that people are able to hypnotize ourselves. The human body scan is a widely recognized technique for self-hypnosis. Beginning at probably the highest point of the entire body with your eyes shut, filter down steadily from the mind to the foot. Notice each sensation your breath growing the ribcage, the seat pressing against the back of yours, the agony in the elbow of yours, each finger expanded, legs on the ground. Rehash the process from base to top. Keep looking over and down unless you get into a stupor. You might have known about controlled relaxing for contemplation. Nevertheless, it could be an easy kind of self-hypnosis. Here is the way it works:

- Close the eyes of yours and sit upright in a seat, arms on the lap of yours.
- Inhale with the nose and out through the lips.
- Utilizing average controlled breaths, count down from hundred.
- Each breath out counts as one meanwhile.
- Toward the end, you may stay in a stupor. If it wasn't, move with the exercise by tallying down by a greater number.

CHAPTER 13 NEURO-LINGUISTIC PROGRAMMING

Neuro-Linguistic Programming is actually an approach to influencing people's behavior as well as thinking. It emerged in the 1970s after Richard Bandler and John Grinder learned that they could link neurological procedures in addition to language to get particular behavioral changes they needed. To be able to know what NLP is actually truly, let us break down the acronym.

Neuro is actually in reference to just how the mind of our works. This's inclusive of all the aspects of the brain of ours, like the cerebrum, cerebellum, and the brain stem of yours. The cerebrum of yours has two distinct areas also, the left and the proper side. These're many exceptional first people to the biology of ours, as well as the genetics which we carry. The mind shapes of ours will also be significantly impacted by the encounters we have been through as well as the lives that we've lived. Although we are able to alter the way we think, the manner by which the mind of ours works takes a bit longer to really influence. The neurology of yours provides insight into the way you are able to alter the way in which the brain of your functions.

Linguistic is actually inclusive of all of the reasons that we express ourselves. It will have the way we speak as well as speak with other people. Ways the voice sounds of ours, the firmness of what we are thinking, as well as the facial expressions we make use of our many vital to the linguistic nature of ours. The body language of ours is an element of this, also. The way you hold the way, your posture, and your arms you fidget could be a part of the linguistic conduct of yours, also.

Last but not least, your programming refers to the way in which you've basically been programmed. You are wired a particular way as you grew into the person you're right now. NLP is going to be about just how you are able to reprogram yourself, so you believe a particular way. You are able to utilize these programs on yourself, though they're additionally handy tools when influencing others also. Someone taught in neuro-linguistic programming realizes how such tasks are actually organized in the psyche and the way to access them via language with the aim that used tasks, as well as autopilot methods, might be transformed.

Factors of NLP's methodologies have been co-opted by mainstream culture. For instance, there's been a whole lot made about the supposed capability to recognize lies by looking at an individual's eye moves. Since many self-improvement manuals have been composed on the basis of NLP methods, it's sensible to deal with it and the way the instruction capabilities, and it is invaluable to find out which conditions it's ideal for treating.

Neuro-linguistic programming is a psychological methodology which declares that an individual may set techniques employed by highly effective individuals to do one's own goals. It leads the individual to glean from their really individual encounters of frustration and achievement for the objective of determining which thought practices, sentiments, and processes are beneficial. No exercise is actually negative, no matter if it prompts obvious distress, as it's just a phase at the learning procedure.

By surveying an individual's emotions, musings, activities, and discourse, neuro-linguistic programming experts assemble a photograph of the individual's interaction with real life. NLP techniques are, in that case, utilized to allow the person to duplicate the procedures employed by others to utilize them rather than methods that haven't demonstrated as fruitful. NLP bases several of the opinions behind the methods on the point that people are able to predict some amount of certainty in the way humans will react. Many people are going to act in ways that are the same methods to one another, despite any differences they've.

NLP management is actually seated in the concept that people are able to anticipate what could end up happening by playing out a scenario in the brain of ours as we'd imagine it to occur. From there, we are able to understand the potential results better, understanding what persuasion strategies will work best to get the scenario that we wish. NLP tactics surround suggestions based in what we see from the planet based in what we have been taught throughout different academic as well as expert institutions. Each map of the planet of ours, what's created by the perspective of ours, is actually unusual, unique, and containing shifting dimensions of what could be thought to be real.

As one's NLP abilities develop, they are able to identify better the framework that others make use of to make choices. The greater you are able to understand, this particular, the easier it is going to be changing the person's mind, and basically, the manner by which they make choices.

Discreet Neuro-Linguistic Programming

NLP has techniques that have become popular and successful globally, and if you learn and use them properly, it will break you free from the chains that are tying you down at the moment. NLP is a realistic subject that involves face-to-face contact and the practice of the skill. Certainly, by delving into these pages or the many books available, you can enhance your knowledge of it, but if you want to develop the skills for yourself, you will want to attend an NLP practitioner's course face to face? Please read on to whatever you wish to do. This substantial book contains considerable help and encouragement from you. Discreet NLP, also known as conversational hypnosis, is the ability to hypnotize others and to communicate with their unconscious mind without them knowing they have been hypnotized. Discreet NLP is a remarkable tool that enables you to attract others to you and stir them to follow you and go out to please you.

You can secretly sway people with Discreet NLP to buy from you, persuade them to do things for you, and be in command of conversations. It is an incredible tool that, in simple day to day conversations, can change your life. You can access the unconscious mind of the subject by passing the vital conscious mind with careful use of vocabulary and specific body language, and can dramatically influence their actions. Since the subject is unaware of being affected by hypnosis, they believe they have come up with the concept themselves. Discreet NLP gives you the secret to planting ideas, hypnotizing subjects, and interacting with their subconscious mind. Once you enter their subconscious mind, you can make suggestions and influence their thinking and beliefs in a conversational way. People will be enthralled by what you have to say and drawn like a magnet to you.

Without them knowing it, you can use the power of suggestion on anyone, and they will believe it was their inspiration. You can make suggestions to just about anyone by modifying your voice tone and your body language, and they will do whatever you want them to do (as long as it doesn't go against their morals or their ethics). Discreet NLP is incredibly powerful when collectively utilizing three extraordinary disciplines. Each one alone is very effective on its own, but the results will amaze you when you combine all three into Discreet NLP. Hypnosis, NLP (Neurological Linguistic Programming), and mentalism are the three fields. Hypnosis is the power to hypnotize people and interact with their unconscious brain in order to change their behavior, opinions, or thoughts.

Neurological Linguistic Programming is the art of communication or discourse. NLP teaches you how to make a positive relationship with people and then get them to WILL please you. Mentalism shows you how to bring out false truths. Those false perceptions will make subjects believe everything you tell them. When you learn and execute these three disciplines as Discreet NLP, you have the ability within you to change not only your life but the lives of those around you as well. Once you communicate with their subconscious mind, you can make use of the power of suggestion to improve your life, but you can also use it to make your life better.

Apparently, normal conversation can produce rapid induction (putting someone into a trance state). You can then make suggestions and put ideas into their subconscious minds within that conversation. You should act differently. Discreet NLP is just one type of hypnosis. It is a practice that gives you the benefit of having the full power of your life so that you can achieve grandeur. You don't have to be a wizard, mystic, or talented in any way to master Discreet NLP. Once you've mastered the necessary skills to excel in Discreetly hypnotizing others, you're on the road to achieve everything you may want or need in life, not only for yourself but for your loved ones as well.

The Conscious Mind

Hypnotism is round about us. A lot of that's hidden or Discreet. We also think of hypnosis as stage hypnosis, as occurring only when we go to a show. Yet the fact is that hypnosis is just the conscious mind's diversion so that the unconscious mind works. This is what trance state means. Maybe you're driving down the freeway, and all of a sudden realize you're passing two exits where you intended to get off. Or you're running out and breaking through the wall to the height of that runner. You get to that point where you are not consciously aware of what's going on. You are out of the mind for the minute when you are aware of how much fun you are having. The child playing a game is not watching himself play the game. The musician who is practicing 8 hours a day doesn't see it as a chore, rather they see it as a pleasurable activity where they get lost.

The Secret of Hypnosis

This is the secret of hypnosis, in order to bring the subject into a pleasurable state where some intention can be achieved. And the purpose is both the secret to the trance state's success, and the form of hypnosis used. There's a lot of talk about conversational hypnosis and Discreet NLP. What makes hypnosis Discreet is the word Discreet, hidden, obvious meaning. The hypnotist's techniques are hidden down.

So the hypnotist uses hypnotic techniques to bring about the state of trance without the subject being aware of it. That's mind control attraction. It's the desire to control somebody else to get them to do something they want. Before we jump to any moral conclusions, we should understand that everyone uses Discreet NLP every day, all of the time.

Daily Hypnosis

Sure, you can think of a man who seduces a woman as Discreet NLP. And there are certainly plenty of books, DVDs and courses. And that may be morally reprehensible to you. But what's that Discreet NLP about a woman flirting? Isn't "the game" part of using perfume, lipstick, and languid moves? That's the reason the fanatic wants to ban such behavior. Because it does work. The problem with the obsessive is their part of the problem of mind control. They want to take control of you too. A better solution is to be aware of the techniques used in mind control. You will be in control by being aware of how your mind is being worked on by being conscious of how distracted you are.

Discreet NLP-How to lose friends and alienate individuals

Use hypnosis in everyday situations is usually called Conversational Hypnosis, most sometimes Discreet NLP. This could be discreet because you don't want people to know you 're doing something for them or simply because revealing them wouldn't add anything to the conversation. NLP and Hypnosis are closely related. A general concept for how the mind works is that you have pieces of the mind that are conscious and unconscious. The conscious part is moral and logical, which is the part of your mind in which you think. Your unconscious mind is the part where your memories and feelings are processed. This also has power over the muscle movements and automatic functions that we all have, such as keeping blood pumping across the body, routines, and automatic behavioral parts.

If you could give your unconscious mind clear recommendations bypassing your conscious mind's discerning and logical thinking faculties, you could possess tremendous power over men. Limitations are evident. Your unconscious mind is geared towards self-preservation, and, for example, stopping breathing does not obey commands. But what if you could make suggestions for getting excited about a particular product, or feel attracted to particular people or even vote in an election in a particular way?

It would be easier to get a wavering voter to vote for a specific party than someone who has spent their entire life voting for an opposing group. It is much more difficult to get someone with a different sexual orientation to fall in love with you than to tell someone who already considers you attractive. Although it is increasingly less successful, the more discreet and the more you are going to go against others, using Discreet NLP, it is possible to push people a great distance. A good NLP Practitioner Course will train you in all the strategies you need to be able to use.

The argument, though, is that while you can bypass the aware, logical, thinking mind of a human, you can't completely get rid of it. This means they'll remember what you've done to them at some point. They may not know how, but because of how they feel, they are likely to breed resentment towards you. Say you use Discreet NLP to mis-sell the goods.

Initially, your customers might go away happy because that was the hypnotic state you induced in the ... but when they come out of it, they'll probably feel cheated, manipulated and conned to buy something they don't want. The net result is returns, complaints, and a huge reputational loss. Used correctly, Discreet NLP techniques will get people to access and start fulfilling their deep desires and motivations. If I take the example of sales when I find a customer with a product need, if I can find a way to link the product to meet their needs at a profound psychological level, they will feel great about the sale, the product, and about me. The net result is extremely happy customers and a strong reputation.

I think you can start thinking about some great applications for yourself, such as presenters raising their charisma, linking fun and enjoyment to meeting friends, or satisfying your employees at work. Learning how to connect the core values of people to the things you want them to do is a crucial part of Discreet NLP, and it's very strong.

If you do that with things that aren't right for them, they're going to feel cheated, if you do this in a way that takes them to where they want to go, you're going to build life mates. A good course for NLP practitioners should demonstrate that you can use Hidden NLP to get people to do what you want and to thank you for it, so they get what they want too.

HOW ARE PEOPLE USING NLP ON YOU?

Communication is a program by which an individual offers vague allusions as well as indications using nonverbal prompts. For instance, if a male inquires as to whether the spouse of his is actually okay and she answers Yes with a moan and a shrug of the shoulders of her, this's unmistakably showing she is not alright, but the spoken answer of her is actually complete. Does your partner demand preposterous expectations on the way of yours of living? In case you're pressured to comply with impossible time constraints, have controlled eating times as well as restroom breaks, or maybe no access to your companions or money, at that time, this's mind control and could likely be considered misuse of NLP practices.

In order to fight this behavior, recognize assistance from dear loved ones with respect to this particular circumstance, as when it gets to this point, you are going to have presumably been used out with confidence that is low. NLP is not a thing that's constantly going to be apparent. Anybody who's using NLP is very likely a specialist that has practiced the method regularly. Several warning signs may include specific attention being paid for you, feeling as you've realized the ideal partner of yours, or perhaps that the person you've rather lately met is flawlessly coordinated for you. Look out for an individual that remains reflecting the non-verbal correspondence of yours or even uses ambiguous expressions. They might not bode very well.

If you're speaking to somebody who may be an NLP specialist, and they're relaxing in the very same position as you or perhaps are actually holding the hands of theirs in the exact same fashion as you're, evaluate them by intentionally moving or even talking in a specific manner and then examine if they to perform a comparable idea. Skilled NLP experts are going to have greater ability compared to others at veiling this behavior. Nevertheless, many will faster duplicate the behavior you initiate.

In the underlying phases of compatibility acceptance, an NLP client can give good concern to the eyes of yours. You might believe this's since they're severely inspired by what you're saying. Rather they're viewing your eye developments to perceive the way you store and access data.

Quickly, they will have the capability to make sure when you're lying or perhaps acting purposefully. They will likewise have the capability to determine what aspects of the cerebrum of yours you're utilizing when you're speaking. These people learn from what they see you are doing, and also from the perspective of yours, and it may look they've deep information about just how you think and what you're wondering. A wise hack for this's dashing the eyes of yours around haphazardly - jump the right, back to the various other sides, side to side, up-down. Make it appear to be regular; however, do it arbitrarily. This can get an NLP specific nuts since you will be distracting them from the research of theirs of you.

Suppose you end up in the organization of an NLP specialized, and also you wind up in a heightened psyched condition - potentially you start snickering tough or maybe get furious or perhaps something similar - as well as the person you're conversing with throws the hand of theirs on you while you're acting in this particular fashion. They might touch the arm of yours or even provide you with a gentle tap on the shoulder. By doing this, the NLP specialist has a method of returning one to that status when the need is, simply by touching you in the exact same fashion once again.

One of the important methods that NLP specialists make use of is actually questionable language to prompt an entrancing daze. It's discovered that the more questionable language is actually, the more it drives people to a trance, on the grounds that there's much less than a person is actually subject to differ with or perhaps react to. On the flip side, explicit language is going to remove a person from the stupor. Be sure you're being mindful of controlling language as well. "Don't wait to unwind." "You are actually no cost to test drive this particular vehicle on the off chance you like." "You are able to value this almost as you are able to imagine." Look out for this.

These examples of trance inducers. Probably the most excellent strategy to get somebody to achieve a thing, like moving into a stupor, is actually by authorizing them to do it while not telling them to. Together these lines, proficient hypnotherapists won't ever point one to achieve something. They are going to say such things as "Don't wait to move toward getting as comfortable as you are able to imagine."

Phrases as "As you discharge this inclination much more, you are going to wind up moving into an existing plan with the audio of the prosperity of yours to an ever-increasing extent." This kind of jabber is actually the bread as well as butter of the pacing-and-driving notions of NLP; the trance inducer is not truly saying anything; they're merely endeavoring to program the inspiration of yours and move you towards exactly where they require one to go.

Continuously state, "Would you be in a position to make clear what you mean?" This achieves two things: it interferes with this whole process, and it moves the talk into explicit language, breaking the stupor inducing usage of ambiguous language.

NLP people are going to utilize language with layered or disguised implications. For instance, "Diet, healthy living and submit yourself to me are actually probably the most crucial conditions, would not you say?" Superficially, in case you noticed this sentence spoken in a fast fashion, it'd seem to be an indisputable articulation which you'd presumably concur with unthinkingly.

Really, healthy living, as well as diet, are actually conditions that are serious, beyond any doubt. At any rate, what is the layered in the message? "Diet, healthy living, and submit yourself to me are actually probably the most crucial conditions, would not you say?" That's appropriate, and also you only unknowingly consented to it. Skilled NLP experts may be daring with this particular kind of issue.

Be exceptionally watchful about daydreaming around NLP people - it's an encouragement for these people to go in with an unnoticed trigger. Here is an example: An NLP client that was endeavoring to help you to compose for the blog of his at no cost noticed you weren't putting much effort into the project.

He then started using the technique of adding secret meanings to the words of his by talking about exactly how he never ever wants to purchase anything at all since information energy sources send him collections as well as publications at no cost.

Should you end up being directed to settle rapidly on something and think you're being controlled, leave the circumstance. Keep up twenty-four hours prior to settling on any choices, especially monetary ones. Don't get swept up into an off the cuff choice. Sales reps are actually equipped with NLP systems explicitly to design spur-of-the-moment purchases. Don't get it done. Leave do not permit yourself to be manipulated, and prevent authority over the life of yours.

In addition, the essential and preeminent standard: If you think someone is actually manipulating you or maybe you are feeling the individual is actually attempting to manipulate you, go with the instincts of yours. NLP people frequently appear dodgy. Escape, or even allow it to be acknowledged that they shouldn't practice NLP techniques on you while speaking with you.

Practical Steps to achieve These Skills

Now you fully understand what it may are like if a person is actually using NLP on you, it's some time to find out the way you are able to make use of it on others. The same as any other methods of persuasion in this particular book we have talked about thus far, make sure that you're not making use of this in a dangerous way. Instead of attempting to fool folks into doing everything you need, do these effective methods to make sure you're getting an area of pleasure for the both of you.

First, let us start by checking out the basic language you are able to use. Right now, there are apparently limitless words we are able to work with, so as somebody who wishes to affect others, you have to make sure that you're conscious of the typical ones seen in the strategies of probably the highest competent NLP influencers. The very first word is, "don't." When somebody says, "don't look over here," the very first thing you should do is generally look exactly where they said not to. This's since the mind of ours isn't acknowledging that "don't." Instead, it's concentrated solely on the particular issue of the discussion, and that is the sight which is present to the area you are told not to appear.

In case you're seeking a person to take action for you, you may say "don't" first, but just in a little setting. "Don't think about this right now," is actually a great thing to point out when you really want the individual to think regarding a product. Possibly you're conversing with the boss of yours regarding how fun it will be to arrange a holiday for the holidays instead of investing cash on one easy party. You may say, "We should think about a little trip rather than a party for the holidays this season. Do not think about this today, although, since we are very active with all of the other jobs at the moment." What would you believe that the supervisor will do then? As a way to distract herself from the stress of work, she may begin to consider the trip and just how fun it might be for the workers.

You would not always want to make use of this word in case you're really attempting to get something physical. To tell a spouse, "Don't get me flowers for Valentine's day," is not going to do the job, regardless of how often times you may have noticed it do so on TV. As well as films, they'll merely believe you do not wish flowers. You may instead say, "Don't make a huge deal; I do not want much." It's not guaranteed, though it may work to persuade them they need to create a big problem, so they exceed the expectations of yours.

The largest word that an NLP master will make use of is actually "you." When you are able to include things like "you/I" statements, it can help the other individual visualize themselves. The crucial to getting a person to listen to you are talking about them! As self-centered as it may seem, humans just like chatting about themselves. This's since it's exactly who they're as well as the standard for just how they perceive the world. One more NLP tactic is using "because," "however," or any other explanatory words. In case you are saying something such as, "I demand 5 dollars," to your partner or maybe parents, they may just believe nothing of it and never choose to provide you with the cash. In case you say, "I require five money since I wish to purchase a little food," chances are they are going to be much more likely to provide you with the cash, as easy as that.

Consumers want a sizable explanation, proof, and evidence when they're making a choice. Even in case, they're being affected to make that choice, in the end, they are going to want facts to back up the determining factors of theirs. The greater number of info you are able to offer to them, the much more likely it is going to be to really get what you would like from this particular individual.

Not merely does this help build the case of yours since you're offering evidence for the choice of theirs, though you're additionally ensuring you are going to be in a position to show them you're confident in which you're conscious of real evidence as well as the facts.

When you are able to link the level of yours of persuasion to a thought pattern that somebody may already have, it is going to be simpler to affect them. Do not only look for things on the surface level when attempting to gain influence. Truly learn the cognitive skills which lie behind decision making. Not everybody will fall for the original influence. Therefore you are going to have to appear deeper into what could keep them up to discover the answers necessary to sway them successfully.

Always place yourself in the shoes of theirs. How about the request of yours that might keep them up? Precisely why can they be going to say no? From there, look at the part of the mind of theirs, the cognitive ability, which is going to emerge whenever they begin to make specific choices. You then are able to greatly look at the language that had to affect the behavior of theirs adversely.

Powerful Leadership

Today you already know the best essential components involved in NLP tactics; it's some time to have a look at the way you are able to make use of these techniques to turn into a good leader. To influence individuals in the daily life of yours could be important, but when you're in a position of power, or perhaps at the very least would like to be, you have to seek out the balance between control and expert. A strong leader knows the way to encourage the followers of theirs, not always handle them. Can your choices impact the life of yours as well as the individuals who are respecting as well as listening to you?

Foremost and first, be sure you are concerned about the company of yours. Whatever you're the leader of, you've to have confidence in it and truly know how it is able to correctly make it easier to as well as your followers live a happier and better life. If perhaps you've no interest in what you're doing, then why should anybody else?

All of us have moments where we're less passionate compared to others, though it's crucial as a leader that you do not show that. Consistently guarantee you're invested in the work of yours, and you're focused. You cannot look for something more from individuals in case you're not placing these fundamental works available.

Then, make sure you're efficiently talking with the staff of yours. Have constant meetings as well as assessment periods, so they're provided the chance to voice some issues they may be having. In case you're unavailable, do not in the workplace, refuse to answer calls, or maybe outright ignore the staff members of yours or any other followers, next they're not going to listen to you successfully.

They'll still meet your needs, but just since they've to. To get individuals to actually believe in you, to actually know how you are able to make them pay attention to you, then you have to guarantee you're listening to them initially!

At exactly the same time, you've to make sure you have a high amount of emotional intelligence for your followers or staff members, too. Show empathy, and you're inclined to say that when you're wrong. Naturally, you do not wish to apologize when you're not at fault outwardly, but constantly show you're prepared to tune in as well as self-reflect on the choices that you are making.

Being a leader, the focus is not simply about getting the task finished. That's what the staff is there for. Being a leader, the job of yours is usually to make sure they're competent to obtain the task finished efficiently since they're happy; the requirements of theirs are actually achieved, and they're being taken care of. You'll additionally be a much better supervisor as well as a leader in case you're proficient. Always be ready to learn something totally new, as well as ensure you're in line with the development which you're exhibiting to others. The more you are able to accomplish this, the easier it is going to be for individuals to begin to believe in as well as trust in you and what you're attempting to affect these to do.

CHAPTER 14 THE ART OF PERSUASION

Persuasion is another form of mind control that will be debated. While there may not be as much media hype about this form of mind control as there is with brainwashing and hypnosis, when done correctly, it can be just as effective. The issue with this form is that there are just so many different forms of persuasion present in everyday life that it can be difficult for any single source to get through to the subject and make a difference.

While persuasion works to change the subject's thoughts and beliefs like the other forms of mind control, it seems as though everyone is trying to persuade you about something so that it becomes easier to ignore the persuasion that comes to the subject. For example, television advertisements, when an argument is going on, or even when a conversation is going on, there is some sort of persuasion going on. People often use persuasion without noticing, to their advantage. This chapter will go into more depth on persuasion and how it can be used effectively as a method of mind control.

What is Persuasion?

When people think of persuasion, they sometimes come up with a lot of different answers. Some may think of the commercials and advertisements they see all around them, urging the purchase of a particular product over another. Others can think about political persuasion, and how politicians can seek to sway the opinion of the electorate to get another vote. Both are examples of persuasion because the message attempts to change the way the subject thinks. There is justification in everyday life, and it is a very powerful force and a major influence on the topic and society. Advertising, mass media, legal decisions, and politics will all be informed by how persuasion works and, in effect, will also seek to convince the subject.

As can be shown, some main differences exist between persuasion and the other types of mind control that have been addressed in this guidebook so far. Brainwashing and hypnosis may involve isolation of the subject in order to alter its mind and identity. Manipulation will also work toward the final goal of just one person. While persuasion can be done on just one subject to change their mind, persuasion can also be used on a larger scale to persuade a whole group or even society to change the way they think. This can make it even more effective, and possibly dangerous because it has the ability to change many people's minds at once rather than just a single subject's mind.

Many people fall under the mistaken illusion of being resistant to persuasion. They think they'd be able to see any pitch of sales that's thrown their way, whether the manipulator is actually selling a product or some new idea, and then be able to understand the situation that's going on and come to a conclusion with their own logic. This will be true in some scenarios; nobody is falling for everything they hear all the time when they use logic, especially if it goes completely against their beliefs, no matter how strong the argument may be. Therefore, most subjects should be able to skip the notifications about buying TVs and fancy cars or the newest product on the market. The act of persuasion can also be even more subtle, and it will be easier for the audience to develop their own views on what they are being told.

When the act of persuasion arises, most people will see it in a negative light. They'll think of a salesman or conman who's trying to persuade them to change all their beliefs and who'll push and bother them until the change happens. While this is certainly one way of thinking about persuasion, it is often possible to use this process in a positive way rather than just a negative one. Public service campaigns, for example, can persuade people to avoid smoking, or recycle can be ways of persuasion that can benefit the subject's lives. It's all in how the persuasion process is used.

Elements of Persuasion

As with other forms of mind control, when it comes to persuasion, there are certain elements to be watched for. These elements help define exactly what persuasion is to make it more knowledgeable. According to Perloff in 2003, persuasion is defined as "a symbolic process in which communications attempt to persuade other people to change their attitudes or behaviors regarding a problem by transmitting a message in a free-choice atmosphere." This is one of the things that distinguish persuasion from the other forms of mind control; the subject is often allowed to make their own free choices in the matter, even if the persuasion tactics are going to work to shift the mind of the subject in a particular direction. The subject may choose the way they want to think, whether they want to purchase a product or not, or whether they believe the evidence behind the argument is good enough to change their minds. There are a few elements present in persuasion which help to define it further. These features include:

Forbearance is symbolic

That means that to get the point across, it uses sounds, images, and words. Persuasion will involve the manipulator intent on deliberately influencing the subject or group.

Self-persuasion is an essential part of that process. Usually, the subject is not coerced, and instead, they are given the freedom to choose their own choice. There are many ways to convey convincing messages, including face-to-face, email, radio, and television. Communication may also take place either nonverbally or verbally.

Let's look in a little more depth at each of these issues. The first aspect of persuasion is that symbolically, it is necessary. To convince somebody to think or act in a certain way, you need to be able to show them why they should change their minds. This will include using words, sounds, and images to convey a new point. To show your point, you can use the words to start a debate or argument. Pictures are a perfect way of presenting the facts needed to persuade us to go one direction or the other. Some nonverbal clues are possible, but they won't be as successful as using words and pictures.

The second key is that persuasion will be used in a deliberate way to influence the way others act or think. This one is fairly clear if you don't want to manipulate someone, you don't use manipulation to alter them. The persuader will try out different tactics to get the subject to think the same way they do. It may be anything as easy as actually holding a conversation with them or providing facts that support their perspective. On the other hand, it might require a lot more and include more complicated ways to change the mind of the subject. More information on the techniques used in persuasion will be discussed later in this chapter.

The unique thing about persuasion is that it allows for some form of free will to the subject. In that way, the subject is allowed to make his own choice. Usually, no matter how hard someone is trying to convince them of something, they don't have to go for it. The subject might listen to a thousand commercials about the best car to buy, but if they don't like that brand or don't need a new vehicle, then they won't go out and buy it. If so,

The subject is against abortion, and it won't matter how many people come out and say how great abortion is, it won't change their minds. This allows much more freedom of choice than is found in the other forms of mind control, which could explain why, when asked, many people don't see this as a kind of mind control.

Persuasion is a type of control of the mind that can take place in several different ways. While brainwashing, hypnosis and manipulation must occur face to face, and in some cases in complete isolation, persuasion may occur otherwise. Examples of persuasion can be found all over the place, including when you're talking to people you know, on the Internet, and via radio and TV. Convincing messages can also be delivered through nonverbal and verbal means, although it is much more effective when using verbal techniques.

Modern Persuasion

Over time, persuasion has evolved from its original beginnings and has changed. For many years Persuasion has been around; in fact, it has been around since ancient Greece. This doesn't mean the art and persuasion process is exactly the same as they were back then. In fact, quite a few changes have been made to the art of persuasion and how it is used in modern times. This section will address some of the key elements of modern-day persuasion. Richard M. Perloff spent quite some time studying modern persuasion, how it is used, and how it can affect the whole of society. He wrote a book entitled The Persuasion Dynamics: Contact and Attitudes in The 21st Century, which outlines the five ways in which the use of modern persuasion differs from the way it had been used in the past. These five ways cover:

The number of messages considered persuasive has grown by leaps and bounds: persuasion was used in ancient Greece's times only in writing and in elite debates. Convincing was not a big thing, and you wouldn't see it very often. In modern times, taking you around is hard to get to somewhere without any message of persuasion. Think of the various forms and sources of ads out there; the average person in the U.S. can see up to 3000 of these every day. Besides that, people are always knocking at your door trying to get you to buy something, believe their ideas, or try something new. Persuasion is far more a part of modern life than it has been in history at any other time.

- Persuasion travels really fast: back in ancient Greece times, it might take weeks or longer to get from one point to another for a persuasive message. This limited the impact of persuasion since most people could not get the message. In the context of face-to-face communication, most acts of persuasion had to be done. In modern times, thanks to the use of the internet, radio, and television, persuasive messages can cover a large distance in hardly any time at all. Political leaders will meet the electorate in only seconds at once, and any message can be quickly distributed. Persuasion assumes a far greater role when it can spread so fast. Persuasion can mean a lot of money: now that businesses have discovered the power of persuasion, they are doing all they can to make it work. The more effective they are in persuading customers to purchase their goods, the more money they receive.

Some companies are primarily due to the convincing mechanism, such as public relations firms, marketing firms, and advertising agencies. Other firms will be able to use the persuasive techniques offered by those firms to reach and exceed the sales goals they set.

- Persuasion has become more subtle than in the past: the manipulator would announce their views loudly at the beginning of persuasion for the entire group to hear in the hopes of getting them all to change their minds. Those days are over, and the persuasion process has become a lot more discreet. Although it is possible to find persuasive acts that are still very loud and in your face, as in some forms of advertising, many others follow a more subtle route. An example of this is when companies are creating a certain image of themselves, such as being family-friendly, to get consumers to buy their products. You will also note that instead of engaging in discussion with your friend about going to a party, they're going to use peer pressure or maybe list a few things to try to get you to come along. Despite being more subtle, persuasion is still as powerful today as it has ever been. The persuasion process has become more complicated: along with persuasion being more nuanced and even more difficult to figure out, it is also moving down the road to becoming more complicated. The topic being targeted is more diverse than in the past, and they have to make a lot more choices. For example, where once a person has just gone to the one store in town to buy anything they need, now they can choose from various stores from the hardware store to the grocery store to the clothing store for their needs. Besides that, there is often more than one option available in the area for each of these shopping categories. All those choices make it harder for the manipulator to find a good message of persuasion for the consumer or any other subject.

Methods of persuasion

Methods of persuasion can often come under other names and be referred to in ways such as strategies of persuasion and tactics of persuasion. There is not only one method that can be used to persuade somebody to think or to act in some way. The manipulator may be able to talk to the subject while presenting evidence to change the mind of the subject, they may be able to use some kind of force or pull against the subject they have, and they may be able to perform some kind of service for the subject or use another tactic. This section will go into more detail on the different methods of persuasion available and how each one of them could be to be successful in the persuasion process uses force depending on the situation, the manipulator may decide that using some force to persuade the subject to think its way is a good idea. This can happen when the ideas don't fit correctly, daily communication doesn't work, or when the manipulator is irritated or unhappy with the communication change. Sometimes coercion is used as a form of scare tactic as it allows the target less time to think about what happens compared to when a normal discussion takes place objectively. Usually, the force will be used when the manipulator has had less success using the other available means of persuasion, although sometimes it is also done starting with the use of force. At certain times, coercion can be used when the manipulator feels like they are losing control or when the subject can present the manipulator with conflicting facts, and the manipulator becomes angry. Often when it comes to the persuasion process, it is not the best idea to use force. This is because a lot of subjects will see the use of force as a threat because the manipulator won't give other options to the request they make. The whole appeal of persuasion is that it offers a choice of paths to the subject, but once force is put into the mix, freedom of choice is gone, and the subject is more likely to feel threatened. Once the subject feels threatened, they're less likely to listen and consider anything the manipulator says so that the process won't go on. Because of these reasons, the use of force in the art of persuasion is generally discouraged and avoided, unlike the other forms of mind control discussed.

Influence Arms

Another method that can be used to persuade the subject to lean a particular way is to utilize the available weapons of influence. Robert Cialdini developed those six influences in his book Influence. This book discusses the art of persuasion and defines the six weapons of influence that are capable of making the manipulator successful in its objectives. Reciprocity, commitment, and consistency, social proof, liking, authority, and scarcity are the six weapons of influence. These six weapons of influence are significant to the manipulator as they are a part of their subjects' change process. We'll discuss each of these six-guns below.

Mutuality

The primary weapon of control is the reciprocity principle. This principle states that if one person, the manipulator, provides something of value to the other person, the subject, then the subject will try to repay the manipulator in kind. It simply means that when the manipulator performs some sort of service to the subject, at some stage, the subject may feel they have an obligation to perform a similar service to the manipulator. While the two services may not be the same, they have the same value to match each other's obligations.

The act of reciprocation ends up giving the subject a sense of duty, which the manipulator can then use as a powerful weapon when they choose to use persuasion. The rule of reciprocity is very effective because it helps the manipulator get the subject into the right frame of mind for the act of persuasion by instilling the subject with a sense of obligation and overpowering it. The manipulator will be more likely to persuade the subject to do or behave in any way, because the subject may have that feeling of duty hanging over them. Another added benefit for the manipulator in using reciprocity is that it's not just a moral standing that puts the obligation on the subject; it's also a standing that's held up by social codes. The manipulator won't have to worry if the subject has the right moral code to return the favor. If the subject does not feel the need to do so, the manipulator should have some means at their fingertips to drive it into action.

As a society, people don't like individuals who neglect to return a favor or payment when a free gift or service is offered to them. If the manipulator does not feel the subject will reciprocate with them, they can turn them into their social group. They can do this by telling other friends or coworkers how they did a favor for the subject, but when it was needed, the subject never returned it. Now, by asking the favor, the manipulator has placed social expectations on the subject, making it much more likely that they can convince the subject to do something. The subject would be able to reciprocate to the manipulator for the most part without having any outside powers. When the favor is granted, the subject will start looking for ways to repay the manipulator so that the score is even, and they don't seem greedy or egoistic. The manipulator will then be able to provide the subject with an easy solution on how to repay this debt; the subject will be grateful for having this easy solution and will be more likely to go the way the manipulator wants.

Commitment and Continuity.

The next weapon of power to be discussed is commitment and continuity. If they wish to persuade anyone to change their point of view, the manipulator will need to use both of these. They are easier to understand when things are clear, which can help the subject make better decisions. It's not fair for the manipulator to constantly change the details they 're using, or alter other information needed to help the subject process the information. Rather than helping with the persuasion process, keeping away constantly from consistency will make the manipulator look like a liar and someone who can't be trusted, resulting in the persuasion process failing.

Consistency is highly valued in society: people like things to stay a certain way the way most of the time. While there is a lot of variety in daily life, people feel safe knowing that overall, things remain pretty constant. It lets them understand what has happened, know what to expect, and be prepared if any changes happen. If consistency were not available, it would be very hard to plan things, and there would always be chaos issues going around. If you want to persuade a particular subject, then you have to make sure that your facts are consistent, and that they make sense. Consistency results in benefiting most people 's approach to everyday life. Ever tried planning a day out when something unexpected comes up? It can make things nearly impossible to do, and will eventually feel like a disaster.

People like consistency because it gives them the opportunity to know what to expect and what to do. They know when it's time to eat when it's time for work, and when there will be other things going on all day. Consistency offers a very useful solution due to the complexities inherent in modern life. Life is hard enough without referring to other stuff that doesn't render ever after. It makes things a lot easier when people are able to have consistent lives. Consistency is a great tool, as it enables the subject to be able to make the right decisions and process information. If the manipulator wants to succeed in persuading the subject, they need to make sure their message is consistent. There is no room for false evidence that may later appear and ruin the entire process. Keep the facts truthful and concise, and to persuade the subject much better. The act of commitment is something that ties in with consistency. It is important to have some kind of engagement in place to know that the subject is actually persuaded and that the effort has paid off. This can mean, in advertising, that the subject will buy the product or in politics, it can mean that the subject will vote for a particular candidate. The commitment that is made varies according to the nature of persuasion. According to the concept of consistency, if a person commits, either in writing or orally, they are far more likely to honor their commitment.

It has been found that this is much more true in terms of written promises because the topic would be mentally more tangible, and there is some hard evidence that they have committed to the undertaking. That makes a lot of sense; many people are going to pledge verbally that they are going to repair it or do anything, only to turn around and not. Yeah, some people are going to do what they're doing, and they're more likely to do so if they're promising orally than not promising at all, but sometimes it's still hard to get the results you want in that way. Moreover, there's no way to back it up because an oral compromise just becomes a dispute he said she said and no one can win. On the other hand, if the manipulator is in a position to provide a written promise from the subject, they would have the proof that they need the thing done.

The reason why it is so vital for the manipulator to get the subject to consent to an undertaking is that after the subject has committed to the new role, they have more of a propensity to behave in a manner that suits that commitment. The topic will move on after that point and begin to engage in self-persuasion for the cause. They must have numerous justifications and reasons for endorsing the undertaking along with others to prevent any problems with the manipulator. If the manipulator can bring the subject to that stage, the manipulator would have far less work to do.

Democratic Protests

Persuasion is a form of social interaction, and so the social rules where it happens will have to be followed. The topic will be affected by the people around them; they will be more likely to want to do what others are doing, instead of doing their own thing. The topic will base their views and behaviors on what others are doing around them, how these same people are behaving and believing. For instance, if the subject grows up in a city, they are more likely to behave like those from that area; on the other hand, those who grow up in a very religious community that spend most of their time praying, studying, and helping those.

The expression "strength of the crowd" can be very powerful under this belief. The subject would want to know at all times what other people around you are doing. In this country, it has become almost an obsession to be able to do what others are doing to fit in, given the fact that people would be saying how they want to be special and be a person. An explanation is given of how people are going to do something if others do it can be found with a phone-a-thon. If the host says something like "Operators are waiting, please call now," then the subject may feel like there are operators sitting around with nothing to do because nobody is calling them. This would make the topic less likely to call because they feel that if someone else does not call, then they will not call either. If the host changes only a few words and then says, "If operators are busy, please call again," a very different outcome can be obtained. The subject would now presume that the operators are occupied with several other subjects' calls, so the organization must be successful and legitimate. The topic would be far more likely to call in whether they get through immediately or not, or if they have to be put on hold.

The persuasive strategy of social evidence is the most powerful in circumstances where the subject is unaware of what they are going to do or when circumstances tend to have several parallels. The subject would always prefer to adhere to what those around them are doing in unclear or unpredictable circumstances that have several options or possibilities to make. This is because the options are so similar that all of them would work, but they're going to believe that the option the others make is the right one. The other way social evidence can be used is when such comparisons arise. The subject, for example, is much more likely to adapt and shift to others who are in some way similar to them. If there is someone close to the subject in charge, the subject would definitely listen to them and obey them rather than if the person in charge is somewhat different from the subject matter.

The manipulator should be able to use the concept of social evidence to help in their convincing process. The first way they will do this is to analyze the language they say. With the example given from the game show, both quotes said the same thing, but they came up with two different interpretations by flipping the wording up. None of them was a lie; they were only successful in inducing a different kind of response. Whether the manipulator behaves the way, they say things may get the right answer from their subjects and convince the subject to follow the same ideas and beliefs. Furthermore, the manipulator will find that there is more progress in getting people that are close to them to share in the ideas. That's why politicians are going to try to appeal to communities with similar ideas. If they intend to enter a wider audience, they will change their ideas to make them more appealing to those new audiences.

Attractiveness Factor

The manipulator will be working really hard to get them to like the subject. There is a very clear explanation or this; they 're far more likely to say yes to them if the subject likes the handler. There are two principal factors that will lead to how well the manipulator likes the subject. The former is physical beauty, and the latter is the resemblance. For the first, if the manipulator is physically more appealing to the subject, they would have the feeling of becoming more convincing because they can more easily get what they want while also shifting attitudes of others. This attractiveness factor has been shown to be successful in sending favorable messages and perceptions of other qualities the manipulator may have, including intellect, kindness, and talent. All of this works together to make an attractive person more likely to be able to convince the subject more easily.

The second element, similitude, is a little simpler. The theory is that if the subject is identical to the manipulator, they are far more likely to respond in the affirmative to what the manipulator is asking. This method is very normal, and most of the time, the subject isn't going to have to worry about whether it's the best thing to do because they enjoy it and are close to the manipulator.

Authority

One way the manipulator can succeed in persuading the subject is by being an authority. In most people, there is a propensity to assume that what an expert says about a subject is real. The subject is more likely to enjoy listening to a trustworthy and competent manipulator; this means that if the manipulator can bring these two things to the table, then they are already on the way to getting their subject to listen and believe in them. Studies have been done to demonstrate how this strategy of authority will succeed in persuading the subject to listen to what the manipulator has to say. The research that was performed was known as the study of Milgram, which was basically a whole series of experiments that began in 1961. The participants were composed of two topics, and each was put in separate rooms. The first subject was then attached to an electric harness that was capable of delivering the shock. The second topic was told by the manipulator, who had been dressed in the coat of a scientist and looked official, to ask the first topic questions and then to punish them whenever a question was answered wrongly. The manipulator asked the second subject to deliver electrical shocks that came from a panel that was under the control of the second subject. The second subject had to select the next highest voltage to use the next time after providing a shock and would continue to do so until it reached the maximum voltage of 450 volts. One thing the second subject didn't know was that the first subject was merely an actor who caused the pain; this first subject wasn't personally hurt in the process. This experiment was performed in order to see how well someone in power can follow the second subject and not hurt anyone intentionally. The statement that accompanied this study was, "When an authority tells ordinary people that it is their job to do harm, how much suffering will the subject be willing to inflict upon a completely innocent individual if the orders come from above? "According to this report, most of the second subjects were willing to bring as much pain as was available to the first subject. This led to the conclusion that most subjects are willing to inflict pain on others if an authority figure of some sort tells them to do so. Of course, when it comes to persuasion, discomfort isn't something that's really needed to change the way people think. This study was merely an example of how the subject would respond to the manipulator if the manipulator can show they are some kind of authoritarian individual. Keeping that in mind may help the manipulator reach its own agenda.

Scarcity

Scarcity is another method of persuasion with which people might be familiar but which is often undervalued. When the concept or idea has minimal supply, so a higher value is more likely to be attributed. "People want more of something they can't get," according to Cialdini. While that may sound like describing a kid who wants to get into the cookie jar when they're told no, it can also explain how normal adults behave. When there's the scarcity question to remember, the context will also matter. This basically implies that the notion of scarcity may really be a benefit within different contexts. The persuasion manipulator should use the scarcity idea to their advantage. They would have to find a way to make the subject think the item is rare by describing why it is so different and what it does that nothing else can do. The manipulator would have to operate their subject in a proper manner. The manipulator can also opt to go the other way; instead of explaining what the item or concept will earn the customer may demonstrate what they will lose by not getting the item. For instance, the manipulator might say something like, "you 're going to lose $5" instead of "you could save $5." This is just another way the manipulator will be able to make something as scarce as it is.

There are two explanations about why the scarcity theory works. First off, when goods or products are hard to get, they typically gain more interest. The more interest an object has, even though that is not real, the higher quality it would tend to have. The second point is that when anything is not as easily available as it once was, the subject will begin to understand that in the future, they will lose the chance of obtaining something. If this begins to happen, the subject will start giving the service or object that is scarce a higher value, simply because it will become more difficult to procure.

The concept behind this theory is that the subject should want the things which are beyond their control. If anything is easy to get, nobody wants it as much as when the object is harder. If the manipulator can plant the idea that their opinions, values, or things are scarce and hard to come by, they would have a far better chance of finding success in their attempts of persuasion.

Techniques for Persuasion

If the manipulator wants to be successful in persuading the subject into something, certain strategies will have to be learned, which will help them out. The subject will be presented each day with different types of persuasion. Food producers will try to get the subject to buy the new items, or more of the old while studios will advertise their latest blockbusters. Since persuasion can be found almost anywhere, finding a way to impose their point of view on the matter would be a major challenge for the negotiator. For many years the techniques which come with persuasion have been observed and studied all the way back to ancient times. It is because power is so beneficial to a wide variety of different individuals. The systematic study of these techniques has evolved beginning in the early 20th century.

Because the ultimate aim of using persuasion is to convince the subject to take the convincing point, internalize it, and then accept it as a new mindset, there is tremendous value in finding out which persuasion methods are the most effective ones. The three persuasion methods that give the manipulator the most value and that will be addressed in this section build a desire, appeal to the social needs, and use loaded images and expressions.

Create a Need

One way the manipulator can get the subject to change their way of thinking is to establish a need, or they can respond to a need that has already developed within the subject. If performed correctly, this form of persuasion must appeal to the subject; this means that in order for the manipulator to be successful, they would need to appeal to the subject's basic needs, such as their need for self-actualization, self-esteem, affection, food, and shelter. The reason this approach will work so well for the manipulator is that the subject will really need certain things. Food is not something they will live for long without. Whether the manipulator can persuade the subject that their shop is the best, or whether they can get more food or shelter by modifying their values, there's a better likelihood of success.

Appealing to Social Needs

Next, the manipulator should refer to the subject's social needs. Although social needs can not be used as frequently as the primary needs, they are still an essential resource to use. People like being wanted and being part of the crowd. They like the prestige that certain items can give them and feel as if they belong to a higher social standing. The idea of appealing to the subject's social needs can be seen in most on-line television advertisements; in these ads, the audience may be persuaded to buy an item so that they can become well-known or just like anyone else. When the manipulator responds to the subject's social needs, they may enter a new area that might be of interest to the subject.

Use Loaded Images and Phrases

If it comes to persuasion, having a choice of words will make all the difference. There are several different ways of doing the same thing, but one way might push the subject into action while the other is not going to. If it comes to using persuasion, using the right words the right way would make all the difference. Earlier in this chapter, the discussion of the phone-a-thon is a perfect example of how words can be used to persuade people to leap into practice. Persuasion is a strong instrument of mind control that is often misunderstood and underestimated. Maybe that is because it gives the subject more options compared to the other forms of mind control. In the other choices, the subject is coerced into submission by the negotiator, often in isolation, and ends up with no say in What is happening in the process. The facts are framed in terms of persuasion so that the audience can make up its own mind, even though the facts are put in a way to portray them in the best light.

CHAPTER 15 PERSUASION TECHNIQUES TO HELP YOU INFLUENCE OTHERS

Persuasion methods that are widely used to include the "foot-in-the-entryway," as well as "entryway in-the-face" procedures. In the foot-in-the-entryway process, someone starts with a sensible and small need - "Do you've enough money?" - which at that time leads into a far more significant need - "I need ten dollars for a taxi." The entryway in-the-face process is actually the inverse - it provides someone making a major demand, having it rejected, and next retreating to a bit of need. Someone doing contract work, for example, might deal with you for a considerable length of money in advance, then after you refuse, will ask for a smaller amount. This works since, adopting the more substantial demand, the small request seems to be sensible. The degree of the effect an individual has on you is connected to management. Envision having the capability to influence cases if the circumstance calls for it. These two strategies, which we discussed, are actually simple enough. However, they may have a big effect on just how much we're in a position to manage others and also the circumstances in which we find ourselves with them.

Based on a large body of investigation, the capability to put in control over other folks is simpler than you might have thought. A guide has had the best substantial impact in this particular field: Robert Cialdini's Influence. From it, Cialdini provides the six resources of influence, which will allow you to persuade others: shortage, authority, liking, social verification, consistency, and correspondence. Through the majority of this particular chapter, we look at these power tools of influence and just how you are able to employ them to the benefit of yours to be able to get everything you would like.

Resources of Influence

The top reason people will make use of the six resources of influence is usually to help you to do whatever they would like you to do. We by now discussed the typical motives that others will have to affect you, but let us have a look at exactly why you may want to utilize these persuasive tactics on others.

The chance to impact people usually emerges out of apparent needs. Several of them include:

- The need to make alterations to a workplace scenario
- Authoritative cultural change
- Tempting more customers to buy through you
- Urging co-workers to adopt new abilities

Using these six techniques of persuasion will enable one to amplify the capacity of yours for influence. Just before we proceed any further, a powerful word of warning is required in this case. We simply invest the very first one-half of this particular publication profiling the despicable methods manipulators feed off others as parasites. Do not be a manipulator. Don't to mishandle these capabilities. Generally, there can easily be a fine line between manipulating others and exerting control. The essential determiner is an inspiration. Use these tools the appropriate manner, and also you and some are going to receive benefits.

Humans, as an entire, have the capability to operate within autopilot. Similar to a bird sing, a cow creates hounds bark or milk, we adopt respond and sessions in predictable ways, whether mastered or perhaps instinctive, as though it is the DNA of ours. We're provided with brand new info all the time. However, many of it passes us by. We cannot take everything living presents everything at the same time. If perhaps we did, we will be overburdened, and the brains of ours could not adapt fast enough. That's exactly where subconscious regimes are available in.

The cerebrum of ours intentionally picks a target to focus on and disposes of whatever it deems non-essential for the emphasis. For that reason, many activities are carried out with no conscious thought, and the psychological faculties of ours help us lead the daily lives of ours, by which we react to info that is brand new without knowing about this purposely. You are able to use these resources as well as influence techniques to break into people's autopilot plans and point them to conform to certain conduct. It is crucial to recall these things:

- Begin in light of the end. Understand the targets of yours and what you're looking for to achieve. Just what does achievement are like?
- Consider the individuals whom you're trying to impact and select the proper influence techniques to suit the circumstance.
- Utilize the methods that suit the condition.

Reciprocity

This's the very first device, and it's commonly linked with reciprocity. It's the thought that in case you take action for an individual, they're going to be highly very likely to do exactly the same thing for you in exchange. Part of this's created from obligation and also the rules which we utilize to govern the modern society of ours. On the flip side, it's likewise used to make them afraid that in case they don't return the favor, they will not continue on getting the benefits from you.

Reciprocity is actually a very helpful tool to jumpstart a scenario whenever we want a thing done. The supposition of it is the fact that by acting first and doing a thing for one more individual, then you definitely are going to improve the likelihood of the various other party doing everything you need to be achieved. When we want to go first and give before we make an effort to get, we have a much better shot of engaging others. What helpful but unexpected element would we have the ability to accomplish for the partners of ours, which could acquire us a sympathetic ear whenever we have to deal with these to attain a thing for us? Doing very well by others is actually a shrewd strategy to get others to do exactly the same task for you down the road. The sole way one might be damaged in this particular scenario is whether they are not reciprocated. It nonetheless is not a terrible thing to do something great for another person. Obtaining what you would like is not the very best explanation, though it's at times an adequate inspiration to help you ensure both parties are actually satisfied.

You will find a number of different methods to generate a correspondence job for you. To give others small blessings, approaching others with deference, and performing favors for people in need are actually a number of ways in which you are able to earn points with people that are different.

Consider the objectives of yours once more & identify the best way to be of assistance to individuals. It may be just a vague notion of just how you've been of assistance before. You are able to start little to find out how the efforts of yours are received before risking or perhaps committing much more. Whenever you see that the gifts of yours or maybe favor have been received favorably, then simply, you are able to wait often to enable reciprocation, or maybe you are able to provide another kindness. Though it is essential to maintain a fragile balance of the relationship. The basic principle is all about correspondence. In the event that you go far in providing without the various other party having a chance to give back, you are able to cause alienation or discomfort.

The standard strategy is helping various other individuals and be benevolent when you have the opportunity since nobody is able to tell exactly how it may allow you to down the line. Also, it's these small demos of thoughtfulness that could be recollected as well as prove to be helpful once you want help in the future. Think about if you have an existing or perhaps a birthday card from someone you're not generally utilized to accepting one from. What sway did that have on you? Just how did that impact the head of yours? Did it lead you to take any certain action? You might have sent them a birthday card as well as an existing back. For what explanation is it? It's generally due to the principal weapon of impact: the standard of reaction. This regular state in which we must make an effort to reimburse, in type, what another person has supplied to us.

For example, if a good friend sends us a birthday present, we ought to identify the birthday of his with our own gift; if two or perhaps 3 welcome us to a gathering, we ought to make certain to welcome them to one of our own. By trying to keep the correspondence rule, we're dedicated to the future reimbursement of favors, solicitations, blessings, and so forth.

For what reason do we accomplish this? It's straightforward; we think it is right to react in kind due to a sentiment of obligation. In addition, it's the ingrained culture of ours as well as conviction frameworks that constrain us within compensating these kinds of debt.

Make sure you are not doing sort items for other people just to purchase a thing from an individual. We still must be considerate of others, giving and considerate in all facets of life. In case you simply do things since you want something back out of the other individual, then this is able to result in a great deal of disappointment, and this also can turn into a kind of manipulation. Generally, there can easily be a subtle distinction between offering as well as purchasing.

However, correspondence is actually a principle of thumb we have to have in most of the relationships of ours, both romantic and as close friends. Exactly how might we expect understanding, love, and respect from others if we are not prepared to provide them the same? It's been said that the most effective marriage isn't one in which each side provides fifty percent, but where each partner provides a hundred percent. That's the concept of correspondence.

This particular "bribery" type can continue to be extremely effective when used properly. In case you're likely to ask for something from the employer of yours, then you definitely will wish to hold back until the conclusion of the day and conduct the greatest capabilities of yours to be able to rather "butter them up." If you desire to ask your partner or parents for some cash to purchase one thing you would like, you may make them dinner first. These are methods of locating the "opportune moment" which offer the very best conditions for one to get the outcome you wish. It's shrewd, but not always manipulative.

The key difference between making use of this for impact as well as not manipulation is usually to make sure you are not expecting them to take action that's going to damage them, which might then be considered threatening or perhaps in certain situations, blackmailing. Rather, just have intentions that are good and make certain you're never influencing an individual to do things that are going to cause them to become uncomfortable.

Consistency

Among the primary reasons behind manipulation is actually the pursuit of self-devised expectations. Manipulators take extreme actions due to their insecurities or anxieties that they won't be what they believe they need. You are able to assist every one of the individuals who are around you - not only those that are actually manipulative - by ensuring consistency in everything you do. Once you come to be a reliable and dependable individual, it'll instantly allow you to a lot additional important.

If you stick to the word of yours or perhaps do everything you say, now individuals are aware that they are able to depend on you to obtain the end result, which they're envisioning. When you've established some trustworthiness, it gets easier to affect the actions of others. They are going to trust you; then when you provide guidance and begin to guide them in a specific path, it'll get so much easier for these people to listen to the words of yours.

You will find three elements to consistency: intentionality, sincerity, and responsibility. The very first part is functioning duty. By this, Cialdini implies that a person should make a certain decision to accept responsibility for whatever matter is actually at hand. In the event that you're unwilling to commit completely what about an individual way, but make a contingency plan when things go container or even make certain that there's an escape route, then you haven't embraced duty, and it is up to simple possibility whether you'll succeed. Surely, you won't acquire an impact with other people due to the quality of consistency.

When you've created an individual dedication to be accountable for concern or maybe a problem, you have to make the commitment public of yours. Stating to others that you are going to accomplish a specific job is an excellent start to getting it done. It shows the sincerity of yours about the job at hand. The public declaration of yours of the duty of yours demonstrates you're inclined to risk the reputation of your track record of the outcome. Next, if you understand others are actually watching, there's basic accountability of others knowing that you're accountable, which causes you too much more susceptible to complete.

Third, you have to follow through on what you've dedicated to yourself as well as to others. You have to work to the outcome deliberately. The great thing about this particular facet of consistency is the fact that even in case you don't be successful in the reasons that you and some expected, whenever you exert focused hard work to bring about the end result you have envisioned, you'll still make the credibility related to consistency. The payoff might not be as great as in case you did just as hoped, or perhaps more effective, though you are going to earn points for trying.

Consider this: when you have placed a wager on a bet or perhaps bought a lottery ticket, perhaps you have at any point felt much more certain you're planning to win than you did right before acting on that threat? Did the perspective shift of yours from vulnerability to conviction? Pro athletes have long used the method of visualization, frequently imagining themselves accomplishing their desired results, to advertise the good results of theirs on the area, as well as the basic principle is actually akin if an individual has the drive, optimism, and confidence to attain an end result, the probability of financial success increases.

The brains of ours are extremely adaptable, though we might also think about them sluggish. That's when there's a predetermined course of action, and it gets the default training course for the brains of ours. This particular truth originates from the innate preference of ours for predictability as well as steadiness about us. The concept of consistency leverages this particular tendency. Instead of expending power to strike off in a brand new path, we're a lot more apt to expend energy on something that we currently feel accountable. If a particular person settles on a choice, the mind of his is going to align with the conclusion of that course of action. He reacts in manners that legitimize the previous option of his. Even in the face of difficulty, he persuades himself he's settled on the appropriate choice and can persevere in it. To do otherwise brings about cognitive dissonance as well as emotional stress.

Have a glimpse at the following example: An play around in New York was carried out to identify human behavior in a few instances. Because of this experiment, a regular radio was left on a towel close to a big group of beachgoers. A staged snatch-and-grab was carried out to find out how individuals will react. For the very first part of the experiment, if the staged robbery occurred, only 4 out of 20 people responded to the theft. For the next part of the analysis, a selected unique asked certain bystanders to view the stereo of his while he attended to a situation someplace else.

In this 2nd situation, it was discovered that 19 out of 20 individuals started to be aware of the surroundings of theirs and reacted if the staged robbery occurred. Right here we come across the illustration of consistency in life that is real.

This particular kind of belief is so ingrained in us; it creates a bias for just how we look at individuals. Nearly universally, people that are responsible, rational, and steady in daily life situations are actually regarded with respect, trust, and admiration. Consistency shows up frequently in the informal social circumstances of ours, also. We quite often, as being a kind gesture, question people just how they're doing. Whether they're doing okay or otherwise, you expect to have them to let you know all is okay. Through consistency, we have a tendency to take the basic concept of something without honestly considering or perhaps responding to it.

It's typical for somebody to question a friend, "If I try this, might you do it too?" Whether the point in question is actually safe or maybe not, people are going to be far more comfortable doing something simply because someone else, with whom they have a connection or even sense of duty, is actually doing the work. The concept of consistency, thus, has helped describe the strength of peer pressure.

So would you employ this truth of consistency as a tool? If you demonstrate the character of a reliable and consistent individual, subsequently, others will be far more likely to have confidence in you and also to look for you for details that are vital. And by going on record as responsible, you are making the success of yours much more likely. Furthermore, you boost the odds of yours of influencing someone else and top them to your preferred destination in case you are able to get them to embrace even the smallest type of duty as well as to do this in an interpersonal or public means. In a product sales atmosphere, surveys, or maybe product testing are excellent ways to accomplish this, particularly in the context of enhancing the product's security or performance for others' advantage. Your subject then turns into an ally, allowing you to achieve the goal of yours of having a much better item. The private investment of theirs can, after that, turn into a means for these people to get a desire to have the item or maybe service you're giving.

In a setting in which you have to lead a meeting, you are able to create buy-in even before you get into the boardroom by providing the peers of yours a little but engaging job or maybe a problem to think about as preparation. When done very well, this can develop enthusiasm and make a foundation for these people to publicly commit to investing as you want in the task of yours. Make sure you look for means to verify as well as integrate whatever each individual ready in order to provide them a feeling of contribution.

In coaching or perhaps a mentoring role, you must encourage the pupil of yours to embrace duty in the proper circumstances and, after that, stick to these facets of the consistency tool. She must inform others of the determination of her, and then work diligently to make it happen. As you guide her, you are able to help her to recognize the fantastic worth of the deposits toward creating her standing and character amongst others - and alternatively, long-lasting damage and the damage which can take place from being inconsistent. This kind of inconsistency is able to take the form of both disengagements, an unwillingness to commit to being accountable, and negligence, not effectively following through whenever a commitment has been made.

Community Verification

We have all noticed the saying, "If so-and-so jumped off a bridge, might you do it too?" There are several cases where we could even say, "Yes!" since we're so trusting of that individual. This's basically what societal verification is. If you are able to demonstrate that others are actually thinking the exact same manner, they've exactly the same confidence of a concept, and that there's community proof to confirm the proposition, then it is going to be simpler to have influence over others.

Often, people rely on substantial gestures from others to guide the way they think, feel, and act. Not everybody is a reputable tool for that type of guidance; we are likely to lend far more credibility to others that are very similar to us.

You have most likely heard about or even observed in action the thought of a "plant" at a crowd, who's created to jumpstart a certain desired reaction to a chance. When that specific proclaims a wish to invest in a secret tomato slicer, then someone else that actually did want one but was afraid has the courage to call out. And also, the force of several voices accumulates, convincing others that are undecided. From the ugliest form of it, we come across the basic principle of interpersonal verification take place in the "mob mentality," every time a crowd forms to do damage with very little regard for the effects. Specific standards end up blurred in favor of the mob's unrestrained power as well as intensity.

In a far more private setting, the basic principle of interpersonal verification is used every one of the time periods to rally support for a concept or perhaps initiative. When initiating change, it's a typical technique to separately seek out influential individuals to the community or maybe workspace, trying to win them over to the technique, as well as asking them to allow for the energy by talking very well of it to others. Whenever the others see a representative, who's akin to themselves offering help, they're far more apt to go by in the exact same way. Getting that very first unique create a move has a tremendous impact and also triggers the device of interpersonal verification.

Consider the previous time you shopped for something on the internet, maybe a guide through Amazon, or maybe a holiday rental on the beach via TripAdvisor. What did you do before you decided to buy? You checked out the surveys, right? Though it is a relatively high amount of trust that people place in the views of various other individuals - folks whom we've never met before as well as about whom we understand almost nothing. However, we make big choices that affect our careers, our finances, our families, and personal lives, based on the pithy feedback provided by anonymous people on the web (where you are able to believe in everything, right?). This's quite an incredible model of the strength of social verification to guide as well as influence our choices and actions. It reveals that one strategy we utilize to determine what's right is discovering what others think is right.

The rule of interpersonal verification is effective since it is able to use, especially to the way in which we pick what establishes proper conduct. We quite often see conduct as more and more right to the degree that we come across others performing it. And so, when we're in a problem of uncertainty or vulnerability, it's human instinct for us to appear to individuals around us for guidance on which move to make. You will find a selection of methods you are able to make use of social verification to the benefit of yours, particularly as a company person or maybe someone in charge of marketing. One effective technique is taping into internet based life stages. Think about when you're trying to find a product or even finding out about something totally new. Both the first investigations of ours and the best choices of ours could be seriously affected by the number of fans, recommendations, and supporters. Profiles or pages with a lot of devotees are regarded as specialists in the specialty of theirs and, in most cases, develop far more and get specific factors due to the access to theirs as well as wide impact. Exploit these life stages as well as towns with concentrated promotion.

Compliments, testimonials, and reviews are another amazing advantage for utilizing the device of interpersonal verification, particularly in a web-based environment. It's a fundamental rule of advertising. You accumulate comments and surveys from the satisfied clients of yours and use those to assemble trust with new clients. Statements coming from the horse's mouth are actually the best.

To make sure, the basic principle of interpersonal verification is typically at its most important of cases where someone seeks a solution or a resolution to a question. Think, for example, of a person traveling worldwide for the very first time. As she encounters odd cultural phenomena & can't understand what's created or maybe the points folks say, she glances around. She watches what other individuals are actually doing, and she follows suit. Often it ends up in embarrassment, nearly all almost all of the time, it is the road to success.

Still, cultural verification could likewise get scans no matter if individuals have what they consider a perfectly good, fixed behavior and also have no issue in the thought process of theirs. Cialdini, as well as a research team directed an exam to perceive what information type on signs would lead to inn visitors reusing the washroom towels of theirs.

- Sign one referred to ecological motives.

- Sign two said the inn would provide a donation to an ecological cause.

- Sign three said the inn had by now launched a donation and asked: "Will you please go along with us?"

- Sign four said most inn visitors reused the towels of theirs just once while staying at the inn.

At the stage when guests had been informed that other lodging site visitors had been reusing the towels of theirs, they had been certain to agree to the solicitation. Sign #4 received forty-eight percent of participants to reuse the towels of theirs.

Liking

Offering compliments, sharing praise, and typically being a buddy to somebody is actually sufficient to persuade them on several levels. This's the reason why social media has a lot of influence. When we are able to shoot for "likes" from other individuals and get those likes, we're reassured within the choices of ours. It's the validation required to be able to affect us to continue going.

Individuals love the people that love them or perhaps whom they see as companions. It's a fundamental but impressive thought. The equipment of preference may be employed in a few ways.

One method is actually discovering shared values with anybody you meet. When you are able to connect with them all over their interests or pastimes, you will have a firm ground to work through. All this calls for is asking questions that are good and listening effectively. An additional technique of creating affinity with other people is providing support as well as sincere compliments. Particularly when the points you notice as well as affirm in others offer them sharp insight in themselves, you are able to play a crucial role in influencing them to develop as well as create the areas of theirs of strength. The key here's genuine commendation rather than flattery. Insincere or even embellished praise is able to come off as creepy and will simply do as much damage as genuine compliments offer advantages.

Give good criticism as well as a genuine commendation to the colleagues of yours. Start by watching yourself and noting how often you provide good versus negative criticism in one day. Just like the vast majority of us, you may be astonished! Make an effort to provide good words of flattery three times as frequently as you are doing bad ones. To become an excellent friend, concentrate even more on giving than on receiving. While you connect with others, be reasonable and consistent with the things which you're asking of them. In the event you are not prepared to get it done yourself, why must another person do it for you? Let individuals feel you're there for these people when they require you. Be transparent; act normally, and do not create a specific attempt to be winsome or popular. Just treat others just how you'd love to be viewed, and the majority of reasonable folks are going to be satisfied in the profile of yours. These are components that are crucial in creating trust.

Have you driven two times as much to create an easy food buy only since you love the staff members of one establishment better compared to the shops closer to you? Whether or maybe not you feel at ease in an area and as the experience, while you're there could be as vital a consideration as choice or cost of things. Look at salespeople. The most significant thing a sales rep can do is get a feeling of just who you're and things you need first. Only next will he or maybe she goes on to provide you with products or maybe services which could help the unique requirements of yours and desires. Oftentimes, we are able to see a salesperson's maneuvers a mile away, as he definitely attempts to locate a location of common ground. The most effective salespeople have a knack for cracking by resistance, although, and finding a method to create a relationship with a buyer, flat when the attempts of his to be likable is actually evident.

In order to make use of the instrument of liking, keep in mind that you'll most likely sabotage the efforts of yours in case you try out way too difficult and system a lot of. If the device works its best, you're competent to make use of an all-natural point of commonality with somebody else. You should not fabricate info about yourself to build these kinds of connections. Though you identify a place in common with someone else, you are able to artfully accentuate this point and construct the connection close to it. An exchange about a most loved game or maybe sports crew is actually an exceptional case of that. It's just human to be engaging or maybe love somebody much more in case they show interest in us or perhaps compliment us on something. With that said, we're far more susceptible to agree about or maybe buy something by someone based on them liking us.

This particular device is additionally handy in big team settings. If perhaps you have the event to talk before a crowd, you need to believe in advance about the simplest way to represent yourself. What must you wear? Will there be any modifications you ought to make to the strategy you talk about? What accounts is it possible to tell which will particularly resonate with the team? You do not wish to become a sell-out, however, if there's a version of yourself which suits best in this crowd, then simply employ that individual to produce probably the highest level of affinity. Ultimately, in case you make use of this device properly, you are going to provide advantages for yourself as well as the individuals who just like you.

Authority

Authority figures are able to have several of the best influence. In case you're driving, and there's a cop behind you, which influences you to visit the speed limit, just due to the profile of theirs. When you're going for a test, the authority figures at the front side of the room are actually influencing one not to cheat as well as take a look at the papers of various other pupils. This could be the simplest tool to develop influence, though it's additionally the most misused.

In case you're going about being authoritative in the wrong way, not merely will others fail to listen to you, though they may wind up being actively insubordinate. Parents that are way too hard on the children of theirs are able to wind up driving them out, and this teen could rebel just for the benefit of angering the parents of theirs. It's essential to get the line in between too stringent & too permissive when making use of this device of persuasion.

We have a tendency to think of expert in phrases of a person with a commanding character or maybe a high-level job barking out orders and commands to underlings. To make sure that impression is but one facet of authority. But there's yet another method to be an expert in a way that's much more subtle and maybe much more important in the long haul. When you're viewed as a specialist or maybe a specialist for an area, the knowledge of yours or maybe knowledge establishes you as an authority, and some will seek you since they wish the possibility you provide to influence the development of theirs. Individuals trust individuals who understand what they're intending and therefore are comfortable in what they're about to do since they've completed it often before.

Various other individuals are going to have less noble aspirations and might just seek to make the most of your network or perhaps prestige. Because of this, thought leaders and individuals with notoriety need to be discerning. In contrast to the various other resources for persuasion that we've discussed, this's one where various other individuals will seek you out much more than you've to try out as well as exert impact on others. After this, you run the danger of finding yourself manipulated.

Many of us have a little aspect of ability or may be information that may gain others still with no widespread appeal. With this situation, what you've to provide might traveling by word of mouth with an extended time. True, in a workplace environment, you are able to send out your resume out to the entire staff of yours on the 1st day of yours of the workplace as well as screen certificates as well as plaques on the walls of the workplace of yours. But this kind of actions reek of pride and turn away likely the most teachable people, who'd be probable to place to good use any expertise you share. Yet another technique to create your capabilities known in a less demonstrative option is actually to pepper the chats of yours with small bits as well as pieces of info associated with your knowledge and interests. When individuals are listening very well and also have a concern in the exact same region, they'll ultimately request more info. These informal ways of sharing your skill place you in the very best place to make use of the expert of yours in an influential and persuasive means.

Be an authority and do everything you like working on most. The more you understand & do properly, the much more important the authority of yours is going to be. And do not be deceived into believing that impact just fallen into the laps of the best individuals you notice in the public eye. Many of them have worked relentlessly and tirelessly to be much better at the region of theirs compared to anybody else. Work hard, and also, you are going to have the expertise that is excellent from which to guide others.

Scarcity

"While items last," "limited edition," "exclusive," along with other phrases this way, are usually utilized as advertising techniques to get individuals much more curious. Dunkin Donuts could come out with a brand new device and then point out its limited edition like it were several exceptional flavors of coffee never to be replicated once again. In truth, the particular ingredient may not differ a lot from something they currently have, and they're merely making use of this strategy to obtain more folks enthusiastic about the service.

Scarcity, as well as shortage, may be extremely beneficial when you're trying to influence others. This makes them think as though they have a rare opportunity is going to make them much more apt to jump on the offer, pressuring them and offering them the sense that they've to act now, or maybe they'll discover they're way too late to enjoy something wonderful.

People value what's unusual, and worth typically boosts when scarcity increases. Imagine just how you will think in the event that you urgently need a gadget & scurry to buy it just to discover out it's no longer available?

Think about a lack of gas, a very sensible & consequently invaluable commodity in the modern society of ours. A mass lack of gas - and it's occurred in the past - signifies costs skyrocketing, lines that are long for actually a gallon of gas and emergency protocols for companies, agencies, and citizens as brand new techniques of obtaining things that are small completed would have to be started.

The greater uncommon a thing is, the more prominent the desire to acquire it. A dread of lacking one thing is able to stir people to a free-for-all, which makes them frantic never to pass up a fantastic ability. Ironically, the impulse to stay away from missing out on food is actually stronger compared to the desire to have something. And so this's a tool which will come with a good deal of potential.

Lines for probably the most recent iPhone, show tickets, computer games, as well as the franticness of the shopping extravaganza following Thanksgiving are actually additional examples of the measures to which people will go if the weapon of shortage comes into play. You will find a few techniques that you are able to use the standard of shortage to induce others. These include things like making provide constrained to time, restricting supply, or perhaps offering one-time offers, every one of which produces feelings of deficiency.

One of the ways scarcity plays on the human psychology of ours is we have an all-natural bias toward thinking that one thing that's scarce or rare is a bit better. Possibly the concept is actually affected somewhat by the thought of social verification - if more and more people wanted one thing that there's very little left, then it has to be exceptional. Scenarios in which there seems to be a selection process play on human pride as well as charm to the ego. This's the reason why individuals spend exorbitant charges to be members of extraordinary country clubs as well as elite societies. There's a sensation of status as well as the value that will come from this kind of association.

In case you're promoting an item, buyers will be moved to react much more urgently when provided a time limit or even when warned that supplies are actually limited. Still, those elements by themselves won't finish the persuasive component of scarcity. You have to additionally aid prospective customers to envision the effects in case they don't act fast.

Likewise, the tactic of shortage could be utilized as an easy way of top individuals to make a choice. Just simply, they have to evaluate whether the lives of theirs will be much better with a product or perhaps without an item, in a problem of shortage. When you are able to assist them to picture these scenarios, preferably with the acquisition as good as well as the shortage as bad, then you definitely are going to help them to create the choice of theirs. Naturally, you do not wish to be dishonest, and also you mustn't confuse the motivation of yours for benefit with the inspiration to bring about good in the life of another. Or else, you are going to twist this influential ability in manipulation.

The equipment of shortage is able to assist in a sales setting and also when creating company pitches, though you do not wish to use it on an individual fitness level constantly. For instance, you may wish to express to the friends of yours you cannot hang out this usually, although the routine of yours is free so that they are going to be much more likely to reach out for you. This will be seen as manipulation.

Simply because making use of a shortage in the private life of ours in deceitful does not imply there will not be individuals that attempt to make use of it. Think of those people that appear to have a lot of friends, but very few they're close with. This particular "popular" status has permitted them to have admiration from others constantly. A primary reason that they may be in a position to attain this status is due to scarcity. Perhaps they often show up late to a party as well as leave before others too. Maybe they hardly ever text back, causing you to feel eager for a solution while you do the texting initially. They may withhold emotion so that when they're compassionate, feels like a rare and special treat.

You may think about this in the private life of yours, but continually be conscious of who's on the additional side. An easy method to carry out the technique will be doing so via social networking, or even in case you are attempting to establish the brand of yours as well as gain recognition in this sense.

Posting less would mean that if you do post an image on social networking, for instance, everybody will be a little more excited as well as probable to click "like" than they'd for an individual that posts three times one day. Others are going to be far more excited for brand new articles in case you delay to smartly release it instead of in case you're continually providing things away at no cost.

Some people as a task or perhaps love to feel as if they're working for something. Therefore they are going to be much more likely to try harder to win you over to have the endorsement of yours when you're limited instead of extremely offering. This may be most just seen by a female waiting until the sixth or fifth date to participate in romantic tasks to be able to create a partner of theirs a lot more curious. Be careful as this particular approach does not constantly work. There'll be a few people who become just tired of waiting about, and they will not constantly be as ready to pay out higher costs for things which appear "exclusive" or "rare."

CHAPTER 16 ALL YOU NEED TO KNOW ABOUT PERSUASION

What comes to mind when you talk about persuasion? Some people may think of advertising ads that encourage audiences to purchase a particular product, and others may think of a political candidate seeking to persuade voters to pick his or her name from the ballot box. Persuasion is a strong force in daily life and has a huge influence on society and on the individual. Politics, legal rulings, mass media, news, and advertisement are all influenced and affect us in turn by the power of persuasion. We like to believe that sometimes we are immune to persuasion. That we have a natural ability to see beyond the advertising of sales, understand the facts in a situation, and come to conclusions all by ourselves. For certain cases, that might be accurate, but persuasion isn't just a pushy salesman trying to sell you a car, or a tv ad that urges you to purchase the latest and greatest product. Persuasion can be subtle, and it can depend on a variety of factors how we respond to those influences.

Negative examples are always the first to come to mind when we think about persuasion, but persuasion can often be used as a positive power. Community service initiatives that encourage people to recycle or stop smoking are excellent examples of persuasion used to make life easier for people. How is persuasion, then? According to Perloff (2003), persuasion can be described as ".. a symbolic process in which communicators attempt to convince other people to alter their attitudes or behaviors about a problem by transmitting a message in a free-choice atmosphere."

The key elements of this convincing definition are:

- Symbolic persuasion, using words, images, sounds, etc.
- This requires a deliberate effort to manipulate others.
- Crucial to self-persuasion. People are not coerced; instead, they are free to make choices.

Methods of persuasive message transmission can occur in a variety of ways, including verbally and nonverbally through television, radio, the Internet, or face-to-face contact.

How is Personality Different Today?

Although persuasion art and science have been of interest since the Ancient Greeks' period, there are major variations in how persuasion occurs today and how it occurred in the past. Richard M. Perloff, in his book The Dynamics of Persuasion: Communication and Attitudes in the 21st Century, outlines the five main ways in which modern persuasion differs from past:

The amount of persuasive messages has gone up tremendously. For a moment, think about how many advertisements you receive on a regular basis. The number of ads the average U.S. person is subjected to every day varies from about 300 to over 3,000 according to different sources. Persuasive communication is traveling far faster. Television, radio, and the Internet, all help to very easily, distribute convincing messages.

- Persuasion is a major enterprise. In addition to the corporations that are in business solely for persuasive reasons (such as advertising agencies, marketing firms, public relations corporations), and many other businesses are dependent on persuasion to sell goods and services.
- Contemporary persuasion is far more subtle. There are, of course, plenty of advertisements using very simple persuasion tactics, but other messages are far more subtle. For example, marketers often carefully create a very specific picture designed to encourage viewers to buy goods or services to achieve the expected lifestyle.
- Persuasion becomes more complex. Consumers are more complex and have more options, so when it comes to choosing their compelling medium and message, marketers must be savvier.

Modern Form of Persuasion

Pratkanis & Aronson (1991) argue convincingly that even more than other societies do, Western societies prefer persuasion. Marriages aren't arranged and are left to each couple's persuasive tactics. Unlike communist countries that regulate trade, it is left to the advertiser to establish consumer tastes and choices. Arguments are not resolved by members of tribes or religious officials, but by lawyers' wrangling. Rulers are not born royally or chosen because of their ability, but emerge through one of the greatest rituals of persuasion of all, the election campaign. Almost always the nominee with both good looks and a confident personality wins.

The ancient Greeks had a more rational approach toward persuasion. A national of Greece could employ a Sophist to help him learn to argue. Sophists were itinerant, knowledge-dedicated lecturers, and writers — you might say they were the graduate students of the old world. The sophists contended that persuasion was a useful tool for discovering the truth. They figured the cycle of arguing and questioning would uncover myths and discover the correct ones. A sophist didn't really know which side of an argument he was talking on. Yes, often, Sophists will switch sides in the middle of a discussion. Their stated purpose was a reasoned argument that revealed the facts. We had accepted new ideas in the free market.

Sounds like our world? No-we rely even more on the use of persuasion strategies and enforcement than the ancients did. The modern approach to persuasion, however, takes the form of logical reasoning and debate? Difficult. Today's persuaders are calling on the public to achieve their goals "through the use of symbols and of our most simple human emotions."

Since the ability to convince and avoid persuasion is directly linked to one's life-long success, you would think the subject should be taught in school. One might assume people know their methods of persuasion as well as learning the letters of the alphabet, or the ten commandments, or how to conduct CPR. Yet how many of us can recite ten convincing principles? How many of us can evaluate a situation and choose the best persuasive method for the job at hand? Too many of us are still aware of the thousands of times we are affected by someone else every day?

Do this: take a look at your medicine box, or fridge, or workshop. Every item you see is a trophy of war, which represents the victory of some company over its competitors. They persuaded you to trade your hard-earned money for their commodity for some reason— or maybe for no reason at all. Why exactly did they do that?

Don't make mistakes. There are legions of agents of power working in our society. They thrive-at the pinnacles of power they exist-by having you think things and do things they want you to think and do. Many people are either ignorant of these forces or greatly overestimate the amount of space they need to make up their own minds when they are. But the good influence agent knows that the answer to his technique would be as effective as the springing of a mousetrap if he can handle the situation and choose the appropriate technique.

Persuasive Techniques

The end aim of persuasion is to encourage the client to internalize the convincing point and accept the new mindset as part of their core belief system. Those are only a handful of the extremely successful forms of persuasion. Other methods include, and many others, the use of rewards, punishments, positive or negative expertise.

- **Create a Need**

One form of persuasion involves generating a desire or an appeal to a need that exists beforehand. This sort of persuasion appeals to the basic needs of a person for shelter, affection, self-esteem, and self-actualization. Marketers often use this technique to sell their goods. Consider, for example, how many commercials say people need to buy a specific product to be content, healthy, loved, or admired.

- **Asking for Social Needs**

Another rather successful form of persuasion appeals to the imperative of being famous, influential, or similar to others. Television advertisements include many examples of this kind of persuasion, where audiences are persuaded to purchase things so that they can be like anyone else or like a well-known or well-respected person. Television ads are a massive source of convincing provided that some reports say the average American watches between 1,500 and 2,000 hours of television per year.

- **Using Loaded Images and Words**

Persuasion often takes advantage of loaded words and pictures. The power of encouraging words is well known to advertisers, which is why so many ads use phrases like "fresh and improved" or "all good."

- **Get Your Foot in the Door**

Another method that is also successful in getting people to meet a request is known as the strategy of "foot-in-the-door" This technique of persuasion involves getting a person to consent to a small request, such as asking them to buy a small item, followed by making a much greater request. The requester already has its "foot in the door" by getting the person to consent to the small initial favor, making the individual more likely to comply with the larger request. A friend, for example, asks you to have her two children babysit for an hour or two. She then asks if you should only babysit the children for the rest of the day until you consent to the smaller offer.

Since you have already agreed to the smaller request, you may feel obligated to agree to the bigger request as well. This is a perfect example of what psychologists call the commitment law, and advertisers also use this tactic to persuade customers to buy goods and services.

- **Go big and then tiny**

The foot-in-the-door approach is the reverse of that approach. A salesperson may start by making an unreasonable, sometimes large request. The person reacts by refusing, slamming the door figuratively on the deal. The salesperson responds by making a much smaller offer, which sometimes turns out to be conciliatory. People often feel obligated to answer these offers. Because they rejected the original request, people still feel obligated to approve the smaller request to support the salesperson.

- **Utilize the Power of Reciprocity**

You probably feel an almost overwhelming responsibility when people do you a favor, to return the favor in kind. This is known as reciprocity rule, social duty to do something for someone else because they did something for you at first. Marketers may use this tendency by making it appear as if they're doing you a kindness, including "extras" or discounts, which then force people to accept the offer and make a purchase.

- **Create a point of anchor for your negotiations**

The anchoring bias is a subtle cognitive bias that can affect agreements and decisions in a powerful way. When attempting to arrive at a decision, the first bid appears to become a point of anchorage for all subsequent negotiations. So, if you're trying to negotiate an increase in pay, being the first person to propose a figure, particularly if that figure is a bit high, will help to leverage your favor in future negotiations. The first number is the point of departure. Although you may not get the number, starting high can result in your employer getting a higher bid.

- **Limit your Accessibility**

Psychologist Robert Cialdini is well known for the six common concepts he first presented in his best-selling book Influence: The Psychology of Persuasion. One of the key principles that he identified is known as scarcity or limiting something's availability. Cialdini suggests things get more appealing when they're scarce or limited. People are more likely to buy anything if they know that it's the last one or the sale is about to end. For example, an artist could only produce a limited run of a given print. Because there are only a few prints available for sale, people will have a better chance of making a purchase until they go abroad.

The above examples are just a few of the many techniques of persuasion which social psychologists identify. Look at your everyday life for signs of persuasion. A fascinating experiment is to watch a random television show for half an hour and remember any instance of convincing ads. You can be surprised at the sheer amount of convincing strategies employed in such a short period of time.

CHAPTER 17 DECEPTION – A FORM OF MIND CONTROL

The next form of mind control to be addressed is Deception. This method of mind control may have some parallels to coercion in the sense that manipulators will be using a lot of deceit to achieve their final target. This chapter will go into more depth about how manipulation operates, the strategies used in it, and some of the results.

What is Deception?

Deception, along with mystification, manipulation, and beguilement, is an act the manipulator uses to perpetuate ideas about facts that are falsehoods or are just partial truths in the subject matter. Deception may include a number of different items like concealment, disguise, diversion, hand sleight, deception, and concealment. The manipulator should be able to monitor the subject 's mind because the subject will have faith in them. The subject may believe what the manipulator says, and might even base future plans and shape their world based on the things the manipulator has told them. Unless the manipulator follows the deception procedure, the statements that they told the subject are going to be false. If the subject finds out, confidence can quickly be broken, which is why the manipulator must be skilled at the process of deceit and good at turning it around if they want to stay with their subject.

Deception often occurs in terms of partnerships, and it may contribute to feelings of mistrust and deception between the two partners in the relationship. This is because deceit is in violation of the rules of most partnerships and is often seen as having a negative effect on the perceptions that come with that connection. Many people hope to be able to have a straightforward discussion with their spouse; if they had known that their spouse is manipulative, they would have to learn how to use misdirection and deception to get the honest and accurate details they need. The faith will still be gone from the relationship, making it impossible to restore the relationship back to where it once was. The subject would always question the things the manipulator was telling them, questioning whether the story was true or something made up. Despite this current mistrust, most relationships end when the subject finds out about the manipulator's deceit.

Misleading Types

Deception is a type of communication that relies on omissions and lies to persuade the manipulator to best suit the topic of the universe. Because communication is involved, there may also be various forms of deception that may occur. Similar to the Interpersonal theory of deception, there are five different forms of deception to be identified. Some of these have been seen in the other types of mind regulation, suggesting that similarities can occur. The five major disappointments include:

- Lies: this is when the manipulator compiles information or offers facts entirely different from what the reality is. They will pose this information as fact to the subject, and the subject will find it the facts. It can be risky because the subject does not know that they are being fed fake information; if the subject realized the information was fake, they would certainly not speak to the manipulator, and there would be no manipulation.
- Equivocations: It is where the manipulator makes comments that are contradictory, vague, or indirect. This is done to lead the topic to become confused and to fail to understand what is happening. This can also help the manipulator save face if the subject returns later and tries to blame them for the misinformation.
- Disguises: It is one of the most common types of Deception used. Disguises are when the manipulator deliberately omits information relevant or important to the context or engages in any behavior that would hide information relevant to the subject for that particular context. The manipulator may not have lied explicitly to the subject, but they will have made sure the crucial information that is needed never makes it to the subject.
- Exaggeration: This is when the manipulator overestimates a fact or stretches the facts a little to transform the story the way they want. Although the manipulator may not be lying explicitly to the subject, they may make the situation sound like a bigger deal than it actually is, or they can change the facts a little so the subject can do what they want.

- Modesty: modesty is the exact opposite of the method of an exaggeration since the manipulator is to consider downplaying or diminishing aspects of reality. They'll tell the subject that an incident isn't that big deal when it might potentially be the thing that decides whether the subject gets to graduate or gets such a major promotion. The manipulator would be able to go out later and say how they didn't know how big a deal it was, making them look nice, and the topic looks practically insignificant if they whine about it. Those are only a handful of different forms of deception. The manipulator of deception will use any method available to them to reach their ultimate goal, much like what happens in the other forms of mind control. If they can accomplish their goal using another approach against the subject, then they can do so, and the above list is not exclusive in any way. The deception manipulator may be very dangerous because the target will not be able to say what is the truth and what is an act of deception; the manipulator will be so good at what they are doing that it will be almost difficult to decide what is the truth and what is not.

Motives for Deception

Researchers have found that three major motivations are present in deceptions contained in close relations. This may include motives based on friends, motives based on oneself, and motives centered on relationships. Let's look at the motivations that centered on the partner first. The manipulator may use deception in this kind of motive to avoid causing harm to the subject, or to his wife. They may also use the deception to preserve the relationship between the subject and an outside third party, to avoid making the subject worry about it, or to keep the subject's self-esteem intact. That kind of motive for deceit can also be seen as both relationally advantageous and socially friendly.

That sort of deceit is not as terrible as any of the others. When the manipulator hears something negative that the best friend of the subject has said about them, then the manipulator may prefer to keep it to himself. Although this is a form of deceit, it helps the subject retain the relationship, although preventing the subject from feeling sorry for itself. It is the most commonly found type of deceit in relationships, and may not cause too much harm if it is found out. Many couples will prefer to use this type of Deception to protect their partner.

First, is the self-focused manipulation motive. That one is not considered as honorable as the first and is thus regarded as more downward than the other approaches. Rather than thinking about the subject matter and how they feel, the manipulator will actually think about how they feel and their own self-image. Through this purpose, the manipulator uses the deception to defend or improve its own self-image. This form of deception is used to shield off criticism, embarrassment, or frustration from the manipulator. When used in the partnership, this deception is generally viewed as a more severe problem and transgression than what is seen in the partner-focused deception. This is because the manipulator wants to behave in an egoistic way, instead of trying to protect the partnership or the other partner.

Lastly, the connection centered on deception motives. The manipulator will use this deception in the hope of limiting any harm that could come to the relationship simply by avoiding the trauma and conflict in relationships. This type of deceit, depending on the situation, often benefits the relationship, and at other times, it can be the cause of damaging the relationship as it can make things more difficult. For instance, if you want to hide how you feel about supper because you don't want to get into a confrontation, it might improve the relationship. On the other hand, if you have an affair and chose to keep the knowledge to yourself, it would only complicate things in the end.

It is not recommended regardless of the purpose of Deception in the relationship. The manipulator withholds information that may be important to the subject; if the subject finds out about it, they may start losing trust in the manipulator and wondering what else the manipulator hides from them. For a reason behind the lie, the target won't be too worried; they'll only be annoyed that something has been hidden from them and that the relationship will start to crumble. Perhaps it's best to adhere to the relationship's integrity policy and associate yourself with others who don't practice deceit in your social circle.

Detecting Deception

When the subject is interested in preventing deceit in their life to prevent the games of mind that come with it, it is always a good idea to learn how to detect deceit when it occurs. Also, it is difficult for the subject to ascertain whether deception is happening until the manipulator slips up and either reveals a lie that is apparent or blatant, or they refute something that the subject already knows to be real. While it may be difficult for the manipulator to deceive the subject for a long period of time, it is something that will occur commonly between people who know each other in everyday life. Detecting when deception occurs is always difficult, as there are really no ways to say when deception occurs that are absolutely accurate. Deception, however, is capable of putting a significant burden on the manipulator's cognitive functioning because they will have to find out how to remember all the comments they made to the subject so that the tale remains plausible and accurate. One slips up, and the subject will tell you something isn't right. Regardless of the pressure of keeping the story straight, the manipulator is much more likely to spill out information to tip the subject by either nonverbal or verbal signals.

Researchers agree that detecting deception is a cognitive, dynamic, and nuanced mechanism that often differs depending on what message is being exchanged. According to the theory of interpersonal deception, deception is an iterative and complex cycle of manipulation between the sender, who works to manipulate the information as they want it to be different from the reality, and the subject, who will then try to find out whether or not the message is true. The acts of the manipulator will be interrelated with the actions taken by the subject after it receives the message. The manipulator must reveal, during this exchange, the nonverbal and verbal information that will guide the participant in the deception. The subject may be able to tell you at some points that the manipulator was lying to them.

If the manipulator is dishonest, it's not always possible to say. According to Aldert Vrij, a noted scholar of deception, there are no specifically linked nonverbal attitudes to deception. Although there are many nonverbal actions that can be associated with the act of deceit, such signals can also occur when certain actions are present, and it is difficult to ascertain if the manipulator is using deceit unless they are performing an outright lie. Another scholar of deception, Mark Frank, puts forward another idea of deception, which includes how it can be detected at the cognitive level of the subject. If deceit happens, it involves a conscious act on the part of the participant that is intentional, so listening to words and paying attention to the language of the body that is going on is both important in trying to decide whether anyone is deceiving you. When someone asks a question and the manipulator is not able to answer it explicitly, rather than use some sort of interruption, has a weak reasoning structure, repeats a lot of phrases, and takes less time to speak about that particular question, they are more likely to lie. Basically, when trying to find out when deceit happens, there are not many signs which can be considered. There are a couple of nonverbal signs that may be present when someone is deceiving, but they may also have some other problems like nervousness or shyness.

Key Deception Elements

Although deciding which factors indicate when deception happens can be difficult, there are some components that are characteristic of deception. Sometimes, the subject would not know that these components happened unless the manipulator revealed an outright lie or was caught in the deceiving act. These are components that will be remembered later if the manipulator uses the deception mechanism in the appropriate manner. Camouflage, mask, and simulation are the three principal components of deception.

• **Camouflage**

Camouflage is the first element of deception. That is where the manipulator tries to conceal the facts in a certain way so that the target does not know that the detail is missing. This technique will also be used when the manipulator uses half-truths when they say facts. The subject will not realize that the camouflaging has occurred until later when these truths are revealed in some way. The manipulator must be an expert at camouflaging the facts so that by chance, the subject finding out about the deception is very difficult for him.

• **Disguise**

Disguise is yet another part that can be found in the deception process. When this happens, the manipulator works to create an impression that he is something or someone else. This is when the manipulator hides everything about himself from the subject, such as his real name, what they do for a job, who they were with, and what they are up to when they go out. This goes beyond just altering the outfit that someone wears in a play or movie; when the disguise is used in the act of deception, the actor tries to change their entire appearance to confuse and deceive the subject matter. There are many examples that can demonstrate the use of disguise in the deception method. The first is in self-disguising relationships with the partner, usually as another male, so that they are not identifiable. This could be done by the manipulator to get back into a crowd of people who don't like them, alter their personality to make others like them, or for some motive to advance their goals. The word disguise may, in some cases, apply to the manipulator disguising the true nature of a proposal in the hopes of avoiding an impact or purpose unpopular with that proposal. This type of disguise is often used in advertising or in political spin. Disguise can be dangerous in that it masks the true essence of what is happening. When the manipulator hides who they are from the subject, then it can be very hard for the subject to decide who they really are. If information is excluded from the subject, it clouds the way they can think because they do not have the correct information to make rational choices. Although the subject may think it makes rational choices of its own free will, the manipulator took away key details that could change the mind of the subject.

Modeling

The third part of the Deception is called simulation. It consists of revealing the details about the subject that is incorrect. For simulation, there are three methods that can be used, including diversion, distortion, and mimicry. Through mimicry, or copying another pattern, the manipulator may unintentionally represent something similar to itself. You will have an idea close to someone else's, and they'll say it's all theirs, instead of offering credit. Sometimes this type of simulation can occur through auditory, visual, and other means. Fabrication is another method that can be used by the manipulator when using deception. What this means is the manipulator's going to take something that's found in reality and alter it to be special. They can say a story that didn't happen or add embellishments to make it sound better or worse than it really was. Whilst the heart of the story might be real, yes they got a bad grade on a test, some extra items are going to be thrown in because the teacher intentionally gave them a bad grade. The truth is that the manipulator did not research, and that is why in the first place, they got a bad score.

Lastly, diversion is just another form of deception simulation. It is when the manipulator tries to get the target to concentrate their attention on something other than the truth; usually by baiting or providing something more enticing than the hidden truth. For instance, if the husband cheats and feels the wife is beginning to find out, he might carry a diamond ring home to distract her from the issue for a brief while. The problem with this strategy is that it always doesn't last long, and the manipulator needs to find some way of deceiving the subject to keep the cycle going.

Detecting Deception

Deception has become an important part of daily life. Whether or not the manipulator aims to inflict harm, there are several instances where deception creeps into all kinds of relationships. To get more time to finish a job, the manipulator may deceive their boss; a spouse may deceive their partner so as not to hurt their feelings. While many cases do not cause harm, they are still present within society. Because of this occurrence, work has been undertaken to try to understand why it occurs, and who is more likely to commit the acts.

Social study

Socially, some work has been conducted to see the impact of Deception on culture. Many methodologies are used in social science, for example, in psychology, which deals specifically with deception. In such methodologies, the researchers would intentionally misinform or deceive their participants about what is actually going on in the experiment. It leaves the subjects unaware of What is going on and can help produce better outcomes.

A research completed in the year 1963 by Stanley Milgram explains how frustration works on individuals. The manipulators assured the subjects that they should help out in a study that dealt with learning and memory; in fact, this test looked at how eager the subjects were to obey the orders of those in charge, even though that obeying meant that one of the other subjects would have to suffer. While the person who received the pain was merely an actor and did not really get harmed in the experiment, it was found that if the authority told him to do so, the subjects would inflict the highest possible pain on the actor. By the conclusion of this research, the participants were told the true essence of the research, and they ensured the individuals left in a state of well-being. The use of deception in this position has brought up a lot of research ethics issues. The American Psychological Association and other professional bodies are now governing, ensuring that the subjects are handled equally and do not in the process undo the harm.

Psychology Study

Psychological research is the division that would often use manipulation because it is important to assess the outcomes that will actually occur. The reasoning for doing this deception is that humans are very sensitive to the way they may look to others, as well as to themselves, and the self-consciousness they experience can distort or interfere with the way the subject might act in normal circumstances outside of doing the research where they would not experience scrutinized. The deception is intended to make the subjects feel more comfortable so that the manipulator can get more accurate results.

The manipulator may be interested, for example, in figuring out what circumstances could make a student cheat on a test. If the manipulator asks the student outright, the subjects would not most likely admit to cheating because there will be no way the manipulator will find out who is telling the truth and who is not. In this scenario, the manipulator will need to use provocation to get a precise picture of how much the cheating takes place. Instead, the manipulator might say the study is to find out how intuitive the subject is; the subject may even be told during the process that they may be given the opportunity to look at the answers of someone else before they give their own. At the end of this research involving deception, the manipulator is required to tell the subject what the study's true nature is, and why the deception was necessary. Often, after the work is all completed, most manipulators will also have a short description of the findings that happened with all the participants.

While deception is commonly used in these kinds of research studies, they are bound by the American Psychological Association's ethical guidelines; there are some disputes over whether deception is something that should be allowed at all. Many claim it is not appropriate to encourage deceit, and it is causing harm to the participating subjects. Some assume that if the participants understood the precise essence of the analysis in advance, the findings would be distorted. The biggest problem with the use of deception in a study is often not the actual deception itself. Actually, it is the unpleasant treatment that is used in a study of this nature, as well as the negative consequences of what will happen in the research. Typically this is the underlying reason why others are against using these kinds of studies and why they are considered immoral in nature.

Another reason against the ethics of using deception in these types of research is that the subject has already given its informed consent to the study. They've been reading the rules and regulations that go with the research and feel like they're being told enough about the end results they want to sign a waiver to get going. This is argued that if the researcher deceives the subject and leaves crucial details about the study out, regardless of whether it is in the study's best interest, then the subject is not really told to begin with. Because of this, the participant would not be included in the research because they did not specifically give consent to the actual test being performed.

Regardless of the claims that are out there on this issue, some fascinating observations have been made when the participants are misled about the essence of the research. For instance, with regard to the above research on cheating, if the participants had been told about the true nature of the test, it is not possible that any of them would have cheated. That would be because none of the people around them would want to be seen as deceptive or fake. The manipulation gave the researchers the chance to see what will happen in a real-world scenario. Therefore, if the memory test subjects listed earlier in the guidebook knew about the true nature of the research, they would not have been as likely to listen to the figure of authority and deliver the results they did. Despite the questions posed about using deception in science, the use of deception has produced a lot of interesting results for researchers. Such findings may not have been possible without the use of manipulation as the subject might have responded to the study in a different way.

Psychology

Psychology may be the main explanation of why frustration is used in science, but there is still a lot of dissatisfaction that has arisen in modern philosophy. Yes, in philosophy, deceit is a very common phenomenon. For example, in the meditations of Descartes that was written in 1641, the notion of Deus deception was introduced; this notion was something that was able to trick the ego, while it was thinking objectively about what was going on in fact. This notion continued to be used as part of his hyperbolic doubt; this is where the subject then begins to doubt everything that can be doubted because, in the past, they were deceived. Sometimes, cynical claims would use this Deus manipulation as their basis to doubt or challenge one person's understanding of truth. The key part of the claim argues that because it is easy to track the subject, anything the subject knows might be incorrect.

It is only one of the examples of intellectual deceit. A lot of works have been written on this subject, attempting to clarify just what it is, how it impacts the subject and ways the topic should stop coming into contact with it. A lot of work has also been done trying to decide when deceit could be good, and when it could be detrimental. This is the subject of considerable debate; some people agree that all deceit is bad, while others see deceit to save somebody's feelings as good in some cases as a husband hiding them the fact that somebody has said something about his wife means something.

CHAPTER 18 LESSONS ON DECEPTION

Deception refers to the act of causing someone to believe something which is untrue-big or small, cruel, or kind. Even the most honest people practice deceit, with different studies showing the average person is multiple times a day. Some of those lies are major ("I've never fooled you!"), but more often than not, they are little white lies ("That dress looks good,") that are implemented to escape uncomfortable situations or to spare somebody's feelings. Deception is not always an act that looks outward. There are also the lies people say to themselves, for reasons that range from healthy self-esteem maintenance to extreme delusions beyond their control. Although lying to oneself is generally perceived as dangerous, some experts argue that there are certain types of self-deception-such as believing that one can accomplish a challenging goal even if there is evidence to the contrary that can have a positive effect on overall wellbeing.

Researchers have long found ways to detect unequivocally when someone is lying. One of the most well-known, the polygraph test, has been controversial for a long time, and evidence suggests that those with certain psychiatric disorders such as Antisocial Personality Disorder can not be accurately measured using polygraphs or other commonly used methods of lie detection. Will lies have the meaning of working in life? Despite what your parents told you, psychologists think that telling the whole truth can potentially set you back in some circumstances. Evidence not only indicates that lying is more popular than you might expect. A study conducted by Dr. Bella DePaulo found that people are lying twice a day on average. The average person tells a lie over the course of a week to about one out of every three people they talk to one-on-one. Like it or not, we have built a world in which speaking the truth doesn't always take you forward. In reality, lies can make it easier to get along with the people around you, as shown by the findings of a study showing that people routinely lie for the benefit of others.

DePaulo found that it's very normal for people to lie for no other reason than to make others more confident. Women do this much more frequently than people who have been found lying more to boost their own reputations. In reality, usually, a conversation between two men includes eight times as many lies about themselves as anything else.

Only those telling little white lies profit from the lies. Research published in the Journal of Consumer Research's April 2012 edition found that the people who were lied to were later viewed with more compassion and generosity. It's not like we don't know we're lying; we know, and we feel guilty enough many times to let it affect our future behavior.

The ease with which we can deceive each other and the prevalence of lying render dishonesty an aspect in our culture, which is not to be overlooked and which will not go away anytime soon. However, do most people tell lies for success? The financial benefit doesn't seem to be the reason behind most lies, and repetitive lies in your professional and personal life will definitely come back to haunt you. Instead, research generally shows that we lie more for others and for everyone's sake — rather than getting ahead.

Nobody likes being misled, and it can become a big scandal when public figures are caught in a lie. But though many people take pride in their scrupulous integrity and seek to distinguish themselves from individuals who are more comfortable with the falsehoods-the fact is that for a number of reasons, everyone is lying. In reality, some experts say that it can take a certain amount of deceit to maintain a stable, functioning society. Formerly the domain of ethicists and theologians was the systematic study of deceit, but more recently, psychologists have turned their attention to why people lie and the circumstances that make them more likely to do so.

Social Psychology

Were they more greedy meat eaters than vegetarians? Do chaotic conditions perpetuate stereotypes? Will we feel smarter about winning awards for those close to us? The work of prominent Dutch psychologist Diederik Stapel recently dealt with these and other interesting questions. Just fifteen years after earning his Ph.D. with honors in 1997, Stapel had published more than 130 research articles, received a career trajectory award from the Society of Experimental Social Psychology, and risen to become the faculty dean at his university. However, it started to dawn on his students in 2011, that his work had only one problem: he was making up the results.

His university's investigation has so far revealed that for no less than 55 of his papers, Stapel fabricated the results. This has contributed to the problem of retractions in many popular academic journals like Science. Stapel has since apologized publicly to his employers and students. He also wrote a memoir, Derailed, in which his personal fall into scientific misconduct was recounted. It was described by fellow psychologists as "priceless and revealing," particularly its "unexpectedly beautiful" final chapter, though they also note that it is riddled with plagiarized lines from Raymond Carver and James Joyce's writings.

Why did such an internationally known psychologist become enmeshed in such a web of deceit, a man whose work was published in The New York Times and Time? Most of us would like to assume that a fluke, the work of a rogue researcher on the fringes of the discipline, is the appearance of deception in a scientific field such as psychology. And the true origins of the problem are pervasive and deep. The question goes to the core of contemporary psychology: Deception was recognized as a necessary evil in the pursuit of truth by many psychological researchers.

Find the account below.

Beth is a student in sophomore psychology at a large university in urban research. As a prerequisite for her introductory psychology course, she volunteered as a participant for a study exploring the disparity between online and in-person contact. A couple of graduate students dressed in white lab coats led her to a small cubicle, where she read a short article on medical history and discussed it with someone she was told another student in a chat room. She was shocked when her chat partner expressed skepticism about an African American researcher 's achievements, but she shrugged off the comment and completed her task. A third graduate student later took her into another room and told her that this was, in fact, an analysis of contemporary racism. Beth then recalled the other graduate students making openly negative comments about another student, who was also African American. The debriefing graduate student gave her some papers to read about the procedures and goals of the report, and sent her along the way. Reflecting on her past, Beth felt discouraged and regretful. How has she led astray?

There is something that is profoundly troublesome about using deception in the search for reality. Yet deceit has played a prominent role in psychological science for well over a century-and many would argue fundamental — A participant who enrolls in a research study is sometimes confused about his actual intent, the researchers' answers are in fact tracking, and the true identity of fellow "subjects." In some situations, participants are not even told that they are participating in a research study. Why has the deception tradition grown in psychological science, where is it today, and what are the issues with its continuing use?

We may offer growing rationals for deception. One is that there's deceit around us, permeating fields like ads and politics. There is no need to hold psychological researchers to a higher degree, the proponents say. One is the point that it is not necessarily harming subjects. Feelings can be damaged, but under false pretenses no one is forced to donate blood or sacrifice a limb. The most common statement is that it would be difficult to do any work without deceit. Just as doctors monitor the respiratory levels without calling attention to a patient's breathing, while subjects are unaware, psychologists will track behavior. Deception is rationalized in the laboratory environment as the only way to replicate the natural behavior.

Deception was a hallmark of psychological science in the first two-thirds of the 20th century. According to a new study of social science deception, only about 10 percent of the publications in social psychology papers before 1950 contained difficult approaches. Through the 1970s, the use of deception had reached more than 50 percent, and the figure reached two-thirds of studies in some papers. This means that subjects in social psychology experiments — at least those that survived the peer-review process and made it to publication — had a better than 50-50 chance of having the truth withheld from them, being told things that were not true, or being manipulated in Discreet ways.

Disappointment advocates say they use little lies to reveal great truths. Many subjects voice no objection and readily provide sophisticated ethical defenses of the action. In a perfect world, perhaps, deception would be scrupulously avoided, but ours is not perfect, so proponents argue that compromises must be made. Of course, they admit, researchers should do their best to avoid deception wherever possible, employing it only as a last resort. In some cases, alternative methodologies may be developed that don't require it. However, in the end, deceit is an essential tool in the search for information.

The American Psychological Association gives explicit support to the argument that dishonesty is necessary for scientific progress. The view that the ends justify the means in apparent in the APA's Ethical Principles of Psychologists and Code of Conduct, which reads as follows: "Psychologists do not conduct a study involving deception unless they have determined that the use of deceptive techniques is justified by the study 's significant prospective scientific, educational or applied value and that effective non-deceptive alternatives are not feasible." Moreover, the APA code explicitly forbids the use of deception in research that is reasonably expected to cause "physical pain or severe emotional distress." The implication seems to be that deception by itself is not harmful or objectionable.

Psychology is the second most popular undergraduate specialty in the nation and has numbered about 90,000 students since the mid-2000s. Many introductory psychology courses are permeated by permissive attitudes towards deception. In several psychological studies, including the one mentioned above, students are often forced to serve as subjects in order to obtain a passing grade. In the beginning, a lot of students have no idea that researchers, teachers, and fellow students can deceive them. As the course progresses, they learn that many of the best-known psychological experiments of the 20th century were founded on deceptions of one kind or another. Students may be persuaded by the end of the semester that deceit is a valid technique.

Suppose an undergraduate psychology student goes home to visit her family during a school break. During the visit, a friend poses a question that the student would prefer, for one reason or another, not to answer truthfully. Having been told by textbook authors and professors that deception is often justified for the sake of higher ends, might such a student be more likely to withhold information, provide false information, or distort the truth? After all, if deception is permitted in scientific experiments in the pursuit of knowledge, why should it be impermissible in the context of everyday relationships? Where is the harm in a white lie?

Remember how a used car salesman deals with a client. Does the buyer blindly trust whatever the seller says? Of course not. But should this same principle apply in the domains of research and higher learning? "Buyer concern" may be the industry slogan, but "Let test subjects' lookout" is not the sign we want to see hanging over the door of the laboratory. Research's practice of deceit undermines the relationship between research and the society it studies. The more suspiciously research subjects look, the less scientifically important their involvement would become. The more we hope to be fooled, the less our answers authentically reflect what we actually think and feel.

Yet the impact of manipulation on research is not even at stake much. In the end, the essence of our entire society is a fundamental concern. Scientists are extremely self-confident. When these trusted figures regularly turn out to be engaged in fraud, confidence is gradually diminishing in them and even in everyone else. Deception in psychological science destroys the idea that those entrusted with the discovery of facts should demand authenticity from us.

Deception can be habit-forming, like telling the facts. The more often we indulge in dishonesty, the simpler it is, and the more normal it is. Do we really believe the process of deception can be handled safely in the laboratory? Are we prepared to sacrifice the standard of truthfulness and the habit of honesty for the sake of a misguided conception of scientific advancement? We have to recognize scientifically accepted deception, which is fundamentally inconsistent with the pursuit of truth.

CHAPTER 19 BODY LANGUAGE - UNDERSTANDING HOW OUR BODIES COMMUNICATE

There are a variety of people in the world who are truly kind, compassionate, and caring for other people's needs. Many of these people are that way, and there are just as many people behind the things they do and do, who have ulterior motives. And how do you know someone who seems kind and compassionate but is manipulative under the surface? This is not a simple case. You know, when you see someone with a badge and a gun on their belt, they're a police officer. If a person wears a blue button-up with an embroidered name on the breast, you can assume that they are some sort of mechanic. Nor do manipulators wear uniforms. Occasionally, you won't know whether anyone is sincere or trying to persuade you.

Individuals don't come in with a book of informal rules. If they did, so we should probably not listen to them anyway. Winding up blinded to the actual nature of someone is easy, as it is a natural part of our relationship to need something from them. Sociopaths, for instance, maybe the most utterly enchanting people on the planet. They have a way to make you believe in their intentions, rather than your own. You do not know just how charming a narcissist can be until after realizing their true colors; you look back on the relationship. Such people are great at enticing their victims in a few seconds, while in the next few seconds making a 180-degree turn for the worse. Therefore, it's important to keep an eye out for these people without even having to rub heads with them. It could very well be difficult to discern the difference between someone captivating because he is sincere or someone who is an expert manipulator. So here is a guide for reading deceptive body language when determining whether or not you're dealing with such a guy.

Signals and Reactions

The first thing many manipulators are trying to do is imitate your body language in any way they can. They can begin by sitting in the same position as you and even move their arms or legs the same way you are. We do that because they want you around them to feel more responsive and vulnerable. Your mind takes these similarities on board and is conscious of a kind of mirroring effect. Which makes it think it can trust this person more as you understand better who that person is. Rather than thinking it might be a technique of coercion, our minds conclude that if that person is like us, they must be someone we can trust. Which ends up happening is that we get lost in their language and don't know the real tricks they could do to try to persuade us. You may wonder if we need to know whoever sits the same way we do. This is indeed a technique of coercion, but that doesn't mean that every person who does this tries to persuade us. The easiest way to determine whether or not this is someone who tries to exploit us is to look at the essence of the chat. Often when we're feeling nervous, we subconsciously mimic the other person. It's a way for our bodies to seek to relate more to the other person, and we don't feel like sitting next to them as awkward. When you've seen someone mirroring the way you're sitting, consider looking at the essence of the interaction.

When the other person tries to convince you to believe something, or you spoke about a change-related topic. There's a possibility they've tried to get you on their side. Whether it was more of a friendly chat or one where you did most of the talking, then it was either a misunderstanding or a sign that the other person was feeling nervous. One indication that someone may try to persuade you is that they stand as high as possible, possibly with their arms on their hips. It may be the other person trying to make sure they look as big as they can. In severe cases, this is a cause of intimidation. Most of the time, it is simply the attempt by the individual to display power, and among others, a sense of strength.

Note, this may also be a sign of anxiety again. If a person feels like being underestimated or someone doesn't listen to them, then this technique can be a way of boosting strength. It is also important to be mindful of other people's body language so we can get the real context of the situation rather than what is happening on the surface level. Don't be scared of someone who's like a superhero, but remember not letting yourself slip under the influence of someone who's just trying to make your body look bigger. Some of the main body language signs that will not be the most encouraging interaction is that the other person is closed off, keeping his arms crossed or even his hand over his mouth. Like anything else in this segment, it might once again be a sign that you don't want to open up or feel afraid and defenseless. If a person is being faced with something bad or told some horrible news, they may have this kind of body language.

When the situation is one where you are addressing yourself more freely, and the other person is sitting like this, they can seek to gather personal information about you, which they may use later. When the scenario would be one where you're both opening up, and they're sitting like this, make sure to hold off on some of the juicy secrets until they're just as ready to open up. Likewise, they can be more subtle than that, and can even give up their body language to be more convincing. They might be opening their arms and putting their arm around you even though the relationship isn't personal and sitting with a large chest to say you're welcome. This is safe to do in other discussions, but if they are trying to get more personal details out of you, don't let yourself fall for this tactic.

What Others see in the language of the body

If anyone tries to convince us, they'll probably consider our body language. It's important to be mindful of the stuff that could give them the signal we feel vulnerable, frightened, or anxious about them. When they can feel these kinds of feelings, so other people will find it easy to manipulate others. Let's start from the top of our bodies first, and then work our way down. When you wrinkle your forehead, this is a sign you might be nervous. This may lead others to think you're nervous and may take advantage of this weakness. They can start thinking about stuff that has you even more stressed out, which can lead to misunderstanding. It can encourage them to make the most of what you're thinking. They can also use your uncertainty to put in your head more ideas and get you to think about them. When they're good ideas, that can be especially convincing, because you'll be more interested in listening to positive stuff to divert you from what caused stress.

The manipulators will then look into your eyes and see what you think. Squinted eyes can reflect concentration, and it can be manipulated by others as if they were a wrinkled face. Bright and open eyes will display concentration that you are an open-minded person to new ideas. Others may see this and can presume your good intentions, trying to take advantage and manipulate your level of empathy. The same goes for wide smiles and open smiles. Often happy people can seem easier to manipulate since they are less aggressive and more open to persuasion.

They'll look at the way you carry your weapons, too. Closed weapons mean you could be a little more suspicious about what they've got to say. You can see that, and perhaps you might need to try a little harder to persuade you. A more transparent attitude will show them they have a chance to convince you. It can also be a warning when you exhibit certain signs of anxiety that you feel anxious and insecure around them. They know you could be worried about them if you fidget with your hands, twist your hair, pick fingers, shake legs, or look around a lot. This will help them get the impression that it's going to be easier to take advantage of and a certain way to sway you.

You don't have to be nervous all the time about how you sit or hold on to yourself, because not everyone can research your body language closely. When you're in a situation where people seem to be trying to manipulate you or to control you at all costs, then it's important to make sure you defend yourself. Stand strong and comfortable, maintain the correct amount of eye contact, and remain focused on the situation's background indicators rather than just when the words come out of their mouths.

We will go into the other forms in the rest of the book that manipulators take advantage of you in their actual words, and the acts they take to try to keep you under their spell. Then we will give you the resources you need to find positivity from this and make yourself a convincing individual. More strategies about body language will also be covered in the NLP chapter.

CHAPTER 20 WAYS TO PROTECT YOURSELF FROM EMOTIONAL MANIPULATION

We all love pursuing the other sex every now and then-both men and women. It's fun and a good sport, as long as we're frank about it and bear in mind that it's all about passion. Why? For what? Since it's deceit to try and love can not be exploited-we don't find love; love finds us. So we should view a relationship of love as sacred ground.

Sadly, so many people believe in deception – both in relationships and in industry. In my early twenties, I read something that stuck for good in my subconsciousness: if you can align yourself with the universe, it's easy to achieve success. What does this mean for this topic? Which means manipulations are pointless at the end of the day. Manipulations may potentially offer a short-term benefit, but in the long run it will eventually lead to consequences as manipulations are opposed by the universe. But if we go with the celestial wind, we'll gravitate toward our target – more or less effortlessly. Too good to be real? Every one of us is playing a part in the cosmic game. In the scheme of things, we just have to know our position and let it play out. And Jesus said his cross is as light as a feather. Of course, this means giving up several wishes and aspirations that aren't part of our cameo; however, our celestial intent typically turns out to be much more grandiose than our puny, selfish ambitions.

That being said, we also need to defend ourselves from other people's childish manipulations, including those around us. Don't take this lightly; it's painful emotional coercion and can leave deep wounds on people 's psyche and soul. And once you are in a state of exploitation, it is very difficult to get out. But don't either take this affair too seriously, we 're doing a lot of things subconsciously, and your partner may not even know that she's manipulating you.

There will always be people trying to shake your trust-people trying to instill seeds of self-doubt inside you. Such people would do their utmost to trick you into thinking that their beliefs are facts that are objective. They 're trying to tell you everyone in the world thinks you're rude, nuts, or not nice enough. Then they'll tell you how much they're worried about you-how you're living your life, spending your money, raising your children, on and on.

If you don't really change the way they want you to change, then your life will be destroyed. This is what they want to believe in you. The truth is you don't want to help these people. They want to get you under control. We want you to adjust, not to make your life easier, but to affirm their lives and prevent you from overgrowing them.

Don't get angry. Manipulative people are not preoccupied with your needs. They worry about their own interests. Once you allow manipulative people in your life, it can be extremely difficult to get rid of them. The trick is to have enough self-control to send the boot to dishonest people as soon as you see them. Here are a few ways to get rid of manipulative people from your life:

Don't Fall Into Their Trap

Most of us come across instances where others seek to manipulate our thoughts, attitudes, or actions and take advantage of them to their own advantage. In one such case, you fail to understand the true motive. The person mentally dominates you, and you step into the pit. Often this emotional abuse costs you a lot when you make some critical decisions under another person's control, and when it is too late, you know it later.

You have to be conscious when a relationship sounds too good to be true. They are showering you with compassion, gratitude, admiration, congratulations, and affection. You feel like you live in a dream where everything seems perfect. They don't give you a reason to worry. You simply can not find any flaws in them. Also, if anything goes wrong, they can begin to weep or feel sorry. You can have become the object of extreme intimacy and have the feeling of a passion for the fairy tale.

It is the outcome because you actually began the relationship with love bombing, and all of a sudden, you start feeling ignored. You are receiving gratitude, presents, and recognition, but rarely. You feel like you're losing your hold, or having someone else in your life. You get another gift from them, the moment you make up your mind to move on. You find it hard to make your own mind up. They are trying to get leverage over you in one situation like this. For most instances, this works to your amazement. You approach them much more.

Individuals often succeed in manipulating their victims after intermittent reinforcement. We can avoid behaving in the same way while fighting back or demanding an answer. The explanation is that they are really taking complete care of you now, so they say goodbye to the intermittent strengthening. We no longer really need it. Manipulators have many different faces, and in the same manner, they can use many different ways to get things done. The person may make an undertaking, and later deny that you begin to doubt your own perception. They do make you feel bad when you try hard to make them aware of their promise. They can employ shallow sympathy and burst into crocodile tears. Eventually, you end up trusting them and even doubting whether you listened correctly.

You can't believe smiling faces that seem confident and strong. Manipulative people often have self-serving prejudice, so they think less for the other person's feelings. We have a reason to look for others who affirm them and make them even feel superior.

Steer straight wherever possible

A manipulator 's actions typically vary according to the situation they 're in. For instance, a manipulator may speak rudely to one person, and act respectfully towards another the next moment. When you see these extremes frequently in a person, it would be advisable to stay away from them. And you really have to communicate with this guy. That will prevent you from becoming a deceptive victim.

One way to identify a manipulator is to see if a person is behaving in different circumstances and before different people with different faces. Although we all have a degree of this sort of social distinction, some psychological manipulators seem to dwell in extremes habitually, being highly polite to one person, and totally gross to another-or totally helpless at one moment, and fiercely violent at another. If you frequently experience this form of behavior from an adult, keep a healthy distance away, and avoid interacting with the person unless you absolutely have to. As described earlier, there are nuanced and deep-seated causes for persistent psychological abuse. Saving or saving these is not your job.

There are some circumstances in which you can't fully leave a relationship-most, usually whether that person is a parent or an extended family member. You probably can not go cold turkey unless the individual causes serious harm or psychological damage. Next, you need to accept this person completely for who they are and change your relationship standards accordingly. If they were someone you needed validation from before, then you would have to quit looking for their validation. Recognize that their advice is not something you need in your life if they were someone you received advice from. When they keep offering it, you can thank them for it, and then politely dump it. When setting these limits, be as discreet as you can, and do not tell the other person you are setting them. Creating this shift at your end will take some time, and when you get upset with the other person in the process, you will have to deal with their reaction on top of that.

Knowing this will drain your energy a little bit, setting limits around the time you spend with that person. If you've been hanging out every Saturday with your manipulating mother-in - law, cut it down to once a month and plan something for that day so that there is a definite end time for your hangout.

Call them out on their actions

Manipulators are always difficult to deal with, but the worst are Discreet manipulators. They will stay cool as a cucumber when confronted, and yet rigid and unbending. You may start to get frustrated when you start seeing their faulty reasoning. When you keep fighting with them, you'll find it hard not to raise your voice a bit. You 're going to start looking like the irrational one, and they're going to try to take back control in remaining calm, based on their "maturity."

Defending yourself is tempting and trying to get the other person to see what is really going on. But a true manipulator will not change their tune, and the more you give in to that urge to protect yourself, the more they will twist your words more. It will not be long before you get stuck in this twisted web of myths and false expectations. If you are in a situation with a true manipulator, the two goals for any conflict that is taking place should be to resolve and leave, whether that means leaving the current conversation or exiting the relationship. Evite threats, accusations, lose patience, accuse the other person of coercion, or become excessively emotional. Stick to honest, factual, and respectful declarations when you speak.

There are things that require a high degree of intelligence, flexibility, or self-discipline when dealing with a manipulative person. You might not have the self-control to react without losing your temper and making things worse. If that's the case, accept this about yourself and take extra steps to avoid a tense confrontation (invite a mediator into the conversation, for example, or send an email instead of meeting in person, so you have time to think through what you say).

For me, it can cause a bit of tension to deal with someone who loses their temper. I needed to have a friend with me in order to feel secure in circumstances where there was a lot of blow-up risks. However, much as I wished I could handle the conflict myself, I realized that I wasn't quite in a position to do so. I would have felt a lot of needless discomforts if I had failed to acknowledge this about myself because of my decision to act better than I was. Wouldn't you be better at handling the problem than you are? Others will be attacking the vulnerable points, and trying to make it seem like the problem will be easier for you to deal with than it is. Do not equate your reaction to someone else's reaction in one case.

Ignore what they do and say

It is intended to ignore the dishonest men. These people flip flop over things, they 're slippery when you try to keep them accountable, they promise support that never comes, they 're always making you feel guilty-everything you don't want in person. The greatest mistake you can make when dealing with a dishonest person is trying to correct him or her. You sink deeper into their pit, by correcting them. Humans will use anger and misunderstanding to lure you into a confrontation. We want to make you feel nervous so that they can see how you tick. When they learn the triggering factors, you are going to use them to affect your actions. A smarter approach is to ignore them entirely. Only erase them from your life if you can't delete them instantly-even if they 're a supervisor, coworker, or member of the family agree with what they're doing and then carry about doing your own thing anyway.

Touch Their Centre of Gravity

Manipulative people actively take advantage of their own tactics against you. Through your enemies, they will become enemies, and turn them against you. They 're going to dangle some small reward in front of you and make you chase it relentlessly-they 're going to take it away any time you get close to it. You will forever keep past acts above your head. And on and on. Avoid letting those who exploit you use their tactics against you. Switch the tables in, instead. Build your own plan, and hit them where it hurts. When you are forced to deal with a dishonest person who, no matter how hard you try to avoid them, tries to make your life miserable, you have only one choice, find their center of gravity and destroy it. This center may be associates, followers, or subordinates to the deceptive individual. It may be a high-level talent or advanced knowledge of a particular area. They can manage it as a particular resource.

Figure out what their center of gravity is, and make it yours anyway. Creating alliances with those close to them, hiring people to replace them with their skillsets and knowledge base, or siphoning away their precious assets. This will throw them off balance and push them to concentrate on managing their life, not yours.

Believe in your decision

You know better than anyone else what is best for your future. So many people are going around asking for the views of other people on anything. How do I want to do with my life? What am I fantastic at? Where am I, then? Avoid searching for other people so you can describe yourself. Define yourself. Believe in yourself.

What distinguishes winners from losers is not the ability to listen to other people's opinions; it's the ability to listen to one's own opinions. You prevent dishonest people from influencing your life by setting up your own values and keeping them tightly onto them. This will serve as a firewall to your convictions, keeping manipulators ostracized and out of your way.

Try not to fit right in

Keep reinventing yourself. One myth is the belief that continuity is somehow admirable or related to achievement. Manipulative people want you to be consistent so that they can count on you to advance their agendas. They want you to show up at 9 am every day and work at minimum wage for them. We want you to come home on time and make them feel good about themselves and clean the house.

Consistent assembly lines. The prison is uniform. Consistency is how they trap you in a shell. It's their way of manipulating you. The only way to stop being exploited is by consciously going against all the barriers other people seek to create for you. Hold on trying to blend in. Instead, they're looking to stand out. Act to be different in some way, and never remain the same for too long. By design, personal growth needs a lack of consistency. Constant change is expected-constant reinvention.

Avoid Concession

Guilt is an emotion to no use. But this is a powerful tool. Guilt is one of those weapons that would be used against you by dishonest men. They will make you feel bad for past defeats and small mistakes, or they will make you feel guilty for being overconfident and prideful. They'll use it against you if you spend feeling happy or sure of yourself. One will ever feel too good about themselves, they would claim. Another tool that is being used against you by manipulators is doubt. We will work to instill within you a sense of self-doubt-doubts about your ability and your worth. Their ultimate goal is to take you off balance and make you guess yourself in second place. Within this state of confusion, manipulators gain control.

Their power is getting greater and twice as likely to convince you to compromise on your principles, ambitions, and yourself.

Simple solution-avoid feeling guilty. Avoid asking yourself. When it comes to your own life, you owe nothing to anyone. You deserve to feel good about yourself and to be stunned by your achievements. You deserve to have a good sense of confidence and self-belief in what you do. It is neither moral nor enlightened to compromise on either of these issues. This is then the path to self-destruction.

Never ask for permission

Asking for forgiveness is better than asking for permission. The problem is that we have been conditioned to ask for permission constantly. As a boy, we had to ask for everything we wanted — to be fed, changed, and burped. We had to ask permission to go to the bathroom in the day, and we had to wait to eat lunch at a designated time, and wait for our turn to play with toys. As a result, most people never cease to expect permission.

Employees around the world are waiting for a promotion and waiting for their turn to talk. Most are so used to being chosen that they sit in meetings in silence, afraid to talk out of turn or even lift their hands. It's a different way of living.

Even if you did it whenever you wanted to do it? And if you quit being too worried about politeness and feeling relaxed with others? What if, instead, exactly the way you want to live your life? They are all things you can do whenever you want.

Manipulative people want you to feel constrained by some abstract law or principle that says you can't behave freely without consulting an authority figure or a party. The reality is that at any given moment, you can miss this feeling of confinement. You will continue living a completely different life today than you lived it yesterday. Your decision is yours.

Build a greater sense of mission

Destiny driven people aren't easily fooled. The reason manipulators in this world tend to prosper is that so many people lead a purposeless life. If there is no reason in your life, you can not believe something. They 're going to do anything. Because, somehow, nothing matters. People who lack intent literally waste time. There is no rhyme or explanation behind the manner in which they live their lives. We don't know where to go, or why they are here. So, to avoid going insane, they 're working in meaningless jobs and stuffing their minds full of celebrity gossip, reality television, and other useless types of media. They remain busy to avoid the desperate feeling of emptiness growing inside them. This profession and loneliness empower deceptive individuals.

Every minute, a sucker is born. When you are constantly distracted, constantly consuming pointless stuff, trying to stay busy constantly-you are the sucker. By peddling meaningless knowledge and events to them, manipulators manipulate purposeless people. The only way to escape that destiny is by cultivating a sense of destiny. Destiny is doing away with distraction. The manipulators can't hurt you because you think you're going. They can not confuse you or lead you astray.

Take New Opportunities

The universe want to put your eggs in one bowl. Someone and all around you ask you to lock yourself upon and on in a mortgage, a car payment, a secure relationship, a single position at the office. They want you staked down to a single chance for the rest of your life. Nowadays, it is also looked down on being optimistic. Staying hungry is also seen as a sign of weakness. How can't you just be happy with what you have? Why should you be so greedy? If you show a desire for more, this is what dishonest people would ask you. They 're going to call you vain, greedy, prideful. They'll make you feel cold and uncomfortable like you're heartless and inhumane. The reality is that they want to keep you in your place. They want you to stay at the same job and spend the rest of your life living in the same place. They want you and the structures they control to remain dependent upon them.

The only way to stay autonomous is to look for new possibilities and build new ones actively. Continue applying for new jobs, continuing to start new companies, developing new partnerships, and seeking new experiences.

Avoid being an infant

When you ever get fooled by someone, shame on them. When you're fooled by someone ten times, you're an idiot. Avoid making manipulators walk around you all over from being a snap pack. Nobody feels sorry for you, and you're always being humiliated. Have enough self-consciousness and reverence for yourself to say no to dishonest men.

You can not just walk around life, blaming the troubles on others. You can not simply walk away from the people trying to control you through life, either. Yes, there are people who are negative and manipulative. And yes, these people are going to try to use you. Yet that doesn't mean that you have a free pass to make mistakes and exploit them. Without your permission, no-one can control you. You are to blame for your own achievements and defeats. If others outstrip you, it's your fault, not theirs, be smart. Learn from wrongs. Don't want to believe the same slippery person again and again. Slice them free. Remove them from life. Commit to connecting yourself with like-minded people who will not be exploiting you.

Betting on Yourself

Take a gamble on the one thing in life that you can control yourself. Too many people restrict themselves to considering only external factors when making difficult decisions. They consider the financial consequences of a situation and its relationships. Yet they fail to acknowledge the impact on their personal satisfaction and sense of self-worth that their choice would have. As a result, when they should be taking chances on themselves, they take chances on other people. Then, they wonder why they are sad.

If you just take chances on strangers and things, you put yourself at the mercy of those people and stuff. It makes you weak and ready to exploit. You should take chances on yourself instead. In any tough situation you find yourself facing, don't ask questions like, "Who's the right one to side with? "Or" What choice would be more likely to succeed? "Rather, say," What am I most likely to do? "So go out and do that. For example, if you face an opportunity to start your own company or keep working at the same dead-end job, don't keep in the job only because the pay is just slightly pathetic. Don't just live, because the relationships are slightly unpleasant. You are betting on external factors when you do so. This is also a mistake. Betting on yourself is a safer Plan.

You would never regret making a bet on yourself. You will, of course, have to take full responsibility for any mistakes that you make. Sure, you need to stick to a higher standard. Yet you, too, must be solely responsible for your own victories. You will continue to rise and achieve greater and higher rates of success.

Stop getting emotionally attached to them

All you do with a manipulator is false. Every fight you have been going through is your fault. Manipulating will wreak havoc on your feelings. You go from crying to being furious to in the short term feeling guilty and indignant. Then you are sorry you have not stuck up for yourself. You are ashamed to let them get started again on you. Your emotions are more stable once you've left a manipulator.

Life is a journey into an adventure. On the way, many people come to give us company at various times for a certain amount of time and go after they play their part in our lives. There is no problem with the persons coming and going in themselves, but the difficulties occur when you are emotionally attached to the persons and feel powerless, tense, and worried when the relationship ends with an emotional manipulator particularly. Therefore, if you want to stay healthy and make progress in life, you need to resolve the emotional connection as soon as possible. There is no doubt that some individuals will become the driving force for you to move towards the path chosen. But being separated from them, you should be careful not to get distracted. You need to make judicious use of the relationships. Be attached to individuals with a detached approach and take care of them to create a confident atmosphere. However, when you let them go out of your life for being a manipulator because some other relationship is waiting on your way to your journey, you should not be dependent on that person for your growth and stop your life. You need to re-focus on your journey, which leaves past memories behind.

Handling emotional connection measures the degree of sophistication of one's journey down the desired direction and its gravity. Treat yourself to the moment you share with friends. Learn from them, love them, and look after them, but don't make them walk sticks. Much of the time, people are usually afraid to lose anyone because of their incapacity to go on in life alone. So, if you dare walk alone on the chosen path, you no longer have to conquer the emotional connection.

Meditate Frequently

Were you keen on feeling calmer? More Focused? All in managing the emotions? If so, meditation will offer mental relaxation, which is something that many people long for in the fast-paced, high-tech busy world today. When you're dealing with depression, mood swings, tension, or other related problems, meditation will help provide the relaxation and clarity you're looking for in just a few minutes a day.

Anyone will benefit from frequent meditation if the challenges you face are related to depression and stress, childhood trauma, or chemical alteration in brain function. There is really no better time to start meditating than there is now! Through time, the effects of meditation grow, but you can almost instantly feel a sense of calm, quiet, and peace. Meditation takes the body into a state of deep relaxation and offers the requisite tools and resources to cope with stress. While the body and mind learn to relax through the exercises and methods of deep breathing, the mind calms, and the body enters a state of tranquility.

In fact, meditation can neutralize the negative consequences of stress hormones, which overtax your body and emotional state. The feelings relax and regulate as hormone levels return to normal. And you'll be better able to cope with strong feelings and circumstances the next time you feel frustrated or nervous, use your breath to calm down and relax. Emotions can also keep you, hostage, making you feel like you're living your life on an uncontrollable roller coaster of ups and downs, twists, and turns. On the other hand, meditation involves a lot of visualization-a powerful tool that can help you reshape your current thinking and create a more positive, stable emotional environment.

Meditation can help you build self-esteem, heal from past traumas, and in the present moment, experience more joy. During meditation, visualization not only provides you with the resources to cope with emotional distress by providing equilibrium, but it can also help you plan a path of transition for your future. Meditation will alter your inner life and help you cope with emotional manipulators.

Inspiring them

Using all the experience you've acquired to become your best self to help them to become your best self. If you are having trouble improving their behavior, work with a counselor. It can be very difficult to change their behavior, and you may not be able to do it on your own. A psychologist or therapist may help him recognize habits that need to alter and discuss the feelings that are behind him. These will also help him develop new, healthy behaviors.

Tell them "You 're OK."

This begins with the way you used to not respond to their techniques anymore. If you don't want to, you say "no," or you speak your mind even though they don't like it. Work on feeling ok with how negatively they may react. When they're not yours, don't pick them up.

You can only keep your acts under control. That's crucial because you won't be able to alter a manipulator 's behavior, however, you can avoid being their victim. That happens when you start saying, "no." The first step in breaking the cycle is to manipulate us because we allow it and to refuse to be manipulated. Manipulators are good at what they do, so watch out for their reaction. You would probably say or do things that tug at the heartstrings. We will stand firm in our "no," realizing we are taking the first step to free ourselves from its power.

Let go of nasty relationships

Toxic partnerships can be hard to let go of. Many people find themselves caught in a cycle of returning to relationships that are not good for them. This just creates a cycle of hurt and grief. Toxic relationships can be let go of there. Psychologists have worked with people who have had enough of this issue to be able to write a whole handbook about it. The very first step to getting out of a toxic relationship is admitting to yourself that the relationship isn't perfect. You might note and try to explain the signs of a toxic relationship with yourself. It's called 'cognitive dissonance' if you notice that uncomfortable feeling in the back of your mind, and it's your brain trying to protect you from what you know is true. Take note of the things that make you feel this way in a relationship. The first step is to recognize that your connection is toxic. You have to be conscious of all the things that affect you before you can truly be free.

Relationships are a side lane. Two people are involved in the relationship, meaning that two people are involved in all the disagreements, arguments, and behavior. You can not fully take the blame on yourself. If you blame yourself for all of the relationship problems, you'll find yourself going back to trying to fix them. Recognize that both parties are sometimes at fault for a dysfunctional relationship. Recognize your responsibilities-but your responsibilities alone. Within a toxic relationship, you don't need to be up to anyone else's issues. There's no need to hoist it on yourself because you aren't to blame.

Some of the best things you can do while trying to let go of a controlling partner is to cut off the touch. Holding in touch would just make the letting go harder. This involves searching out toxic people that are no longer in your life. Resist scrolling through their social media or questioning how they are doing with your mutual friends. You should still follow your intuition when it comes to cutting people out of your life, according to Sarah Newman, M.A. Although it may sound drastic, Newman advises loosening the bonds when it comes to a toxic relationship. You need to be in a position to move on, where you can feel optimistic about the lack of touch, rather than pain.

Mariana Bockarova, Ph.D., says the closure is one of the best things to move on from a manipulative and broken relationship. Bockarova understands that closure will help people reconstruct their whole lives in a safe and positive way. One way to help you let go of a toxic relationship is to find closure. Healing comes from inside for many people and considers all the ways the relationship went wrong in the first place. Writing one more letter or making the other party recognize the toxicity will provide closure for some. Whatever it is, it's necessary for closure to move on.

The most important thing in quitting and letting go of an abusive relationship is getting someone there to catch you if you fall. It can be unsettling to let go, mainly if it is a long-term one. Keep in contact with friends and relatives who will support you through the more stressful moments. These will also help to hold you accountable when it comes to not searching out those you've cut off. Aid networks are essential in allowing dysfunctional partnerships to go away. Don't fear to reach out to people who love you the most.

Develop a strong mindset

Although one toxic person may use coercion and lies, another may have recourse to intimidation and incivility. And if you're not patient, you can take a serious toll on your life for people like this. Nevertheless, mentally healthy people deal skillfully with manipulative people. They refuse to give away their strength, and no matter who surrounds them, they continue to be their best self.

Putting a name on your sensations reduces their intensity. So whether you feel sad, nervous, frustrated, or afraid, confess it — at least to yourself. Pay attention also to how those emotions can affect your choices. You can be less likely to take chances when you are feeling nervous. You may get more impulsive when you're excited. Increasing the understanding of the feelings will reduce the risk that you will make only emotionally driven unreasonable decisions.

Listing your emotions is just part of the fight — you need skills to control your emotions as well. Think of your current abilities to cope. Should you eat something when you're nervous? Should you drink to keep yourself calm? When you're mad, will you sell it to your friends? If you're anxious, you stay home? These conventional strategies can make you feel better right now, but they will make you feel worse in the long run. Search for long-term coping strategies that are perfect for you. Keep in mind that what works for one person doesn't always work for another, and you need to figure out what's best for you to manage your emotions. Experimenting with various coping mechanisms to figure out what works for you, deep breathing, exercising, meditating, reading, painting, and spending time in nature are only a few of the techniques that could help.

The way you think has an impact on how you feel and how you behave. You are deprived of intellectual energy by saying things like, "I can't take this," or "I'm such an idiot." Pay attention to what you think. You'll probably note rising trends and themes. Maybe you're telling yourself about things you feel uncomfortable about doing. Or maybe you're telling yourself you're not in control of your life.

Respond with something more constructive to the unproductive and unreasonable feelings. But instead of saying, "I'm going to screw this up," think, "This is my chance to shine, and I'm going to do my best." Changing the interactions, you're having with yourself can be the most instrumental thing you can do to improve existence. Changing your attitude is the only way to teach your brain to think differently. Do tough things — and keep doing them even though you don't think you should. You will be demonstrating to yourself that you are stronger than you think. Set up healthy daily habits too. Practice appreciation, exercise, get plenty of sleep, and follow a balanced diet in order for the brain and body to be at its best. Seek out individuals who inspire you to be your best. And create an atmosphere that helps you develop a balanced lifestyle.

Many of the world's positive habits won't work if you practice them alongside your bad habits. It is like eating donuts on a treadmill while you're running. Pay attention to your bad habits (we all have them) that rob you of the mental strength. Whether you feel bad for yourself or envy the success of other people, it takes only one or two to keep you stuck in life. Once you realize your bad habits, spend energy, replacing them with healthier alternatives. You will then be able to step out of the hamster wheel and actively work towards your goals.

Just as it takes time and practice to become physically strong, so too, it takes dedication to build mental strength. But the key to feeling your best and reaching your most significant potential is to build mental muscle.

Give yourself constructive self-appraisal all day long

An emotional manipulator will totally tarnish your mood, so make sure you restore yourself during the day with uplifting self-talks. Each of us has a set of messages that keep playing in our minds over and over. Our responses to life and its circumstances are represented by this internal dialog or personal commentary. One way to recognize, encourage, and maintain optimism, hope, and happiness is to fill our minds with optimistic self-talking consciously. Far too often, because of our manipulative partner, the self-talk pattern that we have formed is negative. They recall the derogatory things our friends, parents, siblings, or teachers told us as children. We remember other children's adverse reactions, which undermined the way we felt about ourselves. Such messages have been playing in our minds over the years, strengthening our feelings of rage, fear, guilt, and hopelessness.

Some of the most important approaches used in dealing with those suffering from depression are to determine the root of these messages and to work with the individual to "overwrite" them deliberately. If a person learned he was worthless as a child, we'd show him how special he really is. If a person has learned to expect disasters and catastrophic events while growing up, we will teach her a better way to predict the future.

Check the exercise below. Within your head, write down some of the negative thoughts that hinder your desire to resolve your circumstances. Whenever possible, be precise, and include everyone you know who contributed to the post. Now, take a moment to consciously combat the negative messages in your life with constructive truths. Don't give up when you're not quick to find them. There is an actual truth for every negative message which will override the weight of despair. There are always those truths; keep looking until you find them.

You can get a negative message replaying in your mind if you make a mistake. You've been told as a child, "You're never going to amount to anything" or "You can't do anything right." When you make a mistake and you're going to because we all do-you can choose to overwrite that message with a positive one, such as "I choose to accept and grow from my mistake" or "As I learn from my mistakes, I become a better person." Good self-conversation isn't self-deception. It's not looking at circumstances mentally with eyes that just see what you want to see. Instead, positive self-talk is about acknowledging the truth in situations and within you. One of the fundamental truths is that you will be making mistakes. It is unfair to expect perfection in yourself or someone else. It's also unrealistic to expect no difficulties in life, whether by your own actions or by pure circumstances.

When adverse events or mistakes occur, positive self-talk is aimed at bringing the positive out of the negative in order to help you do better, go further, or simply move forward. The practice of constructive self-talk is also the mechanism that helps you to discover in any given situation the hidden happiness, hope, and joy.

CONCLUSION

The guidebook took some time to discuss the different forms of mind control prevalent in today's world, as well as some of the strategies and techniques that go along with each form. Each of the techniques of mind control works in a different way. Brainwashing aims to convince the target to alter his or her whole identity by using isolation, intimidation, and eventually providing a way to feel better that conforms to the new identity they want. Hypnosis lets the participant enter a new altered state of mind where they are more likely to be perceptive and open to new ideas. On the other hand, coercion and deception can alter the subject's current thought process by using subterfuge as a primary strategy, while persuasion includes manipulating the values, attitudes, expectations, motives, or behaviors of a person.

Except for brainwashing and manipulation, mind control is a tool that can be used to accomplish one's objectives or ambitions in a positive way. It all depends on the type of mind control involved, and the individual's intent to apply it. This also depends on whether it would help the goal or subject of mind control.

Thanks for reading this book.

If you enjoyed the content, please leave a good review, it will be useful to me. Thanks in advance!

www.ingramcontent.com/pod-product-compliance
Lightning Source LLC
Chambersburg PA
CBHW081152020426
42333CB00020B/2483